P9-DWJ-950

# Great Taste for 20 Years...and Counting!

After two decades of sharing **favorite family recipes** from cooks like you, *Taste of Home* just keeps getting better. See for yourself in this **exciting new cookbook**!

Since 1993, *Taste of Home* magazine has brought you thousands of scrumptious recipes shared by families just like yours. We gathered together these dishes in our *Taste of Home* annual cookbook series, and this all-new 20th edition keeps the delicious tradition going.

In *2013 Taste of Home Annual Recipes,* you'll enjoy a full year's worth of flavorful favorites from the magazine—plus dozens of bonus dishes never before seen in *Taste of Home.* It all adds up to 503 recipes in one convenient collection!

Everything you love about this best-selling cookbook series is back, from the "Mom's Best" and "Field Editor Favorites" chapters to "Potluck Pleasers" and "Just Desserts." Plus, you'll find these exciting new features:

- **Three At-a-Glance Recipe Icons**
  Handy icons next to the recipes will help you quickly pinpoint the best choices for you:
  FAST FIX = Recipes that take 30 minutes or less to fix
  MAKE AHEAD = Recipes prepared in advance
  SLOW COOKER = Recipes made in a slow cooker
- **Weeknight Dinners in a Dash**
  Thanks to the "Weeknight Solutions" chapter, Monday-through-Friday suppers are a cinch to serve no matter how time-crunched you are. Enjoy family dinners on even your busiest days.
- **Breakfast and Brunch Made Easy**
  For the first time, you'll find sensational morning recipes together in one convenient chapter. Page through "Breakfast & Brunch" to choose from dozens of sunrise specialties.
- **Step-by-Step Recipe Directions**
  To make it even simpler to whip up the delicious dishes in this book, we've numbered the steps in our recipes. Never lose your place again!
- **Stories About Cooks Like You**
  Get to know the personal stories behind the recipes. We've included photos and quotes from family cooks not only in the "Field Editor Favorites" and "Mom's Best" chapters, but throughout the book.

Featuring 18 big chapters, this can't-miss cookbook also includes hundreds of gorgeous full-color photos, helpful hints from family cooks as well as the pros in the Taste of Home Test Kitchen, and two handy indexes to help you find every recipe you need.

So dig in! Turn the page and start savoring all there is to find inside *2013 Taste of Home Annual Recipes.*

**TASTE-TEMPTING BEST**
Whether you're looking for a special main course, standout side dish or sweet treat, you just can't go wrong with the flavor-packed favorites inside *2013 Taste of Home Annual Recipes.* Indulge in scrumptious specialties such as (above, from top) juicy Santa Fe Strip Steaks (p. 65), fresh-tasting Olive Caprese Salad (p. 26) and rich Greek Honey Nut Pie (p. 120).

# 2013 taste of home ANNUAL RECIPES

■ EDITORIAL
Editor-in-Chief **Catherine Cassidy**

Executive Editor/Print & Digital Books **Stephen C. George**
Creative Director **Howard Greenberg**
Editorial Services Manager **Kerri Balliet**

Senior Editor/Print & Digital Books **Mark Hagen**
Editor **Michelle Rozumalski**
Associate Creative Director **Edwin Robles Jr.**
Art Director **Gretchen Trautman**
Content Production Manager **Julie Wagner**
Layout Designers **Catherine Fletcher, Nancy Novak**
Copy Chief **Deb Warlaumont Mulvey**
Copy Editors **Mary C. Hanson, Dulcie Shoener, Joanne Weintraub**
Recipe Content Manager **Colleen King**
Assistant Photo Coordinator **Mary Ann Koebernik**
Recipe Testing **Taste of Home Test Kitchen**
Food Photography **Taste of Home Photo Studio**
Editorial Assistant **Marilyn Iczkowski**

Editor, *Taste of Home* **Jeanne Ambrose**
Art Director, *Taste of Home* **Erin Burns**
Food Editor, *Taste of Home* **Karen Berner**
Recipe Editor, *Taste of Home* **Irene Yeh**

■ BUSINESS
Vice President, Publisher **Jan Studin, jan_studin@rd.com**
Regional Account Director **Donna Lindskog, donna_lindskog@rd.com**
Eastern Account Director **Joanne Carrara**
Eastern Account Manager **Kari Nestor**
Account Manager **Gina Minerbi**
Midwest & Western Account Director **Jackie Fallon**
Midwest Account Manager **Lorna Phillips**
Michigan Sales Representative **Linda C. Donaldson**
Southwestern Account Representative **Summer Nilsson**

Corporate Digital & Integrated Sales Director, N.A. **Steve Sottile**
Associate Marketing Director, Integrated Solutions **Katie Gaon Wilson**
Digital Sales Planner **Tim Baarda**

General Manager, Taste of Home Cooking Schools **Erin Puariea**

Direct Response Advertising **Katherine Zito, David Geller Associates**

Vice President, Creative Director **Paul Livornese**
Executive Director, Brand Marketing **Leah West**
Senior Marketing Manager **Vanessa Bailey**
Associate Marketing Manager **Betsy Connors**

Vice President, Magazine Marketing **Dave Fiegel**

■ READER'S DIGEST NORTH AMERICA
Vice President, Business Development **Jonathan Bigham**
President, Books and Home Entertaining **Harold Clarke**
Chief Financial Officer **Howard Halligan**
Vice President, General Manager, Reader's Digest Media **Marilynn Jacobs**
Chief Content Officer, Milwaukee **Mark Jannot**
Chief Marketing Officer **Renee Jordan**
Vice President, Chief Sales Officer **Mark Josephson**
General Manager, Milwaukee **Frank Quigley**
Vice President, Chief Content Officer **Liz Vaccariello**

■ THE READER'S DIGEST ASSOCIATION, INC.
President and Chief Executive Officer **Robert E. Guth**

■ COVER PHOTOGRAPHY
Photographer **Rob Hagen**
Food Stylists **Shannon Roum, Sue Draheim**
Set Styling Manager **Stephanie Marchese**


5400 S. 60th St., Greendale WI 53129



International Standard Book Number (13): 978-1-61765-129-8
International Standard Serial Number: 1094-3463


Printed in U.S.A.

1 3 5 7 9 10 8 6 4 2

**PICTURED ON THE BACK COVER** Tangerine-Glazed Turkey (p. 207), Brown Rice Chutney Salad (p. 22) and All-American Bacon Cheeseburgers (p. 32).

**PICTURED AT LEFT** Black-Eyed Susan Cookies (p. 104), Thin-Crust Gluten-Free Pepperoni Pizza (p. 289) and Honey Chipotle Ribs (p. 302).

# contents



**PICTURED ON THE COVER** Wilted Spinach Salad with Butternut Squash (p. 21), Mustard & Cranberry Glazed Ham (p. 210), Parmesan Potatoes Au Gratin (p. 192) and Sauteed Spring Vegetables (p. 192).

# Appetizers & Beverages

When **a little refreshment** is just what you need, turn to this sized-right chapter. You'll find **special snacks and drinks** for holiday dinners, casual parties and family munching anytime.

"Toasted baguette slices burst with flavor when I top them with blue cheese, roasted tomato jam, caramelized onion and balsamic vinegar. They're worth the effort!"

—**DEBBIE REIL** CLEARWATER, FLORIDA

## Herb & Roasted Pepper Cheesecake

Roasted red peppers and fresh herbs lend my savory cheese spread a touch of sweetness, a hint of licorice and a bit of a peppery finish. Top it off with a drizzle of olive oil just before serving, then pass the pita chips.

—**LAURA JULIAN** AMANDA, OHIO

**PREP:** 20 MIN. **BAKE:** 35 MIN. + CHILLING
**MAKES:** 24 SERVINGS

- **3 packages (8 ounces each) cream cheese, softened**
- **¾ cup whole milk ricotta cheese**
- **1½ teaspoons salt**
- **¾ teaspoon pepper**
- **3 eggs, lightly beaten**
- **1½ cups roasted sweet red peppers, drained and finely chopped**
- **¾ cup minced fresh basil**
- **⅓ cup minced fresh chives**
- **3 tablespoons minced fresh thyme**
- **3 tablespoons crumbled cooked bacon**
- **3 garlic cloves, minced**
- **1 tablespoon olive oil**
- **Roasted sweet red pepper strips and additional minced chives, optional**
- **Baked pita chips**

**1.** Place a greased 9-in. springform pan on a double thickness of heavy-duty foil (about 18 in. square). Securely wrap foil around pan.

**2.** Place the cream cheese, ricotta cheese, salt and pepper in a food processor; cover and process until smooth. Add eggs; pulse just until combined. Add the red peppers, herbs, bacon and garlic; cover and pulse just until blended. Pour filling into prepared pan. Place springform pan in a large baking pan; add 1 in. of boiling water to larger pan.

**3.** Bake at 350° for 35-45 minutes or until center is just set and top appears dull. Remove springform pan from water bath; remove foil. Cool cheesecake on a wire rack for 10 minutes; loosen edges from pan with a knife. Cool 1 hour longer. Refrigerate overnight.

**4.** Remove the rim from pan. Just before serving, drizzle cheesecake with oil; top with red pepper strips and chives if desired. Serve with pita chips.

## FAST FIX Ginger Pear Sipper

Here's a refreshing thirst-quencher for brunch or cocktail hour. The fruity sipper will please nearly any palate.

—**SUSAN WESTERFIELD**
ALBUQUERQUE, NEW MEXICO

**PREP/TOTAL TIME:** 5 MIN.
**MAKES:** 1 SERVING

- **3 ounces ginger ale, chilled**
- **3 ounces pear nectar, chilled**
- **1 slice fresh pear**

In a tall glass, combine the ginger ale and pear nectar; garnish with pear slice.

Herb & Roasted Pepper Cheesecake

## FAST FIX Mulled Red Cider

Red wine brings a rosy glow to this warm, holiday-perfect beverage. The spices are a wonderful complement to both the wine and apple cider.
**—STEVE FOY** KIRKWOOD, MISSOURI

**PREP/TOTAL TIME:** 20 MIN.
**MAKES:** 7 SERVINGS (¾ CUP EACH)

- **Cinnamon-sugar, optional**
- **1¾ cups apple cider or juice**
- **½ cup sugar**
- **3 cinnamon sticks (3 inches)**
- **4 whole cloves**
- **1 bottle (750 milliliters) dry red wine**

**1.** If desired, moisten the rims of seven mugs with water. Sprinkle cinnamon-sugar on a plate; dip rims in cinnamon-sugar. Set mugs aside.
**2.** In a large saucepan, combine the cider, sugar, cinnamon sticks and cloves. Cook and stir over medium heat until sugar is dissolved.
**3.** Add wine and heat through. Remove from the heat. Cover and steep for 10 minutes; strain. Serve in prepared mugs.

## FAST FIX After-Dinner Mocha White Chocolate

Give a childhood favorite a grown-up makeover and enjoy a rich, luscious treat. If you'll be serving kids, simply leave out the coffee granules.
**—SCARLETT ELROD**
NEWNAN, GEORGIA

**PREP/TOTAL TIME:** 15 MIN.
**MAKES:** 2 SERVINGS

- **1½ cups 2% milk**
- **3 ounces white baking chocolate, chopped**
- **2 tablespoons instant coffee granules**
- **1 teaspoon vanilla extract**
- **Optional toppings: whipped cream and baking cocoa**

**1.** In a small saucepan, heat milk over medium heat until bubbles form around the sides of the pan (do not boil).
**2.** Place the remaining ingredients in a blender. Add hot milk; cover and process until frothy. Serve in mugs. Top with whipped cream and cocoa if desired.

## Cheddar Gougeres

Gougeres are usually prepared with Gruyere cheese, but I often substitute the sharpest cheddar I can find for bolder flavor. Make this recipe your own with the cheese of your choice.
**—BRIDGET KLUSMAN**
OTSEGO, MICHIGAN

**PREP:** 30 MIN. **BAKE:** 15 MIN.
**MAKES:** 3 DOZEN

- **1 cup water**
- **¼ cup butter, cubed**
- **2½ teaspoons kosher salt, divided**
- **1 cup all-purpose flour**
- **4 eggs**
- **1½ cups shredded sharp cheddar cheese**
- **½ cup minced fresh chives**
- **2 garlic cloves, minced**

**1.** In a large saucepan, bring the water, butter and ½ teaspoon salt to a boil. Add flour all at once and stir until a smooth ball forms. Remove from the heat; let stand for 5 minutes. Add eggs, one at a time, beating well after each addition. Continue beating until mixture is smooth and shiny. Stir in cheese, chives and garlic.
**2.** Drop by tablespoonfuls 1 in. apart onto greased baking sheets. Sprinkle with remaining salt. Bake at 375° for 14-16 minutes or until golden brown. Serve warm.

After-Dinner Mocha White Chocolate

Cheddar Gougeres

## Dress Your Drink

When it comes to special-occasion beverages, garnishes are half the fun. Here are some celebratory ideas to get you started:

- Add extra "yum" to chocolaty drinks by dipping rims of glasses into Irish cream or water, then into powdered hot chocolate.
- Use the same technique to rim drinks with superfine sugar or very finely crushed graham crackers, cookies or candies.
- Chill and enhance beverages with flavored ice cubes made from fruit juice, brewed tea or water mixed with small chunks of fruit.

## FAST FIX Raspberry Hot Cocoa

Garnished with raspberry-flavored marshmallows, whipped cream and chocolate curls, this cool-weather favorite goes from everyday to extra-special in a snap.
—**ANDREW MCDOWELL** LAKE VILLA, ILLINOIS

**PREP/TOTAL TIME:** 10 MIN. **MAKES:** 4 SERVINGS

- **3 cups 2% milk**
- **1 cup frozen unsweetened raspberries, thawed**
- **6 ounces semisweet chocolate, chopped**
- **2 teaspoons sugar**
- **Optional toppings: whipped cream, marshmallows and chocolate curls**

**1.** In a small saucepan, heat milk over medium heat until bubbles form around sides of pan (do not boil).
**2.** Place the raspberries, chocolate and sugar in a blender; cover. While processing, gradually add hot milk in a steady stream. Strain; discard seeds. Serve in mugs; top with whipped cream, marshmallows and chocolate if desired.

## FAST FIX Frosty Pumpkin Nog

Here's a creamy delight for the Christmas season. Once you serve chilled glasses of this nicely spiced beverage to holiday guests, you're sure to get frequent requests.
—**CRYSTAL BRUNS** ILIFF, COLORADO

**PREP/TOTAL TIME:** 10 MIN. **MAKES:** 5 SERVINGS

- **3 cups 2% milk**
- **⅔ cup low-fat vanilla frozen yogurt**
- **½ cup canned pumpkin**
- **¼ cup sugar**
- **1 teaspoon each ground nutmeg, mace and cinnamon**
- **Whipped cream, optional**

In a blender, combine all ingredients; cover and process for 30 seconds or until smooth. Pour into chilled glasses; top with whipped cream if desired. Serve immediately.

Mini Veggie Wagon

## FAST FIX Mini Veggie Wagon

For our family reunion at my sister's farmhouse, I created miniature wagons out of fresh veggies to place on the tables. Even the youngsters had fun eating their vegetables, right down to the cucumber wagon wheels.
—**NELLA PARKER** HERSEY, MICHIGAN

**PREP/TOTAL TIME:** 15 MIN. **MAKES:** 4 SERVINGS

- **2 celery ribs**
- **1 medium cucumber**
- **2 wooden skewers (6 inches)**
- **Fresh baby carrots, broccoli florets and purple cauliflowerets or vegetables of your choice**
- **Vegetable dill dip**

**1.** Cut celery ribs in half lengthwise and then into 6-in. pieces. Cut cucumber into 1/2-in. slices. Place one cucumber slice on the end of each skewer; place celery pieces lengthwise across skewers to form wagon frame.
**2.** Pile carrots, broccoli, cauliflowerets and remaining cucumber on wagon. Serve with dip.

## FAST FIX Butterscotch Martinis

Decadent chocolate and butterscotch schnapps pair up for a nightcap that will satisfy any sweet tooth.
—**CLARA COULSON MINNEY**
WASHINGTON COURT HOUSE, OHIO

**PREP/TOTAL TIME:** 10 MIN. **MAKES:** 2 SERVINGS

- **Ice cubes**
- **¼ cup clear creme de cacao**
- **¼ cup creme de cacao**
- **3 tablespoons vodka**
- **3 tablespoons butterscotch schnapps liqueur**
- **6 semisweet chocolate chips**

**1.** Fill a shaker three-fourths full with ice. Add the creme de cacao, vodka and schnapps.
**2.** Cover and shake for 10-15 seconds or until condensation forms on outside of shaker. Divide chocolate chips between two chilled cocktail glasses; strain butterscotch mixture over chips.

British Tenderloin & Pumpernickel Crostini

## British Tenderloin & Pumpernickel Crostini

I like to use an ovenproof skillet when searing my tenderloin. That way, all the wonderful beef juices stay in the pan while the meat finishes—and it makes for easy cleanup, too!

**—SHARON TIPTON**
WINTER GARDEN, FLORIDA

**PREP:** 20 MIN.
**BAKE:** 30 MIN. + STANDING
**MAKES:** 3 DOZEN

- **1 tablespoon olive oil**
- **1 beef tenderloin roast (2 pounds)**
- **1 teaspoon salt, divided**
- **½ teaspoon coarsely ground pepper**
- **1 cup (8 ounces) sour cream**
- **¼ cup prepared horseradish**
- **2 tablespoons lemon juice**
- **¼ teaspoon paprika**
- **18 slices pumpernickel bread, halved**
- **3 tablespoons butter, melted**
- **1 bunch watercress**

**1.** Rub oil over tenderloin; sprinkle with 3/4 teaspoon salt and pepper. In a large skillet, brown beef on all sides. Place roast on a rack in a shallow roasting pan.
**2.** Bake, uncovered, at 425° for 25-35 minutes or until meat reaches desired doneness (for medium-rare, a meat thermometer should read 145°; medium, 160°; well-done, 170°). Let stand for 10 minutes before slicing thinly.
**3.** In a small bowl, combine the sour cream, horseradish, lemon juice, paprika and remaining salt. Chill until serving.
**4.** Brush both sides of bread with butter; place on baking sheets. Bake at 425° for 4-6 minutes or until toasted, turning once.
**5.** Spread with chilled sauce; top with sliced beef. Garnish with watercress sprigs.

## MAKE AHEAD Kalamata Cheesecake Appetizer

Even if you normally shy away from Kalamata olives, you'll be glad you tried this cheese spread. The other ingredients "tame" the Kalamatas. Prefer a milder flavor? Substitute the more common black or green olives.

**—THERESA KREYCHE**
TUSTIN, CALIFORNIA

**PREP:** 30 MIN.
**BAKE:** 25 MIN. + CHILLING
**MAKES:** 24 SERVINGS

- **1¼ cups seasoned bread crumbs**
- **½ cup finely chopped pecans**
- **⅓ cup butter, melted**

**FILLING**

- **2 packages (one 8 ounces, one 3 ounces) cream cheese, softened**
- **1 cup (8 ounces) sour cream**
- **1 tablespoon all-purpose flour**
- **¼ teaspoon salt**
- **¼ teaspoon pepper**
- **1 egg, lightly beaten**
- **1 egg yolk**
- **½ cup pitted Kalamata olives, chopped**
- **2 teaspoons minced fresh rosemary**
- **Halved pitted Kalamata olives and fresh rosemary sprigs, optional**

**1.** In a small bowl, combine bread crumbs and pecans; stir in butter. Press onto the bottom of a greased 9-in. springform pan. Place pan on a baking sheet. Bake at 350° for 12 minutes. Cool on a wire rack.
**2.** In a large bowl, beat the cream cheese, sour cream, flour, salt and pepper until smooth. Add egg and egg yolk; beat on low speed just until combined. Fold in chopped olives and minced rosemary. Pour over crust. Return pan to baking sheet.
**3.** Bake for 25-30 minutes or until center is almost set. Cool on a wire rack for 10 minutes. Loosen edges of cheesecake from pan with a knife. Cool 1 hour longer. Refrigerate overnight.
**4.** Remove rim from pan. Top cheesecake with halved olives and rosemary sprigs if desired.

Kalamata Cheesecake Appetizer

# CAN'T GET ENOUGH NACHOS!

Everyone loves that party mainstay—nachos loaded with terrific toppings. Next time, take your taste buds on a trip with these recipes inspired by cuisines from around the world.

## Islander Nachos

**PREP:** 40 MIN.
**BAKE:** 10 MIN. + COOLING
**MAKES:** 16 SERVINGS

- **⅓ cup plus 1 tablespoon sugar, divided**
- **2 teaspoons ground cinnamon**
- **⅓ cup honey**
- **¼ cup butter, cubed**
- **8 flour tortillas (8 inches)**
- **4 ounces cream cheese, softened**
- **1 teaspoon vanilla extract**
- **1 container (8 ounces) frozen whipped topping, thawed**
- **½ cup drained crushed pineapple**
- **4 medium bananas, sliced**
- **1 cup flaked coconut, toasted**
- **½ cup chopped macadamia nuts, toasted**

**1.** In a small bowl, combine 1/3 cup sugar and the cinnamon; set aside. In a small saucepan, combine the honey and butter. Cook and stir over medium heat until blended. Brush onto both sides of tortillas; sprinkle tops with sugar mixture.

**2.** Stack tortillas, top sides up; cut into sixths. Arrange wedges, sugared sides up, in a single layer on ungreased baking sheets. Bake at 400° for 6-8 minutes or until crisp and golden brown. Cool completely on wire racks.

**3.** In a large bowl, beat cream cheese, vanilla and remaining sugar until creamy. Beat in whipped topping until blended. Fold in pineapple. Arrange tortilla wedges on a large serving platter. Spoon cream cheese mixture over wedges. Top with bananas, coconut and macadamia nuts. Serve immediately.

## Mediterranean Nachos

To give nachos a Mediterranean twist, smother seasoned pita wedges with ground lamb or beef, feta cheese and a creamy cucumber sauce.
**—ZAZA FULLMAN-KASL**
VENTURA, CALIFORNIA

**PREP:** 30 MIN.+ STANDING
**COOK:** 15 MIN. **MAKES:** 12 SERVINGS

- **2 medium cucumbers, peeled, seeded and grated**
- **1½ teaspoons salt, divided**
- **½ teaspoon ground cumin**
- **½ teaspoon ground coriander**
- **½ teaspoon paprika**
- **¾ teaspoon pepper, divided**
- **6 whole pita breads (6 inches)**
- **Cooking spray**
- **1 pound ground lamb or beef**
- **2 garlic cloves, minced**
- **1 teaspoon cornstarch**
- **½ cup beef broth**
- **2 cups plain Greek yogurt**
- **2 tablespoons lemon juice**
- **¼ teaspoon grated lemon peel**
- **2 cups torn romaine**
- **2 medium tomatoes, seeded and chopped**
- **½ cup pitted Greek olives, sliced**
- **4 green onions, thinly sliced**
- **½ cup crumbled feta cheese**

**1.** In a colander set over a bowl, toss cucumbers with 1/2 teaspoon salt. Let stand 30 minutes. Squeeze and pat dry. Set aside. In a small bowl, combine the cumin, coriander, paprika, 1/2 teaspoon pepper and 1/2 teaspoon salt; set aside.

Mediterranean Nachos

**2.** Cut each pita into eight wedges; arrange in a singer layer on ungreased baking sheets. Spritz both sides of pitas with cooking spray; sprinkle with 3/4 teaspoon seasoning mix. Broil 3-4 in. from the heat for 3-4 minutes on each side or until golden brown. Cool on wire racks.

**3.** In a large skillet, cook lamb and remaining seasoning mix over medium heat until lamb is no longer pink. Add garlic; cook 1 minute longer. Drain. Combine cornstarch and broth until smooth; gradually stir into the pan. Bring to a boil; cook and stir for 2 minutes or until thickened.

**4.** In a small bowl, combine the yogurt, lemon juice, lemon peel, cucumbers and remaining salt and pepper. Arrange pita wedges on a serving platter. Layer with lettuce, lamb mixture, tomatoes, olives, onions and cheese. Serve immediately with cucumber sauce.

You'll feel like you've escaped to the tropics when you munch Hawaiian-style Islander Nachos. Pineapple, bananas, macadamia nuts and coconut combine for the sweet flavors of paradise.
**—JENNIFER HEASLEY** YORK, PENNSLVANIA

## Sicilian Nachos

I serve a homemade meat sauce and Parmesan cheese over crispy bread instead of tortilla chips. To turn this appetizer into a main course, simply add a green salad on the side.

**—SONYA LABBE**
WEST HOLLYWOOD, CALIFORNIA

**PREP:** 20 MIN. **COOK:** 35 MIN.
**MAKES:** 12 SERVINGS

- **1 pound ground beef**
- **1 small red onion, finely chopped**
- **1 small carrot, finely chopped**
- **4 garlic cloves, minced**
- **¾ teaspoon crushed red pepper flakes**
- **½ cup dry red wine or beef broth**
- **1 can (15 ounces) crushed tomatoes, undrained**
- **1 can (8 ounces) tomato sauce**
- **½ cup vegetable broth**
- **1 bay leaf**
- **¼ teaspoon salt**
- **¼ teaspoon pepper**
- **2 tablespoons minced fresh basil or 2 teaspoons dried basil**
- **48 slices French bread baguette (¼ inch thick)**
- **2 garlic cloves, halved**
- **⅓ cup olive oil**
- **1 cup shaved Parmesan cheese**

**1.** In a large skillet, cook the first five ingredients over medium heat until beef is no longer pink; drain. Add wine, stirring to loosen browned bits from pan.
**2.** Stir in the tomatoes, tomato sauce, broth, bay leaf, salt and pepper. Bring to a boil. Reduce heat; simmer, uncovered, for 20-25 minutes or until thickened. Discard bay leaf. Stir in basil.
**3.** Rub baguette slices with garlic halves; place on ungreased baking sheets. Brush lightly with oil. Bake at 400° for 3-5 minutes or until lightly browned.
**4.** Arrange toast on serving platters; top with beef mixture and cheese. Serve immediately.

Beer and Brats Nachos

When it's time for the big game, savor a taste of the Midwest with a platter full of cheesy Beer and Brats Nachos. It's a guaranteed winner with meat lovers.
**—KELLY BOE** WHITELAND, INDIANA

## Beer and Brats Nachos

**PREP/TOTAL TIME:** 30 MIN.
**MAKES:** 12 SERVINGS

- **1 package (14 ounces) fully cooked smoked bratwurst links, sliced**
- **2¼ cups frozen pepper and onion stir-fry blend**
- **3 cups (12 ounces) shredded cheddar cheese**
- **2½ teaspoons all-purpose flour**
- **1 cup chopped onion**
- **1 tablespoon olive oil**
- **1 garlic clove, minced**
- **¾ cup beer or beef broth**
- **12 cups tortilla chips**

**1.** In a large skillet, saute bratwurst for 1 minute. Add stir-fry blend; cook 3-5 minutes longer or until vegetables are tender. Set aside and keep warm.
**2.** In a large bowl, combine cheese and flour. In a large saucepan, saute onion in oil until tender. Add garlic; cook 1 minute longer. Stir in beer; heat over medium heat until bubbles form around sides of pan.
**3.** Reduce heat to medium-low; add a handful of cheese mixture. Stir constantly, using a figure-eight motion, until almost completely melted. Continue adding cheese, one handful at a time, allowing cheese to almost completely melt between additions.
**4.** Arrange the tortilla chips on a large serving platter. Spoon the cheese mixture over the chips. Top with the bratwurst mixture. Serve immediately.

## Miniature Shepherd's Pies

Hearty and sized just right, mini meat pies are perfect for nibbling at holiday parties. Want an alternative to ground beef? Substitute ground lamb and a teaspoon of dried rosemary.

**—SUZANNE BANFIELD**
BASKING RIDGE, NEW JERSEY

**PREP:** 40 MIN. **BAKE:** 15 MIN.
**MAKES:** 4 DOZEN

- **½ pound ground beef**
- **⅓ cup finely chopped onion**
- **¼ cup finely chopped celery**
- **3 tablespoons finely chopped carrot**
- **1½ teaspoons all-purpose flour**
- **1 teaspoon dried thyme**
- **¼ teaspoon salt**
- **⅛ teaspoon ground nutmeg**
- **⅛ teaspoon pepper**
- **⅔ cup beef broth**
- **⅓ cup frozen petite peas**
- **2 packages (17.3 ounces each) frozen puff pastry, thawed**
- **3 cups mashed potatoes**

**1.** In a large skillet, cook the beef, onion, celery and carrot over medium heat until beef is no longer pink; drain. Stir in the flour, thyme, salt, nutmeg and pepper until blended; gradually add the broth. Bring to a boil; cook and stir for 2 minutes or until sauce is thickened. Stir in peas; heat through. Set aside.

**2.** Unfold pastry. Using a floured 2¼-in. round cutter, cut 12 circles from each sheet (save scraps for another use). Press circles onto the bottoms and up the sides of ungreased miniature muffin cups.

**3.** Fill each with 1½ teaspoons beef mixture; top or pipe with 1 tablespoon mashed potatoes. Bake at 400° for 13-16 minutes or until heated through and potatoes are lightly browned. Serve warm.

Miniature Shepherd's Pies

FAST FIX

## Cauliflower Popcorn

Roasting transforms cauliflower into a delectable snack so mellow, your family will gobble it up like popcorn. This snack from the Taste of Home Test Kitchen is a terrific side dish, too.

**PREP/TOTAL TIME:** 30 MIN.
**MAKES:** 4 SERVINGS

- **1 large head cauliflower, broken into small florets**
- **1 tablespoon olive oil**
- **½ teaspoon garlic salt**
- **1 tablespoon grated Parmesan cheese**

Place the cauliflower in a greased 15-in. x 10-in. x 1-in. baking pan. Drizzle with oil and sprinkle with garlic salt; toss to coat. Bake, uncovered, at 400° for 15-18 minutes or until tender, stirring once. Sprinkle with cheese.

## Curried Cranberry Snack Mix

At Christmastime or any time, give loved ones the gift of great flavor with a canister full of this simple-to-make, mouthwatering munchie. Tangy dried cranberries combine wonderfully with French-fried onions, honey mustard, peanuts, spices and more.

**—ROBIN HAAS**
CRANSTON, RHODE ISLAND

**PREP:** 10 MIN.
**COOK:** 15 MIN. + COOLING
**MAKES:** 4 QUARTS

- **6 cups Corn Chex**
- **3 cups Rice Chex**
- **1 can (6 ounces) French-fried onions**
- **2 cups miniature pretzels**
- **1½ cups honey-roasted peanuts**
- **⅓ cup butter, cubed**
- **3 tablespoons honey**
- **2 tablespoons honey mustard**
- **1½ teaspoons curry powder**
- **1 teaspoon garlic powder**
- **1½ cups dried cranberries, divided**

**1.** In a large bowl, combine the first five ingredients. Place the butter, honey, honey mustard, curry powder and garlic powder in a small microwave-safe bowl.

Microwave, uncovered, on high for 1 to 1½ minutes, stirring every 30 seconds or until the mixture is smooth. Pour over cereal mixture and toss to coat.

**2.** Place half of the mixture in a large microwave-safe bowl. Microwave, uncovered, on high for 2-3 minutes, stirring after each minute. Stir in ¾ cup cranberries. Immediately spread onto waxed paper; cool completely. Repeat with remaining cereal and cranberries. Store in an airtight container.

## FAST FIX Citrus Champagne Sparkler

Here's a festive, citrusy Champagne beverage to enjoy at a bridal shower.

**—SHARON TIPTON**
WINTER GARDEN, FLORIDA

**PREP/TOTAL TIME:** 10 MIN.
**MAKES:** 11 SERVINGS

- **1¼ cups orange juice**
- **⅓ cup orange liqueur**
- **⅓ cup brandy**
- **¼ cup sugar**
- **¼ cup lemon juice**
- **¼ cup unsweetened pineapple juice**
- **6 cups chilled Champagne**

In a pitcher, combine the first six ingredients, stirring until sugar is dissolved. Pour ¼ cup into each champagne flute or wine glass. Top with Champagne.

FAST FIX

## Cranberry-Lime Sangria

Tart and fruity, this special sangria is always a hit. Try it with a Cinco de Mayo spread or any Mexican meal.

**—KATY JOOSTEN**
LITTLE CHUTE, WISCONSIN

**PREP/TOTAL TIME:** 20 MIN.
**MAKES:** 13 SERVINGS (¾ CUP EACH)

- **2 cups water**
- **1 cup fresh or frozen cranberries, thawed**
- **1 bottle (750 milliliters) white wine, chilled**
- **¾ cup frozen limeade concentrate, thawed**
- **1 each medium orange, lime and apple, peeled and diced**
- **1 bottle (1 liter) citrus soda, chilled**

**1.** In a small saucepan, combine water and cranberries. Cook over medium heat until berries pop, about 5 minutes. Drain and discard liquid; set cranberries aside.

**2.** In a pitcher, combine the wine and limeade concentrate. Stir in the diced fruit and reserved cranberries; add the soda. Serve over ice.

## Margarita Chicken Quesadillas

Layer flour tortillas with marinated and grilled chicken, sauteed veggies, two kinds of cheese and lime butter. Quesadillas never tasted so good!

**—STEPHANIE BRIGHT**
SIMPSONVILLE, SOUTH CAROLINA

**PREP:** 35 MIN. + MARINATING
**BAKE:** 10 MIN. **MAKES:** 16 WEDGES

- **4 boneless skinless chicken breast halves (5 ounces each)**
- **¾ cup thawed frozen limeade concentrate**
- **1 large onion, sliced**
- **1 medium sweet orange pepper, julienned**
- **1 medium sweet yellow pepper, julienned**
- **2 tablespoons canola oil**
- **¼ teaspoon salt**
- **¼ teaspoon pepper**
- **4 flour tortillas (10 inches)**
- **1 cup (4 ounces) shredded Monterey Jack cheese**
- **1 cup (4 ounces) shredded cheddar cheese**
- **2 tablespoons butter, melted**
- **1 tablespoon lime juice**
- **1 tablespoon chopped fresh cilantro**
- **Lime wedges, optional**

**1.** Place chicken in a large resealable plastic bag; add limeade concentrate. Seal bag and turn to coat. Refrigerate for 6 hours or overnight.

**2.** In a large skillet, saute the onion and sweet peppers in oil until tender; season with salt and pepper. Set aside.

**3.** Moisten a paper towel with cooking oil; using long-handled tongs, lightly coat the grill rack. Drain and discard marinade. Grill chicken, covered, over medium heat or broil 4 in. from the heat for 5-8 minutes on each side or until a thermometer reads 170°. Cut chicken into ¼-in. strips; set aside.

**4.** On one half of each tortilla, layer Monterey Jack cheese, chicken, pepper mixture and cheddar cheese; fold over. Place quesadillas on a baking sheet. Combine butter and lime juice; brush over tortillas. Bake at 350° for 8-10 minutes or until cheese is melted.

**5.** Cut each quesadilla into 4 wedges. Sprinkle with cilantro; serve with lime wedges if desired.

Cranberry-Lime Sangria

Margarita Chicken Quesadillas

## FAST FIX Chipotle Avocado Dip

If you have any of this yummy dip left over, try spooning it on tacos.

—BARBARA OLIPHANT
VALLEY CENTER, KANSAS

**PREP/TOTAL TIME:** 15 MIN.
**MAKES:** 3 CUPS

- **3 medium ripe avocados, peeled**
- **1 cup reduced-fat mayonnaise**
- **¼ cup finely chopped onion**
- **1 tablespoon finely chopped banana pepper**
- **1 tablespoon minced pickled hot cherry peppers**
- **1½ teaspoons garlic powder**
- **1 to 1½ teaspoons ground chipotle pepper**
- **1 teaspoon onion powder**
- **1 teaspoon seasoned salt**
- **Assorted fresh vegetables**

In a small bowl, mash avocados. Stir in mayonnaise, onion, peppers and seasonings. Chill until serving. Serve with vegetables.

**Editor's Note:** *Wear disposable gloves when cutting hot peppers; the oils can burn skin. Avoid touching your face.*

## Shallot-Blue Cheese Dip

Here's a party-perfect appetizer you'll love on baked potatoes, too.

—ALISA PIRTLE
BROWNS VALLEY, CALIFORNIA

**PREP:** 10 MIN.
**COOK:** 30 MIN. + CHILLING
**MAKES:** 2 CUPS

- **1½ cups thinly sliced shallots**
- **1 tablespoon canola oil**
- **¾ cup reduced-fat mayonnaise**
- **¾ cup reduced-fat sour cream**
- **1½ cups (6 ounces) crumbled blue cheese**
- **Assorted fresh vegetables**

**1.** In a large skillet, saute shallots in oil until softened. Reduce heat to medium-low; cook for 25-30 minutes or until deep golden brown, stirring occasionally. Cool to room temperature.

**2.** In a small bowl, combine mayonnaise and sour cream. Stir in blue cheese and caramelized shallots. Cover and refrigerate for at least 2 hours. Serve with vegetables.

Nutty Berry Trail-Mix

## FAST FIX Garlicky Peanut Dip

Enhance fresh vegetables—or perk up your family's dinnertime stir-fry—with this nutty, well-spiced blend.

—SADIE BUECKSLER
ASHLAND, WISCONSIN

**PREP/TOTAL TIME:** 20 MIN.
**MAKES:** 1 CUP

- **1 small onion, chopped**
- **2 tablespoons olive oil**
- **¼ cup sunflower kernels**
- **3 garlic cloves, minced**
- **⅔ cup water**
- **⅓ cup creamy peanut butter**
- **3 tablespoons brown sugar**
- **2 tablespoons reduced-sodium soy sauce**
- **¼ teaspoon ground ginger**
- **¼ teaspoon ground cumin**
- **¼ teaspoon pepper**
- **Dash cayenne pepper**
- **Assorted fresh vegetables**

In a small skillet, saute onion in oil until tender. Add sunflower kernels and garlic; cook 2 minutes longer. Add the water, peanut butter, brown sugar, soy sauce and spices. Bring to a boil; cook and stir until blended. Serve with vegetables.

## FAST FIX Nutty Berry Trail-Mix

My son's favorite trail mix got an "A" in my early childhood nutrition course.

—CHERI MAJORS
CLAREMONT, CALIFORNIA

**PREP/TOTAL TIME:** 5 MIN.
**MAKES:** 10 CUPS

- **1 can (15 ounces) mixed nuts**
- **2 cups (12 ounces) semisweet chocolate chips**
- **1 package (9 ounces) raisins**
- **1 package (6 ounces) chopped dried pineapple**
- **1 jar (5.85 ounces) sunflower kernels**
- **1 package (5 ounces) dried cranberries**

In a large bowl, combine all ingredients; mix well. Store in an airtight container.

**Garlicky Peanut Dip**

**Shallot-Blue Cheese Dip**

**Chipotle Avocado Dip**

## Ranch Spread Snowman

Let your children use colorful veggies and their imagination to decorate a snacktime snowman. They may want to make an extra to leave out for Santa, too.

**—SHERRY AL-TAMIMI** SUGAR VALLEY, GEORGIA

**PREP:** 20 MIN. + CHILLING **MAKES:** 2⅔ CUPS

- **2 packages (8 ounces each) cream cheese, softened**
- **½ cup butter, softened**
- **1 envelope ranch salad dressing mix**
- **1 tablespoon spicy brown mustard**
- **1 garlic clove, minced**
- **Assorted decorations: small pitted ripe olives, pretzel sticks and sweet red and/or orange pepper**
- **Assorted crackers and fresh vegetables**

**1.** In a small bowl, beat cream cheese and butter until smooth. Add the dressing mix, mustard and garlic; mix well. Shape into two balls, one slightly larger than the other. Cover and refrigerate for at least 4 hours.

**2.** Remove from the refrigerator 15 minutes before serving. On a serving plate, stack the small cheese ball on top of the larger ball to make a snowman.

**3.** Cut ends from olives to make small circles; attach to snowman for eyes and buttons. Insert pretzel sticks for arms. Cut top hat from pepper; place on top of snowman. Trim pepper to make a nose; insert into face. Serve with crackers and vegetables.

## MAKE AHEAD Wonton Pot Stickers with Soy Reduction

These special appetizers filled with ground pork freeze so well, I always prepare large batches. That way, I have extras to pull out of the freezer at a moment's notice. If you don't have bok choy—a type of Chinese cabbage with white stems and dark green leaves—regular cabbage will do.

**—MICHAEL ANGELO** SPRING, TEXAS

**PREP:** 45 MIN. + FREEZING **COOK:** 15 MIN./BATCH
**MAKES:** ABOUT 3½ DOZEN (¾ CUP SAUCE)

- **½ cup mirin (sweet rice wine)**
- **½ cup balsamic vinegar**
- **¼ cup reduced-sodium soy sauce**
- **2 fresh basil leaves**

**POT STICKERS**

- **1½ cups finely chopped bok choy**
- **2 tablespoons minced fresh cilantro**
- **1 tablespoon minced fresh gingerroot**
- **1 tablespoon chopped green onion**
- **1 tablespoon oyster sauce**
- **¾ teaspoon toasted sesame oil**
- **1 pound ground pork**
- **45 wonton wrappers**

**ADDITIONAL INGREDIENT**

- **¼ cup toasted sesame oil**

**1.** In a small saucepan, combine the mirin, balsamic vinegar and soy sauce. Bring to a boil; cook until liquid is reduced by half, about 15 minutes. Add basil; cover and steep for 2 minutes. Remove basil and discard. Cool sauce and transfer to a freezer container.

**2.** For pot stickers, combine the first six ingredients in a large bowl. Crumble pork over mixture and mix well.

**3.** Place about 1 tablespoon pork mixture in the center of each wonton wrapper. (Keep remaining wrappers covered with a damp paper towel until ready to use.) Moisten edges with water. Fold one corner diagonally over filling and press edges to seal.

**4.** Place on a waxed paper-lined 15-in. x 10-in. x 1-in. baking sheet; freeze until firm. Transfer to resealable plastic freezer bags. May be frozen for up to 3 months.

**5. TO USE POT STICKERS:** Thaw sauce in the refrigerator overnight. Arrange a fourth of the pot stickers 1 in. apart in a greased steamer; place in a large saucepan over 1 in. of water. Bring to a boil; cover and steam for 12-14 minutes or until a thermometer inserted into filling reads 160°. Repeat with remaining pot stickers.

**6.** In a large skillet, cook pot stickers in oil in batches over medium-high heat for 1-2 minutes on each side or until golden brown. Serve with sauce.

**Editor's Note:** *Look for mirin in the Asian condiments section.*

## Steak & Blue Cheese Bruschetta with Onion & Roasted Tomato Jam

Toasted baguette slices burst with flavor when I top them with blue cheese, roasted tomato jam, caramelized onion and balsamic vinegar. They're worth the effort!

**—DEBBIE REID** CLEARWATER, FLORIDA

**PREP:** 45 MIN. **GRILL:** 10 MIN.
**MAKES:** 16 APPETIZERS (¾ CUP TOMATO JAM)

- **1 large sweet onion, halved and thinly sliced**
- **5 tablespoons olive oil, divided**
- **1 cup grape tomatoes, halved**
- **½ teaspoon kosher salt, divided**
- **¼ teaspoon freshly ground pepper, divided**
- **6 ounces cream cheese, softened**
- **3 ounces crumbled blue cheese**
- **3 garlic cloves, minced**
- **16 slices French bread baguette (½ inch thick)**
- **2 beef ribeye steaks (¾ inch thick and 8 ounces each)**
- **1½ teaspoons Montreal steak seasoning**
- **2 tablespoons balsamic vinegar**

**1.** In large skillet, cook and stir onion in 2 tablespoons oil over medium-high heat until softened. Reduce heat to medium-low; cook 30 minutes or until golden brown, stirring occasionally.
**2.** Place the tomatoes in a shallow baking pan. Add 1 tablespoon oil, 1/4 teaspoon salt and 1/8 teaspoon pepper; toss to coat. Bake at 400° for 10-15 minutes or until softened. Lightly mash tomatoes; stir into onions.
**3.** In small bowl, mix cream cheese, blue cheese, garlic and remaining salt and pepper until blended.
**4.** Brush both sides of baguette slices with remaining oil. Grill over medium heat 1-2 minutes on each side or until toasted.
**5.** Sprinkle both sides of steaks with seasoning. Grill, covered, over medium heat for 3-5 minutes on each side or until meat reaches desired doneness (for medium-rare, a thermometer should read 145°; medium, 160°; well-done, 170°). Let stand 5 minutes before slicing.
**6.** Spread cheese mixture onto toasts; top with steak and onion mixture. Drizzle with vinegar.

**Steak & Blue Cheese Bruschetta with Onion & Roasted Tomato Jam**

## Greek-Style Pizza

Savor the tastes of Greece with this appetizing pie. To ensure a crisp, flaky crust, drain the tomato slices on a paper towel to soak up extra moisture before assembling the pizza.

**—CLAIRE TORRICE** OSWEGO, NEW YORK

**PREP:** 25 MIN. **BAKE:** 25 MIN. **MAKES:** 18 SERVINGS

- **¼ cup butter, cubed**
- **¼ cup olive oil**
- **½ pound sliced fresh mushrooms**
- **1 medium onion, sliced**
- **3 garlic cloves, minced**
- **1 package (10 ounces) fresh spinach, trimmed and coarsely chopped**
- **1 tablespoon lemon juice**
- **1 teaspoon dried basil**
- **1 teaspoon dried oregano**
- **1 package (16 ounces, 14-inch x 9-inch sheet size) frozen phyllo dough, thawed**
- **2 cups (8 ounces) shredded part-skim mozzarella cheese**
- **1 cup (4 ounces) crumbled feta cheese**
- **3 medium ripe tomatoes, sliced**
- **½ cup seasoned bread crumbs**

**1.** In a large skillet, melt butter. Transfer to a small bowl; add oil and set aside. In the same skillet, saute the mushrooms, onion and garlic until tender. Add spinach; saute until wilted. Add the lemon juice, basil and oregano; set aside.
**2.** Brush a 13-in. x 9-in. baking dish with reserved butter mixture. Place one sheet of phyllo dough in baking dish; brush lightly with butter mixture. (Keep remaining phyllo covered with plastic wrap and a damp towel to prevent it from drying out.) Repeat layers with remaining phyllo, brushing each layer.
**3.** Top with the spinach mixture; sprinkle with cheeses. Coat both sides of tomato slices with bread crumbs; arrange over top. Bake at 375° for 25-30 minutes or until cheese is melted and crust is golden brown.

# Salads & Dressings

**Toss together** any of the fresh-tasting recipes in this chapter. Whether you need a dish for a potluck or a side to round out a family dinner, **these special medleys** are the perfect picks.

"Here's a light, refreshing blend to enjoy on a summer day...or anytime! The made-from-scratch vinaigrette comes together quickly with just olive oil, jalapeno pepper jelly, raspberry vinegar and allspice."

—**ROXANNE CHAN** ALBANY, CALIFORNIA

## Green Bean and Walnut Salad

Cranberries give these dressed-up green beans a tasty twist. Everyone loves the crunchy walnuts, too.

**—DEBORAH GIUSTI**
HOT SPRINGS, ARKANSAS

**PREP:** 15 MIN. **COOK:** 5 MIN. + CHILLING
**MAKES:** 12 SERVINGS

- **3 pounds fresh green beans, trimmed**
- **¾ cup chopped walnuts**
- **⅓ cup dried cranberries**

**VINAIGRETTE**

- **6 tablespoons olive oil**
- **6 tablespoons red wine vinegar**
- **3 garlic cloves, minced**
- **½ teaspoon salt**
- **½ teaspoon pepper**

**1.** Place beans in a Dutch oven and cover with water. Bring to a boil. Cover and cook for 4-7 minutes or until crisp-tender; drain.
**2.** In a large bowl, combine the beans, walnuts and cranberries. In a small bowl, whisk the vinaigrette ingredients. Pour over bean mixture; toss to coat. Cover and refrigerate until chilled. Toss before serving.

Green Bean and Walnut Salad

## FAST FIX Honey-Orange Broccoli Slaw

When you need coleslaw quickly, here's a great choice. Hints of honey and citrus make it special.

**—DEBBIE CASSAR**
ROCKFORD, MICHIGAN

**PREP/TOTAL TIME:** 15 MIN.
**MAKES:** 6 SERVINGS

- **1 package (12 ounces) broccoli coleslaw mix**
- **⅓ cup sliced almonds**
- **⅓ cup raisins**
- **2 to 3 tablespoons honey**
- **2 tablespoons olive oil**
- **2 tablespoons orange juice**
- **4 teaspoons grated orange peel**
- **¼ teaspoon salt**

In a large bowl, combine the coleslaw mix, almonds and raisins. In a small bowl, whisk the remaining ingredients. Pour over salad; toss to coat.

## FAST FIX Goat Cheese Lettuce Cups

The slightly peppery bite of a radish goes surprisingly well with a juicy apple. Bring the two together in a light, lemony dressing and sprinkle it all with crumbled goat cheese.

**—TOM FAGLON**
SOMERSET, NEW JERSEY

**PREP/TOTAL TIME:** 20 MIN.
**MAKES:** 4 SERVINGS

- **12 radishes, thinly sliced**
- **1 large apple, peeled and thinly sliced**
- **2 tablespoons olive oil**
- **2 tablespoons lemon juice**
- **1 teaspoon grated lemon peel**
- **¼ teaspoon salt**
- **⅛ teaspoon pepper**
- **4 Bibb or Boston lettuce leaves**
- **1 package (4 ounces) herbed fresh goat cheese, crumbled**

In a small bowl, combine radishes and apple. In another bowl, whisk the oil, lemon juice, lemon peel, salt and pepper. Add to radish mixture; toss to coat. Just before serving, place radish mixture in lettuce leaves; top with cheese.

Turkey Pinto Bean Salad with Southern Molasses Dressing

## Turkey Pinto Bean Salad with Southern Molasses Dressing

Loaded with lean protein, this filling main course that uses leftover turkey is a welcome alternative to the usual post-Thanksgiving Day fare.

**—LILY JULOW** GAINESVILLE, FLORIDA

**PREP:** 35 MIN. + CHILLING
**MAKES:** 6 SERVINGS

- **½ cup oil-packed sun-dried tomatoes**
- **1 garlic clove, peeled and halved**
- **½ cup molasses**
- **3 tablespoons cider vinegar**
- **1 teaspoon prepared mustard**
- **½ teaspoon salt**
- **¼ teaspoon coarsely ground pepper**
- **3 cups cubed cooked turkey breast**
- **2 cans (15 ounces each) pinto beans, rinsed and drained**
- **1 medium green pepper, diced**
- **2 celery ribs, diced**
- **1 cup chopped sweet onion**
- **¼ cup minced fresh parsley**

**1.** Drain tomatoes, reserving 2 tablespoons oil. Place garlic and tomatoes in a food processor; cover and process until chopped. Add the molasses, vinegar, mustard, salt, pepper and reserved oil. Cover and process until smooth.
**2.** In a large bowl, combine the turkey, beans, green pepper, celery, onion and parsley. Add dressing and toss to coat. Cover and refrigerate for at least 2 hours.

## Wilted Spinach Salad with Butternut Squash

Round out a special autumn or winter dinner with this warm, tongue-tingling salad full of harvesttime ingredients. The made-from-scratch cranberry dressing and butternut squash spiced with chili powder add amazing flavor!

**—MARGEE BERRY**
WHITE SALMON, WASHINGTON

**PREP:** 20 MIN. **COOK:** 25 MIN.
**MAKES:** 4 SERVINGS

- **1 cup cubed peeled butternut squash**
- **½ teaspoon chili powder**
- **½ teaspoon salt, divided**
- **4 teaspoons olive oil, divided**
- **⅓ cup balsamic vinegar**
- **2 tablespoons dry red wine or chicken broth**
- **2 tablespoons whole-berry cranberry sauce**
- **5 cups fresh baby spinach**
- **4 slices red onion**
- **½ cup dried cranberries**
- **⅓ cup slivered almonds, toasted**
- **⅓ cup crumbled goat cheese**
- **Coarsely ground pepper, optional**

**1.** In a small skillet, saute the squash, chili powder and 1/4 teaspoon salt in 2 teaspoons oil for 11-13 minutes or until tender. Set aside; keep warm.

**2.** In a small saucepan, bring vinegar to a boil. Reduce heat; simmer for 4-6 minutes or until reduced to 1/4 cup. Stir in the wine, cranberry sauce, remaining oil and remaining salt. Bring to a boil; cook 1 minute longer.

**3.** Place spinach on a serving platter; top with red onion, dried cranberries and squash mixture. Drizzle with warm dressing. Sprinkle with slivered almonds, goat cheese and pepper if desired. Serve immediately.

**Wilted Spinach Salad with Butternut Squash**

Wilted Spinach Salad with Butternut Squash is a holiday-worthy treat. To make quick work of peeling the squash, prick it with a fork and give it 45 seconds in the microwave. Then, trim an inch from the base of the squash, making it stand up straight and tall while you run the peeler from top to bottom.

**—MARGEE BERRY** WHITE SALMON, WASHINGTON

## Brown Rice Chutney Salad

A simple rice salad in a cafe inspired me to add chutney and Indian spices to this dish. To fire things up even more, mix in a small amount of hot chili oil, tasting often as you go.

**—BROOKE MARTIN**
GREENFIELD, MINNESOTA

**PREP:** 30 MIN. + CHILLING
**MAKES:** 8 SERVINGS

- **8 cups cooked brown rice, cooled**
- **3 medium carrots, shredded**
- **¾ cup dried cranberries**
- **1 small sweet red pepper, chopped**
- **3 green onions, sliced**
- **½ cup mango chutney**
- **3 tablespoons olive oil**
- **2 tablespoons red wine vinegar**
- **2 teaspoons curry powder**
- **½ teaspoon salt**
- **½ teaspoon garam masala**
- **3 cups fresh baby spinach, chopped if desired**
- **1 medium apple, chopped**
- **1 cup salted cashews**

**1.** In a large bowl, combine the first five ingredients. In a small bowl, whisk the chutney, oil, vinegar, curry powder, salt and garam masala. Pour over rice mixture; toss to coat. Refrigerate for several hours.

**2.** Just before serving, add spinach and apple; toss to combine. Sprinkle with cashews.

**Editor's Note:** *Look for garam masala in the spice aisle.*

Brown Rice Chutney Salad

## FAST FIX Apple, Blue Cheese & Bibb Salad

Red or Golden Delicious apples bring a burst of fall flavor to ordinary lettuce. Tossing in toasted walnuts and blue cheese makes it even more special.

**—REBEKAH BEYER** SABETHA, KANSAS

**PREP/TOTAL TIME:** 20 MIN.
**MAKES:** 9 SERVINGS

- **4 cups torn Bibb or Boston lettuce**
- **3 medium Red and/or Golden Delicious apples, chopped**
- **½ cup olive oil**
- **1 tablespoon white balsamic vinegar or white wine vinegar**
- **1 tablespoon honey**
- **1 tablespoon mayonnaise**
- **½ teaspoon mustard seed, toasted**
- **½ teaspoon stone-ground mustard (whole grain)**
- **¼ teaspoon salt**
- **⅛ teaspoon coarsely ground pepper**
- **1 cup crumbled blue cheese**
- **¾ cup walnut halves, toasted**
- **½ cup golden raisins**

In a salad bowl, combine the lettuce and apples. In a small bowl, whisk the oil, vinegar, honey, mayonnaise, mustard seed, mustard, salt and pepper. Drizzle over salad and toss to coat. Sprinkle with cheese, walnuts and raisins. Serve immediately.

## Pasta & Sun-Dried Tomato Salad

The beauty of orzo is that it can be served warm or cold. This is an ideal contribution to picnics and cookouts.

**—DAWN WILLIAMS**
SCOTTSBORO, ALABAMA

**PREP:** 20 MIN. **COOK:** 15 MIN.
**MAKES:** 8 SERVINGS

- **1 can (49 ounces) reduced-sodium chicken broth**
- **1 package (16 ounces) orzo pasta**
- **¼ cup chopped oil-packed sun-dried tomatoes plus 2 teaspoons oil from the jar**
- **1 garlic clove, minced**
- **¾ teaspoon salt**
- **¼ teaspoon pepper**
- **⅓ cup shredded Parmesan cheese**
- **4 fresh basil leaves, thinly sliced**
- **Optional toppings: crumbled feta cheese and canned garbanzo beans**

**1.** In a large saucepan, bring broth to a boil. Stir in orzo; return to a boil. Cook for 8-10 minutes or until tender, stirring occasionally.

**2.** Drain orzo; transfer to a large bowl. (Discard broth or save for another use.) Stir in the tomatoes, oil from sun-dried tomatoes, garlic, salt and pepper; cool completely.

**3.** Add Parmesan cheese and basil; toss to combine. Cover and refrigerate until serving. Serve with toppings if desired.

## FAST FIX Turkey Spinach Salad with Cranberry-Raspberry Dressing

Savor your leftover turkey in this hearty medley. For a variation, replace the nuts with fried wonton strips.

**—ELIZABETH KING**
DULUTH, MINNESOTA

**PREP/TOTAL TIME:** 30 MIN.
**MAKES:** 6 SERVINGS (⅔ CUP DRESSING)

- **½ cup whole-berry cranberry sauce**
- **2 tablespoons raspberry vinegar**
- **2 tablespoons seedless raspberry jam**
- **¼ teaspoon salt**
- **⅓ cup olive oil**

**SALAD**

- **8 cups fresh spinach, torn**
- **3 medium kiwifruit, peeled and sliced, divided**
- **1 cup fresh raspberries, divided**
- **½ cup whole-berry cranberry sauce**
- **2 cups diced cooked turkey breast**
- **¾ cup coarsely chopped macadamia nuts, toasted**

**1.** In a blender, combine the cranberry sauce, vinegar, jam and salt. Cover and process until smooth. While processing, gradually add oil in a steady stream. Refrigerate until chilled.
**2.** To serve, combine the spinach, half of the kiwi, ½ cup raspberries and cranberry sauce in a large bowl. Add ½ cup dressing; toss to coat. Transfer to a serving platter. Arrange the turkey, macadamia nuts and remaining fruit over top; drizzle with remaining dressing. Serve immediately.

## FAST FIX All-Spiced-Up Raspberry and Mushroom Salad

Here's a light, refreshing blend to enjoy on a summer day...anytime! The made-from-scratch vinaigrette comes together quickly with just olive oil, jalapeno pepper jelly, raspberry vinegar and allspice.

**—ROXANNE CHAN**
ALBANY, CALIFORNIA

**PREP/TOTAL TIME:** 30 MIN.
**MAKES:** 4 SERVINGS

- **2 tablespoons raspberry vinegar**
- **2 tablespoons olive oil, divided**
- **1 tablespoon red jalapeno pepper jelly**
- **¼ teaspoon ground allspice**
- **1 pound small fresh mushrooms, halved**
- **4 cups spring mix salad greens**
- **1 cup fresh raspberries**
- **2 tablespoons chopped red onion**
- **2 tablespoons minced fresh mint**
- **2 tablespoons sliced almonds, toasted**
- **¼ cup crumbled goat cheese**

**1.** In a small bowl, whisk the vinegar, 1 tablespoon oil, pepper jelly and allspice; set aside.
**2.** In a large skillet, cook and stir mushrooms in remaining oil over medium-high heat until tender; cool slightly.
**3.** In a large bowl, combine the salad greens, raspberries, onion, mint and almonds. Add mushrooms and vinaigrette; toss to combine. Sprinkle with goat cheese; serve immediately.

Turkey Spinach Salad with Cranberry-Raspberry Dressing

All-Spiced-Up Raspberry and Mushroom Salad

### Key to Kiwi

To quickly peel kiwifruit, try using a teaspoon. This method works best with fruit that is ripe but not too soft.

First, cut off both ends of the kiwi and slip a teaspoon just under the skin, matching the spoon's curve to the curve of the fruit. Then slide the spoon around the kiwi to separate the fruit from the skin. Once the spoon has been run around the fruit, it will easily slip out of the skin in one piece.

### Mushroom Matters

Select mushrooms with fresh, firm, smooth caps with closed gills. Avoid mushrooms that are shriveled or moist or that have cracks, brown spots or blemishes.

To clean mushrooms, gently remove dirt by rubbing them with a mushroom brush or wiping them with a damp paper towel. Or quickly rinse them under cold water, drain and pat dry with paper towels. Do not peel mushrooms.

## FAST FIX Lemon Dijon Dressing

**PREP/TOTAL TIME:** 10 MIN.
**MAKES:** ABOUT 1 CUP

- ½ cup lemon juice
- ⅓ cup light corn syrup
- ¼ cup canola oil
- 1 tablespoon finely chopped red onion
- 2 teaspoons Dijon mustard
- ½ teaspoon salt

Place all ingredients in a jar with a tight-fitting lid; shake well. Just before serving, shake dressing and drizzle over salad; toss to coat.

With plenty of citrus and mustard, my super-fast Lemon Dijon Dressing has a nice tang that's balanced by a hint of sweetness. Try it over spinach or mixed greens with cucumber and tomatoes.
—**BRYAN BRAACK** ELDRIDGE, IOWA

## Ruby Raspberry Slaw

Give ordinary coleslaw a "berry" good twist. It's sure to get rave reviews.
—**DEBORAH BIGGS**
OMAHA, NEBRASKA

**PREP:** 15 MIN. + CHILLING
**MAKES:** 6 SERVINGS

- 2 cups shredded red cabbage
- 2 cups shredded cabbage
- 1 cup shredded carrots
- ¼ cup prepared raspberry vinaigrette
- 3 tablespoons mayonnaise
- ¼ teaspoon pepper
- ½ cup fresh raspberries

**1.** In a large bowl, combine cabbages and carrots. In a small bowl, whisk the vinaigrette, mayonnaise and pepper. Pour over cabbage mixture; toss to coat. Cover and refrigerate for 10 minutes.
**2.** Top with raspberries and serve.

## Cobb Salad

The Taste of Home Test Kitchen put a fresh spin on this all-American dish.

**PREP/TOTAL TIME:** 40 MIN.
**MAKES:** 6 SERVINGS (1¼ CUPS DRESSING)

- ¼ cup red wine vinegar
- 2 teaspoons salt
- 1 teaspoon lemon juice
- 1 small garlic clove, minced
- ¾ teaspoon coarsely ground pepper
- ¾ teaspoon Worcestershire sauce
- ¼ teaspoon sugar
- ¼ teaspoon ground mustard
- ¾ cup canola oil
- ¼ cup olive oil

**SALAD**

- 6½ cups torn romaine
- 2½ cups torn curly endive
- 1 bunch watercress (4 ounces), trimmed, divided
- 2 cooked chicken breasts, chopped
- 2 medium tomatoes, seeded and chopped
- 1 medium ripe avocado, peeled and chopped
- 3 hard-cooked eggs, chopped
- ½ cup crumbled blue or Roquefort cheese
- 6 bacon strips, cooked and crumbled
- 2 tablespoons minced fresh chives

**1.** In a blender, combine the first eight ingredients. While processing, gradually add canola and olive oils in a steady stream.
**2.** In a large bowl, combine the romaine, endive and half of the watercress; toss lightly. Transfer to a serving platter. Arrange the chicken, tomatoes, avocado, eggs, cheese and bacon over the greens; sprinkle with chives. Top with remaining watercress. Cover and chill until serving.
**3.** To serve, drizzle 1 cup dressing over salad and toss to coat. Serve with remaining dressing if desired.

## Grandma's Potato Salad

Our Fourth of July feast just wouldn't be complete without a bowl of Grandma's cool, creamy classic.
—**SUE GRONHOLZ**
BEAVER DAM, WISCONSIN

**PREP:** 45 MIN. + COOLING
**COOK:** 15 MIN. + CHILLING
**MAKES:** 24 SERVINGS (¾ CUP EACH)

- 6 pounds medium red potatoes
- Water

**DRESSING**

- 1 cup water
- ½ cup butter, cubed
- ¼ cup white vinegar
- 2 eggs
- ½ cup sugar
- 4½ teaspoons cornstarch
- ¾ cup heavy whipping cream
- ¾ cup Miracle Whip

**SALAD**

- 1 small onion, finely chopped
- 2 green onions, sliced
- 1 teaspoon salt
- ½ teaspoon pepper
- 3 hard-cooked eggs, sliced
- Paprika

**1.** Place potatoes in a stockpot and cover with water. Bring to a boil. Reduce heat; cover and cook for 15-20 minutes or until tender. Drain. When cool enough to handle, peel and slice potatoes; cool completely.
**2.** For dressing, in the top of a double boiler or metal bowl over barely simmering water, heat water, butter and vinegar until butter is melted. In a small bowl, beat eggs; add sugar and cornstarch. Add to butter mixture; cook and stir for 5-7 minutes or until thickened. Transfer to a large bowl; cool completely.
**3.** In a small bowl, beat cream until stiff peaks form. Stir Miracle Whip into cooled dressing mixture; fold in whipped cream. Stir in onion, green onions, salt and pepper. Add potatoes; toss lightly to combine. Refrigerate, covered, until chilled.
**4.** To serve, top with hard-cooked eggs; sprinkle with paprika.

Grandma's
Potato Salad

## Olive Caprese Salad

When heirloom tomatoes arrive, enhance them with red onions, green olives and a surprising twist—star anise.
—**JULIE MERRIMAN** COLD BROOK, NEW YORK

**PREP:** 35 MIN. **COOK:** 5 MIN. + MARINATING
**MAKES:** 10 SERVINGS

- **1 cup plus 2 tablespoons red wine vinegar, divided**
- **½ cup sugar**
- **1 whole star anise**
- **¾ cup thinly sliced red onion (about ½ medium)**
- **2 pounds medium heirloom tomatoes, cut into wedges**
- **2 cups heirloom cherry tomatoes, halved**
- **1 cup pitted green olives, halved**
- **8 ounces fresh mozzarella cheese, sliced and halved**
- **1 tablespoon each minced fresh basil, tarragon, mint and cilantro**
- **1 serrano pepper, thinly sliced**
- **¼ cup olive oil**
- **2 tablespoons lime juice**
- **1½ teaspoons grated lime peel**
- **¼ teaspoon salt, optional**

**1.** In a small saucepan, combine 1 cup vinegar, sugar and star anise. Bring to a boil, stirring to dissolve sugar. Remove from the heat. Cool slightly; stir in onion. Let stand for 30 minutes.
**2.** In a large bowl, combine the tomatoes, olives, cheese, herbs and serrano pepper. Remove star anise from onion mixture; drain onion, reserving 2 tablespoons marinade. (Discard remaining marinade or save for other use.) Add onion to tomato mixture.

Olive Caprese Salad

Summer Corn Salad

**3.** In a small bowl, whisk the oil, lime juice, lime peel and remaining vinegar; pour over tomato mixture. Drizzle with reserved marinade; toss gently to coat. Season with salt if desired. Serve immediately.
**Editor's Note:** *Wear disposable gloves when cutting hot peppers; the oils can burn skin. Avoid touching your face.*

## FAST FIX Summer Corn Salad

The tastes of summer are on full display in this beautiful dish. It's loaded with colorful vegetables and basil. Plus, crumbled feta cheese tops it all off in a rich, tangy way.
—**PRISCILLA YEE** CONCORD, CALIFORNIA

**PREP:** 20 MIN. + STANDING **MAKES:** 4 SERVINGS

- **5 teaspoons olive oil, divided**
- **1 tablespoon lime juice**
- **¼ teaspoon salt**
- **¼ teaspoon hot pepper sauce**
- **1½ cups fresh or frozen corn, thawed**
- **1½ cups cherry tomatoes, halved**
- **½ cup finely chopped cucumber**
- **¼ cup finely chopped red onion**
- **2 tablespoons minced fresh basil or 2 teaspoons dried basil**
- **¼ cup crumbled feta cheese**

**1.** In a small bowl, whisk 4 teaspoons oil, lime juice, salt and pepper sauce; set aside.
**2.** In a large skillet, cook and stir corn in remaining oil over medium-high heat until tender. Transfer to a salad bowl; cool slightly. Add the tomatoes, cucumber, onion and basil. Drizzle with dressing and toss to coat.
**3.** Let stand for 10 minutes before serving or refrigerate until chilled. Sprinkle with cheese just before serving.

## FAST FIX ▸ Chicken & Rice Salad with Peanut Sauce

A dinner worthy of a Thai restaurant just doesn't get much speedier than this 10-minute entree. Want a bit of extra heat? Sprinkle it with crushed red pepper flakes.
—**SHERRI MELOTIK** OAK CREEK, WISCONSIN

**PREP/TOTAL TIME:** 10 MIN. **MAKES:** 6 SERVINGS

- **2 packages (8.8 ounces each) ready-to-serve long grain rice**
- **⅔ cup Thai peanut sauce**
- **2 tablespoons canola oil**
- **2 tablespoons water**
- **1 package (16 ounces) coleslaw mix**
- **2 packages (6 ounces each) ready-to-use grilled chicken breast strips**
- **½ cup torn cilantro leaves**
- **1½ cups dry roasted peanuts**

**1.** Prepare rice according to package directions; remove to a large bowl. Meanwhile, in a small bowl, whisk the peanut sauce, oil and water until blended; set aside.
**2.** Add the coleslaw mix, chicken and cilantro to the rice. Drizzle with the peanut sauce mixture; toss to combine. Sprinkle with peanuts; serve immediately.

## FAST FIX ▸ Grilled Chicken on Greens with Citrus Dressing

If you love salads with the flavors of the Southwest—cumin, chili powder and a little cayenne heat—here's the recipe you've been waiting for. The combination of grilled chicken strips, fresh veggies and cheddar cheese makes a delicious, satisfying main course. You won't want to skip the spicy homemade dressing, which keeps well in the refrigerator.
—**THERESE ANDERSON** PINE CITY, MINNESOTA

**PREP/TOTAL TIME:** 30 MIN. **MAKES:** 8 SERVINGS

- **1 pound boneless skinless chicken breasts**

**DRESSING**

- **1 cup mayonnaise**
- **1 cup (8 ounces) sour cream**
- **⅓ cup orange juice**
- **2 tablespoons lemon juice**
- **4 teaspoons grated orange peel**
- **1 tablespoon ground cumin**
- **1 tablespoon chili powder**
- **1 teaspoon pepper**
- **1 garlic clove, minced**
- **¼ teaspoon salt**
- **¼ teaspoon cayenne pepper**

Grilled Chicken on Greens with Citrus Dressing

**SALAD**

- **4 cups torn leaf lettuce**
- **1 medium tomato, seeded and chopped**
- **1 medium red onion, chopped**
- **1 medium sweet red pepper, chopped**
- **1 medium green pepper, chopped**
- **½ cup shredded cheddar cheese**

**1.** Moisten a paper towel with cooking oil; using long-handled tongs, lightly coat the grill rack. Grill chicken, covered, over medium heat or broil 4 in. from the heat for 5-7 minutes on each side or until a thermometer reads 170°.
**2.** Meanwhile, in a small bowl, combine the dressing ingredients; set aside. In a large bowl, combine the lettuce, tomato, onion, peppers and cheese; divide among eight plates. Cut chicken into bite-size pieces; place over salad. Serve with dressing.

Grating fresh orange peel is a lot easier when you place the orange in the freezer the night before. I also wear a pair of clean gloves to protect my fingertips while grating.
—**JENNIFER BENSON** SHEBOYGAN, WISCONSIN

# Soups & Sandwiches

When it comes to **comforting combos**, it's hard to beat a steaming bowl of soup and stacked-high sandwich. So go ahead and treat yourself to the **rave-winning recipes** in this chapter.

"Want to enjoy a sensational burger without paying high restaurant prices? This recipe beefs up a juicy patty with bacon, cheddar cheese and more."

—**JACKIE BURNS** KETTLE FALLS, WASHINGTON

MAKE AHEAD

## Roasted Tomato Soup

Just before the first frost of the season, we gather up all of the tomatoes from my mother's garden to create this flavor-packed favorite. We serve slices of toasted bread spread with pesto on the side.

**—KAITLYN LERDAHL**
MADISON, WISCONSIN

**PREP:** 30 MIN. + FREEZING **COOK:** 30 MIN.
**MAKES:** 6 SERVINGS (1½ QUARTS)

- **15 large tomatoes (5 pounds), seeded and quartered**
- **¼ cup plus 2 tablespoons canola oil, divided**
- **8 garlic cloves, minced**
- **1 large onion, chopped**
- **2 cups water**
- **1 teaspoon salt**
- **½ teaspoon crushed red pepper flakes, optional**
- **½ cup heavy whipping cream**
- **Fresh basil leaves, optional**

1. Place tomatoes in a greased 15-in. x 10-in. x 1-in. baking pan. Combine 1/4 cup oil and garlic; drizzle over tomatoes. Toss to coat. Bake at 400° for 15-20 minutes or until softened, stirring occasionally. Remove and discard skins.
2. Meanwhile, in a Dutch oven, saute onion in remaining oil until tender. Add the tomatoes, water, salt and, if desired, pepper flakes. Bring to a boil. Reduce heat; cover and simmer for 30 minutes or until flavors are blended. Cool slightly.
3. In a blender, process soup in batches until smooth. Stir in cream; heat through. Cool; transfer to freezer containers. Cover and freeze for up to 3 months.
4. **TO USE FROZEN SOUP:** Thaw in the refrigerator overnight. Place in a large saucepan; heat through. Garnish with basil if desired.

Roasted Tomato Soup

## Best Beefy Burgers with Roasted Onion & Peppercorn Mayo

Red onions and mayonnaise blended with crushed peppercorns make an extra-special, gotta-try-it burger.

**—MELISSA JELINEK**
MENOMONEE FALLS, WISCONSIN

**PREP:** 20 MIN. **COOK:** 15 MIN.
**MAKES:** 4 SERVINGS

- **1 small red onion, chopped**
- **1 tablespoon olive oil**
- **1¼ teaspoons salt, divided**
- **½ cup mayonnaise**
- **½ teaspoon whole peppercorns, crushed**
- **1½ pounds ground beef**
- **4 kaiser rolls, split and toasted**
- **Optional ingredients: tomato slices and lettuce leaves**

1. Place onion on a greased baking sheet. Drizzle with oil and sprinkle with 1/4 teaspoon salt; toss to coat. Bake at 400° for 8-12 minutes or until tender. Cool slightly. In a small bowl, combine the mayonnaise, crushed peppercorns and onion mixture; set aside.
2. Sprinkle beef with remaining salt; gently mix. Shape into four patties. In a large skillet, cook patties over medium heat for 6-8 minutes on each side or until a thermometer reads 160° and juices run clear. Serve on rolls with mayonnaise mixture and, if desired, tomato and lettuce.

Prosciutto Provolone Panini

FAST FIX

## Prosciutto Provolone Panini

On busy days, I like to fix this "uptown" take on grilled cheese sandwiches for a quick lunch or dinner. If you don't have fresh sage handy, substitute 1 tablespoon of Italian seasoning.

**—CANDY SUMMERHILL**
ALEXANDER, ARKANSAS

**PREP/TOTAL TIME:** 25 MIN.
**MAKES:** 4 SERVINGS

- **8 slices white bread**
- **8 slices provolone cheese**
- **4 thin slices prosciutto**
- **3 tablespoons olive oil**
- **3 tablespoons minced fresh sage**

1. On four slices of bread, layer a slice of cheese, a slice of prosciutto and a second slice of cheese. Top with remaining bread.
2. Brush both sides of sandwiches with oil; sprinkle with sage. Cook in a panini maker or indoor grill until bread is toasted and cheese is melted.

Roasted vegetables and tomatoes will get even more flavor from herbs. Try tossing 2 pounds of vegetables with 1-2 tablespoons of chopped fresh rosemary, thyme, sage or oregano. If you are using dried herbs, go with 1 tablespoon.

# Beef Barley Soup with Roasted Vegetables

**PREP:** 25 MIN. **COOK:** 1 HOUR
**MAKES:** 8 SERVINGS (3 QUARTS)

- **¼ cup all-purpose flour**
- **1 teaspoon salt**
- **½ teaspoon pepper**
- **1 pound beef stew meat (¾-inch cubes)**
- **5 tablespoons olive oil, divided**
- **1 large portobello mushroom, stem removed, chopped**
- **1 medium onion, chopped**
- **1 fennel bulb, chopped**
- **1 garlic clove, minced**
- **8 cups beef stock**
- **2 cups water**
- **2 cups cubed peeled butternut squash**
- **1 large baking potato, peeled and cubed**
- **2 large carrots, cut into ½-inch slices**
- **⅔ cup quick-cooking barley**
- **2 teaspoons minced fresh thyme**
- **Dash ground nutmeg**
- **¼ cup minced fresh parsley**

1. In a small bowl, mix the flour, salt and pepper; sprinkle over beef and toss to coat. In a Dutch oven, heat 2 tablespoons oil over medium heat. Add beef; brown evenly. Remove from the pan.
2. In same pan, heat 1 tablespoon oil over medium-high heat. Add the mushroom, onion and fennel; cook and stir for 4-5 minutes or until tender. Stir in garlic; cook 1 minute longer. Add stock and water, stirring to loosen browned bits from pan. Return beef to pan. Bring to a boil; reduce heat. Cover and simmer for 40-60 minutes or until meat is tender.
3. Meanwhile, place the squash, potato and carrots on a greased 15-in. x 10-in. x 1-in. baking pan; drizzle with remaining oil and toss to coat. Bake at 425° for 20-25 minutes or until vegetables are almost tender, stirring twice.
4. Add barley, thyme, nutmeg and vegetables to soup; return to a boil. Reduce heat; cover and simmer for 10-12 minutes or until barley is tender. Sprinkle with parsley.

**Beef Barley Soup with Roasted Vegetables**

The beauty of Beef Barley Soup with Roasted Vegetables is that you can roast the veggies separately in the oven while the soup simmers. Then you simply toss them in during the last minutes on the stove. I love that they keep their own bright, distinctive flavors.

—**GAYLA SCOTT** WEST JEFFERSON, NORTH CAROLINA

## MAKE AHEAD Mushroom Beef Stew

I sprinkle blue cheese on Mushroom Beef Stew just before serving to add even more flavor. Serve some now and store the rest in the freezer for another meal.
**—NANCY LATULIPPE** SIMCOE, ONTARIO

**PREP:** 45 MIN. + FREEZING
**COOK:** 1½ HOURS **MAKES:** 9 SERVINGS

- **1 carton (32 ounces) beef broth**
- **1 ounce dried mixed mushrooms**
- **¼ cup all-purpose flour**
- **1 teaspoon salt**
- **1 teaspoon pepper**
- **1 boneless beef chuck roast (2 pounds), cubed**
- **3 tablespoons canola oil**
- **1 pound whole baby portobello mushrooms**
- **5 medium carrots, chopped**
- **1 large onion, chopped**
- **3 garlic cloves, minced**
- **3 teaspoons minced fresh rosemary or 1 teaspoon dried rosemary, crushed**

**ADDITIONAL INGREDIENTS**

- **2 tablespoons cornstarch**
- **2 tablespoons water**
- **Hot cooked egg noodles, optional**
- **¼ cup crumbled blue cheese**

1. In a large saucepan, bring broth and dried mushrooms to a boil. Remove from the heat; let stand 15-20 minutes or until mushrooms are softened. Using a slotted spoon, remove mushrooms; finely chop. Strain remaining broth through a fine mesh strainer. Set aside mushrooms and broth.
2. In a large resealable plastic bag, combine the flour, salt and pepper; set aside 1 tablespoon for sauce. Add beef, a few pieces at a time, to the remaining flour mixture and shake to coat.
3. In a Dutch oven, brown beef in oil in batches. Add the portobello mushrooms, carrots and onion; saute until onion is tender. Add the garlic, rosemary and rehydrated mushrooms; cook 1 minute longer. Stir in reserved flour mixture until blended; gradually add mushroom broth.
4. Bring to a boil. Reduce heat; cover and simmer for 1½ to 2 hours or until beef is tender. Cool stew; transfer to freezer containers. Freeze for up to 6 months.
5. **TO USE FROZEN STEW:** Thaw in the refrigerator overnight. Place in a Dutch oven; bring to a boil. Combine cornstarch and water until smooth; gradually stir into the pan. Return to a boil; cook and stir for 2 minutes or until thickened. Serve with egg noodles if desired; top with blue cheese.

## FAST FIX All-American Bacon Cheeseburgers

Want to enjoy a sensational burger without paying high restaurant prices? This recipe beefs up a juicy patty with bacon, cheddar cheese and more.
**—JACKIE BURNS**
KETTLE FALLS, WASHINGTON

**PREP/TOTAL TIME:** 30 MIN.
**MAKES:** 4 SERVINGS

- **2 tablespoons finely chopped onion**
- **2 tablespoons ketchup**
- **1 garlic clove, minced**
- **1 teaspoon sugar**
- **1 teaspoon Worcestershire sauce**
- **1 teaspoon steak sauce**
- **¼ teaspoon cider vinegar**
- **1 pound ground beef**
- **4 slices sharp cheddar cheese**
- **4 hamburger buns, split and toasted**
- **8 cooked bacon strips**
- **Optional toppings: lettuce leaves and tomato, onion and pickle slices**

1. In a large bowl, combine the first seven ingredients. Crumble beef over mixture and mix well. Shape into four patties.
2. Grill burgers, covered, over medium heat or broil 3 in. from the heat for 4-7 minutes on each side or until a thermometer reads 160° and juices run clear. Top with cheese. Grill 1 minute longer or until cheese is melted. Serve on buns with bacon and toppings of your choice.

All-American Bacon Cheeseburgers

## FAST FIX Southwestern Shrimp Bisque

I enjoy both Cajun and Mexican food, and my 30-minute bisque combines the best of both worlds. I round out the menu with a crispy green salad for a simple but special dinner.

**—KAREN HARRIS**
CASTLE ROCK, COLORADO

**PREP/TOTAL TIME:** 30 MIN.
**MAKES:** 3 SERVINGS

- **1 small onion, chopped**
- **1 tablespoon olive oil**
- **2 garlic cloves, minced**
- **1 tablespoon all-purpose flour**
- **1 cup water**
- **½ cup heavy whipping cream**
- **2 teaspoons chicken bouillon granules**
- **1 tablespoon chili powder**
- **½ teaspoon ground cumin**
- **½ teaspoon ground coriander**
- **½ pound uncooked medium shrimp, peeled and deveined**
- **½ cup sour cream**
- **Chopped fresh cilantro and sliced avocado, optional**

1. In a small saucepan, saute onion in oil until tender. Add garlic; cook 1 minute longer. Stir in flour until blended. Stir in the water, cream, bouillon and seasonings; bring to a boil. Reduce heat; cover and simmer for 5 minutes.
2. Cut shrimp into bite-size pieces if desired; add shrimp to soup. Simmer 5-10 minutes longer or until shrimp turn pink. Place sour cream in a small bowl; gradually stir in 1/2 cup hot soup. Return all to the pan, stirring constantly. Heat through (do not boil). Top with cilantro and avocado.

## MAKE AHEAD Italian Sausage Minestrone

This fuss-free minestrone is perfect family fare on chilly autumn or winter days. I love dipping slices of warm, crusty French bread into the broth.

**—ELIZABETH RENTERIA**
VANCOUVER, WASHINGTON

**PREP:** 20 MIN. + FREEZING
**COOK:** 1¼ HOURS
**MAKES:** 13 SERVINGS (3¼ QUARTS)

- **1 pound bulk Italian sausage**
- **2 large carrots, chopped**
- **2 celery ribs, chopped**
- **1 medium onion, chopped**
- **6 garlic cloves, minced**
- **3 tablespoons olive oil**
- **7 cups reduced-sodium chicken broth**
- **2 cans (15 ounces each) cannellini or white kidney beans, rinsed and drained**
- **2 cans (14½ ounces each) fire-roasted diced tomatoes, undrained**
- **2 bay leaves**
- **1 tablespoon Italian seasoning**
- **1 tablespoon tomato paste**

**ADDITIONAL INGREDIENTS**

- **1 cup ditalini or other small pasta**
- **Shredded or shaved Parmesan cheese**

1. In a Dutch oven, cook sausage over medium heat until no longer pink; drain.
2. In the same pan, saute the carrots, celery, onion and garlic in oil until tender. Stir in the chicken broth, beans, tomatoes, bay leaves, Italian seasoning, tomato paste and sausage. Bring to a boil. Reduce heat; cover and simmer for 30 minutes.
3. Cool soup; transfer to freezer containers. Freeze for up to 3 months.
4. **TO USE FROZEN SOUP:** Thaw in the refrigerator overnight. Transfer to a Dutch oven. Bring to a boil. Stir in ditalini; return to a boil. Reduce heat and cook, uncovered, for 6-8 minutes or until pasta is tender. Serve with cheese.

**Southwestern Shrimp Bisque**

**Italian Sausage Minestrone**

When making Southwestern Shrimp Bisque, be sure to keep an eye on your cooking time. Shrimp turn a blushing pink color when they're done, and they'll be chewy if overcooked. If you prefer, substitute any shellfish for the shrimp. Clams, lobster and mussels are all good alternatives. Have a shellfish allergy or aversion? Replace the shrimp with a mild fish—or even chicken. If you choose chicken, use bite-size pieces and replace the water in the recipe with chicken stock.

# TIMEOUT FOR TURKEY

A golden, juicy bird is a must for many on Thanksgiving. But turkey isn't just for the holidays anymore! Enjoy these sensational soup and sandwich recipes any time of year.

Stuffing Dumpling Soup

## Stuffing Dumpling Soup

**PREP:** 20 MIN. **COOK:** 25 MIN.
**MAKES:** 5 SERVINGS

- **1 cup sliced fresh mushrooms**
- **1 medium onion, chopped**
- **1 tablespoon olive oil**
- **3 garlic cloves, minced**
- **4 cups reduced-sodium chicken broth**
- **1½ cups chopped fresh carrots**
- **2 teaspoons Creole seasoning**
- **2 eggs**
- **½ cup all-purpose flour**
- **2 cups cooked stuffing**
- **2 cups cubed cooked turkey**
- **1½ cups cut fresh green beans**

1. In a Dutch oven, saute the mushrooms and onion in oil until tender. Add garlic; cook 1 minute longer. Add the broth, carrots and Creole seasoning. Bring to a boil. Reduce heat; simmer, uncovered for 5-8 minutes or until carrots are tender.
2. Meanwhile, in a large bowl, whisk eggs and flour until smooth. Crumble stuffing over mixture; mix well. If necessary, add water, 1 teaspoon a time, until mixture holds its shape.
3. Add turkey and green beans to soup; return to a boil. Drop stuffing mixture by heaping tablespoonfuls onto simmering soup. Cover and simmer for 8-10 minutes or until a toothpick inserted in a dumpling comes out clean (do not lift the cover while simmering).

**Editor's Note:** *The following spices may be substituted for 1 teaspoon Creole seasoning: 1/4 teaspoon each salt, garlic powder and paprika; and a pinch each of dried thyme, ground cumin and cayenne pepper.*

I've always liked turkey, dumplings and stuffing, so I put them all together in Stuffing Dumpling Soup. My family loves it—even my little ones. It's got some kick, but a dollop of sour cream mellows it.
**—RELINA SHIRLEY** RENO, NEVADA

## Turkey Sandwich with Pineapple Salsa

Here's the very first recipe I created on my own. I think the fresh pineapple really brightens up the flavors of the other ingredients. If you prefer, use rolls in place of the French bread.
**—ANDREA BOYER** LENORE, IDAHO

**PREP:** 25 MIN. **BAKE:** 15 MIN.
**MAKES:** 6 SERVINGS

- **1¼ cups finely chopped fresh pineapple**
- **2 roma tomatoes, finely chopped**
- **½ cup finely chopped onion**
- **⅓ cup minced fresh cilantro**
- **1 loaf (1 pound) French bread**
- **1 pound thinly sliced cooked turkey**
- **6 slices part-skim mozzarella cheese**

**AIOLI**

- **¾ cup mayonnaise**
- **2 tablespoons lemon juice**
- **2 garlic cloves, minced**
- **½ teaspoon pepper**

1. In a small bowl, combine the pineapple, tomatoes, onion and cilantro; set aside.
2. Cut bread in half horizontally; place cut sides up on an ungreased baking sheet. Bake at 350° for 4-5 minutes or until toasted; remove top half from pan. Layer bottom half with turkey and cheese. Bake 10-13 minutes longer or until turkey is heated through and cheese is melted.
3. Meanwhile, combine the aioli ingredients in a small bowl. Carefully spread over cheese; top with salsa. Replace bread top; cut into six slices.

## Saucy Onion Meatball Subs

**PREP:** 40 MIN. **COOK:** 30 MIN.
**MAKES:** 8 SERVINGS

- **1 egg, lightly beaten**
- **¼ cup dry bread crumbs**
- **¼ cup finely chopped onion**
- **¼ cup grated Parmesan cheese**
- **2 tablespoons chicken broth**
- **1 teaspoon salt**
- **½ teaspoon pepper**
- **¼ teaspoon dried thyme**
- **1½ pounds ground turkey**
- **2 tablespoons olive oil**

**SAUCE**

- **3 cups sliced onions**
- **2 tablespoons olive oil**
- **2 garlic cloves, minced**
- **½ teaspoon dried thyme**
- **¼ cup all-purpose flour**
- **2 cups beef broth**
- **1 cup chicken broth**
- **¾ teaspoon salt**
- **¼ teaspoon pepper**
- **¼ teaspoon Worcestershire sauce**

**SANDWICHES**

- **8 submarine buns**
- **1½ cups (6 ounces) shredded Monterey Jack cheese**

1. In a large bowl, combine the first eight ingredients. Crumble turkey over mixture and mix well. With wet hands, shape turkey mixture into 1½-in. balls. In a large skillet, brown meatballs in oil in batches; drain and set aside.
2. For sauce, in the same skillet, saute onions in oil until tender. Add garlic and thyme; cook 1 minute longer. Stir in flour until blended; gradually add the beef and chicken broths. Stir in the salt, pepper and Worcestershire sauce. Bring to a boil; cook and stir for 2 minutes or until thickened.
3. Add meatballs; return to a boil. Reduce heat; cover and simmer for 9-11 minutes or until meatballs are no longer pink.
4. Meanwhile, cut each bun in half lengthwise, leaving one side attached. Place buns, cut sides up, on baking sheets. Broil 3-4 in. from the heat for 2-3 minutes or until toasted.
5. Top buns with meatballs and onions; sprinkle with cheese. Broil 2-4 minutes longer or until cheese is melted. Serve with remaining sauce for dipping if desired.

For people who don't care for tomato sauce—and anyone who's craving a great sandwich—Saucy Onion Meatball Subs are a fantastic, satisfying choice.

**—ANDRIA GASKINS**
MATTHEWS, NORTH CAROLINA

Saucy Onion Meatball Subs

## FAST FIX Buffalo Sloppy Joes

**PREP/TOTAL TIME:** 30 MIN.
**MAKES:** 8 SERVINGS

- **2 pounds extra-lean ground turkey**
- **2 celery ribs, chopped**
- **1 medium onion, chopped**
- **1 medium carrot, grated**
- **3 garlic cloves, minced**
- **1 can (8 ounces) tomato sauce**
- **½ cup reduced-sodium chicken broth**
- **¼ cup Louisiana-style hot sauce**
- **2 tablespoons brown sugar**
- **2 tablespoons red wine vinegar**
- **1 tablespoon Worcestershire sauce**
- **¼ teaspoon pepper**
- **8 hamburger buns, split**
- **1 cup (4 ounces) crumbled blue cheese, optional**

1. Cook the first five ingredients in a Dutch oven over medium heat until turkey is no longer pink. Stir in tomato sauce, broth, hot sauce, sugar, vinegar, Worcestershire sauce and pepper; heat through.
2. Serve on buns; sprinkle with cheese if desired.

Buffalo Sloppy Joes

Lean ground turkey makes my Buffalo Sloppy Joes lighter than the standard ground beef version. Hot sauce and blue cheese provide the authentic taste.

**—MARIA REGAKIS**
SOMERVILLE, MASSACHUSETTS

## Grilled Prosciutto-Cheddar Sandwiches with Onion Jam

For a modern variation of grilled cheese full of comfy farmhouse flavors, try my recipe for Grilled Prosciutto-Cheddar Sandwiches with Onion Jam.
**—SUSAN ANDRICHUK** NEW YORK, NEW YORK

**PREP:** 1¼ HRS. **COOK:** 5 MIN.
**MAKES:** 4 SANDWICHES (½ CUP ONION JAM)

**ONION JAM**
- **2 large sweet onions, sliced**
- **1 cup dry red wine**
- **2 tablespoons honey**
- **1 tablespoon red wine vinegar**
- **¼ teaspoon crushed red pepper flakes**
- **¼ teaspoon salt**
- **¼ teaspoon pepper**
- **4 teaspoons apricot preserves**

**SANDWICHES**
- **8 slices cinnamon-raisin bread**
- **8 thin slices prosciutto or deli ham**
- **4 slices aged cheddar cheese**
- **3 tablespoons butter, softened**

1. For jam, place onions and wine in a large skillet; bring to a boil. Reduce heat; cover and simmer for 30 minutes. Stir in the honey, vinegar, pepper flakes, salt and pepper. Simmer, uncovered, for 30 minutes or until liquid is evaporated.
2. Stir in preserves; cook 3-5 minutes longer or until onions are glazed. Remove from the heat; cool slightly.
3. Spread four bread slices with onion jam. Layer with prosciutto and cheese. Top with remaining bread. Butter outsides of the sandwiches.
4. In a large skillet over medium heat, toast the sandwiches for 2-3 minutes on each side or until golden brown and the cheese is melted.

Grilled Prosciutto-Cheddar Sandwiches with Onion Jam

## Sunday Supper Sandwiches

The pork and sauerkraut for these home-style favorites can also be prepared in a 4-quart slow cooker. Just cover and cook on low for 8-10 hours or until the meat is tender.
**—LIBBY WALP** CHICAGO, ILLINOIS

**PREP:** 25 MIN. **BAKE:** 2 HOURS 30 MIN.
**MAKES:** 8 SERVINGS

- **1 can (14 ounces) sauerkraut, rinsed and well drained**
- **1 boneless pork shoulder butt roast (2½ to 3 pounds)**
- **½ teaspoon salt**
- **¼ teaspoon pepper**
- **¼ cup stone-ground mustard, divided**
- **1 cup apple cider or juice**
- **¼ cup sweetened applesauce**
- **8 slices rye bread, toasted**
- **1 cup (4 ounces) shredded Swiss cheese**

1. Place the sauerkraut in an ovenproof Dutch oven. Sprinkle the pork with salt and pepper; brush with 2 tablespoons mustard. Place over sauerkraut. Add apple cider and applesauce.
2. Cover and bake at 325° for 2½ to 3 hours or until pork is tender. Remove roast; cool slightly. Drain sauerkraut mixture; set aside. Shred pork with two forks.
3. Place toast on an ungreased baking sheet. Spread with the remaining mustard. Top with pork, then sauerkraut mixture; sprinkle with cheese. Broil 4-6 in. from the heat for 2-3 minutes or until the cheese is melted.

## FAST FIX Chicken Gnocchi Pesto Soup

**PREP/TOTAL TIME:** 25 MIN.
**MAKES:** 4 SERVINGS

- **1 jar (15 ounces) roasted garlic Alfredo sauce**
- **2 cups water**
- **2 cups cubed rotisserie chicken**
- **1 teaspoon Italian seasoning**
- **¼ teaspoon salt**
- **¼ teaspoon pepper**
- **1 package (16 ounces) potato gnocchi**
- **3 cups coarsley chopped fresh spinach**
- **4 teaspoons prepared pesto**

In a large saucepan, combine the first six ingredients; bring to a gentle boil, stirring occasionally. Stir in gnocchi and spinach; cook 3-8 minutes or until the gnocchi float. Top each serving with pesto.

**Editor's Note:** *Look for potato gnocchi in the pasta or frozen foods section.*

After sampling a similar concoction at a restaurant, I came up with Chicken Gnocchi Pesto Soup. It's a quick version I can whip up in my own kitchen.
—**DEANNA SMITH** DES MOINES, IOWA

## Neighborhood Bean Soup

I like to make big-batch recipes, such as this tasty soup. That tendency has helped me get to know my neighbors.
—**CHERYL TROWBRIDGE**
WINDSOR, ONTARIO

**PREP:** 30 MIN. + STANDING
**COOK:** 2¼ HOURS
**MAKES:** 10 SERVINGS (2¾ QUARTS)

- **2 cups dried great northern beans**
- **5 cups chicken broth**
- **3 cups water**
- **1 meaty ham bone or 2 smoked ham hocks**
- **2 to 3 tablespoons chicken bouillon granules**
- **1 teaspoon dried thyme**
- **½ teaspoon dried marjoram**
- **½ teaspoon pepper**
- **¼ teaspoon rubbed sage**
- **¼ teaspoon dried savory**
- **2 medium onions, chopped**
- **3 medium carrots, chopped**
- **3 celery ribs, chopped**
- **1 tablespoon canola oil**

1. Sort beans and rinse with cold water. Place beans in a Dutch oven; add water to cover by 2 in. Bring to a boil; boil for 2 minutes. Remove from the heat; cover and let soak for 1-4 hours or until beans are softened.
2. Drain and rinse the beans, discarding liquid. Return beans to pan; add chicken broth, 3 cups water, ham bone, chicken bouillon and seasonings; bring to a boil. Reduce heat; cover and simmer for 1½ hours.
3. Meanwhile, in a large skillet, saute the onions, carrots and celery in oil until tender; add to soup. Cover and simmer 45-60 minutes longer or until beans are tender.
4. Remove ham bone; cool slightly. Remove meat from bone and cut into chunks; return to soup. Discard bone. Skim fat from soup.

## FAST FIX Beef & Spinach Gyros

Here, traditional gyros get a twist with ground beef, spinach and ripe olives.
—**MARY JOHNSON**
COLOMA, WISCONSIN

**PREP/TOTAL TIME:** 25 MIN.
**MAKES:** 6 SERVINGS

- **1 pound lean ground beef (90% lean)**
- **1 package (10 ounces) frozen chopped spinach, thawed and squeezed dry**
- **6 green onions, chopped**
- **1 can (2¼ ounces) sliced ripe olives, drained**
- **2 teaspoons lemon-pepper seasoning, divided**
- **1 large tomato, chopped**
- **1 cup (8 ounces) fat-free plain yogurt**
- **½ cup reduced-fat mayonnaise**
- **6 pita breads (6 inches), halved**
- **12 lettuce leaves**
- **1 cup (4 ounces) crumbled feta cheese**

1. In a large skillet, cook beef over medium heat until no longer pink. Add the spinach, onions, olives and 1 teaspoon lemon-pepper; heat through. Stir in tomato; set aside.
2. In a small bowl, combine yogurt, mayonnaise and remaining lemon-pepper. Line the pita halves with lettuce; fill with beef mixture and cheese. Serve with yogurt sauce.

**Beef & Spinach Gyros**

SLOW COOKER

## Pork & Green Chile Stew

**PREP:** 40 MIN. **COOK:** 7 HOURS
**MAKES:** 8 SERVINGS (2 QUARTS)

- **2 pounds boneless pork shoulder butt roast, cut into ¾-inch cubes**
- **1 large onion, cut into ½-inch pieces**
- **2 tablespoons canola oil**
- **1 teaspoon salt**
- **1 teaspoon coarsely ground pepper**
- **4 large potatoes, peeled and cut into ¾-inch cubes**
- **3 cups water**
- **1 can (16 ounces) hominy, rinsed and drained**
- **2 cans (4 ounces each) chopped green chilies**
- **2 tablespoons quick-cooking tapioca**
- **2 garlic cloves, minced**
- **½ teaspoon dried oregano**
- **½ teaspoon ground cumin**
- **1 cup minced fresh cilantro**
- **Sour cream, optional**

1. In a large skillet, brown pork and onion in oil in batches. Sprinkle with salt and pepper. Transfer to a 4-qt. slow cooker.
2. Stir in potatoes, water, hominy, chilies, tapioca, garlic, oregano and cumin. Cover and cook on low for 7-9 hours or until meat is tender, stirring in cilantro during the last 30 minutes of cooking. Serve with sour cream if desired.

**Pork & Green Chile Stew**

The tender chunks of pork, green chilies, hominy and spices in Pork & Green Chile Stew bring some welcome heat to those long, cold winter evenings.
—**PAUL SEDILLO** PLAINFIELD, ILLINOIS

## Creole-Spiced Shrimp Po' Boys

I sometimes use oysters or crawfish in addition to—or instead of—the shrimp in my po' boys.
—**STACEY JOHNSON**
BONNEY LAKE, WASHINGTON

**PREP:** 30 MIN. **COOK:** 5 MIN./BATCH
**MAKES:** 4 SANDWICHES (1 CUP SAUCE)

- **¾ cup mayonnaise**
- **½ cup ketchup**
- **1 teaspoon prepared horseradish**
- **1 teaspoon hot pepper sauce**
- **Oil for frying**
- **¾ cup all-purpose flour**
- **¾ cup cornmeal**
- **1 tablespoon Creole seasoning**
- **1 teaspoon salt**
- **1 pound uncooked medium shrimp, peeled and deveined, tails removed**
- **4 French rolls, split**
- **2 cups shredded lettuce**
- **2 medium tomatoes, sliced**

1. In a small bowl, mix the mayonnaise, ketchup, horseradish and pepper sauce. Cover and chill until serving.
2. In an electric skillet, heat ½ in. of oil to 375°. In a resealable plastic bag, combine the flour, cornmeal, Creole seasoning and salt.
3. Add shrimp; seal bag and toss to coat. Fry shrimp in oil for 2-3 minutes on each side or until golden brown. Drain on paper towels.
4. Spread rolls with some of the sauce. Layer bottoms with lettuce, shrimp and tomatoes; serve with remaining sauce.

**Editor's Note:** *The following spices may be substituted for 1 teaspoon Creole seasoning: ¼ teaspoon each salt, garlic powder and paprika; and a pinch each of dried thyme, ground cumin and cayenne pepper.*

MAKE AHEAD

## Zesty Chicken Tortellini Soup

After a busy day, it's so nice to come home to this heartwarming soup.
—**NANCY LATULIPPE**
SIMCOE, ONTARIO

**PREP:** 40 MIN. **COOK:** 10 MIN. + FREEZING
**MAKES:** 6 SERVINGS (2½ QUARTS)

- **4 cups reduced-sodium chicken broth**
- **4 cups reduced-sodium beef broth**
- **6 boneless skinless chicken thighs (about 1½ pounds)**
- **4 medium carrots, sliced**
- **2 celery ribs, sliced**
- **1 small onion, chopped**
- **1 envelope reduced-sodium onion soup mix**
- **1½ teaspoons dried parsley flakes**
- **½ teaspoon garlic powder**
- **½ teaspoon crushed red pepper flakes**
- **½ teaspoon poultry seasoning**
- **½ teaspoon pepper**
- **2½ cups frozen cheese tortellini**

1. In a Dutch oven, bring chicken broth and beef broth to a boil; reduce heat. Add chicken and poach, uncovered, for 25-30 minutes or until a meat thermometer reads 170°. Remove chicken; cool slightly.
2. Add carrots, celery, onion, soup mix, parsley and seasonings to broth. Bring to a boil. Reduce heat; cover and simmer for 10-15 minutes or until vegetables are tender.
3. Cool soup. Meanwhile, chop chicken. Add tortellini and chicken to soup. Transfer to freezer containers; freeze for up to 3 months.
4. **TO USE FROZEN SOUP:** Thaw in the refrigerator overnight. Place in a saucepan; bring to a boil. Reduce heat; cook, uncovered, for 5-10 minutes or until heated through and tortellini are tender.

Baked Potato Cheddar Soup

## FAST FIX Baked Potato Cheddar Soup

Here's comfort food that requires just a handful of kitchen staples. Choose a better-quality yellow cheddar cheese for a real treat in every bowl.

**—KRISTIN REYNOLDS**
VAN BUREN, ARKANSAS

**PREP/TOTAL TIME:** 30 MIN.
**MAKES:** 4 SERVINGS

- **⅓ cup all-purpose flour**
- **3 cups milk**
- **2 large potatoes, baked, peeled and coarsely mashed (1½ pounds)**
- **⅓ cup plus 2 tablespoons shredded cheddar cheese, divided**
- **½ teaspoon salt**
- **¼ teaspoon pepper**
- **½ cup sour cream**
- **½ cup thinly sliced green onions, divided**
- **Crumbled cooked bacon, optional**

1. In a large saucepan, whisk flour and milk until smooth. Bring to a boil; cook and stir for 2 minutes or until thickened. Stir in the potatoes, ⅓ cup cheese, salt and pepper. Cook over medium heat for 2-3 minutes or until cheese is melted.
2. Remove from the heat. Stir in sour cream and ¼ cup onions until blended. Cover; cook over medium heat for 10-12 minutes or until heated through (do not boil). Garnish with remaining cheese, onions and, if desired, bacon.

## FAST FIX Tuna Ciabatta Melts

Any good crusty bread can be used for this yummy tuna spread. If you like, top the melts with slices of cucumber.

**—BARB TEMPLIN**
NORWOOD, MINNESOTA

**PREP/TOTAL TIME:** 10 MIN.
**MAKES:** 4 SERVINGS

- **1 pouch (11 ounces) light tuna in water**
- **⅓ cup each finely chopped celery, cucumber and red onion**
- **¼ cup mayonnaise**
- **2 teaspoons dill weed**
- **1 teaspoon lemon juice**
- **⅛ teaspoon salt**
- **⅛ teaspoon pepper**
- **4 ciabatta rolls, split**
- **2 cups (8 ounces) shredded cheddar cheese**

1. In a small bowl, combine the tuna, celery, cucumber, onion, mayonnaise, dill, lemon juice, salt and pepper; mix well.
2. Place rolls on a baking sheet. Spread each half with tuna mixture; sprinkle with cheese. Broil 2-3 in. from the heat for 2-4 minutes or until cheese is melted.

## Spring Pea Soup

Truly for the "pea lover," this simple but flavorful recipe originated from an idea in an old cookbook about eating better to live longer. Sauteed potatoes add body to the five-ingredient blend.

**—DENISE PATTERSON**
BAINBRIDGE, OHIO

**PREP:** 10 MIN. **COOK:** 30 MIN.
**MAKES:** 6 SERVINGS

- **2 cups cubed peeled potatoes**
- **2 tablespoons butter**
- **6 cups chicken broth**
- **2 cups fresh or frozen peas, thawed**
- **2 tablespoons minced chives**

1. In a large saucepan, saute the potatoes in butter until lightly browned. Stir in the chicken broth; bring to a boil. Reduce the heat; cover and simmer for 10-15 minutes or until the potatoes are tender. Add the peas; cook 5-8 minutes longer or until the peas are tender. Cool slightly.
2. In a blender, process soup in batches until smooth. Return all to the pan; heat through. Sprinkle with chives.

Tuna Ciabatta Melts

# Side Dishes & Condiments

A special entree calls for equally **special accompaniments**. In this chapter, you'll find comforting veggie medleys, sensational sauces and more to **round out menus** in a memorable way.

"I like to think of this fall-flavored recipe as a labor of love. The risotto requires a bit of extra attention, but once you create that delectable creaminess, your taste buds will thank you!"

—**STEPHANIE CAMPBELL** ELK GROVE, CALIFORNIA

## FAST FIX Dill Green Beans

When I need a family-pleasing side or even a snack, I turn to Dill Green Beans. They make a healthful alternative to salty munchies like potato chips.
—**ALLISON GRAY** FREEPORT, MAINE

**PREP/TOTAL TIME:** 20 MIN.
**MAKES:** 4 SERVINGS

- **1 pound fresh green beans, trimmed**
- **¼ cup rice vinegar**
- **¼ cup reduced-sodium soy sauce**
- **2 tablespoons snipped fresh dill**
- **1 tablespoon sesame seeds, optional**

**1.** Place beans in a steamer basket; place in a large saucepan over 1 in. of water. Bring to a boil; cover and steam for 6-8 minutes or until crisp-tender.
**2.** Meanwhile, in a small bowl, combine the vinegar, soy sauce, dill and sesame seeds if desired. Transfer beans to a serving bowl. Add vinegar mixture and toss to coat. Serve immediately.

## Lentil White Bean Pilaf

I prepare a hearty, meatless grain pilaf when I have extra cooked lentils, rice, barley and quinoa on hand. Vegetarian guests are always thrilled to dig in—and so is everyone else!
—**JULI MEYERS** HINESVILLE, GEORGIA

**PREP:** 35 MIN. **COOK:** 15 MIN.
**MAKES:** 10 SERVINGS

- **1 cup dried lentils, rinsed**
- **½ cup quick-cooking barley**
- **½ cup quinoa, rinsed**
- **⅓ cup uncooked long grain rice**
- **½ pound sliced baby portobello mushrooms**
- **3 medium carrots, finely chopped**
- **3 celery ribs, finely chopped**
- **1 large onion, finely chopped**
- **¼ cup butter, cubed**
- **3 garlic cloves, minced**
- **2 teaspoons minced fresh rosemary or ½ teaspoon dried rosemary, crushed**
- **½ cup vegetable broth**
- **½ teaspoon salt**
- **½ teaspoon pepper**
- **2 cups canned white kidney or cannellini beans, rinsed and drained**

**1.** Cook the lentils, barley, quinoa and rice according to package directions; set aside.
**2.** In a Dutch oven, saute the mushrooms, carrots, celery and onion in butter until tender. Add garlic and rosemary; cook 1 minute longer. Add broth, salt and pepper, stirring to loosen browned bits from pan. Stir in beans and the cooked lentils, barley, quinoa and rice; heat through.
**Editor's Note:** *Look for quinoa in the cereal, rice or organic food aisle.*

Lentil White Bean Pilaf

## MAKE AHEAD Garden Refrigerator Pickles

Canning isn't necessary for these tangy pickles. Just keep them in the fridge and eat them within a month.
—**LINDA CHAPMAN** MERIDEN, IOWA

**PREP:** 20 MIN.
**COOK:** 15 MIN. + CHILLING
**MAKES:** 7 PINTS

- **6 cups sugar**
- **6 cups white vinegar**
- **¼ cup celery seed**
- **¼ cup mustard seed**
- **2 tablespoons canning salt**
- **10 medium carrots, halved and quartered**
- **3 medium cucumbers, sliced**
- **3 medium sweet red peppers, cut into 1-inch pieces**
- **2 large onions, halved and sliced**
- **1 bunch green onions, cut into 2-inch pieces**

**1.** In a Dutch oven, combine the first five ingredients; bring to a boil, stirring to dissolve sugar. Meanwhile, place the remaining ingredients in a large bowl.
**2.** Pour hot liquid over vegetables; cool. Transfer to jars, if desired; cover tightly. Refrigerate for 6-8 hours before serving. Store in the refrigerator for up to 1 month.

## FAST FIX Cheddar Mashed Cauliflower

Want to break away from mashed potatoes? Try cauliflower jazzed up with cheddar cheese and rosemary.

**—CHRYSTAL BAKER**
STUDIO CITY, CALIFORNIA

**PREP/TOTAL TIME:** 15 MIN.
**MAKES:** 6 SERVINGS

- **2 medium heads cauliflower, broken into florets**
- **⅓ cup 2% milk**
- **1 tablespoon minced fresh rosemary**
- **½ teaspoon salt**
- **1 cup (4 ounces) shredded sharp cheddar cheese**

In a Dutch oven, bring 1 in. of water to a boil. Add cauliflower; cover and cook for 5-10 minutes or until tender. Drain; return to pan. Mash cauliflower with the milk, rosemary and salt. Stir in cheese until melted.

## Christmas Cranberries

Bourbon adds bite to this seasonal standby. For a tasty holiday gift, pack it in a small heavy-duty glass storage container with a tight-fitting lid. Wrap the container in a vintage tea towel or cloth napkin, cinch it with ribbon and attach a few small ornaments.

**—BECKY JO SMITH**
KETTLE FALLS, WASHINGTON

**PREP:** 35 MIN. **PROCESS:** 15 MIN.
**MAKES:** 4 HALF-PINTS

- **2 packages (12 ounces each) fresh or frozen cranberries, thawed**
- **1½ cups sugar**
- **1 cup orange juice**
- **¼ cup bourbon**
- **3 teaspoons vanilla extract**
- **1 teaspoon grated orange peel**

**1.** In a large saucepan, combine the cranberries, sugar, orange juice and bourbon. Bring to a boil. Reduce heat; simmer, uncovered, for 18-22 minutes or until berries pop and mixture has thickened.
**2.** Stir in vanilla and peel. Carefully ladle hot mixture into hot half-pint jars, leaving ¼-in. headspace. Remove air bubbles; wipe rims and adjust lids. Process for 15 minutes in a boiling-water canner.

**Editor's Note:** *The processing time listed is for altitudes of 1,000 feet or less. Add 1 minute to the processing time for each 1,000 feet of additional altitude.*

## Sage Sausage Dressing

Port wine is often served as a dessert beverage, but it also lends deep flavor to our family's hearty stuffing.

**—DENISE HRUZ**
GERMANTOWN, WISCONSIN

**PREP:** 40 MIN. **BAKE:** 25 MIN.
**MAKES:** 17 SERVINGS (¾ CUP EACH)

- **¼ cup port wine or 2 tablespoons grape juice plus 2 tablespoons chicken broth**
- **½ cup dried cherries**
- **1 large tart apple, peeled, finely chopped**
- **1 tablespoon lemon juice**
- **1 pound bulk sage pork sausage**
- **1 medium onion, chopped**
- **2 celery ribs, sliced**
- **2 tablespoons olive oil**
- **3 cups chicken broth**
- **½ cup orange juice**
- **¼ cup butter, cubed**
- **1 package (14 ounces) seasoned stuffing cubes**
- **1 cup chopped walnuts, toasted**
- **¼ cup thinly sliced fresh sage**

**1.** In a small saucepan, bring wine to a boil. Stir in cherries; remove from the heat. In a small bowl, combine apple and lemon juice; toss to coat. Set aside cherry and apple mixtures.
**2.** In a Dutch oven, cook sausage over medium heat until no longer pink. Remove from pan with a slotted spoon; drain. In the same pan, saute onion and celery in oil until tender. Add the broth, orange juice and butter; heat until butter is melted.
**3.** Stir in the stuffing cubes, walnuts, sage, cherry mixture, apple mixture and sausage. Transfer to a greased 13-in. x 9-in. baking dish. Bake, uncovered, at 350° for 25-30 minutes or until lightly browned.

Cheddar Mashed Cauliflower

Christmas Cranberries

### Did you know?

There are many varieties of tart apples, including Granny Smith, Ida Red, Rome Beauty, Jonathan and McIntosh.

## FAST FIX Autumn Beans

When it comes to rounding out meals, you can't go wrong with a great bean recipe. Keep some chopped onions in the freezer to shorten the prep time.

**—MARA MCAULEY**
HINSDALE, NEW YORK

**PREP/TOTAL TIME:** 30 MIN.
**MAKES:** 4 SERVINGS

- **8 bacon strips, chopped**
- **¼ cup finely chopped onion**
- **2 cans (16 ounces each) baked beans, undrained**
- **1 cup apple cider**
- **¼ to ½ cup raisins**
- **½ teaspoon ground cinnamon**

In a large skillet, cook bacon over medium heat until crisp. Remove to paper towels with a slotted spoon; drain, reserving 2 tablespoons drippings. Saute onion in drippings. Stir in the remaining ingredients. Bring to a boil; reduce heat and simmer, uncovered, 20-25 minutes to allow the flavors to blend, stirring occasionally.

## Zucchini Stuffing

I've been serving my stuffing for years and always receive compliments on it. If you don't have day-old bread in your pantry, simply slice fresh bread and bake it at 300° for 10 minutes.

**—MARY ANN DELL**
PHOENIXVILLE, PENNSYLVANIA

**PREP:** 25 MIN. **BAKE:** 40 MIN.
**MAKES:** 12 SERVINGS (¾ CUP EACH)

- **1 small onion, chopped**
- **1 celery rib, chopped**
- **3 tablespoons butter**
- **1 cup all-purpose flour**
- **2 tablespoons sugar**
- **1 teaspoon baking powder**
- **1 teaspoon salt**
- **1 teaspoon ground cinnamon**
- **1 teaspoon poultry seasoning**
- **½ cup canned pumpkin**
- **2 eggs**
- **⅓ cup 2% milk**
- **¼ cup butter, melted**
- **4 cups day-old cubed bread**
- **3 medium zucchini, chopped**
- **½ cup shredded cheddar cheese**

**1.** In a small skillet, saute onion and celery in butter until tender; set aside.
**2.** In a large bowl, combine the flour, sugar, baking powder, salt, cinnamon and poultry seasoning. In a small bowl, whisk the pumpkin, eggs, milk and butter; stir into dry ingredients just until moistened. Fold in the bread cubes, zucchini, cheese and onion mixture.
**3.** Transfer to a greased 13-in. x 9-in. baking dish. Cover and bake at 325° for 30 minutes. Uncover; bake 10-15 minutes longer or until lightly browned.

Autumn Beans

## FAST FIX Loaded Cheddar-Corn Potato Patties

For a party appetizer instead of a side dish, shape these into bite-size patties and pile them on a cake platter.

**—DARLENE BRENDEN**
SALEM, OREGON

**PREP/TOTAL TIME:** 30 MIN.
**MAKES:** 1 DOZEN (1 CUP SAUCE)

- **1 cup (8 ounces) sour cream**
- **2 tablespoons plus ⅓ cup thinly sliced green onions**
- **2 cups mashed potato flakes**
- **⅓ cup cornmeal**
- **1¾ teaspoons garlic salt**
- **½ teaspoon smoked paprika**
- **2 cups 2% milk**
- **1 package (10 ounces) frozen corn, thawed**
- **1 cup (4 ounces) shredded extra-sharp cheddar cheese**

**1.** In a small bowl, mix sour cream and 2 tablespoons green onion; refrigerate until serving.
**2.** In a large bowl, mix the potato flakes, cornmeal, garlic salt and paprika. Add the milk, corn, cheese and remaining green onions; mix until blended. Using ½ cupfuls, shape the mixture into twelve 3½-in. patties.
**3.** Heat a large nonstick skillet coated with cooking spray over medium heat. Cook the patties in batches for 2-3 minutes on each side or until golden brown. Serve with sauce.

Loaded Cheddar-Corn Potato Patties

## Southern Black-Eyed Peas

I've discovered that the secret to great black-eyed peas is pork. A double dose of ham for flavor along with slow and gentle cooking gives you perfection in a bowl.
**—EMORY DOTY** JASPER, GEORGIA

**PREP:** 20 MIN. + STANDING **COOK:** 45 MIN. **MAKES:** 6 SERVINGS

- **1 pound dried black-eyed peas, sorted and rinsed**
- **1 large onion, chopped**
- **2 tablespoons olive oil**
- **2 ounces sliced salt pork belly, chopped**
- **6 garlic cloves, minced**
- **2 bay leaves**
- **1 tablespoon minced fresh thyme or 1 teaspoon dried thyme**
- **¼ teaspoon crushed red pepper flakes**
- **¼ teaspoon pepper**
- **1 carton (32 ounces) reduced-sodium chicken broth**
- **2 smoked ham hocks**

**1.** Place peas in a Dutch oven; add water to cover by 2 in. Bring to a boil; boil for 2 minutes. Remove from the heat; cover and let stand for 1 hour. Drain and rinse peas, discarding liquid; set aside.
**2.** In the same pan, saute onion in oil until tender. Add the pork belly, garlic, bay leaves, thyme, pepper flakes and pepper; cook 1 minute longer.
**3.** Add the broth, ham hocks and peas; bring to a boil. Reduce heat; simmer, uncovered, for 35-40 minutes or until peas are tender, stirring occasionally and adding additional water if desired.

Southern Black-Eyed Peas

Gingerbread Spice Jelly

**4.** Discard bay leaves. Remove ham hocks; cool slightly. Remove meat from bones if desired; finely chop and return to pan. Discard bones.

## Gingerbread Spice Jelly

A winner at our county fair, this special spiced jelly has been my homemade gift to friends and family for years. When the jars are empty, people return them for a refill.
**—ROBIN NAGEL** WHITEHALL, MONTANA

**PREP:** 15 MIN. + STANDING **PROCESS:** 10 MIN.
**MAKES:** 5 HALF-PINTS

- **2½ cups water**
- **18 gingerbread spice tea bags**
- **4½ cups sugar**
- **½ cup unsweetened apple juice**
- **2 teaspoons butter**
- **2 pouches (3 ounces each) liquid fruit pectin**

**1.** In a large saucepan, bring the water to a boil. Remove from the heat; add the tea bags. Cover and steep for 30 minutes.
**2.** Discard the tea bags. Stir in the sugar, apple juice and butter. Bring to a full rolling boil over high heat, stirring constantly. Stir in pectin. Boil for 1 minute, stirring constantly.
**3.** Remove from the heat; skim off foam. Carefully ladle hot mixture into hot half-pint jars, leaving ¼-in. headspace. Remove air bubbles; wipe rims and adjust lids. Process for 10 minutes in a boiling-water canner. (Jelly may take up to 2 weeks to fully set.)
**Editor's Note:** *The processing time listed is for altitudes of 1,000 feet or less. Add 1 minute to the processing time for each 1,000 feet of additional altitude.*

## Whipped Vegetable Trio

If you want to serve mashed potatoes but don't have enough potatoes on hand, whip up a delightfully different dish by filling in the gap with carrots and parsnips. The first frost of the season turns the starch in parsnips to sugar, giving them a subtle sweetness. The result is a comforting, memorable side for a holiday dinner or anytime.
—**LEANN BIRD** WEST JORDAN, UTAH

**PREP:** 20 MIN. **COOK:** 20 MIN. **MAKES:** 6 SERVINGS

**8 medium potatoes, peeled and cut into 1-in. cubes**
**4 medium parsnips, peeled and coarsely chopped**
**4 medium carrots, peeled and coarsely chopped**
**8 cups water**
**2 teaspoons salt**
**½ teaspoon pepper**
**Minced fresh chives or parsley, optional**

**1.** Place the first four ingredients in a Dutch oven. Bring to a boil. Reduce heat; cover and simmer for 15-18 minutes or until vegetables are tender.
**2.** Drain, reserving ½ cup cooking liquid. Place vegetables in a large bowl; add the salt, pepper and reserved cooking liquid. Mash until creamy. Garnish with chives if desired.

## Shiitake & Butternut Risotto

I like to think of this fall-flavored recipe as a labor of love. The risotto requires a bit of extra attention, but once you create that delectable creaminess, your taste buds will thank you!
—**STEPHANIE CAMPBELL** ELK GROVE, CALIFORNIA

**PREP:** 25 MIN. **COOK:** 25 MIN. **MAKES:** 2 SERVINGS

**1 cup cubed peeled butternut squash**
**2 teaspoons olive oil, divided**
**Dash salt**
**1¼ cups reduced-sodium chicken broth**
**⅔ cup sliced fresh shiitake mushrooms**
**2 tablespoons chopped onion**
**1 small garlic clove, minced**
**⅓ cup uncooked arborio rice**
**Dash pepper**
**¼ cup white wine or ¼ cup additional reduced-sodium chicken broth**
**¼ cup grated Parmesan cheese**
**1 teaspoon minced fresh sage**

**1.** Place squash in a greased 9-in.-square baking pan. Add 1 teaspoon oil and salt; toss to coat.
**2.** Bake, uncovered, at 350° for 25-30 minutes or until tender, stirring occasionally.
**3.** Meanwhile, in a small saucepan, heat the broth and keep warm. In a small skillet, saute mushrooms, onion and garlic in the remaining oil for 3-4 minutes or until tender. Add rice and pepper; cook and stir for 2-3 minutes. Reduce heat; stir in the wine. Cook and stir until all of the liquid is absorbed.

Shiitake & Butternut Risotto

**4.** Add heated broth, ¼ cup at a time, stirring constantly. Allow the liquid to absorb between additions. Cook just until risotto is creamy and rice is almost tender. (Cooking time is about 20 minutes.) Stir in cheese until melted. Add squash and sage. Serve immediately.

## FAST FIX Roasted Carrot Fries

To transform plain carrot sticks into fun "fries," the Taste of Home Test Kitchen pros simply drizzled them with olive oil, sprinkled on salt and popped them in the oven.

**PREP/TOTAL TIME:** 20 MIN. **MAKES:** 5 SERVINGS

**1 pound fresh carrots, cut into ½-inch sticks**
**2 teaspoons olive oil**
**½ teaspoon salt**

Place carrots in a greased 15-in. x 10-in. x 1-in. baking pan. Drizzle with oil and sprinkle with salt; toss to coat. Bake, uncovered, at 450° for 10-12 minutes or until crisp-tender.

### The Most From Roasting

Want more ideas for enjoying roasted vegetables? Try tossing them in your favorite pasta dishes, soups or even your morning eggs. Or tuck roasted veggies and a slice of mozzarella cheese between two slices of toasted bread for a sensational sandwich.

MAKE AHEAD

## Orange-Smoked Paprika Salt

Your corn on the cob will get a fresh, fragrant boost when you add a hefty pinch of flavored salt from the Taste of Home Test Kitchen pros.

**PREP:** 15 MIN. + STANDING
**MAKES:** 1 CUP

- **¾ cup kosher salt**
- **½ cup grated orange peel (from about 5 large oranges)**
- **½ teaspoon smoked paprika**

Place all ingredients in a food processor; pulse until blended. Transfer to a shallow dish. Let stand at room temperature 3-4 hours or until dry, stirring occasionally. Store in an airtight container in a cool dry place for up to 6 months.

FAST FIX

## White Cheddar Cheese Sauce

Here's one of my best go-to recipes. I make macaroni and cheese, nachos and scalloped potatoes with it.
**—CELESTE NOLAN** GALLIPOLIS, OHIO

**PREP/TOTAL TIME:** 20 MIN. **MAKES:** 3 CUPS

- **¼ cup butter, cubed**
- **¼ cup all-purpose flour**
- **1 teaspoon salt**
- **2 cups 2% milk**
- **2 cups (8 ounces) shredded white cheddar cheese**
- **4 ounces fresh goat cheese, crumbled**

Orange-Smoked Paprika Salt

Lemon-Ginger Salt

In a large saucepan, melt butter over medium heat. Stir in flour and salt until smooth; gradually whisk in milk. Bring to a boil, stirring constantly; cook and stir for 1-2 minutes or until thickened. Stir in cheeses.

MAKE AHEAD

## Lemon-Ginger Salt

Sprinkle a little bit of this unexpected combination from the Taste of Home Test Kitchen staff on hot buttered corn on the cob for a zippy twist.

**PREP:** 15 MIN. **BAKE:** 20 MIN. + COOLING **MAKES:** 1 CUP

- **¾ cup kosher salt**
- **½ cup grated lemon peel (from about 5 large lemons)**
- **1 teaspoon ground ginger**
- **2 tablespoons lemon juice**

**1.** Place salt, lemon peel and ginger in a food processor; pulse until blended. Transfer to an 8-in.-square baking dish. Stir in lemon juice.
**2.** Bake at 200° for 20-25 minutes or until dry, stirring occasionally. Cool completely. Stir with a fork to break up. Store in an airtight container in a cool dry place for up to 3 months.

## Chestnut Stuffing

It just wouldn't be Thanksgiving without a big bowl of our family's favorite stuffing alongside the turkey. If you can't find jarred chestnuts at your grocery store, check gourmet cooking shops or order online.
**—LEE BREMSON** KANSAS CITY, MISSOURI

**PREP:** 40 MIN. **BAKE:** 35 MIN. **MAKES:** 21 SERVINGS

- **1 large onion, chopped**
- **½ cup chopped fennel bulb**
- **1½ cups butter, cubed, divided**

- 2 garlic cloves, minced
- 2 cups peeled cooked chestnuts, coarsely chopped
- 1 large pear, chopped
- 1 cup chicken broth
- ½ cup mixed dried fruit, coarsely chopped
- 2 teaspoons poultry seasoning
- 2 teaspoons minced fresh rosemary
- 2 teaspoons minced fresh thyme
- ½ teaspoon salt
- ½ teaspoon pepper
- 2 loaves day-old white bread (1 pound each), cubed
- 3 eggs
- ¼ cup 2% milk

**1.** In a large skillet, saute onion and fennel in ½ cup butter until tender. Stir in garlic; cook 2 minutes longer. Stir in the chestnuts, pear, broth, dried fruit, seasonings and remaining butter; cook until butter is melted. Bring to a boil. Reduce heat; simmer, uncovered, for 3-4 minutes or until dried fruit is softened.

**2.** Place in a large bowl. Stir in bread cubes. Whisk eggs and milk; drizzle over stuffing and toss to coat.

**3.** Transfer to a greased 13-in. x 9-in. and a greased 8-in.-square baking dish. Bake, uncovered, at 350° for 25 minutes. Uncover; bake 10-15 minutes longer or until lightly browned.

When I'm making apple pie or other treats with fresh apples, I use the small end of a melon baller to scoop out the core from the halved apples. The core comes out neatly and easily.

—HELEN NAGY
SUN CITY CENTER, FLORIDA

Chunky Applesauce

## Chunky Applesauce

There's something extra special about homemade applesauce. This simple version is tart, not too sweet and ideal with pork chops or a pork roast. For a change of pace, try one of the yummy variations listed at the end. They make the same amount—about 3½ cups.

—DEBORAH AMRINE
FORT MYERS, FLORIDA

**PREP:** 15 MIN. **COOK:** 30 MIN.
**MAKES:** ABOUT 3½ CUPS

- 8 cups chopped peeled tart apples (about 3½ pounds)
- ½ cup packed brown sugar
- 1 teaspoon ground cinnamon
- 2 teaspoons vanilla extract

In a Dutch oven, combine apples, brown sugar and cinnamon. Cover and cook over medium-low heat for 30-40 minutes or until apples are tender, stirring occasionally. Remove from the heat; stir in vanilla. Mash apples slightly if desired. Serve warm or cold.

**SPICED APPLESAUCE**
Reduce vanilla to ½ teaspoon. Add 1 tablespoon lemon juice, ½ teaspoon ground ginger, ¼ teaspoon each ground nutmeg and mace and ⅛ teaspoon ground cardamom to apples before cooking.

**NEW ENGLAND APPLESAUCE**
Use Rome Beauty or McIntosh apples. Omit brown sugar and vanilla. Reduce cinnamon to ¼ teaspoon. Add 1 cup each honey and water and ½ cup lemon juice to apples before cooking. If desired, stir 2 tablespoons grenadine syrup into mashed apples.

## FAST FIX Braised Dill Potatoes

Fresh dill, chicken broth and a few other kitchen staples combine for potatoes your family is guaranteed to love.
—**AMIE SCHMIDT** SAN DIEGO, CALIFORNIA

**PREP/TOTAL TIME:** 30 MIN. **MAKES:** 4 SERVINGS

- **1 pound fingerling potatoes**
- **1 cup chicken broth**
- **1 tablespoon butter**
- **3 tablespoons snipped fresh dill**
- **⅛ teaspoon salt**
- **⅛ teaspoon pepper**
- **2 tablespoons sour cream**

**1.** In a large saucepan, arrange potatoes in a single layer. Add broth and butter. Cover and cook over medium-high heat for 12 minutes.
**2.** Uncover; cook 7-10 minutes or until potatoes are tender and broth is evaporated. Press each potato with a turner to crush slightly. Sprinkle evenly with the dill, salt and pepper. Cook 2-3 minutes longer or until bottoms are lightly browned. Serve with sour cream.

## FAST FIX Mushroom & Zucchini Pesto Saute

With purchased or homemade pesto and just five additional ingredients, you can round out your meal with a quick but delicious side dish. It goes together easily on the stove.
—**BENJAMIN SMITH** BEAUMONT, TEXAS

**PREP/TOTAL TIME:** 10 MIN. **MAKES:** 4 SERVINGS

**Mushroom & Zucchini Pesto Saute**

**Tomato Pesto Tart**

- **2 teaspoons olive oil**
- **½ pound sliced fresh mushrooms**
- **1 small onion, chopped**
- **2 medium zucchini, cut into ¼ inch slices**
- **3 tablespoons prepared pesto**
- **¼ teaspoon lemon-pepper seasoning**

In a large skillet, heat oil over medium-high heat. Add mushrooms and onion; cook and stir for 2 minutes. Add zucchini; cook and stir until vegetables are tender. Stir in pesto and lemon-pepper seasoning.

## FAST FIX Tomato Pesto Tart

Try this savory tart for a sophisticated, fresh-tasting treat. It's a great way to use your garden tomatoes.
—**JUDY HANNEBAUM** FREELAND, WASHINGTON

**PREP/TOTAL TIME:** 30 MIN. **MAKES:** 6 SERVINGS

- **1 sheet refrigerated pie pastry**
- **1½ cups (6 ounces) shredded part-skim mozzarella cheese, divided**
- **2 plum tomatoes, thinly sliced**
- **½ cup mayonnaise**
- **¼ cup grated Parmesan cheese**
- **2 tablespoons prepared pesto**
- **½ teaspoon freshly ground pepper**

**1.** On a lightly floured surface, unroll pie pastry. Roll into a 14-in. x 12-in. rectangle; transfer to an ungreased baking sheet. Flute edges; prick bottom with a fork. Bake at 425° for 6-8 minutes or until lightly browned.
**2.** Sprinkle with 1 cup mozzarella cheese; top with tomatoes. In a small bowl, mix the mayonnaise, Parmesan cheese, pesto, pepper and remaining mozzarella until blended; spread over tomatoes. Bake 10-12 minutes longer or until crust is golden brown and filling is bubbly.

## FAST FIX Curry Roasted Potatoes

Here's a fantastic recipe for cooks who want to do some experimenting with new spices and flavors.
—**BRYAN KENNEDY** KANEOHE, HAWAII

**PREP:** 20 MIN. **BAKE:** 20 MIN.
**MAKES:** 6 SERVINGS (1 CUP SAUCE)

- **6 cardamom pods**
- **½ teaspoon whole cloves**
- **2 teaspoons each fennel, cumin, coriander and mustard seeds**
- **2 teaspoons ground turmeric**
- **½ teaspoon salt**
- **¼ teaspoon cayenne pepper**
- **2 tablespoons canola oil**
- **4 medium red potatoes, cut into ¼-inch slices**

**MINT YOGURT SAUCE**

- **1 cup reduced-fat plain yogurt**
- **¼ cup minced fresh mint**

**1.** Remove seeds from cardamom pods. In a small dry skillet over medium heat, toast the cloves and the fennel, cumin, coriander, mustard and cardamom seeds until aromatic, about 1-2 minutes. Cool.
**2.** Transfer to a spice grinder or a mortar and pestle (in batches if necessary); grind until mixture becomes a powder. Stir in the turmeric, salt and cayenne.
**3.** In a large bowl, combine oil and spice mixture. Add potatoes; toss to coat. Arrange in a single layer in an ungreased 15-in. x 10-in. x 1-in. baking pan. Bake at 425° for 16-20 minutes or until golden brown, turning once.
**4.** Meanwhile, combine yogurt and mint in a small bowl. Serve with potatoes.

# Main Dishes

Ring the dinner bell for a **family supper**! Enjoy time with your gang as you sit around the table sharing daily stories and **unforgettable meals** featuring special entrees.

"For a simple dinner in one, turn to Chicken Paillard with Cherry Sauce & Parsley Rice. It cooks up so quickly, we can enjoy it even on busy weeknights."

—**LISA SPEER** PALM BEACH, FLORIDA

MAIN DISHES

## Bubbly & Golden Mexican Beef Cobbler

**PREP:** 20 MIN. **BAKE:** 35 MIN.
**MAKES:** 6 SERVINGS

- **1 pound ground beef**
- **1 envelope taco seasoning**
- **¾ cup water**
- **1 jar (16 ounces) salsa**
- **1 can (8¾ ounces) whole kernel corn, drained**
- **2 cups (8 ounces) shredded sharp cheddar cheese**
- **3⅓ cups biscuit/baking mix**
- **1⅓ cups 2% milk**
- **⅛ teaspoon salt**
- **⅛ teaspoon pepper**

**1.** In a large skillet, cook beef over medium heat for 6-8 minutes or until no longer pink, breaking into crumbles; drain. Stir in taco seasoning and water. Bring to a boil; cook until liquid is evaporated. Transfer to a 11-in. x 7-in. baking dish; layer with salsa, corn and cheese.

**2.** In a large bowl, mix biscuit mix and milk just until blended; drop by tablespoonfuls over cheese (dish will be full). Sprinkle with salt and pepper.

**3.** Bake, uncovered, at 350° for 35-45 minutes or until bubbly and topping is golden brown.

Just like shepherd's pie, Bubbly & Golden Mexican Beef Cobbler is easy to change up. Add some black beans, sour cream, onions, peppers or even guacamole.
**—MARY BROOKS** CLAY, MICHIGAN

## Chicken & Dumplings

After a very long week, I needed some comfort food and made this meal on a whim. Rotisserie chicken drastically cuts the prep time, so we don't have to wait long for dinner to be ready.
**—JESSICA REHS**
CUYAHOGA FALLS, OHIO

**PREP:** 25 MIN. **COOK:** 35 MIN.
**MAKES:** 6 SERVINGS

- **6 cups reduced-sodium chicken broth**
- **3 bay leaves**
- **5 fresh thyme sprigs**
- **4 garlic cloves, peeled**
- **1 teaspoon crushed red pepper flakes**
- **1 cup chopped carrots**
- **1 cup chopped celery**
- **3 tablespoons olive oil**
- **2 tablespoons butter**
- **3 garlic cloves, minced**
- **2 tablespoons all-purpose flour**
- **1 cup frozen peas**
- **1 rotisserie chicken, shredded**
- **¼ cup heavy whipping cream**

**DUMPLINGS**

- **2 cups all-purpose flour**
- **1 tablespoon baking powder**
- **1 teaspoon salt**
- **1 teaspoon cayenne pepper**
- **1 cup buttermilk**
- **2 eggs, lightly beaten**
- **¼ cup minced chives**

**1.** In a large saucepan, combine the first five ingredients. Bring to a boil. Reduce heat; simmer, uncovered, for 30 minutes. Strain and set aside.

**2.** In a Dutch oven, saute carrots and celery in oil and butter until tender. Add minced garlic; cook 1 minute longer. Stir in flour until blended; gradually add prepared broth. Bring to a boil; cook 2 minutes or until thickened, stirring frequently.

**3.** Add peas; return to a boil. Cook 3 to 5 minutes or until peas are tender. Stir in chicken and cream; heat through.

**4.** For dumplings, combine the flour, baking powder, salt and cayenne in a large bowl. In another bowl, combine buttermilk and eggs; stir into dry ingredients just until moistened.

**5.** Drop by tablespoonfuls onto simmering chicken mixture. Cover and simmer for 15-20 minutes or until a toothpick inserted in a dumpling comes out clean. Garnish with chives before serving.

Bubbly & Golden Mexican Beef Cobbler

## FAST FIX Lemon-Orange Shrimp & Rice

Here's an effortless, low-fat version of a favorite dinner standby. It also works well with peach or apricot preserves in place of the orange marmalade.

**—MARY WILHELM**
SPARTA, WISCONSIN

**PREP/TOTAL TIME:** 30 MIN.
**MAKES:** 4 SERVINGS

- **2 packages (6.2 ounces each) fried rice mix**
- **1½ pounds uncooked medium shrimp, peeled and deveined**
- **1 tablespoon canola oil**
- **¼ cup orange marmalade**
- **2 teaspoons grated lemon peel**
- **3 cups frozen sugar snap peas, thawed**

**1.** Prepare rice mix according to package directions, simmering for 10-15 minutes or just until rice is tender. Remove from the pan.
**2.** In the same skillet, cook and stir shrimp in oil over medium-high heat for 4-6 minutes or until shrimp turns pink; stir in orange marmalade and lemon peel. Add snap peas and rice; heat through, mixing gently to combine. Serve.

## FAST FIX Turkey Sausage & Spinach Orecchiette

**PREP/TOTAL TIME:** 30 MIN.
**MAKES:** 4 SERVINGS

- **½ pound uncooked orecchiette or small tube pasta**
- **3 hot Italian turkey sausage links, casings removed**
- **¼ cup chopped onion**
- **2 garlic cloves, minced**
- **¼ teaspoon crushed red pepper flakes**
- **3 cups fresh spinach**
- **½ cup shredded Asiago cheese**
- **¼ cup grated Parmesan cheese**
- **¼ cup rinsed and drained white kidney or cannellini beans**
- **¼ cup chopped roasted sweet red pepper**
- **½ teaspoon Italian seasoning**
- **Additional shredded Asiago cheese, optional**

**1.** Cook orecchiette according to package directions.
**2.** In a large skillet, cook and stir the sausage, onion, garlic and pepper flakes over medium heat for 6-8 minutes or until sausage is no longer pink; drain. Add the spinach, ½ cup Asiago cheese, Parmesan cheese, beans, peppers and Italian seasoning; cook just until spinach is wilted, stirring occasionally.
**3.** Drain pasta; add to sausage mixture and toss to combine. Sprinkle with additional Asiago cheese if desired.

Turkey Sausage & Spinach Orecchiette

## Apple Orchard Pork Roast

Onions and apples meld perfectly to make a sweet and savory treatment for pork roast. Serve it with the accompanying sour cream sauce.

**—VIKKI LEE** GOLD RIVER, CALIFORNIA

**PREP:** 25 MIN.
**BAKE:** 1¼ HOURS + STANDING
**MAKES:** 8 SERVINGS (1 CUP SAUCE)

- **1 boneless whole pork loin roast (3 to 4 pounds)**
- **1 garlic clove, peeled and halved**
- **1 teaspoon salt**
- **½ teaspoon pepper**
- **6 fresh sage leaves**
- **3 fresh rosemary sprigs**
- **3 fresh thyme sprigs**
- **3 large tart apples, cut into wedges**
- **2 medium onions, cut into chunks**
- **4 garlic cloves, thinly sliced**
- **¼ cup butter, cubed**
- **1⅔ cups sparkling apple cider, divided**
- **1 tablespoon soy sauce**
- **¼ cup sour cream**

**1.** Place roast in a shallow roasting pan; rub with garlic halves and sprinkle with salt and pepper. Top with herbs. Arrange the apples, onions and sliced garlic around roast; dot with butter. Combine 1 cup cider and soy sauce; pour over top.
**2.** Bake, uncovered, at 350° for 1¼ to 1½ hours or until a meat thermometer reads 160°, basting occasionally with pan juices. Remove the roast, apples and onions to a serving platter; keep warm. Let stand for 10 minutes before slicing.
**3.** Meanwhile, skim fat from pan juices; transfer juices to a small saucepan. Add remaining cider. Bring to a boil. Remove from the heat; whisk in sour cream until smooth. Serve with pork.

Don't let a funny name like Turkey Sausage & Spinach Orecchiette scare you away. The little ear-shaped pasta makes the perfect partner for spicy turkey sausage and Italian seasoning.
**—ANDREA PHILLIPS** LAKEVILLE, MINNESOTA

## FAST FIX Couscous Tabbouleh with Fresh Mint & Feta

**PREP/TOTAL TIME:** 20 MIN.
**MAKES:** 2 SERVINGS

- **¾ cup water**
- **½ cup uncooked couscous**
- **1 can (15 ounces) garbanzo beans or chickpeas, rinsed and drained**
- **1 large tomato, chopped**
- **½ English cucumber, halved and thinly sliced**
- **3 tablespoons lemon juice**
- **2 teaspoons grated lemon peel**
- **2 teaspoons olive oil**
- **2 teaspoons minced fresh mint**
- **2 teaspoons minced fresh parsley**
- **¼ teaspoon salt**
- **⅛ teaspoon pepper**
- **¾ cup crumbled feta cheese**

**1.** In a small saucepan, bring water to a boil. Stir in couscous. Remove from the heat; cover and let stand for 5-8 minutes or until water is absorbed. Fluff with a fork.
**2.** In a large bowl, combine the beans, tomato and cucumber. In a small bowl, whisk the lemon juice, lemon peel, oil and seasonings. Drizzle over bean mixture. Add couscous; toss to combine. Serve immediately or refrigerate until chilled. Sprinkle with cheese before serving.

**Couscous Tabbouleh with Fresh Mint & Feta**

Using small pasta instead of bulgur for tabbouleh is the speedy key to Couscous Tabbouleh with Fresh Mint & Feta.
**—ELODIE ROSINOVSKY**
BRIGHTON, MASSACHUSETTS

## SLOW COOKER Pineapple Curry Chicken

The curry goes in early in the cooking process, creating the perfect balance.
**—ROBIN HAAS**
CRANSTON, RHODE ISLAND

**PREP:** 25 MIN. **COOK:** 6 HOURS
**MAKES:** 6 SERVINGS

- **2 cans (8 ounces each) unsweetened pineapple chunks, undrained**
- **6 bone-in chicken breast halves, skin removed (12 ounces each)**
- **1 can (15 ounces) garbanzo beans or chickpeas, rinsed and drained**
- **1 large onion, cut into 1-inch pieces**
- **1 cup julienned carrots**
- **1 medium sweet red pepper, cut into strips**
- **½ cup light coconut milk**
- **2 tablespoons cornstarch**
- **2 tablespoons sugar**
- **3 teaspoons curry powder**
- **2 garlic cloves, minced**
- **2 teaspoons minced fresh gingerroot**
- **1 teaspoon salt**
- **1 teaspoon pepper**
- **1 teaspoon lime juice**
- **½ teaspoon crushed red pepper flakes**
- **Hot cooked rice**
- **⅓ cup minced fresh basil**
- **Toasted flaked coconut, optional**

**1.** Drain pineapple, reserving ¾ cup juice. Place chicken, beans, vegetables and pineapple in a 6-qt. slow cooker. In a small bowl, combine milk and cornstarch until smooth. Stir in sugar, curry, garlic, ginger, salt, pepper, lime juice, pepper flakes and reserved juice; pour over chicken.
**2.** Cover and cook on low for 6-8 hours or until chicken is tender. Serve with rice; sprinkle with basil and, if desired, coconut.

## Balsamic Roasted Sausage and Grapes with Linguine

Pasta doesn't have to wear coats of cream and cheese, especially when red grapes and sausage give it lots of sweetness and spice.
**—LAUREN WYLER** AUSTIN, TEXAS

**PREP:** 15 MIN. **BAKE:** 30 MIN.
**MAKES:** 8 SERVINGS

- **¾ pound sweet Italian sausage links**
- **¾ pound hot Italian sausage links**
- **3 cups seedless red grapes**
- **¼ cup balsamic vinegar**
- **2 tablespoons olive oil**
- **2 tablespoons water**
- **½ teaspoon salt**
- **½ teaspoon pepper**
- **1 package (13¼ ounces) multigrain linguine**
- **½ cup prepared pesto**
- **2 cups fresh baby spinach**
- **2 cups spring mix salad greens**

**1.** Place sausage links and grapes in a greased 13-in. x 9-in. baking dish. In a bowl, combine the vinegar, oil and water; pour over sausages. Sprinkle with salt and pepper.
**2.** Bake at 450° for 20 minutes. Turn sausages; bake 10-15 minutes longer or until a thermometer inserted in sausages reads 160°.
**3.** Meanwhile, cook linguine according to package directions. Drain, reserving ½ cup pasta water.
**4.** Cut sausages into ½-in. slices. In a large bowl, combine linguine, reserved pasta water and pesto; toss to coat. Add the sausage, spinach, salad greens and grapes with pan juices; toss to combine. Serve immediately.

## FAST FIX Best-Ever Fried Chicken

Don't wait for a special occasion to prepare this special chicken. It's so good and comes together so easily.
**—LOLA CLIFTON** VINTON, VIRGINIA

**PREP:** 15 MIN. **COOK:** 15 MIN.
**MAKES:** 4 SERVINGS

- **2 cups all-purpose flour**
- **1 tablespoon dried thyme**
- **1 tablespoon paprika**
- **2 teaspoons salt**
- **1 teaspoon pepper**
- **⅓ cup whole milk**
- **1 egg**
- **2 tablespoons lemon juice**
- **1 broiler/fryer chicken (3 to 4 pounds), cut up**
- **Oil for deep-fat frying**

**1.** In a bowl, mix the first five ingredients. In a separate shallow bowl, whisk the milk, egg and lemon juice. Coat chicken pieces, one at a time, with flour mixture; dip in milk mixture, then coat again with flour mixture.
**2.** In an electric skillet or deep-fat fryer, heat oil to 375°. Fry chicken, a few pieces at a time, for 6-10 minutes on each side or until chicken juices run clear. Drain on paper towels.

## MAKE AHEAD Homemade Pierogies

Pierogies are dumplings or tiny pies that are stuffed, boiled and cooked in butter. They're worth the effort!
**—DIANE GAWRYS**
MANCHESTER, TENNESSEE

**PREP:** 1 HOUR + FREEZING
**COOK:** 5 MIN./BATCH **MAKES:** 1 SERVING

- **5 cups all-purpose flour**
- **1 teaspoon salt**
- **1 cup water**
- **3 eggs**
- **½ cup butter, softened**

**FILLING**

- **4 medium potatoes, peeled and cubed**
- **2 medium onions, chopped**
- **2 tablespoons butter**
- **5 ounces cream cheese, softened**
- **½ teaspoon salt**
- **½ teaspoon pepper**

**ADDITIONAL INGREDIENTS (FOR EACH SERVING)**

- **¼ cup chopped onion**
- **1 tablespoon butter**
- **Minced fresh parsley**

**1.** In a food processor, combine flour and salt; cover and pulse to blend. Add water, eggs and butter; cover and pulse until dough forms a ball, adding an additional 1 to 2 tablespoons of water or flour if needed. Let rest, covered, for 15 to 30 minutes.
**2.** Place potatoes in a large saucepan and cover with water. Bring to a boil. Reduce heat; cover and simmer for 10-15 minutes or until tender. Meanwhile, in a large skillet, saute onions in butter until tender; set aside.
**3.** Drain potatoes. Over very low heat, stir potatoes for 1-2 minutes or until steam has evaporated. Press through a potato ricer or strainer into a large bowl. Stir in the cream cheese, salt, pepper and onion mixture; set aside.
**4.** Divide dough into four parts. On a lightly floured surface, roll one portion of dough to ⅛-in. thickness; cut with a floured 3-in. biscuit cutter. Place 2 teaspoons of filling in the center of each circle. Moisten edges with water; fold in half and press edges to seal. Repeat with remaining dough and filling.
**5.** Bring a Dutch oven of water to a boil; add pierogies in batches. Reduce heat to a gentle simmer; cook for 1-2 minutes or until pierogies float to the top and are tender. Remove with a slotted spoon; cool slightly.
**6.** Place on waxed paper-lined 15-in. x 10-in. x 1-in. baking pans; freeze until firm. Transfer to resealable plastic freezer bags. May be frozen for up to 3 months.
**7. TO PREPARE FROZEN PIEROGIES:** In a large skillet, saute four pierogies and onion in butter until pierogies are lightly browned and heated through; sprinkle with parsley.

Spicy Stuffed Peppers with Andouille

## Spicy Stuffed Peppers with Andouille

Eating lighter? Use chicken sausage or cubed chicken instead of andouille.
**—SARAH LARSON**
CARLSBAD, CALIFORNIA

**PREP:** 40 MIN. **BAKE:** 40 MIN.
**MAKES:** 4 SERVINGS

- **1 package (8 ounces) jambalaya mix**
- **4 small green peppers**
- **¾ pound fully cooked andouille sausage links, chopped**
- **1 jalapeno pepper, seeded and minced**
- **1 can (16 ounces) tomato juice**
- **Louisiana-style hot sauce, optional**

**1.** Prepare jambalaya mix according to package directions. Meanwhile, cut peppers lengthwise in half; remove seeds.
**2.** In a skillet, cook and stir sausage over medium-high heat until browned. Add jalapeno; cook 1 minute longer. Using a slotted spoon, remove to paper towels to drain.
**3.** Stir sausage mixture into prepared jambalaya. Spoon into pepper halves. Place in a greased 13-in. x 9-in. baking dish; pour tomato juice over and around peppers.
**4.** Bake, uncovered, at 350° for 40-45 minutes or until peppers are tender.
**Editor's Note:** *Wear disposable gloves when cutting hot peppers; the oils can burn skin. Avoid touching your face.*

MAIN DISHES

FAST FIX

## Seared Scallops with Citrus Herb Sauce

**PREP/TOTAL TIME:** 20 MIN.
**MAKES:** 2 SERVINGS

- **¾ pound sea scallops**
- **¼ teaspoon salt**
- **¼ teaspoon pepper**
- **⅛ teaspoon paprika**
- **3 tablespoons butter, divided**
- **1 garlic clove, minced**
- **2 tablespoons dry sherry or chicken broth**
- **1 tablespoon lemon juice**
- **⅛ teaspoon minced fresh oregano**
- **⅛ teaspoon minced fresh tarragon**

**1.** Pat scallops dry with paper towels; sprinkle with salt, pepper and paprika. In a large skillet, heat 2 tablespoons butter over medium-high heat. Add scallops; sear for 1-2 minutes on each side or until golden brown and firm. Remove from the skillet; keep warm.

**2.** Wipe skillet clean if necessary. Saute garlic in remaining butter until tender; stir in sherry. Cook until liquid is almost evaporated; stir in the remaining ingredients. Serve with scallops.

Plan on making Seared Scallops with Citrus Herb Sauce? Be sure to pat the scallops dry so they go to the table perfectly browned and flavorful.
—**APRIL LANE** GREENEVILLE, TENNESSEE

## Wonton Walnut Ravioli

Roasted butternut squash boasts a sweet, nutty flavor similar to pumpkin but is much easier to prepare. If time is a factor, buy pre-chopped squash that you can find in most grocery stores.
—**NICOLE HOPPING**
SAN FRANCISCO, CALIFORNIA

**PREP:** 45 MIN. + COOLING
**COOK:** 5 MIN./BATCH
**MAKES:** 4 SERVINGS

- **3½ cups cubed peeled butternut squash**
- **1 tablespoon olive oil**
- **¼ teaspoon salt**
- **¼ teaspoon pepper**
- **½ cup half-and-half cream**
- **40 wonton wrappers**
- **1 egg, lightly beaten**
- **½ cup butter, melted**
- **6 tablespoons marinara sauce**
- **⅓ cup finely chopped walnuts**
- **2 teaspoons minced fresh sage**

**1.** Place squash on a greased 15-in. x 10-in. x 1-in. baking pan. Drizzle with oil and sprinkle with salt and pepper; toss to coat. Bake, uncovered, at 425° for 15-20 minutes or until tender, stirring once. Cool slightly.

**2.** Place cream and squash in a food processor; cover and process until pureed. Spoon 1 tablespoon mixture in the center of a wonton wrapper. (Keep wrappers covered with a damp paper towel until ready to use.) Moisten edges with egg; top with another wonton wrapper. Pinch edges to seal, pressing around filling to remove air pockets. Repeat with remaining wrappers and filling.

**3.** In a Dutch oven, bring water to a boil. Reduce heat to a gentle simmer. Cook ravioli in batches for 30-60 seconds or until they float. Remove with a slotted spoon; keep warm.

**4.** Meanwhile, place butter and marinara sauce in a microwave-safe bowl. Cover and microwave on high for 1-2 minutes or until heated through, stirring once. Stir in walnuts. Serve with ravioli; sprinkle with sage.

Wonton Walnut Ravioli

### Did you know?

Unwashed winter squash can be stored in a well-ventilated, dry, cool place for up to 1 month, so take advantage of it when it's on sale!

## Turkey Puffs with Cranberry Cabernet Sauce

Caramelized onions and dried mushrooms revitalize leftover turkey, while sweet and savory cranberry sauce balances the rich pastry and cream cheese. What a delicious way to end the day! Plus, it's a sensational solution for any extra turkey you might have after Thanksgiving dinner.
—**SUZANNE CLARK** PHOENIX, ARIZONA

**PREP:** 40 MIN. **BAKE:** 20 MIN. **MAKES:** 4 SERVINGS

- **1 cup chicken broth**
- **1 cup dried wild mushrooms**
- **1 medium onion, thinly sliced**
- **2 tablespoons butter**
- **1 teaspoon minced fresh tarragon or ¼ teaspoon dried tarragon**
- **¼ teaspoon salt**
- **¼ teaspoon pepper**
- **1 package (17.3 ounces) frozen puff pastry, thawed**
- **8 ounces thinly sliced cooked turkey**
- **½ cup spreadable chive and onion cream cheese**
- **1 egg, beaten**

**SAUCE**
- **1 cup chicken broth**
- **1 cup dry red wine or additional chicken broth**
- **½ cup balsamic vinegar**
- **¾ cup jellied cranberry sauce**

**1.** In a small saucepan, combine broth and mushrooms; bring to a boil. Remove from the heat; let stand for 15-20 minutes or until mushrooms are softened. Using a slotted spoon, remove mushrooms; coarsely chop. Strain remaining broth through a fine mesh strainer. Set aside mushrooms and broth.
**2.** In a large skillet, saute onion in butter until softened. Reduce heat to medium-low; cook, stirring occasionally, for 10 minutes or until golden brown. Add the tarragon, salt, pepper and reserved mushrooms and broth. Bring to a boil; cook over medium heat until liquid is evaporated.
**3.** On a lightly floured surface, unfold puff pastry. Roll each sheet into a 12-in. x 10-in. rectangle; cut each into 2 pieces. Transfer to a greased baking sheet. Spoon mushroom mixture onto each pastry; top with turkey and cream cheese.
**4.** Lightly brush pastry edges with water. Bring long sides over filling, pinching seams and ends to seal. Turn pastries seam side down. Cut small slits into pastry. Brush tops with egg. Bake at 400° for 20-25 minutes or until golden brown.
**5.** Meanwhile, in a small saucepan, combine the broth, wine and vinegar. Bring to a boil; cook until liquid is reduced by half. Stir in cranberry sauce until melted. Serve with pastries.

Turkey Puffs with Cranberry Cabernet Sauce

## Sausage Broccoli Calzone

You know how people drop in unannounced and often a little famished? To remain calm in your own kitchen, reach for packaged French bread dough, sausage, cheese and some veggies—then roll out the red carpet.
—**ANGIE COLOMBO** OLDSMAR, FLORIDA

**PREP:** 20 MIN. **BAKE:** 20 MIN. **MAKES:** 6 SERVINGS

- **12 ounces bulk pork sausage**
- **1½ teaspoons minced fresh sage**
- **1 tube (11 ounces) refrigerated crusty French loaf**
- **2 cups frozen chopped broccoli, thawed and drained**
- **1 cup (4 ounces) shredded part-skim mozzarella cheese**
- **1 cup (4 ounces) shredded cheddar cheese**

**1.** In a small skillet, cook sausage over medium heat until no longer pink; drain. Stir in sage.
**2.** On an ungreased baking sheet, unroll dough starting at the seam; pat into a 14-in. x 12-in. rectangle. Spoon sausage lengthwise across center of dough. Sprinkle with broccoli and cheeses. Bring long sides of dough to the center over filling; pinch seams to seal. Turn calzone seam side down.
**3.** Bake at 350° for 20-25 minutes or until golden brown. Serve warm.

## Cozumel Red Snapper Vera Cruz

Cozumel is home to magnificent Veracruz-style red snapper. Here, I created my own version of the popular seafood dish. Served with couscous, it's a unique meal-in-one favorite.
—**BARBIE MILLER** OAKDALE, MINNESOTA

**PREP:** 25 MIN. **BAKE:** 35 MIN. **MAKES:** 4 SERVINGS

- **4 red snapper fillets (6 ounces each)**
- **½ teaspoon salt**
- **¼ teaspoon pepper**
- **¼ cup white wine or chicken stock**
- **2 large tomatoes, seeded and chopped**
- **1 medium onion, chopped**
- **⅓ cup pitted green olives, chopped**
- **1 jalapeno pepper, seeded and minced**
- **2 tablespoons capers, drained**
- **2 garlic cloves, minced**
- **2 tablespoons olive oil**
- **Hot cooked Israeli couscous and chopped fresh cilantro, optional**

**1.** Sprinkle fillets with salt and pepper. Place in a greased 13-in. x 9-in. baking dish; drizzle with wine. Top with the tomatoes, onion, olives, jalapeno, capers and garlic; drizzle with olive oil.
**2.** Bake at 375° for 35-40 minutes or until fish flakes easily with a fork. If desired, serve with couscous and sprinkle with cilantro.
**Editor's Note:** *Wear disposable gloves when cutting hot peppers; the oils can burn skin. Avoid touching your face.*

Cozumel Red Snapper Vera Cruz

Chicken Portobello Stroganoff

## Chicken Portobello Stroganoff

Stroganov used to be a dish of sauteed beef with sour cream in 19th-century Russia. This modern chicken-and-portobello variation came about when I opened the refrigerator before dinner one night, only to find nothing much but necessity—which truly is the mother of invention!
—**KATIE ROSE** PEWAUKEE, WISCONSIN

**PREP:** 15 MIN. **COOK:** 25 MIN. **MAKES:** 4 SERVINGS

- **1 pound ground chicken**
- **12 ounces baby portobello mushrooms, halved**
- **1 medium onion, chopped**
- **1 tablespoon olive oil**
- **2 garlic cloves, minced**
- **3 tablespoons white wine or chicken broth**
- **2 cups chicken broth**
- **½ cup heavy whipping cream**
- **2 tablespoons lemon juice**
- **¼ teaspoon salt**
- **⅛ teaspoon white pepper**
- **1 cup (8 ounces) sour cream**
- **Hot cooked egg noodles or pasta**

**1.** In a large skillet, cook the chicken, mushrooms and onion in oil over medium-high heat until meat is no longer pink. Add garlic; cook 1 minute longer.
**2.** Stir in wine. Bring to a boil; cook until liquid is almost evaporated. Add the broth, cream, lemon juice, salt and pepper. Bring to a boil; cook until liquid is reduced by half.
**3.** Reduce heat. Gradually stir in sour cream; heat through (do not boil). Serve with noodles.

## Shrimp Scampi Fettuccine with Andouille Butter

We enjoy andouille sausage with pasta. Change up your usual scampi by adding the andouille to a butter sauce.
**—JUDY ARMSTRONG** PRAIRIEVILLE, LOUISIANA

**PREP:** 35 MIN. **COOK:** 20 MIN. **MAKES:** 8 SERVINGS

- **1 package (16 ounces) fettuccine**
- **¾ pound fully cooked andouille sausage links, cut into ¼-inch slices**
- **¾ cup butter, cut up**
- **2 medium leeks (white portion only), thinly sliced**
- **4 garlic cloves, minced**
- **½ cup white wine**
- **¼ cup brandy**
- **1 teaspoon salt**
- **1 teaspoon paprika**
- **½ teaspoon cayenne pepper**
- **2 pounds uncooked large shrimp, peeled and deveined**
- **Minced fresh parsley and lemon wedges, optional**

**1.** Cook fettuccine according to package directions. In a large skillet, cook and stir sausage over medium-high heat until browned, about 5 minutes. Remove from the heat; transfer half of the sausage to paper towels to drain.
**2.** Place butter and drained sausage in a food processor; cover and process until blended. Remove to a bowl; cover and refrigerate.
**3.** Add leeks to remaining sausage in skillet; cook and stir over medium-high heat until leeks are tender. Add garlic; cook 1 minute longer. Add the wine, brandy, salt, paprika and cayenne, stirring to loosen browned bits from pan. Bring to a boil; cook until liquid is reduced by half.
**4.** Stir in shrimp; cook for 5-6 minutes or until shrimp turn pink. Add andouille butter, stirring just until melted.
**5.** Drain fettuccine; place on a large platter. Spoon shrimp mixture over pasta. Sprinkle with parsley and serve with lemon wedges if desired.

Shrimp Scampi Fettuccine with Andouille Butter

## Savory Rubbed Roast Chicken

In general, procedures for roasting meat apply to poultry, too. That means if you use a dry rub on a steak, a dry rub will also work on a chicken. Try a blend of paprika, onion powder, cayenne and garlic powder on the skin and inside the cavity.
**—MARGARET COLE** IMPERIAL, MISSOURI

**PREP:** 20 MIN. **BAKE:** 2 HOURS. + STANDING
**MAKES:** 8 SERVINGS

- **2 teaspoons paprika**
- **1 teaspoon salt**
- **1 teaspoon onion powder**
- **1 teaspoon dried thyme**
- **1 teaspoon white pepper**
- **1 teaspoon cayenne pepper**
- **¾ teaspoon garlic powder**
- **½ teaspoon pepper**
- **1 roasting chicken (6 to 7 pounds)**
- **1 large onion, peeled and quartered**

**1.** In a small bowl, combine the seasonings; set aside. Place chicken breast side up on a rack in a shallow roasting pan; pat dry. Tuck wings under chicken; tie drumsticks together. Rub seasoning mixture over the outside and inside of chicken. Place onion inside cavity.
**2.** Bake, uncovered, at 350° for 2 to 2½ hours or until a thermometer inserted in the thigh reads 180°, basting occasionally with pan drippings. (Cover loosely with foil if chicken browns too quickly.) Cover and let stand for 15 minutes before carving.

### Before You Begin

Make sure whole birds are completely thawed before roasting, or the roasting time will need to be increased and the internal temperature checked often. Remove and discard any pockets of fat in the neck area. Wash the chicken (inside and out) in cold water.

## Orecchiette with Roasted Brussels Sprouts

Featuring pasta and roasted Brussels sprouts, this one-dish specialty has everything I look for in an entree: flavor, texture and a stick-to-your-ribs cream sauce!
—**LILY JULOW** GAINESVILLE, FLORIDA

**PREP:** 45 MIN. **COOK:** 10 MIN. **MAKES:** 6 SERVINGS

- **2 pounds fresh Brussels sprouts, halved**
- **5 tablespoons olive oil, divided**
- **¾ teaspoon salt, divided**
- **¾ teaspoon pepper, divided**
- **3¾ cups uncooked orecchiette or small tube pasta**
- **6 green onions, sliced**
- **3 garlic cloves, minced**
- **¼ cup butter, cubed**
- **¾ cup white wine or chicken broth**
- **4 ounces cream cheese, softened and cubed**
- **Minced fresh parsley**

**1.** In a large bowl, combine the Brussels sprouts, 3 tablespoons oil, 1/4 teaspoon salt and 1/4 teaspoon pepper; toss to coat. Transfer to a greased 15-in. x 10-in. x 1-in. baking pan. Bake, uncovered, at 400° for 30-40 minutes or until tender.
**2.** Meanwhile, cook orecchiette according to package directions; drain, reserving 1 cup pasta water.
**3.** In a small skillet, saute onions and garlic in butter for 1-2 minutes. Stir in wine. Bring to a boil; cook until liquid is reduced by half.
**4.** In a food processor, combine the onion mixture, reserved pasta water and remaining salt and pepper. Cover and process until smooth.

Orecchiette with Roasted Brussels Sprouts

Butternut Squash Risotto

**5.** In a large saucepan, combine the Brussels sprouts, orecchiette, onion mixture, cream cheese and remaining oil. Cook over medium heat until heated through and cream cheese is melted, stirring frequently. Garnish with parsley.

## Butternut Squash Risotto

Change up your risotto any time of year using in-season vegetables—such as butternut squash—spices and broths for a comforting, meatless main course.
—**KATIE FERRIER** WASHINGTON DC

**PREP:** 35 MIN. **COOK:** 30 MIN. **MAKES:** 6 SERVINGS

- **8 cups cubed peeled butternut squash**
- **¼ cup olive oil, divided**
- **½ teaspoon salt**
- **¼ teaspoon pepper**
- **4 to 4½ cups vegetable broth**
- **1 cup water**
- **1 small onion, chopped**
- **2 garlic cloves, minced**
- **2 cups uncooked arborio rice**
- **1 cup lager**
- **2 tablespoons butter**
- **1 teaspoon ground ancho chile pepper**
- **½ teaspoon ground nutmeg**
- **1 cup grated Parmesan cheese**

**1.** In a large bowl, combine the squash, 2 tablespoons oil, salt and pepper; toss to coat. Transfer to a greased 15-in. x 10-in. x 1-in. baking pan. Bake, uncovered, at 450° for 20-25 minutes or until tender, stirring once.
**2.** In a large saucepan, heat broth and water; keep warm. In a large skillet, saute onion and garlic in remaining oil until tender. Add rice; cook and stir for 2-3 minutes. Reduce heat; stir in lager. Cook and stir until all of the liquid is absorbed.
**3.** Add heated broth mixture, 1/2 cup at a time, stirring constantly. Allow the liquid to absorb between additions. Cook just until risotto is creamy and rice is almost tender. (Cooking time is about 20 minutes.) Add the butter, chili pepper, nutmeg and squash; cook and stir until heated through. Remove from the heat; stir in cheese. Serve immediately.

## Chicken Marsala with Gorgonzola

**PREP:** 10 MIN. **COOK:** 30 MIN.
**MAKES:** 4 SERVINGS

- **4 boneless skinless chicken breast halves (6 ounces each)**
- **¼ teaspoon plus ⅛ teaspoon salt, divided**
- **¼ teaspoon pepper**
- **3 tablespoons olive oil, divided**
- **½ pound sliced baby portobello mushrooms**
- **2 garlic cloves, minced**
- **1 cup Marsala wine**
- **⅔ cup heavy whipping cream**
- **½ cup crumbled Gorgonzola cheese, divided**
- **2 tablespoons minced fresh parsley**

**1.** Sprinkle chicken with 1/4 teaspoon salt and pepper. In a large skillet, cook chicken in 2 tablespoons oil over medium heat for 6-8 minutes on each side or until a thermometer reads 170°. Remove and keep warm.
**2.** In the same skillet, saute mushrooms in remaining oil until tender. Add garlic; cook 1 minute longer.
**3.** Add wine, stirring to loosen browned bits from pan. Bring to a boil; cook until liquid is reduced by a third. Stir in cream and remaining salt. Return to a boil; cook until slightly thickened.
**4.** Return chicken to pan; add 1/3 cup cheese. Cook until cheese is melted. Sprinkle with remaining cheese; garnish with parsley.

Chicken Marsala with Gorgonzola

Chicken Marsala with Gorgonzola is a must-have recipe—quick enough for weeknight cooking but also elegant enough for a dinner party.
—**JILL ANDERSON** SLEEPY EYE, MINNESOTA

## Double Layered Souffle

This simple souffle bursts with flavor. The crispy cheese topping hides a creamy layer of turkey underneath. If I don't have turkey on hand, I use chicken instead.
—**SHARON AMIDON**
GUTHRIE, OKLAHOMA

**PREP:** 40 MIN. **BAKE:** 1¼ HOURS
**MAKES:** 8 SERVINGS

- **6 eggs**
- **¼ cup butter, cubed**
- **1 cup chopped fresh mushrooms**
- **¼ cup all-purpose flour**
- **½ teaspoon salt**
- **2 cups 2% milk**
- **3 cups cubed cooked turkey breast**

**SOUFFLE LAYER**

- **⅓ cup butter, cubed**
- **1 shallot, finely chopped**
- **⅓ cup all-purpose flour**
- **½ teaspoon salt**
- **1½ cups 2% milk**
- **1 package (10 ounces) frozen chopped spinach, thawed and squeezed dry**
- **1½ cups (6 ounces) shredded Swiss cheese**

**1.** Separate eggs; let stand at room temperature for 30 minutes. Grease a 2 1/2-qt. souffle dish and lightly sprinkle with flour; set aside.
**2.** Meanwhile, in a large skillet over medium-high heat, melt butter. Add mushrooms; saute until tender. Stir in flour and salt until blended; gradually whisk in milk. Bring to a boil, stirring constantly; cook and stir for 2-3 minutes or until thickened. Add turkey; heat through. Transfer to prepared dish.
**3.** For souffle layer, in a small saucepan over medium-high heat, melt butter. Add shallot; saute until tender. Stir in flour and salt until blended; gradually whisk in milk. Bring to a boil, stirring constantly; cook and stir for 2-3 minutes or until thickened. Transfer to a large bowl; stir in spinach and cheese.
**4.** Stir a small amount of hot spinach mixture into egg yolks; return all to the bowl, stirring constantly. Allow to cool slightly.
**5.** In a large bowl with clean beaters, beat egg whites until stiff peaks form. With a spatula, stir a fourth of the egg whites into spinach mixture until no white streaks remain. Fold in remaining egg whites until combined. Pour over turkey layer.
**6.** Bake at 325° for 1 1/4 to 1 1/2 hours or until the top is puffed and center appears set. Serve.

## Sweet Potato & Caramelized-Onion Shells

Gorgonzola cheese and sweet potatoes put a fun and flavorful spin on my stuffed pasta shells. Delicious with a sprinkle of Parmesan, they're easily topped with gravy.
—**ROBIN HAAS** CRANSTON, RHODE ISLAND

**PREP:** 40 MIN. **BAKE:** 10 MIN.
**MAKES:** 7 SERVINGS

- **2 large onions, chopped**
- **3 tablespoons butter**
- **1 teaspoon garlic powder**
- **¼ teaspoon salt**
- **21 uncooked jumbo pasta shells**
- **¼ cup reduced-sodium chicken broth**
- **1 tablespoon sherry or apple cider**
- **1 teaspoon dried thyme**
- **½ teaspoon pepper**
- **1½ cups mashed sweet potatoes**
- **1½ cups (6 ounces) crumbled Gorgonzola cheese**
- **½ cup grated Parmesan cheese**
- **2 tablespoons minced fresh parsley**
- **1 cup turkey gravy, warmed**

**1.** In a large skillet, saute onions in butter until softened. Add garlic powder and salt. Reduce heat to medium-low; cook, stirring occasionally, for 25-30 minutes or until deep golden brown.
**2.** Meanwhile, cook pasta shells according to package directions. Drain pasta; set aside.
**3.** Stir the broth, sherry, thyme and pepper into onions. Bring to a boil; cook until liquid is almost evaporated. Remove from the heat. Stir in sweet potatoes and Gorgonzola cheese.
**4.** Spoon into shells; place in a greased 11-in. x 7-in. baking dish. Sprinkle with Parmesan cheese. Cover and bake at 375° for 10-15 minutes or until heated through. Sprinkle with parsley. Serve with gravy.

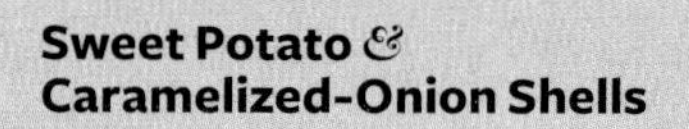
Sweet Potato & Caramelized-Onion Shells

Pretzel-Crusted Chicken with Mixed Greens

## FAST FIX Pretzel-Crusted Chicken with Mixed Greens

The secret to this crunchy coating is grinding the pretzel nuggets until they're finely crushed. Jazz things up using hot buffalo wing- or ranch-flavored pretzels.
—**KERRI BALLIET** MEQUON, WISCONSIN

**PREP/TOTAL TIME:** 30 MIN.
**MAKES:** 4 SERVINGS (⅔ CUP SAUCE)

- **2 cups sourdough pretzel nuggets**
- **½ cup all-purpose flour**
- **2 eggs**
- **¼ cup buttermilk**
- **2 garlic cloves, minced**
- **⅛ teaspoon pepper**
- **5 tablespoons olive oil, divided**
- **4 boneless skinless chicken breast halves (5 ounces each)**
- **⅔ cup mayonnaise**
- **2 tablespoons Dijon mustard**
- **2 teaspoons cider vinegar**
- **⅛ teaspoon salt**
- **⅛ teaspoon pepper**
- **1 package (5 ounces) spring mix salad greens**

**1.** Place pretzels in a food processor; process until finely crushed. Place pretzels and flour in separate shallow bowls. In another shallow bowl, whisk the eggs, buttermilk, garlic and pepper. Pound chicken with a meat mallet to ¼-in. thickness. Dip both sides of chicken in flour, egg mixture and then pretzel crumbs.
**2.** In a large skillet, heat 3 tablespoons oil over medium heat. Add chicken; cook for 4-6 minutes on each side or until no longer pink.
**3.** Meanwhile, in a small bowl, mix mayonnaise and mustard. Remove 2 tablespoons to another bowl for dressing; whisk in remaining oil, vinegar, salt and pepper.
**4.** Place salad greens in a large bowl. Drizzle with dressing; toss to coat. Serve with chicken and remaining mayonnaise mixture.

## Orange Ginger Chicken

This twist on a popular Chinese takeout dish is one of my husband's favorites. We spoon the poultry and citrus sauce over cooked white rice.

**—TONI SCHILZ**
SAN FRANCISCO, CALIFORNIA

**PREP:** 15 MIN. **COOK:** 20 MIN.
**MAKES:** 6 SERVINGS

- **⅓ cup all-purpose flour**
- **6 boneless skinless chicken thighs (about 1½ pounds), cubed**
- **¼ teaspoon salt**
- **¼ teaspoon pepper**
- **2 tablespoons canola oil**
- **½ cup orange juice**
- **½ cup orange marmalade**
- **2 tablespoons reduced-sodium soy sauce**
- **2 tablespoons honey**
- **½ to 1 teaspoon ground ginger**
- **Optional garnishes: thinly sliced green onion and sesame seeds**

**1.** Place flour in a large resealable plastic bag. Season chicken with salt and pepper. Add to bag, a few pieces at a time, and shake to coat. In a large skillet, cook chicken in oil in batches over medium heat until chicken is no longer pink. Remove and keep warm.
**2.** In the same skillet, combine the remaining ingredients. Bring to a boil, stirring to loosen browned bits from pan; cook and stir until thickened. Return chicken to the pan; heat through. Sprinkle with green onion and sesame seeds if desired.

Santa Fe Strip Steaks

We love Southwestern recipes like Santa Fe Strip Steaks. Slice up any leftover meat and use it for fajitas the next day.
**—JOAN HALLFORD**
NORTH RICHLAND HILLS, TEXAS

FAST FIX
## Santa Fe Strip Steaks

**PREP/TOTAL TIME:** 25 MIN.
**MAKES:** 4 SERVINGS

- **½ cup chopped onion**
- **1 tablespoon olive oil**
- **2 cans (4 ounces each) chopped green chilies**
- **½ cup fresh cilantro leaves**
- **1 jalapeno pepper, seeded**
- **2 teaspoons red currant jelly**
- **1 teaspoon chicken bouillon granules**
- **1 teaspoon Worcestershire sauce**
- **1 garlic clove, peeled**
- **½ teaspoon seasoned salt**
- **¼ teaspoon dried oregano**
- **4 boneless beef top loin steaks (1 inch thick and 8 ounces each)**
- **Salt and pepper to taste**
- **½ cup shredded Monterey Jack cheese, optional**

**1.** In a small saucepan, cook and stir onion in oil over medium-high heat until tender. Transfer to a blender. Add the green chilies, cilantro, jalapeno, jelly, bouillon, Worcestershire sauce, garlic, seasoned salt and oregano; cover and process until smooth.
**2.** Return mixture to the same pan; cook over medium heat until heated through, stirring occasionally. Set aside and keep warm.
**3.** Sprinkle steaks with salt and pepper to taste. Broil 4-6 in. from heat for 5-8 minutes on each side or until meat reaches desired doneness (for medium-rare, a thermometer should read 145°; medium, 160°; well-done, 170°). Sprinkle steaks with cheese if desired; serve with green chili sauce.

**Editor's Note:** *Steaks may also be grilled, covered, over medium heat. Top loin steak may be labeled as strip steak, Kansas City steak, New York strip steak, ambassador steak or boneless club steak in your region. When cutting hot peppers, disposable gloves are recommended. Avoid touching your face.*

**top tip** Known for its tart flavor and lovely deep color, red currant jelly is a fruit preserve that works well in savory and sweet dishes. Look for it in the jam and jelly section of the grocery store. If you don't have any on hand, try raspberry jelly instead.

## Gyro Meat Loaf with Tzatziki Sauce

**PREP:** 20 MIN.
**BAKE:** 55 MIN. + STANDING
**MAKES:** 8 SERVINGS

- **1 package (10 ounces) frozen chopped spinach, thawed and squeezed dry**
- **1 cup dry bread crumbs**
- **1 small onion, finely chopped**
- **2 eggs, lightly beaten**
- **¼ cup grated Romano cheese**
- **2 teaspoons dried oregano**
- **1½ teaspoons garlic powder**
- **½ teaspoon salt**
- **2 pounds ground lamb or ground beef**
- **1 cup refrigerated tzatziki sauce**

**1.** In a large bowl, combine the first eight ingredients. Crumble lamb over mixture and mix well. Shape into a loaf and place in a greased 11-in. x 7-in. baking dish.
**2.** Bake, uncovered, at 350° for 55-60 minutes or until no longer pink and a thermometer reads 160°. Let stand for 15 minutes before slicing. Serve with tzatziki sauce.

A spin on classic meat loaf, Gyro Meat Loaf with Tzatziki Sauce allows me to sneak some nutritious spinach into the diet of my meat-and-potatoes family.
—**MANDY RIVERS** LEXINGTON, SOUTH CAROLINA

## Cheese Enchiladas with Green Sauce

To go a bit hotter than a jalapeno, substitute 2 diced fresh serrano peppers for some of the green chilies.
—**MICKEY TURNER**
GRANTS PASS, OREGON

**PREP:** 50 MIN. **BAKE:** 25 MIN.
**MAKES:** 6 SERVINGS

- **1 package (6 ounces) fresh baby spinach**
- **2 tablespoons butter**
- **2 tablespoons all-purpose flour**
- **1 cup half-and-half cream**
- **1 cup 2% milk**
- **1 can (4 ounces) chopped green chilies, drained**
- **3 green onions, chopped**
- **⅓ cup minced fresh cilantro**
- **1 large garlic clove, minced**
- **1¾ teaspoons ground cumin**
- **1½ teaspoons ground coriander**
- **¼ teaspoon crushed red pepper flakes**
- **½ cup reduced-fat sour cream**

**ENCHILADAS**

- **2½ cups (10 ounces) shredded cheddar cheese**
- **1½ cups (6 ounces) shredded Monterey Jack cheese**
- **½ cup finely chopped onion**
- **1 tablespoon minced fresh cilantro**
- **12 corn tortillas (6 inches), warmed**

**1.** In a large skillet, saute spinach until wilted. Drain and remove. In the same pan, melt butter. Stir in flour until smooth; gradually add cream and milk. Bring to a boil; cook and stir for 2 minutes or until slightly thickened.
**2.** Stir in the chilies, green onions, cilantro, garlic, spices and spinach. Remove from the heat; cool slightly. Transfer to a food processor; cover and process until pureed. Stir in sour cream; set aside.
**3.** In a large bowl, combine cheeses; set aside 1 cup for topping. Add onion and cilantro to remaining cheese mixture; toss to combine. Place about ¼ cup cheese-onion mixture down the center of each tortilla. Roll up and place seam side down in a greased 13-in. x 9-in. baking dish.
**4.** Pour sauce over top. Sprinkle with reserved cheese mixture. Bake, uncovered, at 375° for 25-30 minutes or until heated through.

Gyro Meat Loaf with Tzatziki Sauce

Cheese Enchiladas with Green Sauce

## Chicken Paillard with Cherry Sauce & Parsley Rice

For a simple dinner in one, turn to Chicken Paillard with Cherry Sauce & Parsley Rice. It cooks up so quickly, we can enjoy it even on busy weeknights.
—**LISA SPEER** PALM BEACH, FLORIDA

**PREP:** 20 MIN. **COOK:** 20 MIN.
**MAKES:** 4 SERVINGS

- **3¼ cups chicken stock, divided**
- **1½ cups uncooked basmati rice**
- **4 boneless skinless chicken breast halves (4 ounces each)**
- **½ teaspoon sea salt**
- **¼ teaspoon pepper**
- **1½ teaspoons olive oil**
- **½ cup finely chopped sweet onion (about 1 small)**
- **3 tablespoons butter, divided**
- **1 garlic clove, minced**
- **¾ cup dried tart cherries**
- **⅓ cup balsamic vinegar**
- **3 tablespoons tawny port wine**
- **¼ teaspoon Dijon mustard**
- **⅓ cup minced fresh parsley**

**1.** In a large saucepan, bring 2¼ cups stock and rice to a boil. Reduce heat; cover and simmer for 15-20 minutes or until liquid is absorbed and rice is tender.

**2.** Meanwhile, pound chicken with a meat mallet to ¼-in. thickness; sprinkle with salt and pepper. In a large skillet, cook chicken in oil over medium heat for 4-5 minutes on each side or until no longer pink. Remove and keep warm.

**3.** In the same skillet, cook and stir onion in 1 tablespoon butter over medium-high heat for 1-2 minutes or until tender. Add garlic; cook 1 minute longer. Add the cherries, vinegar, wine and remaining stock, stirring to loosen browned bits from pan. Bring to a boil; cook until liquid is reduced by half and cherries are plump, about 6 minutes. Stir in mustard.

**4.** Fluff rice; stir in parsley and remaining butter; serve with chicken and sauce.

Chicken Paillard with Cherry Sauce & Parsley Rice

## FAST FIX Smoked Salmon Quesadillas with Creamy Chipotle Sauce

These extra-special quesadillas take just minutes to make, but you'll want to savor them for as long as possible. I like to sprinkle the cheesy wedges with chopped fresh cilantro.
—**DANIEL SHEMTOB**
IRVINE, CALIFORNIA

**PREP/TOTAL TIME:** 25 MIN.
**MAKES:** 3 SERVINGS (⅔ CUP SAUCE)

- **½ cup creme fraiche or sour cream**
- **2 tablespoons minced chipotle peppers in adobo sauce**
- **2 tablespoons lime juice**
- **⅛ teaspoon salt**
- **⅛ teaspoon pepper**

**QUESADILLAS**

- **¼ cup cream cheese, softened**
- **2 ounces fresh goat cheese**
- **3 flour tortillas (8 inches)**
- **3 ounces smoked salmon or lox, chopped**
- **¼ cup finely chopped shallots**
- **¼ cup finely chopped roasted sweet red pepper**
- **Coarsely chopped fresh cilantro**

**1.** In a bowl, mix the first five ingredients. In another bowl, mix cream cheese and goat cheese until blended; spread over tortillas. Top half side of each with the salmon, shallots and red pepper; fold over.

**2.** Place quesadillas on a greased griddle. Cook over medium heat for 1-2 minutes on each side or until lightly browned and cheeses are melted. Serve with sauce; top with cilantro.

## Basil Polenta with Ratatouille

For our wedding reception, we wanted to provide a vegan menu for guests. They raved about this polenta topped with its colorful ratatouille.

**—KIMBERLY HAMMOND**
KINGWOOD, TEXAS

**PREP:** 25 MIN. + CHILLING
**COOK:** 40 MIN. **MAKES:** 4 SERVINGS

- **4 cups water**
- **1 teaspoon salt, divided**
- **1 cup cornmeal**
- **½ cup minced fresh basil**
- **1 medium eggplant, peeled and cut into ½-inch cubes**
- **1 medium onion, halved and sliced**
- **1 medium green pepper, julienned**
- **5 tablespoons olive oil, divided**
- **4 garlic cloves, minced**
- **1 can (14½ ounces) diced tomatoes, drained**
- **½ cup pitted Greek olives, sliced**
- **1 teaspoon dried oregano**
- **¼ teaspoon pepper**
- **Fresh basil leaves**

**1.** In a large heavy saucepan, bring water and 1/2 teaspoon salt to a boil. Reduce heat to a gentle boil; slowly whisk in cornmeal. Cook and stir with a wooden spoon for 15-20 minutes or until polenta is thickened and pulls away cleanly from the sides of the pan. Stir in basil.
**2.** Spread into an 8-in. square baking dish coated with cooking spray. Refrigerate for 30 minutes.
**3.** Meanwhile, in a skillet, saute the eggplant, onion and green pepper in 2 tablespoons oil until crisp-tender. Add garlic; cook 1 minute longer. Stir in the tomatoes, olives, oregano, pepper and remaining salt. Cook and stir over medium heat for 10-12 minutes or until vegetables are tender.
**4.** Cut polenta into four squares. In another large skillet, cook polenta in remaining oil in batches for 7-8 minutes on each side or until golden brown. Serve with ratatouille; garnish with basil.

## Chicken & Andouille Gumbo

Gumbo is just as hearty when you use andouille sausage. Enjoy this with corn bread or crusty French bread.

**—BILLY HENSLEY**
MOUNT CARMEL, TENNESSEE

**PREP:** 40 MIN. **COOK:** 2 HOURS
**MAKES:** 9 SERVINGS (3¼ QUARTS)

- **2 tablespoons Cajun seasoning, divided**
- **1 teaspoon salt, divided**
- **½ teaspoon pepper, divided**
- **3 pounds bone-in chicken thighs, skin removed**
- **½ cup plus 2 tablespoons canola oil, divided**
- **½ cup all-purpose flour**
- **1 large onion, finely chopped**
- **¾ cup finely chopped green pepper**
- **¾ cup finely chopped sweet red pepper**
- **2 celery ribs, finely chopped**
- **4 garlic cloves, minced**
- **4 cups water**
- **2 cups chicken stock**
- **1½ pounds fully cooked andouille sausage links, sliced**
- **2 tablespoons Worcestershire sauce**
- **2 bay leaves**
- **Hot cooked rice**
- **3 green onions, chopped**

**1.** In a small bowl, mix 1 tablespoon Cajun seasoning, 1/2 teaspoon salt and 1/4 teaspoon pepper; rub over chicken. In a Dutch oven, brown chicken in 2 tablespoons oil in batches; remove chicken from pan.
**2.** Add remaining oil to the same pan; stir in flour until blended. Cook and stir over medium-low heat for 30 minutes or until browned (do not burn). Add onion, peppers and celery; cook and stir for 2-3 minutes or until vegetables are tender. Add garlic; cook 1 minute longer.
**3.** Gradually add water and stock. Stir in the sausage, Worcestershire sauce, bay leaves, chicken and the remaining Cajun seasoning, salt and pepper. Bring to a boil. Reduce heat; cover and simmer for 1 hour or until chicken is very tender.

Basil Polenta with Ratatouille

Chicken & Andouille Gumbo

**4.** Remove chicken from pan; cool slightly. Skim fat from soup and discard bay leaves. Shred chicken and return to soup; heat through. Discard bones. Serve gumbo over rice; top with green onions.

# HAVING PIE FOR DINNER

After a busy-as-can-be day, is your hungry family counting down the minutes to dinnertime? Then treat them to pie—a meat pie, that is! It's sure to satisfy even the heartiest appetites.

Stuffing Crust Turkey Potpie

*MAKE AHEAD*

## Hometown Pasty Pies

I prepare these in advance and freeze them for a quick supper later.

**—JEN HATLEN**
EDGERTON, WISCONSIN

**PREP:** 70 MIN. + CHILLING
**BAKE:** 45 MIN. + STANDING
**MAKES:** 2 PIES (8 SERVINGS EACH)

- **5 cups all-purpose flour**
- **1 tablespoon sugar**
- **1½ teaspoons salt**
- **2 cups butter-flavored shortening**
- **7 tablespoons cold water**
- **1 egg**
- **1 tablespoon white vinegar**

**FILLING**

- **2 cups cubed peeled potatoes**
- **2 cups finely chopped fresh carrots**
- **1 pound ground beef**
- **1 pound bulk pork sausage**
- **1 cup sliced fresh mushrooms**
- **1 medium onion, chopped**
- **1 can (10¾ ounces) condensed cream of mushroom soup, undiluted**
- **1 can (10¾ ounces) condensed cream of chicken soup, undiluted**
- **1 cup frozen peas**
- **1 tablespoon sherry or chicken broth**
- **½ teaspoon salt**
- **½ teaspoon seasoned salt**
- **¼ teaspoon pepper**
- **½ cup shredded Colby cheese**
- **½ cup sour cream**

**1.** In a bowl, combine the flour, sugar and salt; cut in shortening until crumbly. Whisk water, egg and vinegar; gradually add to flour mixture, tossing with a fork until dough forms a ball. Divide dough in quarters so that two of the portions are slightly larger than the other two; wrap each in plastic wrap. Refrigerate for 1 hour or until easy to handle.

**2.** Meanwhile, place potatoes in a large saucepan and cover with water. Bring to a boil. Reduce heat; cover and cook for 5 minutes. Add carrots; cook 6-9 minutes longer or until vegetables are tender. Drain and set aside.

**3.** In a Dutch oven, cook beef and sausage over medium heat until meat is no longer pink. Remove from pan with a slotted spoon; drain, reserving 1 tablespoon drippings. Saute mushrooms and onion in drippings until tender. Add the soups, peas, sherry, salt, seasoned salt, pepper, beef mixture and potato mixture; heat through.

**4.** Roll out one of the larger portions of dough to fit a 9-in. pie plate. Transfer pastry to pie plate. Trim pastry even with edge. Fill with half of the meat mixture. Repeat with remaining larger portion of dough and filling.

**5.** Roll out smaller portions of dough to fit tops of pies. Place over filling. Trim, seal and flute edges. Cut slits in pastry.

**6.** Bake at 375° for 45-50 minutes or until crust is golden brown. Cover edges with foil during the last 15 minutes to prevent overbrowning if necessary. Sprinkle tops with cheese; let stand for 10 minutes. Serve with sour cream.

## Stuffing Crust Turkey Potpie

Prebaking the crust helps to give this satisfying main dish a nice crunch.

**—TAMARA FURDA**
NAPERVILLE, ILLINOIS

**PREP:** 35 MIN. **BAKE:** 20 MIN.
**MAKES:** 6 SERVINGS

- **2 cups cooked cornbread stuffing**
- **3 to 4 tablespoons chicken broth**
- **¼ cup cream cheese, softened**
- **½ cup turkey gravy**
- **2 cups cubed cooked turkey**
- **1 cup frozen broccoli florets, thawed**
- **½ cup shredded Swiss cheese**
- **¼ teaspoon salt**
- **¼ teaspoon pepper**
- **2 cups mashed potatoes**
- **¼ cup half-and-half cream**
- **2 tablespoons butter, melted**
- **½ cup French-fried onions, optional**

**1.** In a small bowl, combine stuffing and enough broth to reach desired moistness; press onto the bottom and up the sides of a greased 9-in. deep-dish pie plate. Bake at 350° for 10-15 minutes or until lightly browned.
**2.** In a large bowl, beat cream cheese and gravy until smooth. Stir in the turkey, broccoli, Swiss cheese, salt and pepper. Spoon over crust.
**3.** In a small bowl, combine potatoes and cream; spread over turkey mixture. Drizzle with butter; sprinkle with onions if desired. Bake 20-25 minutes longer or until heated through and lightly browned.

## MAKE AHEAD Two-Potato Shepherd's Pie

**PREP:** 35 MIN. **BAKE:** 30 MIN.
**MAKES:** 2 CASSEROLES (4 SERVINGS EACH)

- **5 large potatoes and/or sweet potatoes, peeled and cut into chunks**
- **1 pound ground beef**
- **½ pound bulk pork sausage**
- **½ pound medium fresh mushrooms, quartered**
- **2 large carrots, chopped**
- **2 celery ribs, chopped**
- **1 medium onion, chopped**
- **2 garlic cloves, minced**
- **½ cup orange juice**
- **2 teaspoons grated orange peel**
- **1 teaspoon ground nutmeg**
- **¼ teaspoon Worcestershire sauce**
- **½ teaspoon salt, divided**
- **½ teaspoon pepper, divided**
- **¼ cup Dijon mustard**
- **2 teaspoons brown sugar**
- **2 teaspoons rice vinegar**

**1.** Place potatoes in a large saucepan and cover with water. Bring to a boil. Reduce heat; cover and cook for 15-20 minutes or until tender.
**2.** Meanwhile, in a large skillet, cook the beef, sausage, mushrooms, carrots, celery, onion and garlic over medium heat until meat is no longer pink and the vegetables are tender; drain.
**3.** Stir in the orange juice, orange peel, nutmeg, Worcestershire sauce and 1/4 teaspoon each salt and pepper. Bring to a boil; cook until liquid is evaporated. Transfer to two greased 8-in. square baking dishes.
**4.** Drain potatoes and place in a large bowl. Add the mustard, brown sugar, vinegar and remaining salt and pepper; mash until smooth. Spread over meat mixture.
**5.** Bake one casserole, uncovered, at 350° for 30-35 minutes or until heated through. Cover and freeze the remaining casserole for up to 3 months.
**6. TO USE FROZEN CASSEROLE:** Thaw in the refrigerator overnight. Remove from the refrigerator 30 minutes before baking. Cover and bake at 350° for 30 minutes. Uncover and bake 20-25 minutes longer or until heated through.

## Makeover Chicken Potpies

This comforting, lighter potpie uses feel-good ingredients such as peas, carrots and fat-free milk. Your family will want to dive right in on days when it's icy cold outside.
**—JOHN SLIVON** MILTON, FLORIDA

**PREP:** 30 MIN. + CHILLING
**BAKE:** 20 MIN. **MAKES:** 4 SERVINGS

- **1 cup plus 2 tablespoons all-purpose flour, divided**
- **¼ teaspoon baking powder**
- **¼ teaspoon salt**
- **3 tablespoons cold butter, divided**
- **2 tablespoons buttermilk**
- **1 tablespoon canola oil**
- **1 to 2 tablespoons cold water**
- **4 medium carrots, sliced**
- **3 celery ribs, sliced**
- **1 large onion, chopped**
- **2½ cups reduced-sodium chicken broth**
- **⅔ cup fat-free milk**
- **2 cups cubed cooked chicken breast**
- **1 cup frozen peas**
- **⅛ teaspoon pepper**
- **1 egg white, lightly beaten**

**1.** In a small bowl, combine 3/4 cup flour, baking powder and salt. Cut in 2 tablespoons butter until crumbly. Add buttermilk and oil; toss with a fork. Gradually add water, tossing with a fork until dough forms a ball. Cover and refrigerate for 1 hour.
**2.** For filling, in a large skillet, melt remaining butter. Add the carrots, celery and onion; saute until crisp-tender. In a small bowl, combine remaining flour with the broth and milk until smooth. Gradually stir into vegetable mixture. Bring to a boil; cook and stir for 2 minutes or until thickened. Stir in the chicken, peas and pepper. Transfer to four 16-oz. ramekins; set aside.
**3.** Divide dough into four portions. On a lightly floured surface, roll out dough to fit ramekins. Place dough over chicken mixture; trim and seal edges. Cut out a decorative center or cut slits in pastry. Brush with egg white.
**4.** Place ramekins on a baking sheet. Bake at 425° for 20-25 minutes or until crusts are golden brown.

The recipe for Two-Potato Shepherd's Pie allows you to serve one pie right away and freeze a second for a future meal. Sweet potatoes change up the expected topping in this comforting specialty.
**—MARCY-BROOKS SMITH**
FORT COLLINS, COLORADO

## Shrimp Corn Cakes with Soy Mayo

Looking for a change-of-pace dinner tonight? Give these corn cakes a try! The dipping sauce offers a touch of spice.
—**KATTY CHIONG** HOFFMAN ESTATES, ILLINOIS

**PREP:** 30 MIN. **COOK:** 5 MIN./BATCH
**MAKES:** 2 DOZEN (1 CUP SAUCE)

- **½ cup mayonnaise**
- **1 tablespoon reduced-sodium soy sauce**
- **1 tablespoon ketchup**
- **2 teaspoons Dijon mustard**
- **½ teaspoon garlic powder**
- **½ teaspoon hot pepper sauce, optional**
- **⅛ teaspoon pepper**

**SHRIMP CORN CAKES**

- **½ cup chopped onion (about 1 small)**
- **1 tablespoon oil plus additional for frying, divided**
- **2 garlic cloves, minced**
- **½ pound uncooked peeled and deveined shrimp, finely chopped**
- **¾ cup all-purpose flour**
- **¼ cup cornmeal**
- **1 tablespoon cornstarch**
- **1 teaspoon baking powder**
- **¼ teaspoon salt**
- **¼ teaspoon pepper**
- **1 cup cream-style corn**
- **1 cup whole kernel corn**
- **1 egg, lightly beaten**
- **Oil for frying**

Shrimp Corn Cakes with Soy Mayo

Delish Pesto Pasta with Chicken Marsala

**1.** In a small bowl, combine the first seven ingredients. Cover and chill until serving.
**2.** In a large skillet, cook and stir onion in 1 tablespoon oil over medium-high heat until tender. Add garlic; cook 1 minute longer. Add shrimp; cook and stir until shrimp turn pink. Remove from the heat.
**3.** In a large bowl, mix the flour, cornmeal, cornstarch, baking powder, salt and pepper. In a small bowl, mix the corn, egg and shrimp mixture; stir into dry ingredients just until moistened.
**4.** In an electric skillet, heat ¼ in. of oil to 375°. In batches, drop corn mixture by rounded tablespoonfuls into oil; fry 1½ minutes on each side or until golden brown. Drain on paper towels. Serve with sauce.

## FAST FIX Delish Pesto Pasta with Chicken Marsala

Here's my easy, go-to chicken and pasta recipe. It's ready in about 30 minutes, making it ideal for hectic weeknights.
—**LORRAINE FINA STEVENSKI** LAND O LAKES, FLORIDA

**PREP/TOTAL TIME:** 30 MIN. **MAKES:** 6 SERVINGS

- **4 cups uncooked penne pasta**
- **2 tablespoons olive oil, divided**
- **2 pounds boneless skinless chicken breasts, cut into thin strips, divided**
- **3 garlic cloves, minced**
- **2 teaspoons grated lemon peel**
- **1 cup Marsala wine**
- **2 tablespoons lemon juice**
- **1 cup grated Parmesan cheese**
- **1 cup 2% milk**
- **1 envelope creamy pesto sauce mix**
- **1 tablespoon minced fresh basil**
- **1 tablespoon minced fresh parsley**

**1.** Cook pasta according to package directions. In a Dutch oven, heat 1 tablespoon oil over medium-high heat. Add half of the chicken; cook and stir until no longer pink; remove from the pan. Repeat with remaining oil and chicken; remove from the pan.
**2.** Add garlic and lemon peel to the same pan; cook and stir for 30 seconds. Add wine and lemon juice, stirring to loosen browned bits from the pan. Bring to a boil; cook until liquid is reduced by half. Stir in the cheese, milk and sauce mix. Add chicken; cook until sauce is slightly thickened.
**3.** Drain pasta; add to chicken mixture and toss to combine. Sprinkle with herbs.

## Four-Cheese Turkey Pasta Bake

Leftover turkey combines with penne and cheeses to make a classic comfort food. This delicious pasta bake works with chicken, shrimp or beef, too.
**—MARY COKENOUR** MONTICELLO, UTAH

**PREP:** 30 MIN. **BAKE:** 35 MIN. **MAKES:** 6 SERVINGS

- **8 ounces uncooked penne**
- **1 small onion, chopped**
- **2 tablespoons butter**
- **4 garlic cloves, minced**
- **1 can (10¾ ounces) condensed cream of mushroom soup, undiluted**
- **1 package (8 ounces) cream cheese, softened and cubed**
- **1 cup heavy whipping cream**
- **1 cup 2% milk**
- **1 jar (4½ ounces) sliced mushrooms, drained**
- **½ cup shredded part-skim mozzarella cheese**
- **½ cup shredded Parmesan cheese**
- **½ cup shredded Swiss cheese**
- **¼ teaspoon ground nutmeg**
- **¼ teaspoon coarsely ground pepper**
- **2 cups cubed cooked turkey breast**

**TOPPING**

- **½ cup seasoned bread crumbs**
- **3 tablespoons butter, melted**

**1.** Cook penne according to package directions. Drain; set aside.
**2.** Meanwhile, in a large skillet, saute the onion in butter until tender. Add garlic; cook 2 minutes longer. Add the soup, cream cheese, cream and milk; cook and stir just until cream cheese is melted. Stir in the mushrooms, cheeses and spices; cook just until cheeses are melted. Add turkey and penne; heat through.
**3.** Transfer to a greased 2½ qt. baking dish. In a small bowl, combine topping ingredients; sprinkle over pasta mixture. Cover and bake at 350° for 25 minutes. Uncover; bake 10-15 minutes longer or until bubbly and golden brown.

Refried Bean-Taco Pizza

## Refried Bean-Taco Pizza

When I'm in a rush, I take advantage of convenient prepared pizza crust to create this Mexican-style pizza. If you like it spicy, simply add a little chopped jalapeno pepper to the skillet when cooking the ground beef.
**—MARY DETWEILER** MIDDLEFIELD, OHIO

**PREP:** 30 MIN. **BAKE:** 20 MIN. **MAKES:** 8 SERVINGS

- **1¼ pounds ground beef**
- **1 small onion, chopped**
- **½ cup water**
- **1 envelope taco seasoning**
- **1 prebaked 12-inch pizza crust**
- **1 can (16 ounces) refried beans**
- **2 taco shells, coarsely crushed**
- **1 cup (4 ounces) shredded cheddar cheese**
- **1 cup (4 ounces) shredded part-skim mozzarella cheese**
- **2 cups torn iceberg lettuce**
- **2 medium tomatoes, chopped**
- **1 tablespoon sliced ripe olives**

**1.** In a large skillet, cook beef and onion over medium heat until no longer pink; drain. Stir in water and taco seasoning. Bring to a boil. Reduce heat; simmer, uncovered, for 5 minutes.
**2.** Meanwhile, place crust on an ungreased baking sheet. Spread with refried beans. Top with the beef mixture, taco shells and cheeses. Bake at 450° for 10-15 minutes or until cheese is melted. Top with lettuce, tomatoes and olives.

## Eggplant & Zucchini Rollatini

Someone at the table is bound to praise your rollatini dish, then ask what the heck it is. Your simple answer? Thin slices of eggplant that are lightly breaded and fried, covered with cheeses, rolled up, topped with tangy tomato sauce and baked.

**—ANDREA RIVERA**
WESTBURY, NEW YORK

**PREP:** 1 HOUR + STANDING
**BAKE:** 30 MIN. **MAKES:** 8 SERVINGS

- **1 large eggplant**
- **½ teaspoon salt**

**SAUCE**

- **⅓ cup chopped onion**
- **3 garlic cloves, minced**
- **1 tablespoon olive oil**
- **2 cans (28 ounces each) crushed tomatoes**
- **¼ cup dry red wine or vegetable broth**
- **1 tablespoon sugar**
- **2 teaspoons each dried oregano and dried basil**
- **1 teaspoon salt**
- **¼ teaspoon pepper**

**ROLLATINI**

- **4 cups (16 ounces) shredded part-skim mozzarella cheese**
- **1 package (8 ounces) cream cheese, softened and cubed**
- **1 large zucchini, thinly sliced**
- **2 tablespoons plus ½ cup olive oil, divided**
- **2 eggs, lightly beaten**
- **1 cup dry bread crumbs**
- **½ cup grated Parmesan cheese**

**1.** Peel and slice eggplant lengthwise into sixteen ⅛-in. thick slices. Place in a colander over a plate; sprinkle with salt and toss. Let stand for 30 minutes. Rinse and drain.

**2.** In a large saucepan, saute onion and garlic in oil until tender. Add the remaining sauce ingredients. Bring to a boil. Reduce heat; simmer, uncovered, for 20-25 minutes to allow flavors to blend, stirring occasionally.

**3.** In a large bowl, combine mozzarella and cream cheese; mix well. In a large skillet, saute zucchini in 2 tablespoons oil until tender; remove and set aside.

**4.** Place eggs and bread crumbs in separate shallow bowls. Dip eggplant in eggs, then bread crumbs. Fry eggplant in remaining oil in batches for 2-3 minutes on each side or until golden brown. Drain on paper towels.

**5.** Spoon 1 cup sauce into an ungreased 13-in. x 9-in. baking dish. Layer eggplant slices with zucchini; top each with 3 tablespoons cheese mixture. Roll up and place seam side down in baking dish. Top with remaining sauce. Cover and bake at 350° for 30-35 minutes or until bubbly. Sprinkle with Parmesan cheese.

Eggplant & Zucchini Rollatini

## Easy Texas BBQ Brisket

Mom came to visit and said that my brisket was even better than the version we used to eat back home. I use the leftovers for sandwiches.

**—AUDRA RORICK**
BLANCA, COLORADO

**PREP:** 15 MIN. + MARINATING
**BAKE:** 4 HOURS **MAKES:** 10 SERVINGS

- **2 tablespoons packed brown sugar**
- **1 tablespoon salt**
- **1 tablespoon onion powder**
- **1 tablespoon garlic powder**
- **1 tablespoon ground mustard**
- **1 tablespoon smoked paprika**
- **1 tablespoon pepper**
- **2 fresh beef briskets (3½ pounds each)**
- **1 bottle (10 ounces) Heinz 57 steak sauce**
- **½ cup liquid smoke**
- **¼ cup Worcestershire sauce**

**1.** In a small bowl, combine the first seven ingredients. With a fork or sharp knife, prick holes in briskets. Rub meat with seasoning mixture. Cover and refrigerate overnight.

**2.** Place briskets, fat sides up, in a roasting pan. In a small bowl, combine the steak sauce, liquid smoke and Worcestershire sauce; pour over meat.

**3.** Cover tightly with foil; bake at 325° for 4 to 5 hours or until tender. Let stand in juices for 15 minutes. To serve, thinly slice across the grain. Skim fat from pan juices; spoon over meat.

**Editor's Note:** *This is a fresh beef brisket, not corned beef.*

## MAKE AHEAD Molasses-Glazed Baby Back Ribs

**PREP:** 20 MIN. + MARINATING
**GRILL:** 70 MIN. **MAKES:** 4 SERVINGS

- **4½ pounds pork baby back ribs**
- **2 liters cola**
- **½ teaspoon salt**
- **½ teaspoon pepper**
- **¼ teaspoon garlic salt**
- **¼ teaspoon dried oregano**
- **¼ teaspoon onion powder**
- **⅛ teaspoon cayenne pepper**

**BARBECUE SAUCE**

- **¼ cup ketchup**
- **¼ cup honey**
- **¼ cup molasses**
- **1 tablespoon prepared mustard**
- **½ teaspoon cayenne pepper**
- **½ teaspoon salt**

**1.** Place the ribs in large resealable plastic bags; add cola. Seal bags and turn to coat; refrigerate for 8 hours or overnight.
**2.** Drain and discard cola. Pat ribs dry with paper towels. Combine the seasonings; rub over ribs.
**3.** Prepare grill for indirect heat, using a drip pan. Place ribs over pan; grill, covered, over indirect medium heat for 1 hour, or until tender, turning occasionally.
**4.** In a small bowl, combine barbecue sauce ingredients. Brush over ribs; grill, covered, over medium heat 10-20 minutes longer or until browned, turning and basting occasionally.

My sweet-and-sour barbecue sauce is the secret to Molasses-Glazed Baby Back Ribs. Complete your finger-licking menu with buttery corn on the cob.
**—KIM BRADLEY** DUNEDIN, FLORIDA

## Mad About "Meat" Loaf

Meat loaf gets a vegetarian makeover, thanks to plenty of spinach, carrots, zucchini and whole grains. Grind the nuts in your food processor, but be sure to add a little flour so you don't end up with nut butter.
**—SUSAN PRESTON**
EAGLE CREEK, OREGON

**PREP:** 30 MIN. **BAKE:** 50 MIN.
**MAKES:** 6 SERVINGS

- **1 package (6 ounces) fresh baby spinach**
- **1 cup (4 ounces) shredded cheddar cheese, divided**
- **⅔ cup mashed cooked carrots**
- **1 slice whole wheat bread, torn into pieces**
- **2 eggs, lightly beaten**
- **½ cup grated zucchini**
- **½ cup tomato sauce, divided**
- **⅓ cup grated Parmesan cheese**
- **¼ cup finely chopped onion**
- **3 tablespoons ground flaxseed**
- **3 tablespoons ground walnuts**
- **1 tablespoon olive oil**
- **1 garlic clove, minced**
- **1 teaspoon Italian seasoning**
- **½ teaspoon dried sage leaves**
- **¼ teaspoon salt**
- **⅛ teaspoon pepper**

**1.** In a large saucepan, bring 1/2 in. of water to a boil. Add spinach; cover and boil for 3-4 minutes or until wilted. Drain and squeeze dry.
**2.** In a large bowl, combine 3/4 cup cheddar cheese, carrots, bread, eggs, zucchini, 1/4 cup tomato sauce, Parmesan cheese, onion, flaxseed, walnuts, oil, garlic, seasonings and spinach. Pat into a greased 8-in. x 4-in. loaf pan; top with remaining tomato sauce.
**3.** Bake, uncovered, at 325° for 45 minutes. Sprinkle with remaining cheddar cheese. Bake 4-7 minutes longer or until heated through and cheese is melted. Let stand for 5 minutes before slicing.

### Did you know?

Flaxseed is a good source of fiber, and it is packed with heart-healthy oils. Be sure to use the ground or milled variety to enjoy all of the wholesome benefits that flaxseed offers.

Molasses-Glazed Baby Back Ribs

Mad About "Meat" Loaf

SLOW COOKER
## Conga Lime Pork

**PREP:** 20 MIN. **COOK:** 4 HOURS
**MAKES:** 6 SERVINGS

- **1 teaspoon salt, divided**
- **½ teaspoon pepper, divided**
- **1 boneless pork shoulder butt roast (2 to 3 pounds)**
- **1 tablespoon canola oil**
- **1 large onion, chopped**
- **3 garlic cloves, peeled and thinly sliced**
- **½ cup water**
- **2 chipotle peppers in adobo sauce, seeded and chopped**
- **2 tablespoons molasses**
- **2 cups broccoli coleslaw mix**
- **1 medium mango, peeled and chopped**
- **2 tablespoons lime juice**
- **1½ teaspoons grated lime peel**
- **6 prepared corn muffins, halved**

**1.** Sprinkle 3/4 teaspoon salt and 1/4 teaspoon pepper over roast. In a large skillet, brown pork in oil on all sides. Transfer meat to a 3- or 4-qt. slow cooker.
**2.** In the same skillet, saute onion until tender. Add garlic; cook 1 minute longer. Add water, chipotle peppers and molasses, stirring to loosen browned bits from pan. Pour over pork. Cover and cook on high for 4-5 hours or until meat is tender.
**3.** Remove roast; cool slightly. Skim fat from cooking juices. Shred pork with two forks and return to slow cooker; heat through. In a large bowl, combine the coleslaw mix, mango, lime juice, lime peel and remaining salt and pepper.
**4.** Place muffin halves cut side down on an ungreased baking sheet. Broil 4 in. from the heat for 2-3 minutes or until lightly toasted. Serve pork with muffins; top with slaw.
**Editor's Note:** *Wear disposable gloves when cutting hot peppers; the oils can burn skin. Avoid touching your face.*

Conga Lime Pork is a dish that's sure to get extra attention. Nobody steps out of line when a roast slow-cooked in chipotle and molasses moves to the table.
**—JANICE ELDER** CHARLOTTE, NORTH CAROLINA

## Pistachio-Crusted Salmon with Lemon Cream Sauce

Popular pistachios add color and crunch when sprinkled on salmon. The cream sauce gives this dish a lemony smooth finish.
**—ANN BAKER** TEXARKANA, TEXAS

**PREP:** 20 MIN. **BAKE:** 15 MIN.
**MAKES:** 4 SERVINGS

- **4 salmon fillets (1 inch thick and 6 ounces each)**
- **1 teaspoon sea salt**
- **½ teaspoon coarsely ground pepper**
- **¼ cup mayonnaise**
- **½ cup finely chopped pistachios**

**SAUCE**

- **1 shallot, chopped**
- **1 tablespoon olive oil**
- **1 cup heavy whipping cream**
- **2 teaspoons grated lemon peel**
- **¼ teaspoon sea salt**
- **⅛ teaspoon cayenne pepper**

**1.** Place fillets on a greased baking sheet; sprinkle with salt and pepper. Spread with mayonnaise and sprinkle with pistachios.
**2.** Bake at 375° for 15-20 minutes or until fish flakes easily with a fork.
**3.** Meanwhile, in a small saucepan, cook and stir shallot in oil over medium-high heat until tender. Add cream, lemon peel, salt and cayenne; bring to a boil. Reduce heat; simmer, uncovered, for 5-7 minutes or until thickened, stirring occasionally. Serve with salmon.

**Pistachio-Crusted Salmon with Lemon Cream Sauce**

MAKE AHEAD

## Brown Bag Burritos

This recipe made it through the pickiest taste testers: my kids! They absolutely hate beans, but they simply love these plump burritos.

**—MINDY CULVER** POST FALLS, IDAHO

**PREP:** 35 MIN. + FREEZING
**COOK:** 5 MIN./BATCH
**MAKES:** 16 SERVINGS

- **2 pounds ground beef**
- **2 cans (16 ounces each) refried beans**
- **3 cups (12 ounces) shredded Mexican cheese blend or cheddar cheese**
- **1⅓ cups enchilada sauce**
- **½ cup water**
- **⅓ cup chopped onion**
- **2 tablespoons chili powder**
- **1 tablespoon garlic powder**
- **2 teaspoons dried oregano**
- **1 teaspoon salt**
- **16 flour tortillas (10 inches), warmed**
- **Optional toppings: shredded Mexican cheese blend, sour cream, shredded lettuce, chopped tomatoes and sliced ripe olives**

**1.** In a Dutch oven, cook beef over medium heat until no longer pink; drain. Return to pan; add the beans, cheese, enchilada sauce, water, onion and seasonings. Bring to a boil. Reduce heat; cover and simmer for 10 minutes.
**2.** Spoon ½ cup filling off center on each tortilla. Fold sides and end over filling and roll up. Wrap individually in paper towels, then foil. Transfer to a resealable plastic bag. May be frozen for up to 2 months.
**3. TO USE FROZEN BURRITOS:** Unwrap foil. Place paper towel-wrapped burritos on a microwave-safe plate. Microwave on high for 3-4 minutes or until heated through. Serve with toppings of your choice.
**Editor's Note:** *This recipe was tested in a 1,100-watt microwave.*

MAKE AHEAD

## Lone Star Chicken Enchiladas

Start with deli-roasted chicken, and this family-friendly casserole will be ready in no time. For a milder version, simply substitute Monterey Jack cheese for the pepper jack.

**—AVANELL HEWITT**
NORTH RICHLAND HILLS, TEXAS

**PREP:** 30 MIN. + FREEZING
**BAKE:** 35 MIN. **MAKES:** 6 SERVINGS

- **3 cups shredded cooked chicken breast**
- **1 can (10 ounces) diced tomatoes with mild green chilies, drained**
- **¾ cup salsa verde**
- **1 can (4 ounces) chopped green chilies**
- **1 can (2¼ ounces) sliced ripe olives, drained**
- **1 teaspoon ground cumin**
- **2½ cups heavy whipping cream**
- **¾ teaspoon salt**
- **12 corn tortillas (6 inches), warmed**
- **2 cups (8 ounces) shredded pepper jack cheese**

**1.** In a large bowl, combine the first six ingredients. In a shallow bowl, combine cream and salt.
**2.** Dip both sides of each tortilla in cream mixture; top with ¼ cup chicken mixture. Roll up and place seam side down in a greased 13-in. x 9-in. baking dish. Pour remaining cream mixture over top; sprinkle with cheese. Cover and freeze for up to 6 months.
**3. TO USE FROZEN CASSEROLE:** Thaw in the refrigerator overnight. Remove from the refrigerator 30 minutes before baking. Cover and bake at 350° for 35-40 minutes or until heated through.

Brown Bag Burritos

Lone Star Chicken Enchiladas

## Skinny Take on Southwestern

It's a snap to lighten up ethnic foods, and south-of-the-border favorites are no exception. Thanks to bold spices, herbs and seasoning blends, many such foods don't rely on butter and salt to punch up flavor. In addition, light products such as reduced-fat cheeses and sour cream make smart alternatives to their full-fat counterparts. Also keep in mind that yellow and white corn tortillas have less fat and fewer calories than flour tortillas and work well in just about any recipe. Best of all, your family probably won't even notice these savvy substitutions.

FAST FIX

## Greek Chicken Pasta

Artichoke hearts, feta cheese and sun-dried tomatoes lend Mediterranean flair to my Greek Chicken Pasta. I left out the olives, and my family still loved it!
—SUSAN STETZEL GAINESVILLE, NEW YORK

**PREP/TOTAL TIME:** 25 MIN.
**MAKES:** 5 SERVINGS

- **2 cups uncooked penne pasta**
- **¼ cup butter, cubed**
- **1 large onion, chopped**
- **¼ cup all-purpose flour**
- **1 can (14½ ounces) reduced-sodium chicken broth**
- **3 cups shredded rotisserie chicken**
- **1 jar (7½ ounces) marinated quartered artichoke hearts, drained**
- **1 cup (4 ounces) crumbled feta cheese**
- **½ cup chopped oil-packed sun-dried tomatoes**
- **⅓ cup sliced pitted Greek olives**
- **2 tablespoons minced fresh parsley**

**1.** Cook pasta according to package directions.
**2.** Meanwhile, in a large ovenproof skillet, melt butter over medium-high heat. Add onion; cook and stir until tender. Stir in flour until blended; gradually add broth. Bring to a boil; cook and stir for 2 minutes or until thickened. Stir in the chicken, artichoke hearts, cheese, tomatoes and olives.
**3.** Drain pasta; stir into the pan. Broil 3-4 in. from the heat for 5-7 minutes or until bubbly and golden brown. Sprinkle with parsley.

Greek Chicken Pasta

## Chicago Deep-Dish Pizza

I live near Chicago and have managed to sample more than my share of deep-dish pizzas. This recipe lets you re-create the very best of the Windy City—right in your own kitchen.
—LYNN HAMILTON
NAPERVILLE, ILLINOIS

**PREP:** 40 MIN. + RISING **BAKE:** 40 MIN.
**MAKES:** 12 SERVINGS

- **2 to 2½ cups all-purpose flour**
- **¼ cup cornmeal**
- **1 package (¼ ounce) quick-rise yeast**
- **1½ teaspoons sugar**
- **½ teaspoon salt**
- **1 cup water**
- **⅓ cup olive oil**

**TOPPINGS**

- **½ pound sliced fresh mushrooms**
- **4 teaspoons olive oil, divided**
- **1 can (28 ounces) diced tomatoes, well drained**
- **1 can (8 ounces) tomato sauce**
- **1 can (6 ounces) tomato paste**
- **2 to 3 garlic cloves, minced**
- **½ teaspoon salt**
- **¼ teaspoon dried basil**
- **¼ teaspoon dried oregano**
- **¼ teaspoon pepper**
- **3 cups (12 ounces) shredded part-skim mozzarella cheese, divided**
- **1 pound bulk Italian sausage, cooked and crumbled**
- **24 slices pepperoni, optional**
- **½ cup grated Parmesan cheese**
- **Thinly sliced fresh basil leaves, optional**

**1.** In a large bowl, combine 1½ cups flour, cornmeal, yeast, sugar and salt. In a small saucepan, heat water and oil to 120°-130°. Add to dry ingredients; beat just until moistened. Stir in enough remaining flour to form a soft dough.
**2.** Turn onto a floured surface; knead until smooth and elastic, about 6-8 minutes. Place in a greased bowl, turning once to grease the top. Cover and let rise in warm place until doubled, about 30 minutes.
**3.** In a large skillet, cook and stir mushrooms in 2 teaspoons oil over medium-high heat until tender. In a small bowl, mix the tomatoes, tomato sauce, tomato paste, garlic and seasonings.
**4.** Generously grease a 13-in. x 9-in. baking pan or dish with the remaining 2 teaspoons oil. Punch dough down. Roll out into a 15-in. x 11-in. rectangle. Transfer to prepared pan, pressing onto the bottom and halfway up the sides of pan. Sprinkle with 2 cups mozzarella cheese.
**5.** Spoon half of the sauce over the cheese (save remaining sauce for other use or use for dipping). Layer with the sausage, sauteed mushrooms and, if desired, pepperoni; top with the remaining mozzarella cheese and Parmesan cheese.
**6.** Cover and bake at 450° for 35 minutes. Uncover; bake about 5 minutes longer or until lightly browned. Sprinkle with basil if desired.

## Tuscan Artichoke & Spinach Strudel

I decided to put a savory spin on the traditional Austrian pastry with this layered specialty. Tuscan influences such as tomatoes, mushrooms and pesto make this a keeper in my home.

**—JEANNE HOLT**
MENDOTA HEIGHTS, MINNESOTA

**PREP:** 35 MIN. **BAKE:** 30 MIN.
**MAKES:** 12 SERVINGS

- **1¼ cups chopped baby portobello mushrooms**
- **⅓ cup oil-packed sun-dried tomatoes, chopped**
- **4 teaspoons oil from the sun-dried tomatoes, divided**
- **1 package (10 ounces) frozen chopped spinach, thawed and squeezed dry**
- **2 tablespoons prepared pesto**
- **⅛ teaspoon pepper**
- **⅛ teaspoon crushed red pepper flakes, optional**
- **1 cup coarsely chopped thawed frozen artichoke hearts**
- **1 cup (4 ounces) shredded part-skim mozzarella cheese**
- **½ cup shredded Parmesan cheese, divided**
- **1 tube (8 ounces) refrigerated crescent rolls**
- **1 egg**
- **3 tablespoons finely chopped walnuts**

**1.** In a nonstick skillet, saute mushrooms and tomatoes in 2 teaspoons oil from sun-dried tomatoes until mushrooms are tender. Cool to room temperature.
**2.** Meanwhile, in a large bowl, combine the spinach, pesto, pepper and, if desired, pepper flakes. Add the artichokes, mozzarella cheese, 5 tablespoons Parmesan cheese and mushroom mixture; mix well.
**3.** Unroll crescent dough onto a lightly greased baking sheet into one long rectangle; seal seams and perforations. Roll out into a 14-in. x 9-in. rectangle.
**4.** Spread filling in a 3-in.-wide strip down center of rectangle. On each long side, cut 1-in.-wide strips to within ½ in. of filling. Starting at one end, fold alternating strips at an angle across filling. Whisk egg and remaining oil; brush over dough. Sprinkle with walnuts.
**5.** Bake at 350° for 20 minutes. Sprinkle with remaining Parmesan cheese; bake 10 minutes longer or until golden brown. Cool for 5 minutes before cutting into 12 slices.

Tuscan Artichoke & Spinach Strudel

## Chili Mac & Cheese

This comforting Southwestern casserole is big on both simplicity and flavor. What a delicious combination for busy family cooks!

**—MARY AGUILAR** SHELBY, OHIO

**PREP:** 30 MIN. **BAKE:** 20 MIN.
**MAKES:** 8 SERVINGS

- **2 packages (7¼ ounces each) macaroni and cheese dinner mix**
- **2 pounds ground beef**
- **1 small onion, chopped**
- **1 can (14½ ounces) diced tomatoes, undrained**
- **1 can (10 ounces) diced tomatoes and green chilies, undrained**
- **1 can (8 ounces) tomato sauce**
- **2 tablespoons chili powder**
- **1 teaspoon garlic salt**
- **½ teaspoon ground cumin**
- **¼ teaspoon crushed red pepper flakes**
- **¼ teaspoon pepper**
- **2 cups (16 ounces) sour cream**
- **1½ cups (6 ounces) shredded Mexican cheese blend, divided**

**1.** Set aside cheese packets from dinner mixes. In a large saucepan, bring 2 quarts water to a boil. Add macaroni; cook for 8-10 minutes or until tender.
**2.** Meanwhile, in a Dutch oven, cook and stir beef and onion over medium heat for 8-10 minutes or until beef is no longer pink; drain. Stir in the tomatoes, tomatoes and green chilies, tomato sauce and seasonings. Drain macaroni; add to beef mixture. Stir in contents of cheese packets, sour cream and 1 cup cheese.
**3.** Transfer to a greased 13-in. x 9-in. baking dish; top with remaining cheese. Bake, uncovered, at 350° for 20-25 minutes or until bubbly.

## Shrimp Fettuccine with No-Cook Tomato Sauce

**PREP:** 25 MIN. + STANDING
**COOK:** 5 MIN. **MAKES:** 6 SERVINGS

- **5 medium tomatoes (about 1½ pounds), chopped**
- **4 green onions, chopped**
- **¼ cup snipped fresh basil**
- **2 garlic cloves, minced**
- **4 tablespoons olive oil, divided**
- **Salt and pepper to taste**
- **1 package (16 ounces) fettuccine**
- **1½ pounds uncooked medium shrimp, peeled and deveined**
- **Grated Parmesan cheese, optional**

**1.** In a large bowl, combine the tomatoes, green onions, basil, garlic and 1 tablespoon oil; toss lightly. Add salt and pepper to taste. Let stand for 15 minutes, stirring occasionally.
**2.** Meanwhile, cook fettuccine according to package directions. In a large skillet, heat remaining oil over medium-high heat. Add shrimp; cook and stir 2-4 minutes or until shrimp turn pink; add to sauce. Drain fettucine; transfer to a platter. Top with sauce; sprinkle with cheese if desired.

Dressing pasta doesn't get any easier than Shrimp Fettuccine with No-Cook Tomato Sauce. It features lots of fresh basil, and the light sauce is great with almost anything you use it with.
**—SALLY STIEFVATER** PELHAM, NEW YORK

## Kid-Tested Cheeseburger Pizza

If you have picky eaters at the table, you'll want to try this comforting dinner that combines two all-time favorites. My cheeseburger pizza is sure to get thumbs-up approval from big and little diners alike!
**—JENNIFER MILLER**
SMYRNA, TENNESSEE

**PREP:** 30 MIN. **BAKE:** 15 MIN.
**MAKES:** 6 PIECES

- **¾ pound ground beef**
- **1 medium onion, chopped**
- **2 teaspoons garlic powder**
- **2 teaspoons onion powder**
- **⅛ teaspoon crushed red pepper flakes**
- **1 tube (11 ounces) refrigerated thin pizza crust**
- **1 teaspoon Italian seasoning**
- **1 cup marinara sauce**
- **1¼ cups shredded Colby-Monterey Jack cheese**
- **½ cup shredded Parmesan cheese**
- **Sliced pepperoncini, optional**

**1.** In a large skillet, cook the first five ingredients over medium heat until meat is no longer pink; drain.
**2.** Unroll dough into a greased 15-in. x 10-in. x 1-in. baking pan. Bake at 425° for 7-10 minutes or until golden brown. Sprinkle crust with Italian seasoning; spread with marinara. Top with beef mixture; sprinkle with cheeses.
**3.** Bake 6-10 minutes longer or until edges are lightly browned and cheese is melted. Top with pepperoncini if desired.

Kid-Tested Cheeseburger Pizza

## Garden Vegetable Bake

With every spoonful of this vegetable bake, I drift back to a simpler time in my mother's garden. We eagerly filled baskets with ripe tomatoes, crisp pea pods, colorful carrots and green onions. This recipe takes advantage of all such produce, including fresh herbs, which Mom also grew.
**—PAULA MARCHESI**
LENHARTSVILLE, PENNSYLVANIA

**PREP:** 35 MIN. **BAKE:** 25 MIN.
**MAKES:** 6 SERVINGS

- **2 cups chopped carrots**
- **½ cup fresh or frozen lima beans**
- **½ cup cut fresh green beans**
- **2 cups chopped cauliflower**
- **2 cups chopped fresh broccoli**
- **½ cup fresh or frozen whole kernel corn**
- **½ cup fresh or frozen peas**
- **1 large sweet onion, chopped**
- **¼ cup butter, cubed**
- **3 tablespoons all-purpose flour**

- 1 cup half-and-half cream
- 1 cup 2% milk
- 1 package (8 ounces) spreadable garlic and herb cream cheese
- 1 cup (4 ounces) shredded sharp cheddar cheese
- ½ cup shredded part-skim mozzarella cheese
- ½ cup minced fresh parsley
- ¼ teaspoon each salt and pepper
- Dash each white pepper and ground nutmeg
- 1 cup panko (Japanese) bread crumbs
- ½ cup each shredded Parmesan and Romano cheeses

**1.** Place the carrots, lima beans and green beans in a steamer basket; place in a large saucepan over 1 in. of water. Bring to a boil; cover and steam for 4-5 minutes or until crisp-tender, adding the cauliflower, broccoli, corn and peas during the last 2 minutes. Transfer to a large bowl; stir in onion.
**2.** Meanwhile, in a large saucepan, melt butter. Stir in flour until smooth; gradually add the cream and milk. Bring to a boil; cook and stir for 1 minute or until thickened. Stir in the cream cheese, cheddar cheese, mozzarella cheese, parsley and seasonings; cook and stir until blended.
**3.** Pour sauce over vegetables; gently toss to coat. Transfer to a greased 13-in. x 9-in. baking dish. Combine the bread crumbs, Parmesan and Romano cheeses; sprinkle over vegetable mixture. Bake, uncovered, at 350° for 25-30 minutes or until bubbly.

## Skillet-Roasted Lemon Chicken with Potatoes

**PREP:** 20 MIN. **BAKE:** 25 MIN.
**MAKES:** 4 SERVINGS

- 1 tablespoon olive oil, divided
- 1 medium lemon, thinly sliced
- 4 garlic cloves, minced and divided
- ¼ teaspoon grated lemon peel
- ½ teaspoon salt, divided
- ¼ teaspoon pepper, divided
- 8 boneless skinless chicken thighs (4 ounces each)
- ¼ teaspoon dried rosemary, crushed
- 1 pound fingerling potatoes, halved lengthwise
- 8 cherry tomatoes

**1.** Grease a 10-in. cast-iron skillet with 1 teaspoon oil. Arrange lemon slices in a single layer in skillet.
**2.** Combine 1 teaspoon oil, 2 minced garlic cloves, lemon peel, 1/4 teaspoon salt and 1/8 teaspoon pepper; rub over chicken. Place over lemon.
**3.** In a large bowl, combine rosemary and the remaining oil, garlic, salt and pepper. Add potatoes and tomatoes; toss to coat. Arrange over chicken. Bake, uncovered, at 450° for 25-30 minutes or until chicken is no longer pink and potatoes are tender.

Skillet-Roasted Lemon Chicken with Potatoes

Skillet-Roasted Lemon Chicken with Potatoes is a simple, tasty meal I have students prepare in my nutrition class.
—MINDY ROTTMUND
LANCASTER, PENNSYLVANIA

# Breads, Rolls & Muffins

From Blueberry Colada Mini Loaves to Apple Fritters, these **fresh-baked goodies** just can't be beat. Serve them warm from the oven, and they'll disappear before you can say, **"Mmm!"**

"We love this quick and easy morning pastry. For a change of pace, I replace the raspberries with blackberries, marionberries, a mix of raspberries and blackberries, or all three."

—**TRESSA NICHOLLS** SANDY, OREGON

## Best Dinner Rolls

This versatile recipe gives you three different topping choices. It's hard to choose because they're all delicious.
—CHRISTINA PITTMAN
PARKVILLE, MISSOURI

**PREP:** 35 MIN. + RISING **BAKE:** 15 MIN.
**MAKES:** 2 DOZEN

- **4½ to 5 cups all-purpose flour**
- **¼ cup sugar**
- **1 package (¼ ounce) active dry yeast**
- **1¼ teaspoons salt**
- **1 cup whole milk**
- **½ cup water**
- **2 tablespoons butter**
- **2 eggs**
- **1 egg, lightly beaten**

**FOR EVERYTHING DINNER ROLLS**
- **1 teaspoon poppy seeds**
- **1 teaspoon kosher salt**
- **1 teaspoon dried minced garlic**
- **1 teaspoon sesame seeds**
- **1 teaspoon dried minced onion**

**FOR PARM-GARLIC DINNER ROLLS**
- **2 tablespoons grated Parmesan cheese**
- **½ teaspoon dried minced garlic**

**FOR ALMOND HERB DINNER ROLLS**
- **2 tablespoons chopped sliced almonds**
- **½ teaspoon kosher salt**
- **½ teaspoon dried basil**
- **½ teaspoon dried oregano**

**1.** In a large bowl, combine 2 cups flour, sugar, yeast and salt. In a small saucepan, heat milk, water and butter to 120°-130°. Add to dry ingredients; beat on medium speed for 3 minutes. Add 2 eggs; beat on high speed for 2 minutes. Stir in enough remaining flour to form a soft dough (dough will be sticky).
**2.** Turn onto a floured surface; knead until smooth and elastic, about 6-8 minutes. Place in a greased bowl, turning once to grease the top. Cover with plastic wrap and let rise in a warm place until doubled, about 1 hour.
**3.** Punch dough down. Turn onto a lightly floured surface; divide into 24 portions. Shape into balls. Divide between two greased 13-in. x 9-in. baking pans.
**4.** Cover with a clean, lightweight towel and let rise until doubled, about 30 min. Brush with lightly beaten egg. Sprinkle with toppings for rolls of your choice.
**5.** Bake at 375° for 10-15 minutes or until golden brown. Remove from pans to wire racks.

Best Dinner Rolls

FAST FIX

## Almond-Chocolate Crescents

How sweet—breakfast rolls that are yummy enough to be a dessert! They look pretty drizzled with chocolate.
—ROXANNE O'BRIEN
LYNDHURST, VIRGINIA

**PREP/TOTAL TIME:** 30 MIN.
**MAKES:** 8 ROLLS

- **¼ cup almond paste**
- **¾ cup semisweet chocolate chips**
- **1 tablespoon shortening**
- **1 tube (8 ounces) refrigerated crescent rolls**

**1.** Divide almond paste into eight portions; shape each into small logs. Set aside. In a microwave, melt chocolate chips and shortening; stir until smooth.
**2.** Unroll crescent dough; separate into triangles. Spread each with 1 tablespoon chocolate mixture; set aside remaining mixture for drizzling. Place one portion almond paste at wide end of each triangle. Roll up and place point side down 2 in. apart on an ungreased baking sheet; curve ends to form a crescent.
**3.** Bake at 375° for 11-13 minutes or until golden brown. Remove to wire rack to cool completely. Drizzle with reserved chocolate mixture.

## Rosemary-Lemon Scones

My wife and I sampled a scrumptious rosemary-lemon coffee cake at a bed and breakfast many years ago. I tried to capture that flavor combination in a scone, and we loved the results.

**—DAVID BYLAND**
SHAWNEE, OKLAHOMA

**PREP:** 20 MIN. **BAKE:** 15 MIN.
**MAKES:** 8 SCONES

- **2 cups all-purpose flour**
- **3 tablespoons sugar**
- **2 teaspoons baking powder**
- **½ teaspoon baking soda**
- **½ teaspoon salt**
- **5 tablespoons cold butter**
- **1 cup (8 ounces) sour cream**
- **1 egg**
- **2 teaspoons grated lemon peel**
- **1 teaspoon minced fresh rosemary**
- **1 teaspoon coarse sugar**

**1.** In a large bowl, combine the flour, sugar, baking powder, baking soda and salt. Cut in butter until mixture resembles coarse crumbs. Whisk sour cream and egg; stir into crumb mixture just until moistened. Stir in lemon peel and rosemary. Turn onto a floured surface; knead 10 times.

**2.** Pat into an 8-in. circle. Cut into eight wedges, but do not separate. Place on an ungreased baking sheet. Sprinkle with coarse sugar. Bake at 400° for 15-18 minutes or until golden brown. Serve warm.

## Gingerbread Muffin Tops

Ask anyone what the best part of the muffin is, and they'll probably say the top. The Taste of Home Test Kitchen pros created these spiced-up treats that taste like molasses cookies and don't require a special baking pan.

**PREP:** 30 MIN. **BAKE:** 15 MIN.
**MAKES:** 7 MUFFIN TOPS

- **⅓ cup butter, softened**
- **⅓ cup packed brown sugar**
- **1 egg**
- **¾ cup molasses**
- **2 cups all-purpose flour**
- **1½ teaspoons ground ginger**
- **1 teaspoon baking soda**
- **1 teaspoon ground cinnamon**
- **½ teaspoon salt**
- **1 tablespoon coarse sugar**

**1.** In a large bowl, cream butter and brown sugar until light and fluffy. Beat in egg and molasses. Combine flour, ginger, baking soda, cinnamon and salt; gradually add to creamed mixture and mix well.

**2.** Drop by ¼ cupfuls 2 in. apart onto a parchment paper-lined baking sheet. Sprinkle with coarse sugar. Bake at 350° for 15-20 minutes or until set. Cool for 5 minutes before removing from pan to a wire rack. Serve warm.

Gingerbread Muffin Tops

## Zesty Jalapeno Corn Muffins

I make a batch of tender corn muffins at least twice a month. My husband and relatives like the zippy jalapenos.

**—SHARI DORE**
PORT SEVERN, ONTARIO

**PREP:** 20 MIN. **BAKE:** 20 MIN.
**MAKES:** 1 DOZEN

- **2 packages (8½ ounces each) corn bread/muffin mix**
- **¼ cup minced fresh cilantro**
- **1 tablespoon grated lime peel**
- **2 teaspoons ground cumin**
- **2 eggs**
- **⅔ cup buttermilk**
- **4 ounces cream cheese, cubed**
- **2 jalapeno peppers, seeded and minced**
- **4 green onions, finely chopped**

**1.** In a large bowl, combine the muffin mixes, cilantro, lime peel and cumin. Whisk eggs and buttermilk; stir into dry ingredients just until moistened. Fold in the cream cheese, jalapenos and onions.

**2.** Fill greased or paper-lined muffin cups three-fourths full. Bake at 400° for 16-20 minutes or until a toothpick inserted in muffin comes out clean. Cool for 5 minutes before removing from pan to a wire rack. Serve warm.

**Editor's Note:** *Wear disposable gloves when cutting hot peppers; the oils can burn skin. Avoid touching your face.*

Zesty Jalapeno Corn Muffins

### Did you know?

Hot peppers have been eaten in many cultures for at least 400 years. Capsaicin is the heat-producing component in hot peppers and is concentrated in the white membranes and seeds.

## Whole Wheat Cranberry Scones

With a biscuitlike texture, these spiced scones are wonderful spread with butter or jam. Offer them alongside a bowl of fresh berries at your next holiday brunch—or enjoy one as an afternoon pick-me-up with a cup of coffee.
—**PATSYE YONCE** OVID, NEW YORK

**PREP:** 20 MIN. **BAKE:** 15 MIN. **MAKES:** 16 SCONES

- **1½ cups all-purpose flour**
- **1½ cups whole wheat flour**
- **½ cup sugar**
- **3 teaspoons baking powder**
- **½ teaspoon baking soda**
- **½ teaspoon salt**
- **¼ teaspoon ground nutmeg**
- **¾ cup cold butter**
- **1 egg**
- **1 cup vanilla yogurt**
- **½ teaspoon vanilla extract**
- **1 cup dried cranberries**
- **1 tablespoon milk**
- **2 teaspoons cinnamon-sugar**

**1.** In a large bowl, combine the flours, sugar, baking powder, baking soda, salt and nutmeg; cut in butter until crumbly. In a small bowl, combine egg, yogurt and vanilla; stir into dry ingredients just until moistened. Stir in dried cranberries. Turn onto a floured surface, knead 6-8 times.
**2.** Divide dough in half. Transfer each portion to a greased baking sheet. Pat into an 8-in. circle. Cut each circle into 8 wedges, but do not separate. Brush with milk; sprinkle with cinnamon-sugar. Bake at 400° for 15-20 minutes or until golden brown. Serve warm.

Whole Wheat Cranberry Scones

Blueberry Colada Mini Loaves

## Blueberry Colada Mini Loaves

What do you get when you combine a pina colada and quick bread? This delightfully different treat that mixes in plenty of blueberries, too. The recipe makes eight miniature loaves.
—**BRENDA BONN** GENEVA, ILLINOIS

**PREP:** 20 MIN. **BAKE:** 25 MIN. + COOLING
**MAKES:** 8 MINI LOAVES (6 SLICES EACH)

- **⅔ cup shortening**
- **1⅓ cups sugar**
- **4 eggs**
- **1 can (8 ounces) crushed pineapple, drained**
- **½ cup 2% milk**
- **1½ teaspoons lemon juice**
- **3 cups all-purpose flour**
- **2 teaspoons baking powder**
- **1 teaspoon baking soda**
- **½ teaspoon salt**
- **2 cups fresh or frozen blueberries**
- **½ cup flaked coconut**

**1.** In a large bowl, cream shortening and sugar until light and fluffy. Add eggs, one at a time, beating well after each addition. Beat in the pineapple, milk and lemon juice. Combine the flour, baking powder, baking soda and salt; gradually beat into the creamed mixture. Fold in blueberries and coconut.
**2.** Transfer to eight greased 4½-in. x 2½-in. x 1½-in. loaf pans. Bake at 350° for 25-30 minutes or until a toothpick inserted near the center comes out clean.
**3.** Cool for 15 minutes before removing from the pans to wire racks.
**Editor's Note:** *If using frozen blueberries, use without thawing to avoid discoloring the batter.*

## Maple Bubble Bread

Here is my family's all-time favorite breakfast bread. With a scrumptious topping of maple syrup, cinnamon and brown sugar, it's the perfect start to a special day.
—**HANNAH COBB** OWINGS MILLS, MARYLAND

**PREP:** 45 MIN. + RISING **BAKE:** 30 MIN. + COOLING
**MAKES:** 20 SERVINGS

- **1 package (¼ ounce) active dry yeast**
- **¼ cup warm water (110° to 115°)**
- **1 cup warm 2% milk (110° to 115°)**
- **⅓ cup butter, melted**
- **¼ cup sugar**
- **1 egg**
- **1 egg yolk**
- **½ teaspoon salt**
- **5 cups all-purpose flour**

**TOPPING**

- **⅔ cup maple syrup**
- **2 tablespoons butter**
- **1 cup packed brown sugar**
- **½ teaspoon ground cinnamon**
- **3 tablespoons butter, melted**

**1.** In a large bowl, dissolve yeast in warm water. Add the milk, butter, sugar, egg, egg yolk, salt and 3 cups flour. Beat on medium speed for 3 minutes. Stir in enough remaining flour to form a firm dough.
**2.** Turn onto a floured surface; knead until smooth and elastic, about 6-8 minutes. Place in a greased bowl, turning once to grease the top. Cover and let rise in a warm place until doubled, about 1 hour.
**3.** In a small saucepan, combine syrup and butter. Bring to a boil. Cook and stir for 3 minutes; set aside.
**4.** Punch dough down. Turn onto a lightly floured surface; divide into 20 pieces. Shape each into a roll. In a shallow bowl, combine brown sugar and cinnamon. Place melted butter in a separate shallow bowl. Dip buns in butter, then coat in brown sugar mixture.
**5.** Place eight rolls in a greased 10-in. fluted tube pan; drizzle with ⅓ cup syrup. Top with remaining rolls, syrup and brown sugar mixture. Cover and let rise until doubled, about 45 minutes.
**6.** Bake at 350° for 30-35 minutes or until golden brown. Cool for 10 minutes before inverting onto a serving plate. Serve warm.

## FAST FIX Honey-Moon Rolls

Yum! Dress up refrigerated dough with cream cheese, honey and sliced almonds to create delectable crescents.
—**ABBY RUTILA** WHITE LAKE, MICHIGAN

**PREP/TOTAL TIME:** 30 MIN. **MAKES:** 8 ROLLS

- **4 ounces cream cheese, softened**
- **2 tablespoons plus 2 teaspoons honey, divided**
- **¼ cup sliced almonds**
- **1 tube (8 ounces) refrigerated crescent rolls**
- **¼ teaspoon ground cinnamon**

**1.** In a small bowl, beat cream cheese and 2 tablespoons honey until smooth; stir in almonds. Unroll crescent dough; separate into triangles.
**2.** Place 1 tablespoon cream cheese mixture in the center of each triangle. Roll up and place point side down 2 in. apart on an ungreased baking sheet; curve ends to form a crescent. Sprinkle tops with cinnamon.
**3.** Bake at 375° for 12-14 minutes or until golden brown. Drizzle with remaining honey. Serve warm. Refrigerate leftovers.

Maple Bubble Bread

## FAST FIX Chive Garlic Bread

A store-bought loaf of French bread gets a flavorful boost from just a few everyday ingredients—Parmesan cheese, chives, garlic and butter. We serve slices with Italian dinners and munch until every last crumb has vanished.
—**KIM ORR** WEST GROVE, PENNSYLVANIA

**PREP/TOTAL TIME:** 20 MIN. **MAKES:** 12 SERVINGS

- **¼ cup butter, softened**
- **¼ cup grated Parmesan cheese**
- **2 tablespoons minced chives**
- **1 garlic clove, minced**
- **1 loaf (1 pound) French bread, cut into 1-inch slices**

In a small bowl, combine the butter, cheese, chives and garlic; spread on one side of each slice of bread. Wrap in a large piece of heavy-duty foil; seal tightly. Place on a baking sheet. Bake at 350° for 15-20 minutes or until heated through.

# BAKING MIX FROM SCRATCH

Many breads, entrees, desserts and other dishes get a time-saving boost from baking mix. With the recipes here, you can stir up a homemade version and use it to fix scrumptious baked goods.

**Biscuit Baking Mix**
**Flaky Italian Biscuits**
**Cinnamon-Sugar Scones**

## FAST FIX MAKE AHEAD Biscuit Baking Mix

Why spend extra money on a store-bought mix when this one is so easy to make? The homemade blend requires only four common pantry ingredients you can combine in a snap. I use it in recipes that call for biscuit mix and get great results. Try using it to prepare the two treats below—Flaky Italian Biscuits and Cinnamon-Sugar Scones.
—**TAMI CHRISTMAN** SODA SPRINGS, IDAHO

**PREP/TOTAL TIME:** 5 MIN. **MAKES:** 12 CUPS

- **9 cups all-purpose flour**
- **¼ cup baking powder**
- **1 tablespoon salt**
- **2 cups shortening**

In a large bowl, mix the flour, baking powder and salt; cut in shortening until the mixture resembles coarse crumbs. Store in an airtight container in a cool dry place or in the freezer for up to 8 months.

## FAST FIX Flaky Italian Biscuits

Keeping Biscuit Baking Mix (recipe above) on hand makes it a breeze to whip up a batch of tender, golden-brown biscuits anytime. Spread the oven-fresh goodies with butter—or skip the Italian seasoning and serve them with honey.
—**TAMI CHRISTMAN** SODA SPRINGS, IDAHO

**PREP/TOTAL TIME:** 30 MIN. **MAKES:** 8 BISCUITS

- **2 cups Biscuit Baking Mix (recipe above)**
- **1 teaspoon Italian seasoning**
- **½ cup half-and-half cream**

**1.** In a small bowl, mix biscuit baking mix and Italian seasoning; stir in the half-and-half cream just until moistened. Turn onto a lightly floured surface; knead gently 10 times. Pat or roll out to ½-in. thickness; cut with a 2½-in. biscuit cutter.
**2.** Place biscuits 2 in. apart on an ungreased baking sheet. Bake at 425° for 13-16 minutes or until golden brown. Serve warm.

I do the kneading, rolling and cutting of my biscuit dough right on the baking sheet. I remove the scraps and excess flour, then bake. There's no messy counter to clean.
—**PAMELA MAIN** HOPKINTON, MASSACHUSETTS

## Cinnamon-Sugar Scones

I bring my sugar-and-spice scones to every event, and they're a hit with children and adults alike. If you have trouble finding cinnamon chips at your grocery store, look for them online or substitute semisweet chocolate chips.
—**KATHY MONAHAN** JACKSONVILLE, FLORIDA

**PREP:** 20 MIN. **BAKE:** 20 MIN. **MAKES:** 8 SCONES

- **3 cups Biscuit Baking Mix (recipe above left)**
- **¼ cup sugar**
- **½ cup (4 ounces) vanilla yogurt**
- **⅓ cup 2% milk**
- **1 tablespoon vanilla extract**
- **1 cup cinnamon baking chips or semisweet chocolate chips**
- **Cinnamon-sugar or coarse sugar**

**1.** In a large bowl, mix the biscuit baking mix and sugar. In another bowl, whisk yogurt, milk and vanilla; stir into dry ingredients just until moistened. Stir in cinnamon chips. Turn onto a lightly floured surface; knead gently 10 times.
**2.** Pat into a 9-in. circle. Sprinkle with cinnamon-sugar. Cut into eight wedges. Place wedges on an ungreased baking sheet. Bake at 375° for 20-25 minutes or until golden brown. Serve warm.

Cinnamon-Sugar Scones

## Seeded Butternut Squash Braid

Warm up chilly autumn days with a fall-flavored bread. The green hulled pumpkin seeds, better known as pepitas, lend a slightly nutty taste.

**—CHERYL PERRY**
HERTFORD, NORTH CAROLINA

**PREP:** 45 MIN.+ RISING **BAKE:** 20 MIN.
**MAKES:** 1 LOAF (18 SLICES)

- **2¾ cups uncooked cubed peeled butternut squash**
- **1 package (¼ ounce) active dry yeast**
- **⅓ cup warm 2% milk (110° to 115°)**
- **2 tablespoons warm water (110° to 115°)**
- **½ cup pepitas or sunflower kernels**
- **¼ cup butter, softened**
- **1 egg**
- **3 tablespoons brown sugar**
- **½ teaspoon salt**
- **3½ to 4 cups all-purpose flour**

**TOPPING**

- **1 egg**
- **1 tablespoon water**
- **¼ cup pepitas or sunflower kernels**

**1.** Place squash in a large saucepan and cover with water. Bring to a boil. Reduce heat; cover and cook for 15-20 minutes or until tender. Drain and mash squash (you will need 2 cups); cool to 110°-115°.

**2.** In a small bowl, dissolve yeast in warm milk and water. In a large bowl, combine the pepitas, butter, egg, brown sugar, salt, cooked squash, yeast mixture and 2 cups flour; beat on medium speed for 3 minutes. Stir in enough remaining flour to form a soft dough (dough will be sticky).

**3.** Turn onto a floured surface; knead until smooth and elastic, about 6-8 minutes. Place in a greased bowl, turning once to grease the top. Cover with plastic wrap and let rise in a warm place until doubled, about 1 hour.

**4.** Punch dough down. Turn onto a lightly floured surface; divide into thirds. Shape each into a 26-in. rope; braid ropes. Transfer to a greased baking sheet; form into a circle, pinching ends together to seal. Cover with a clean kitchen towel; let rise in a warm place until doubled, about 45 minutes.

**5.** For topping, beat egg and water; brush over braid. Sprinkle with pepitas. Bake at 350° for 18-23 minutes or until golden brown. Remove from pan to wire rack.

Seeded Butternut Squash Braid

## Moist Apple Muffins

These sweet muffins are wonderful anytime. Keep them in mind whenever you need a take-along treat.

**—JEANNE SHERRY**
PUTNAM VALLEY, NEW YORK

**PREP:** 20 MIN. **BAKE:** 20 MIN.
**MAKES:** 2 DOZEN

- **½ cup butter, softened**
- **1¾ cups packed brown sugar**
- **2 eggs**
- **1⅓ cups buttermilk**
- **2⅔ cups all-purpose flour**
- **1¾ teaspoons ground cinnamon**
- **1 teaspoon baking soda**
- **⅛ teaspoon salt**
- **2 cups chopped peeled apples**
- **1 medium apple, peeled and cut into 24 slices**

**TOPPING**

- **⅓ cup all-purpose flour**
- **¼ cup packed brown sugar**
- **¼ teaspoon ground cinnamon**
- **2 tablespoons cold butter**

**1.** In a bowl, beat butter and brown sugar until crumbly, about 2 minutes. Add eggs, one at a time, beating well after each addition. Stir in the buttermilk. Combine the flour, cinnamon, baking soda and salt; add to butter mixture just until moistened. Fold in chopped apples.

**2.** Fill paper-lined muffin cups three-fourths full. Place sliced apples over batter. For topping, combine the flour, brown sugar and cinnamon; cut in butter until crumbly. Sprinkle over tops.
**3.** Bake at 350° for 20-25 minutes or until a toothpick comes out clean. Cool for 5 minutes before removing from pans to wire racks. Serve warm.

## FAST FIX Herb Happy Garlic Bread

The Taste of Home Test Kitchen pros whipped up a quick garlic loaf you'll love serving with meals. The mild cheesy duo on top makes each slice extra rich and delicious.

**PREP/TOTAL TIME:** 15 MIN. **MAKES:** 12 SERVINGS

- **½ cup butter, softened**
- **¼ cup grated Romano cheese**
- **2 tablespoons minced fresh basil or 2 teaspoons dried basil**
- **1 tablespoon minced fresh parsley**
- **3 garlic cloves, minced**
- **1 French bread baguette**
- **4 ounces crumbled goat cheese**

**1.** In a small bowl, mix the first five ingredients until blended. Cut baguette crosswise in half; cut each piece lengthwise in half. Spread cut sides with butter mixture. Place on an ungreased baking sheet.
**2.** Bake, uncovered, at 425° for 7-9 minutes or until lightly toasted. Sprinkle with goat cheese; bake 1-2 minutes longer or until goat cheese is softened. Cut into slices.

Herb Happy Garlic Bread

## Lemon-Thyme Bread

This recipe lends itself to lots of yummy variations. Fresh thyme is best, but if you use dried, use just 1 tablespoon and crush it between your fingers before adding it to the batter.
**—CATHY TANG** REDMOND, WASHINGTON

**PREP:** 25 MIN. **BAKE:** 40 MIN. + COOLING
**MAKES:** 1 LOAF (12 SLICES)

- **½ cup butter, softened**
- **¾ cup sugar**
- **1 egg**
- **½ cup buttermilk**
- **½ cup sour cream**
- **1¾ cups all-purpose flour**
- **2 tablespoons minced fresh thyme**
- **1 tablespoon grated lemon peel**
- **½ teaspoon baking soda**
- **¼ teaspoon salt**
- **Confectioners' sugar**

**1.** In a bowl, cream butter and sugar until light and fluffy. Beat in egg. Combine buttermilk and sour cream. Combine the flour, thyme, lemon peel, baking soda and salt; add to the creamed mixture alternately with buttermilk mixture, beating well after each addition.
**2.** Transfer to a greased 8-in. x 4-in. loaf pan. Bake at 350° for 40-50 minutes or until a toothpick inserted near the center comes out clean. Cool for 10 minutes before removing from pan to a wire rack. Cool completely; sprinkle with confectioners' sugar.

**LEMON-THYME MINI LOAVES**
Use three greased 5¾-in. x 3-in. x 2-in. loaf pans. Bake at 350° for 25-30 minutes or until a toothpick comes out clean.

**LEMON-THYME MUFFINS**
Make batter as directed; fill greased or paper-lined muffin cups two-thirds full. Bake at 400° for 16-20 minutes or until a toothpick comes out clean. Makes: 1 dozen muffins.

**LEMON-THYME MINIATURE MUFFINS**
Make batter as directed; fill greased or paper-lined muffin cups two-thirds full. Bake at 400° for 10-12 minutes or until a toothpick comes out clean. Makes: 4 dozen miniature muffins.

**LEMON-THYME ICING**
In a small bowl, combine ½ cup confectioners' sugar, ½ teaspoon minced fresh thyme and 3 to 4 teaspoons lemon juice, as needed, to achieve a drizzling consistency. Makes: 2 tablespoons.

**LEMONY CREAM CHEESE**
In a bowl, beat 8 ounces softened cream cheese until fluffy. Add ⅓ cup confectioners' sugar, 4 teaspoons lemon juice and 1 teaspoon grated lemon peel; beat until smooth. Makes: 1 cup.

## Almond-Studded Chocolate Loaf

With decadent chocolate and a nutty topping, slices of this luscious bread could be served as an extra-special snack, brunch item or even dessert. I've also given it as a gift.
—**LISA VARNER** EL PASO, TEXAS

**PREP:** 30 MIN.
**BAKE:** 55 MIN. + COOLING
**MAKES:** 1 LOAF (16 SLICES)

- **2 cups all-purpose flour**
- **¼ cup baking cocoa**
- **2 teaspoons baking powder**
- **½ teaspoon salt**
- **¼ teaspoon baking soda**
- **1 egg**
- **1 cup 2% milk**
- **¾ cup packed dark brown sugar**
- **⅓ cup canola oil**
- **½ teaspoon almond extract**
- **1 cup plus 2 tablespoons chopped almonds, divided**
- **¾ cup plus 2 tablespoons miniature semisweet chocolate chips, divided**

**1.** In a large bowl, combine the flour, cocoa, baking powder, salt and baking soda. In a small bowl, whisk egg, milk, brown sugar, oil and extract. Stir into the dry ingredients just until moistened. Fold in 1 cup almonds and ¾ cup chocolate chips.

**2.** Spoon into a greased 9-in. x 5-in. loaf pan. Sprinkle with remaining almonds and chips. Bake at 350° for 55-60 minutes or until a toothpick inserted near the center comes out clean. Cool for 10 minutes before removing from pan to a wire rack.

No-Knead Harvest Bread

Almond-Studded Chocolate Loaf

## No-Knead Harvest Bread

The Taste of Home Test Kitchen pros came up with a fuss-free loaf full of old-fashioned aroma and flavor. It bakes in a 5-quart Dutch oven.

**PREP:** 30 MIN. + RISING
**BAKE:** 30 MIN. + COOLING
**MAKES:** 1 LOAF (16 SLICES)

- **½ cup whole wheat flour**
- **½ cup cornmeal**
- **½ cup assorted seeds, such as sesame seeds, flaxseed, sunflower kernels and/or poppy seeds, divided**
- **1¾ teaspoons salt**
- **¼ teaspoon active dry yeast**
- **3 cups bread flour, divided**
- **2¼ cups cool water (55° to 65°)**
- **2 tablespoons molasses**
- **Additional cornmeal**

**1.** In a large bowl, combine the whole wheat flour, cornmeal, ⅓ cup seeds, salt, yeast and 2½ cups bread flour. Stir in the water and molasses until blended; dough will be wet and sticky.

**2.** Cover dough with plastic wrap and let stand at room temperature until more than doubled in size and bubbles are present on surface, 12 to 18 hours.

**3.** Stir in remaining bread flour. Cover again with plastic wrap; let rise 2 hours longer.

**4.** Lightly oil an oven-safe 5-qt. round Dutch oven; cover and place in oven. Preheat oven to 425°. Carefully remove hot Dutch oven; sprinkle bottom with cornmeal. With a spatula, transfer dough to Dutch oven. Sprinkle with remaining seeds. Cover and bake for 20 minutes.

**5.** Uncover; bake 15-20 minutes longer or until deep golden brown and bread sounds hollow when center is tapped. Remove from pan to a wire rack. Bread may also be prepared in a clay bread baker; prepare baker according to manufacturer's directions and proceed as directed.

## Raspberry Breakfast Braid

We love this quick and easy morning pastry. For a change of pace, I replace the raspberries with blackberries, marionberries, a mix of raspberries and blackberries, or all three.

**—TRESSA NICHOLLS** SANDY, OREGON

**PREP:** 20 MIN. **BAKE:** 15 MIN.
**MAKES:** 12 SERVINGS

- **2 cups biscuit/baking mix**
- **1 package (3 ounces) cream cheese, cubed**
- **¼ cup cold butter, cubed**
- **⅓ cup 2% milk**
- **1¼ cups fresh raspberries**
- **3 tablespoons sugar**
- **¼ cup vanilla frosting**

**1.** Place the biscuit mix in a large bowl. Cut in the cream cheese and butter until the mixture resembles coarse crumbs. Stir in the milk just until moistened. Turn onto a lightly floured surface; knead gently 8-10 times.

**2.** On a greased baking sheet, roll dough into an 18-in. x 12-in. rectangle. Spoon the raspberries down center third of dough; sprinkle with sugar.

**3.** On each long side of rectangle, cut 1-in.-wide strips about 2½ in. into center. Starting at one end, fold alternating strips at an angle across raspberries; seal ends.

**4.** Bake at 425° for 15-20 minutes or until golden brown. Remove to a wire rack to cool slightly. In a microwave-safe dish, microwave the vanilla frosting on high for 5-10 seconds or until of desired consistency; drizzle over pastry.

Raspberry Breakfast Braid

## FAST FIX Pumpkin Butter Pinwheels

Surprising your family with a yummy autumn treat is as easy as rolling up refrigerated dough with pumpkin butter and pecans. Just spread on vanilla frosting and enjoy!

**—LORI MERRICK** DANVERS, ILLINOIS

**PREP/TOTAL TIME:** 30 MIN.
**MAKES:** 4 SERVINGS

- **1 tube (8 ounces) refrigerated crescent rolls**
- **½ cup pumpkin butter**
- **Chopped pecans, optional**
- **½ cup vanilla frosting**

**1.** Unroll the crescent dough into one long rectangle; seal seams and perforations. Spread pumpkin butter to within ½ in. of edges. Sprinkle with pecans if desired. Roll up jelly-roll style, starting with a short side; pinch seam to seal. Place on a greased baking sheet.

**2.** Cut into eight slices to within ½ in. of bottom. Pull slices to the side, alternating left and right. Bake at 375° for 12-15 minutes or until golden brown.

**3.** Spread with frosting; sprinkle with additional pecans if desired. Serve warm.

**Editor's Note:** *This recipe was tested with commercially prepared pumpkin butter.*

## FAST FIX Sweet Potato Biscuits with Honey Butter

Featuring the perfect spread, Sweet Potato Biscuits with Honey Butter are colorful, tender and downright festive for a holiday feast or other special meal.
—**CATHY BELL** JOPLIN, MISSOURI

**PREP/TOTAL TIME:** 30 MIN.
**MAKES:** 10 BISCUITS (ABOUT ½ CUP HONEY BUTTER)

- **2 cups all-purpose flour**
- **4 teaspoons sugar**
- **3 teaspoons baking powder**
- **1 teaspoon salt**
- **1 teaspoon ground cinnamon**
- **½ teaspoon ground nutmeg**
- **¼ cup shortening**
- **1 cup mashed sweet potatoes**
- **½ cup half-and-half cream**

**HONEY BUTTER**

- **½ cup butter, softened**
- **2 tablespoons honey**
- **1 teaspoon ground cinnamon**

**1.** In a small bowl, combine the first six ingredients. Cut in shortening until mixture resembles coarse crumbs. Combine sweet potatoes and cream; stir into crumb mixture just until moistened. Turn onto a lightly floured surface; gently knead 8-10 times.
**2.** Pat or roll out to ½-in thickness; cut with a floured 2½-in. biscuit cutter. Place biscuits 1 in. apart on a greased baking sheet.
**3.** Bake at 400° for 9-11 minutes or until golden brown. Meanwhile, in a small bowl, beat the butter, honey and cinnamon until blended. Serve with warm biscuits.

## Upside-Down Turtle Muffins

If you like traditional turtle candies, you'll love these dessertlike muffins. The ooey-gooey goodies boast a rich caramel center and a glossy chocolate glaze topped with pecans.
—**PATRICE BRUWER-MILLER**
WYOMING, MICHIGAN

**PREP:** 25 MIN. **BAKE:** 15 MIN.
**MAKES:** 8 MUFFINS

- **1 cup all-purpose flour**
- **¼ cup chopped pecans**
- **1 teaspoon baking soda**
- **½ teaspoon salt**
- **½ cup semisweet chocolate chips**
- **3 tablespoons butter**
- **⅓ cup packed brown sugar**
- **⅓ cup buttermilk**
- **1 egg, lightly beaten**
- **1 teaspoon vanilla extract**
- **16 Riesen's chewy chocolate-covered caramels, divided**
- **24 pecan halves**

**1.** In a small bowl, combine the flour, chopped pecans, baking soda and salt; set aside. In a microwave-safe bowl, melt chocolate chips and butter; stir until smooth. Cool slightly. Stir in the brown sugar, buttermilk, egg and vanilla. Stir into dry ingredients just until moistened.
**2.** Fill greased muffin cups three-fourths full. Press one caramel into the center of each muffin cup. Bake at 400° for 12-14 minutes or until a toothpick inserted into the edge comes out clean.
**3.** Cool for 1 minute; invert onto a baking sheet. Top muffins with remaining caramels; return to the oven for 1-2 minutes or until caramel is softened. Place three pecan halves on each muffin. Serve warm.

Upside-Down Turtle Muffins

## FAST FIX Nutty Cranberry Sticky Buns

Dried cranberries and chopped nuts give ordinary sticky buns the taste of Christmastime. But they're so good, you'll want to have them year-round.
—**MARY SHIVERS** ADA, OKLAHOMA

**PREP/TOTAL TIME:** 30 MIN.
**MAKES:** 9 BUNS

- **1 tube (8 ounces) refrigerated crescent rolls**
- **½ cup dried cranberries**
- **¼ cup packed brown sugar, divided**
- **2 tablespoons butter, melted**
- **2 tablespoons maple syrup**
- **⅔ cup chopped pecans**

**1.** Unroll crescent dough into one long rectangle; seal seams and perforations. Sprinkle with cranberries and 2 tablespoons brown sugar. Roll up jelly-roll style, starting with a short side; pinch seam to seal. Cut into nine slices.
**2.** In a small bowl, combine the butter, maple syrup and remaining brown sugar; spread onto the bottom of a greased 8-in. square baking dish. Sprinkle with pecans. Place rolls, cut sides down, over pecans.
**3.** Bake at 375° for 18-22 minutes or until golden brown. Immediately invert buns onto a serving platter.

## FAST FIX Raspberry Cheese Danish

Your guests will think you made these yummy rolls from scratch or bought them from a bakery. No one needs to know you used refrigerated crescent dough and just four other ingredients!
**—KAREN WEIR**
LITCHFIELD, CONNECTICUT

**PREP/TOTAL TIME:** 25 MIN.
**MAKES:** 8 SERVINGS

- **4 ounces cream cheese, softened**
- **¼ cup plus ½ cup confectioners' sugar, divided**
- **1 can (8 ounces) refrigerated crescent rolls**
- **½ cup seedless raspberry jam**
- **2 teaspoons 2% milk**

**1.** In a small bowl, beat the cream cheese and 1/4 cup confectioners' sugar until smooth. Unroll crescent roll dough and separate into four rectangles; seal the perforations. Cut each rectangle in half, making eight squares.
**2.** Transfer squares to a parchment paper-lined baking sheet. Spread 1 tablespoon cream cheese mixture diagonally across each square. Top with 1 tablespoon raspberry jam. Bring two opposite corners of the dough over filling; pinch together firmly to seal.
**3.** Bake at 375° for 10-12 minutes or until golden brown. Combine milk and remaining confectioners' sugar; drizzle over pastries. Serve warm. Refrigerate leftovers.

## Apple Fritters

I've been serving up my golden-brown fritters for over 25 years. My friends and family just can't get enough, so I'm thankful the recipe is easy.
**—MARY SHIVERS** ADA, OKLAHOMA

**PREP:** 15 MIN. **COOK:** 5 MIN./BATCH
**MAKES:** ABOUT 3½ DOZEN

- **3 cups all-purpose flour**
- **½ cup sugar**
- **2 teaspoons baking powder**
- **½ teaspoon salt**
- **1 egg, beaten**
- **1 cup milk**
- **¼ cup orange juice**
- **¼ cup butter, melted**
- **1 teaspoon vanilla extract**
- **1 teaspoon grated orange peel**
- **1 cup grated unpeeled apples**
- **Oil for deep-fat frying**
- **Confectioners' sugar**

**1.** In a large bowl, combine the flour, sugar, baking powder and salt. Combine the egg, milk, orange juice, butter, vanilla and orange peel; add to dry ingredients just until moistened. Fold in the apples.
**2.** In an electric skillet or deep fryer, heat oil to 375°. Drop batter by rounded tablespoonfuls, a few at a time, into hot oil. Fry until golden brown, about 1-2 minutes on each side. Drain on paper towels. Dust with confectioners' sugar.

## Cinnamon-Chip Scones

Here's a wonderful gift idea for the holidays. Pack the scones in a paper bakery box lined with creatively cut tissue, then tie it up with polka-dot ribbon. Tuck a trio of fresh cinnamon sticks into the bow—they'll be a clue to the spiced treasures inside.
**—BONNIE BUCKLEY**
KANSAS CITY, MISSOURI

**PREP:** 25 MIN. **BAKE:** 15 MIN.
**MAKES:** 1 DOZEN

- **2½ cups all-purpose flour**
- **⅓ cup sugar**
- **3 teaspoons baking powder**
- **1 teaspoon ground cinnamon, divided**
- **½ cup cold butter**
- **⅔ cup cinnamon baking chips**

Apple Fritters

Cinnamon-Chip Scones

- **1 cup plus 1 tablespoon heavy whipping cream, divided**
- **1 egg**
- **1 tablespoon coarse sugar**

**1.** In a large bowl, combine the flour, sugar, baking powder and 1/2 teaspoon cinnamon. Cut in butter until mixture resembles coarse crumbs. Stir in cinnamon baking chips. Whisk 1 cup cream and egg; stir into crumb mixture just until moistened.
**2.** Turn dough onto a floured surface; knead 10 times. Pat into a 9-in. circle. Cut into 12 wedges. Separate wedges and place on a greased baking sheet. Brush with remaining cream. Combine coarse sugar and remaining cinnamon; sprinkle over tops.
**3.** Bake at 400° for 14-16 minutes or until golden brown. Serve warm.

# Cookies, Bars & Candies

You'll have **special sweets** well in hand when you make the recipes in this chapter. From Chocolate Raspberry Squares to Saltine Toffee Bark, these goodies get smiles **by the dozens**.

"A cup of tea looks lonely without something yummy beside it. These tangy bars are a wonderful accompaniment. I love the combination of the almond crust and tart lemon curd."

—**DONNA HARDIN** NEW VIRGINIA, IOWA

## Big & Buttery Chocolate Chip Cookies

What's better than a chocolate chip cookie? An even bigger one! My Big & Buttery Chocolate Chip Cookies are a jumbo version of an American classic. They're based on a recipe from a bakery in California called Hungry Bear.
**—IRENE YEH** MEQUON, WISCONSIN

**PREP:** 35 MIN. + CHILLING
**BAKE:** 10 MIN. **MAKES:** 2 DOZEN

- **1 cup butter, softened**
- **1 cup packed brown sugar**
- **¾ cup sugar**
- **2 eggs**
- **1½ teaspoons vanilla extract**
- **2⅔ cups all-purpose flour**
- **1¼ teaspoons baking soda**
- **1 teaspoon salt**
- **1 package (12 ounces) semisweet chocolate chips**
- **2 cups coarsely chopped walnuts, toasted**

**1.** In a large bowl, cream the butter, brown sugar and sugar until light and fluffy. Beat in eggs and vanilla. Combine the flour, baking soda and salt; gradually add to creamed mixture and mix well. Stir in chocolate chips and walnuts.
**2.** Shape quarter cupfuls of dough into balls. Place in an airtight container, separating layers with waxed or parchment paper; cover and refrigerate overnight.
**3.** To bake, place dough balls 3 in. apart on parchment paper-lined baking sheets. Press a shallow indentation in the center of each with your thumb, reshaping sides to smooth any cracks. Let stand at room temperature for 30 minutes.
**4.** Bake at 400° for 10-12 minutes or until the edges are golden brown. Cool for 2 minutes before removing from the pans to wire racks; cool.

Big & Buttery Chocolate Chip Cookies

## Peanut Butter Kiss Cookies

These simple but yummy goodies always please the little ones, and adults are amazed when I tell them the recipe requires just five ingredients.
**—DEE DAVIS** SUN CITY, ARIZONA

**PREP:** 20 MIN.
**BAKE:** 10 MIN. + COOLING
**MAKES:** 2 DOZEN

- **1 cup peanut butter**
- **1 cup sugar**
- **1 egg**
- **1 teaspoon vanilla extract**
- **24 milk chocolate kisses**

**1.** In a large bowl, cream the peanut butter and sugar until light and fluffy. Add egg and vanilla; beat until blended.
**2.** Roll into 1¼-in. balls. Place 2 in. apart on ungreased baking sheets. Bake at 350° for 10-12 minutes or until the tops are slightly cracked.
**3.** Immediately press one chocolate kiss into the center of each cookie. Cool for 5 minutes before removing from pans to wire racks.
**Editor's Note:** *This recipe does not contain flour. Reduced-fat or generic brands of peanut butter are not recommended for this recipe.*

## More The Merrier Orange, Fig & Walnut Bars

Orange cake mix, fig preserves and walnuts may seem like an unusual flavor combination, but they blend wonderfully in these bars.
**—JUDY DALTON** DANVILLE, VIRGINIA

**PREP:** 10 MIN. **BAKE:** 25 MIN.
**MAKES:** 3 DOZEN

- **1 package (18¼ ounces) orange cake mix**
- **1 jar (10 ounces) fig preserves**
- **½ cup canola oil**
- **1 egg**
- **2 cups chopped walnuts**

**1.** In a large bowl, combine the cake mix, preserves, oil and egg; beat on low speed until blended. Stir in walnuts. (Batter will be thick.) Spread into a greased 13-in. x 9-in. baking pan.

2. Bake at 350° for 25-30 minutes or until a toothpick inserted in center comes out clean. Cool on a wire rack. Cut into bars.

## Macadamia & Coconut Caramels

I collect cookbooks from all over the world, and I use them to create new and different dishes. With coconut and macadamia nuts, these smooth caramels go beyond the ordinary.

**—SHARON DELANEY-CHRONIS**
SOUTH MILWAUKEE, WISCONSIN

**PREP:** 25 MIN.
**COOK:** 25 MIN. + CHILLING
**MAKES:** 1½ POUNDS

- **1 teaspoon plus ½ cup butter, divided**
- **1 cup packed light brown sugar**
- **½ cup light corn syrup**
- **¼ teaspoon cream of tartar**
- **¾ cup sweetened condensed milk**
- **½ cup flaked coconut**
- **½ cup chopped macadamia nuts**
- **½ teaspoon vanilla extract**

1. Line an 8-in. square baking dish with foil and grease the foil with 1 teaspoon butter; set aside.

2. In a large heavy saucepan, combine the brown sugar, corn syrup, cream of tartar and remaining butter; bring to a boil over medium heat, stirring constantly. Remove from the heat; gradually stir in milk. Cook and stir over medium-low heat until a candy thermometer reads 244° (firm-ball stage).

3. Remove from the heat; stir in remaining ingredients. Pour into prepared dish. Refrigerate until set, at least 2 hours.

4. Using the foil, lift candy out of dish. Gently peel off foil; cut caramel into 1-in. squares. Wrap individually in waxed paper; twist ends. Store in an airtight container.

**Editor's Note:** *We recommend that you test your candy thermometer before each use by bringing water to a boil; the thermometer should read 212°. Adjust your recipe temperature up or down based on your test.*

## MAKE AHEAD Crunchy Chocolate Mint Balls

Get a jump on the Christmas season by preparing these four-ingredient truffles in advance and tucking them away in the freezer for holiday gift giving. I like to present the cute little candies in miniature cupcake holders for an extra-special touch.

**—AMANDA TRIFF**
DARTMOUTH, NOVA SCOTIA

**PREP:** 45 MIN. + CHILLING
**COOK:** 5 MIN. + FREEZING
**MAKES:** 4½ DOZEN

- **1 package (10 ounces) mint chocolate chips**
- **¼ cup butter, softened**
- **1 can (14 ounces) sweetened condensed milk**
- **1¼ cups chocolate wafer crumbs (about 22 wafers)**
- **White jimmies**

1. In a double boiler or metal bowl over hot water, melt the chocolate chips and butter; stir until smooth. Stir in the sweetened condensed milk. Add wafer crumbs; mix to coat. Refrigerate for 1 hour or until easy to handle.

2. Roll into 1-in. balls; roll in jimmies. Place on a waxed paper-lined 15-in. x 10-in. x 1-in. baking pan; freeze until firm. Transfer to a resealable plastic freezer bag. May be frozen for up to 1 month.

3. **TO USE FROZEN BALLS:** Thaw at room temperature.

Macadamia & Coconut Caramels

Crunchy Chocolate Mint Balls

### REAL VANILLA VS. IMITATION

For many shoppers, choosing between imitation and pure vanilla extract comes down to price—so imitation wins. But in a classic case of you-get-what-you-pay-for, the choice is really about flavor. The organic compounds that bless pure vanilla extract with a deep, alluring flavor give the real product an edge. Our Test Kitchen experts' advice? Especially for special occasions when you want each dish to shine, pure vanilla extract is worth every penny.

## Crunchy Peanut Butter Candy

Anyone who likes peanuts will love this sweet treat loaded with nuts and creamy peanut butter. After breaking the pan of cooled candy into pieces, I add a simple but festive drizzle of melted semisweet chocolate.

**—CONNIE PIETILA** HOUGHTON, MICHIGAN

**PREP:** 20 MIN. **COOK:** 30 MIN. + COOLING **MAKES:** 3½ POUNDS

- **1½ teaspoons butter**
- **2½ cups creamy peanut butter**
- **2 cups salted peanuts**
- **½ teaspoon vanilla extract**
- **2 cups sugar**
- **1½ cups light corn syrup**
- **¼ cup water**
- **1½ teaspoons baking soda**
- **½ cup semisweet chocolate chips**

**1.** Grease a 15-in. x 10-in. x 1-in. pan with butter; set aside. Combine the peanut butter, peanuts and vanilla; set aside.

**2.** In a large heavy saucepan, combine the sugar, corn syrup and water; bring to a boil over medium heat, stirring constantly. Cook, without stirring, until a candy thermometer reads 300° (hard-crack stage). Immediately stir in peanut butter mixture and baking soda. Spread into prepared pan. Cool completely.

**3.** Break the candy into pieces. Melt the chocolate chips; stir until smooth. Drizzle over candy. Store in an airtight container.

**Editor's Note:** *We recommend that you test your candy thermometer before each use by bringing water to a boil; the thermometer should read 212°. Adjust your recipe temperature up or down based on your test.*

## Eyes-Wide-Open Espresso Cookies

Need a pick-me-up to stave off that afternoon sleepiness? Munch on the espresso-laced cookies created by the Taste of Home Test Kitchen team. Each perked-up goodie is topped with a chocolate-covered coffee bean.

**PREP:** 25 MIN. **BAKE:** 10 MIN./BATCH **MAKES:** 45 COOKIES

- **½ cup butter, softened**
- **½ cup sugar**
- **¼ cup packed brown sugar**
- **1 egg**
- **1¼ cups all-purpose flour**
- **6 tablespoons baking cocoa**
- **2 teaspoons finely ground espresso beans**
- **½ teaspoon baking soda**
- **¼ teaspoon salt**
- **1 cup (6 ounces) semisweet chocolate chips**
- **45 chocolate-covered coffee beans**

Crunchy Peanut Butter Candy

1. In a large bowl, cream the butter and sugars until light and fluffy. Beat in egg. Combine the flour, cocoa, ground espresso beans, baking soda and salt; gradually add to the creamed mixture and mix well. Stir in the chocolate chips.
2. Drop by rounded teaspoonfuls 2 in. apart onto parchment-lined baking sheets. Bake at 350° for 8-10 minutes or surface cracks. Immediately press a coffee bean into the center of each cookie. Cool for 2 minutes before removing from pans to wire racks. Store in an airtight container.

## Chocolate Raspberry Squares

My decadent berry bars are very easy to assemble. If you like, sprinkle the finished squares with confectioners' sugar.
—**MARILYN SWISHER** BERRIEN CENTER, MICHIGAN

**PREP:** 15 MIN. **BAKE:** 30 MIN. + COOLING **MAKES:** 16 SERVINGS

- **1½ cups all-purpose flour**
- **1½ cups quick-cooking or old-fashioned oats**
- **½ cup sugar**
- **½ cup packed brown sugar**
- **¼ teaspoon salt**
- **1 cup cold butter, cubed**
- **¾ cup seedless raspberry jam**
- **1 package (11½ ounces) semisweet chocolate chunks**
- **¼ cup chopped walnuts**

1. In a large bowl, combine the flour, oats, sugars and salt. Cut in butter until the mixture resembles coarse crumbs. Set aside 1 cup for topping; press remaining crumb mixture into a greased 9-in. square baking pan. Spread with jam; sprinkle with chocolate chunks.
2. Combine the walnuts and reserved crumb mixture; sprinkle over the top. Bake at 375° for 30-35 minutes or until lightly browned and bubbly. Cool on a wire rack. Cut into squares.

## Amaretto Cream Truffles

The velvety texture of the almond filling makes these truffles absolutely heavenly. I roll them in sweetened baking cocoa.
—**SHERRY DAY** PINCKNEY, MICHIGAN

**PREP:** 30 MIN. + CHILLING **MAKES:** 30 SERVINGS

- **5 ounces semisweet chocolate, chopped**
- **4 ounces milk chocolate, chopped**
- **⅓ cup heavy whipping cream**
- **2 tablespoons Amaretto**
- **1 teaspoon vanilla extract**
- **2 tablespoons sugar**
- **2 tablespoons baking cocoa**

1. Place chocolates in a small bowl. In a small saucepan, bring cream just to a boil. Pour over chocolates; whisk until smooth. Stir in the Amaretto and vanilla. Cool to room temperature, stirring occasionally. Cover and refrigerate for 1½ hours or until easy to handle.

Backwoods Bonfire Bark

2. In a small bowl, combine sugar and cocoa. Shape chocolate mixture into 1-in. balls; roll in cocoa mixture. Store in an airtight container in the refrigerator.

## Backwoods Bonfire Bark

My four-ingredient bark reminds me of being up North at the cabin with my family. The recipe is also great when you're looking for a fast contribution to a bake sale.
—**JAMIE MCMAHON** COLOGNE, MINNESOTA

**PREP:** 10 MIN. **COOK:** 5 MIN. + STANDING
**MAKES:** ABOUT 1½ POUNDS

- **1 pound semisweet chocolate, chopped**
- **1½ cups honey bear-shaped crackers**
- **1½ cups miniature marshmallows**
- **¾ cup dry roasted peanuts**

1. Place the chocolate in a microwave-safe bowl. Microwave on high for 1 minute; stir. Microwave 1 minute longer in 20-second intervals until melted; stir until smooth.
2. Spread to ¼-in. thickness on a waxed paper-lined baking sheet. Immediately sprinkle the crackers, miniature marshmallows and peanuts over the chocolate; press in lightly.
3. Chill until firm. Break or cut into pieces. Store in an airtight container.

## Almond Cheesecake Bars

My sister-in-law gave me the recipe for her scrumptious cheesecake bars. I've brought them to many functions since then, and I always hear raves.

**—MARY COUSER**
MAPLE PLAIN, MINNESOTA

**PREP:** 20 MIN.
**BAKE:** 35 MIN. + COOLING
**MAKES:** 3 DOZEN

- **2 cups all-purpose flour**
- **1 cup butter, softened**
- **½ cup confectioners' sugar**

**FILLING**

- **1 package (8 ounces) cream cheese, softened**
- **½ cup sugar**
- **1 teaspoon almond extract**
- **2 eggs, lightly beaten**

**FROSTING**

- **1½ cups confectioners' sugar**
- **¼ cup butter, softened**
- **1 teaspoon almond extract**
- **4 to 5 teaspoons milk**

**1.** Combine the flour, butter and confectioners' sugar; press onto the bottom of a greased 13-in. x 9-in. baking pan. Bake at 350° for 20-25 minutes or until golden brown.

**2.** For filling, in a bowl, beat the cream cheese, sugar and extract until smooth. Add eggs; beat on low speed just until combined. Pour over crust. Bake for 15-20 minutes or until center is almost set. Cool on a wire rack.

**3.** Combine the frosting ingredients until smooth; spread over bars. Store in the refrigerator.

Almond Cheesecake Bars

## Peppermint Lollipops

The Taste of Home Test Kitchen pros came up with minty pops you'll love sharing for Christmas. Make them extra festive for the holidays using cookie cutters shaped like reindeer, snowmen, gingerbread men, pine trees...the possibilities are endless!

**PREP:** 5 MIN.
**COOK:** 30 MIN. + STANDING
**MAKES:** 10 LOLLIPOPS

- **1½ cups sugar**
- **¾ cup water**
- **⅔ cup light corn syrup**
- **½ teaspoon cream of tartar**
- **½ teaspoon peppermint oil**
- **Red and/or green paste food coloring**
- **10 lollipop sticks**
- **Crushed peppermint candies, optional**

**1.** Butter 10 assorted metal cookie cutters and place on a parchment paper-lined baking sheet; set aside. In a large heavy saucepan, combine the sugar, water, corn syrup and cream of tartar. Cook and stir over medium heat until sugar is dissolved. Bring to a boil. Cook, without stirring, until a candy thermometer reads 300° (hard-crack stage).

**2.** Remove from the heat. Stir in oil, keeping your face away from mixture as odor is very strong. For each color of candy swirls, pour 1/4 cup sugar mixture into a ramekin or custard cup; tint red or green.

**3.** Immediately pour remaining sugar mixture into the prepared cookie cutters. Drizzle with the colored mixtures as desired; cut through with a toothpick to swirl. Remove cutters just before the lollipops are set; firmly press a lollipop stick into each. Sprinkle crushed peppermint candies over the tops if desired.

**Editor's Note:** *This recipe was tested with LorAnn peppermint oil. It can be found at candy and cake decorating supply shops or at www.lorannoils.com. We recommend that you test your candy thermometer before each use by bringing water to a boil; the thermometer should read 212°. Adjust your recipe temperature up or down based on your test.*

Peanut Butter Cereal Treats

## FAST FIX Peanut Butter Cereal Treats

Children can't get enough of this colorful, yummy twist on the usual marshmallow crispy squares. Because these are so simple to fix, older kids could whip up a batch on their own.

**—CHRISTIE PORTER**
SHIPSHEWANA, INDIANA

**PREP/TOTAL TIME:** 30 MIN.
**MAKES:** 2 DOZEN

- **30 large marshmallows**
- **3 tablespoons butter**
- **1 tablespoon peanut butter**
- **6 cups Peanut Butter Cap'n Crunch**
- **1½ cups milk chocolate M&M's**

**1.** In a large saucepan, combine the marshmallows, butter and peanut butter. Cook and stir over medium-low heat until melted. Remove from the heat. Stir in the cereal and M&M's.

**2.** Pat into a 13-in. x 9-in. pan coated with cooking spray. Cool. Cut into bars.

## Monogrammed Cookies

For a fun bridal shower treat, add the bride's monogram to these crisp sugar cutouts from the Taste of Home Test Kitchen staff. Mint and lime zest add a burst of refreshing flavor.

**PREP:** 40 MIN. + CHILLING
**BAKE:** 10 MIN./BATCH
**MAKES:** 4 DOZEN

- **1 cup butter, softened**
- **1 package (3 ounces) cream cheese, softened**
- **1 cup sugar**
- **1 egg yolk**
- **3 tablespoons minced fresh mint**
- **1 teaspoon grated lime peel**
- **1 teaspoon rum extract**
- **1 teaspoon vanilla extract**
- **2¼ cups all-purpose flour**
- **½ teaspoon salt**
- **¼ teaspoon baking soda**

**ROYAL ICING**

- **4 cups confectioners' sugar**
- **6 tablespoons warm water**
- **3 tablespoons meringue powder**
- **Paste food coloring**

Monogrammed Cookies

**1.** In a large bowl, cream the butter, cream cheese and sugar until light and fluffy. Beat in the egg yolk, mint, lime peel and extracts. Combine the flour, salt and baking soda; gradually add to creamed mixture and mix well. Cover and refrigerate for 3 hours or until easy to handle.

**2.** On a lightly floured surface, roll out dough to 1/8-in. thickness. Cut with a floured 2 1/2-in. round cookie cutter. Place 1 in. apart on ungreased baking sheets. Bake at 375° for 8-10 minutes or until edges begin to brown. Cool for 2 minutes before removing from pans to wire racks to cool completely.

**3.** For the icing, in a large bowl, combine the confectioners' sugar, water and meringue powder; beat on low speed just until combined. Beat on high for 4-5 minutes or until stiff peaks form. Tint as desired with food coloring. (Keep unused icing covered at all times with a damp cloth. If necessary, beat again on high speed to restore texture.)

**4.** Frost and decorate cookies as desired. For writing, use round pastry tip #1 or #2. Let dry at room temperature for several hours or until firm. Store in an airtight container.

**Editor's Note:** *Meringue powder is available from Wilton Industries. Call 800-794-5866 or visit wilton.com.*

## Triple-Ginger Gingersnaps

Gingersnaps are especially popular during the holiday season, and mine have three times the spicy delight.

**—JESSICA FOLLEN**
WAUNAKEE, WISCONSIN

**PREP:** 35 MIN. + CHILLING
**BAKE:** 10 MIN./BATCH **MAKES:** 4 DOZEN

- **⅔ cup butter, softened**
- **1 cup packed brown sugar**
- **¼ cup molasses**
- **1 egg**
- **2 teaspoons minced fresh gingerroot**
- **1 cup all-purpose flour**
- **¾ cup whole wheat flour**
- **3 teaspoons ground ginger**
- **1½ teaspoons baking soda**
- **½ teaspoon fine sea salt or kosher salt**
- **½ teaspoon ground nutmeg**
- **¼ teaspoon ground cloves**
- **3 tablespoons crystallized ginger, finely chopped**
- **¼ cup sugar**
- **1½ teaspoons ground cinnamon**

**1.** In a large bowl, cream butter and brown sugar until light and fluffy. Beat in the molasses, egg and fresh ginger.

**2.** Combine the flours, ground ginger, baking soda, salt, nutmeg and cloves; gradually add to creamed mixture and mix well. Stir in crystallized ginger. Cover and refrigerate for 1 hour or until easy to handle.

**3.** In a small bowl, combine sugar and cinnamon. Shape dough into 1-in. balls; roll in sugar mixture. Place 3 in. apart on parchment paper-lined baking sheets. Bake at 350° for 10-12 minutes or until set. Cool for 2 minutes before removing from pans to wire racks. Store in an airtight container.

## Black-Eyed Susan Cookies

Black-eyed Susans attract butterflies when planted in masses—and you'll draw a crowd when you serve these pretty-as-can-be "conversation" cookies. They may take a little extra time to prepare, but their sunny faces and gumdrop centers are worth it!

**—GRACE PACK**
BEAVER, WEST VIRGINIA

**PREP:** 25 MIN. + CHILLING
**BAKE:** 10 MIN./BATCH + COOLING
**MAKES:** 21 COOKIES

- **1 cup butter, softened**
- **1¼ cups sugar**
- **2 eggs**
- **1 teaspoon orange extract**
- **2½ cups all-purpose flour**
- **1 teaspoon baking powder**
- **½ teaspoon salt**

**GLAZE**

- **2 cups confectioners' sugar**
- **¼ cup milk**
- **½ teaspoon orange extract**
- **2 to 3 drops yellow food coloring, optional**
- **Additional confectioners' sugar**
- **Black gumdrops**

Black-Eyed Susan Cookies

1. In a large bowl, cream butter and sugar until light and fluffy. Beat in eggs and extract. Combine the flour, baking powder and salt; gradually add to creamed mixture. Divide dough in half so that one portion is slightly larger than the other; shape each into a disk. Wrap in plastic wrap; refrigerate for 1-2 hours or until easy to handle.
2. On a lightly floured surface, roll larger portion of dough to ⅛-in. thickness. Cut with a floured 3-in. round or scalloped cookie cutter to make flower bottoms. Place 1 in. apart on greased baking sheets. Repeat with remaining dough using a floured 2¾-in. flower or scalloped cookie cutter to make an equal number of flower tops.
3. Bake the larger cookies at 350° for 8-10 minutes or until golden brown; bake the smaller cookies for 5-7 minutes or until golden brown. Remove to wire racks to cool completely.
4. In a small bowl, combine the confectioners' sugar, milk, orange extract and, if desired, yellow food coloring; mix until smooth. Immediately spread over the cooled cookies. Stir additional confectioners' sugar into the remaining glaze to thicken; spread a small amount on bottom of smaller cookies; place over larger cookies. Top with gumdrops.

## Coconut Kisses

Add a light touch to your cookie tray with coconut meringues. Crisp on the outside and chewy on the inside, they go over well year-round.

**—DOROTHY BEAUDRY**
ALBERTVILLE, MINNESOTA

**PREP:** 15 MIN. **BAKE:** 20 MIN./BATCH
**MAKES:** 1 DOZEN

- **1 egg white**
- **½ cup confectioners' sugar**
- **1 cup flaked coconut**

In a bowl, beat egg white on medium speed until stiff peaks form. Gradually add sugar; beat 8 minutes longer. Fold in coconut. Drop by rounded tablespoonfuls 2-in. apart onto a parchment-lined baking sheet. Bake at 325° for 18-20 minutes or until firm to the touch. Cool for 1 minute before removing to a wire rack. Store in an airtight container.

## MAKE AHEAD Chocolate-Nut Pinwheel Cookies

As a young girl, I made these chocolaty pinwheels with my mother every year at Christmastime. Now I enjoy making these treats with my daughters-in-law, daughters and grandchildren.

**—SEDONIE ZEITLER**
LUXEMBURG, WISCONSIN

**PREP:** 1 HOUR + CHILLING
**BAKE:** 10 MIN./BATCH
**MAKES:** ABOUT 5 DOZEN

- **⅔ cup butter, softened**
- **¾ cup sugar**
- **1 egg**
- **1 teaspoon vanilla extract**
- **1¾ cups all-purpose flour**
- **½ teaspoon baking powder**
- **¼ teaspoon salt**
- **⅓ cup ground almonds**
- **¼ teaspoon almond extract**
- **¼ cup baking cocoa**

1. In a large bowl, cream butter and sugar until light and fluffy. Beat in egg and vanilla. Combine the flour, baking powder and salt; gradually add to creamed mixture and mix well. Divide dough in half; add almonds and almond extract to one portion. Add cocoa to the remaining portion.
2. Roll out each portion between two sheets of waxed paper into a 16-in. x 8-in. rectangle. Refrigerate for 30 minutes. Remove waxed paper. Place almond layer over chocolate dough. Roll up tightly jelly-roll style, starting with a long side; wrap in plastic wrap. Refrigerate overnight or until firm.
3. Unwrap and cut into ¼-in. slices. Place 2 in. apart on ungreased baking sheets. Bake at 350° for 9-11 minutes or until set. Remove to wire racks to cool.

Chocolate-Nut Pinwheel Cookies

## Giant Molasses Cookies

My family often asks for a batch of these soft, deliciously chewy molasses cookies. Their extra-large size never fails to make eyes light up.
**—KRISTINE CHAYES**
SMITHTOWN, NEW YORK

**PREP:** 30 MIN. **BAKE:** 15 MIN./BATCH
**MAKES:** 2 DOZEN

- **1½ cups butter, softened**
- **2 cups sugar**
- **2 eggs**
- **½ cup molasses**
- **4½ cups all-purpose flour**
- **4 teaspoons ground ginger**
- **2 teaspoons baking soda**
- **1½ teaspoons ground cinnamon**
- **1 teaspoon ground cloves**
- **¼ teaspoon salt**
- **¼ cup chopped pecans**
- **¾ cup coarse sugar**

1. In a large bowl, cream butter and sugar until light and fluffy. Beat in the eggs and molasses. Combine the flour, ginger, baking soda, cinnamon, cloves and salt; gradually add to creamed mixture and mix well. Fold in pecans.
2. Shape into 2-in. balls and roll in coarse sugar. Place 2½-in. apart on ungreased baking sheets. Bake at 350° for 13-15 minutes or until tops are cracked. Remove to wire racks to cool.

## Lemon Bars

Full of tongue-tingling appeal, lemon bars are always a popular alternative to chocolate-laden desserts. This is a recipe I rely on time and again.
**—ETTA SOUCY** MESA, ARIZONA

**PREP:** 10 MIN. **BAKE:** 45 MIN. + COOLING
**MAKES:** 9 SERVINGS

- **1 cup all-purpose flour**
- **½ cup butter, softened**
- **¼ cup confectioners' sugar**

**FILLING**

- **2 eggs**
- **1 cup sugar**
- **2 tablespoons all-purpose flour**
- **½ teaspoon baking powder**
- **2 tablespoons lemon juice**
- **1 teaspoon grated lemon peel**
- **Additional confectioners' sugar**

1. In a bowl, combine the flour, butter and confectioners' sugar. Pat into an ungreased 8-in. square baking pan. Bake at 350° for 20 minutes.
2. For filling, in a small bowl, beat eggs. Add the sugar, flour, baking powder, lemon juice and peel; beat until frothy. Pour over the crust. Bake 25 minutes longer or until light golden brown. Cool on a wire rack. Dust with confectioners' sugar. Cut into bars.

Giant Molasses Cookies

## Cherry Walnut Squares

I call these my "naughty-but-nice" bars. Packed with dried cherries, white chocolate chips and chopped walnuts, they're indulgent and oh-so-good.
**—LISA SPEER** PALM BEACH, FLORIDA

**PREP:** 25 MIN.
**BAKE:** 25 MIN. + COOLING
**MAKES:** 6½ DOZEN

- **¾ cup butter, softened**
- **⅓ cup packed brown sugar**
- **2 tablespoons plus 1½ teaspoons sugar**
- **⅛ teaspoon almond extract**
- **2 cups all-purpose flour**
- **⅛ teaspoon salt**

**FILLING**

- **1 cup plus 2 tablespoons packed brown sugar**
- **¾ cup butter, cubed**
- **¼ cup light corn syrup**
- **2 tablespoons heavy whipping cream**
- **¼ teaspoon salt**
- **2¾ cups chopped walnuts, divided**
- **1 cup dried cherries, chopped**
- **2½ teaspoons vanilla extract**
- **¾ cup white baking chips**

1. In a large bowl, cream the butter, sugars and extract until light and fluffy. Combine the flour and salt; gradually add to creamed mixture and mix well. Press onto the bottom of an ungreased 13-in. x 9-in. baking pan. Bake at 375° for 8-10 minutes or until the edges begin to brown.
2. Meanwhile, in a large saucepan, combine the brown sugar, butter, corn syrup, cream and salt. Bring to boil over medium heat, stirring constantly. Reduce the heat; cook and stir for 4 minutes or until slightly thickened.
3. Remove from the heat. Stir in 2½ cups walnuts, cherries and vanilla; spread over crust. Bake for 15-20 minutes or until bubbly. Sprinkle with baking chips and remaining walnuts; lightly press into filling. Cool on a wire rack. Cut into bars.

*MAKE AHEAD*

## Cappuccino Brownies

There's something magical in coffee that really enhances chocolate. My java-flavored brownies freeze well, but somehow, most of them disappear before they ever reach the freezer!
**—SUSIE JONES** BUHL, IDAHO

**PREP:** 30 MIN. + CHILLING
**BAKE:** 25 MIN. + COOLING
**MAKES:** 2 DOZEN

- **8 ounces bittersweet chocolate, chopped**
- **¾ cup butter, cut up**
- **2 tablespoons instant coffee granules**
- **1 tablespoon hot water**
- **4 eggs**
- **1½ cups sugar**
- **2 teaspoons vanilla extract**
- **1 cup all-purpose flour**
- **½ teaspoon salt**
- **1 cup chopped walnuts**

**TOPPING**

- **1 package (8 ounces) cream cheese, softened**
- **6 tablespoons butter, softened**
- **1½ cups confectioners' sugar**
- **1 teaspoon ground cinnamon**
- **1 teaspoon vanilla extract**

**GLAZE**

- **4 teaspoons instant coffee granules**
- **1 tablespoon hot water**
- **5 ounces bittersweet chocolate, chopped**
- **2 tablespoons butter**
- **½ cup heavy whipping cream**

1. In a microwave, melt chocolate and butter; stir until smooth. Cool slightly. Dissolve coffee granules in hot water. In a large bowl, beat the eggs and sugar. Stir in vanilla, chocolate mixture and coffee mixture. Combine flour and salt; gradually add to chocolate mixture until blended. Fold in walnuts.
2. Transfer to a greased and floured 13-in. x 9-in. baking pan. Bake at 350° for 25-30 minutes or until a toothpick inserted near the center comes out clean. Cool completely on a wire rack.
3. For the topping, in a large bowl, beat cream cheese and butter until blended. Add confectioners' sugar, cinnamon and vanilla; beat on low speed until combined. Spread over bars. Refrigerate until firm, about 1 hour.
4. For the glaze, dissolve the coffee granules in hot water. In a microwave, melt the chocolate and butter; cool slightly. Stir in the heavy whipping cream and coffee mixture. Spread over cream cheese layer. Let stand until set.
5. Cover and freeze brownies for up to 1 month.
6. **TO USE FROZEN BROWNIES:** Thaw at room temperature. Cut into bars. Refrigerate leftovers.

Cherry Walnut Squares

Cappuccino Brownies

## Trio of Chocolate Truffles

Short on time during the holiday season? Here are three recipes in one. The truffles are smooth, rich and luscious.
**—LURAINE MACLEOD** FEDERAL WAY, WASHINGTON

**PREP:** 45 MIN. + CHILLING **MAKES:** ABOUT 3 DOZEN

- **12 ounces bittersweet chocolate, chopped**
- **⅓ cup butter, cubed**
- **4 egg yolks, beaten**
- **1 tablespoon rum**
- **1½ teaspoons instant coffee granules**
- **⅓ cup raisins**
- **1 tablespoon Cognac or brandy**
- **4½ teaspoons orange liqueur**
- **1½ teaspoons grated orange peel**

**COATINGS**

- **1 tablespoon baking cocoa**
- **3 tablespoons grated chocolate**
- **3 ounces bittersweet chocolate, chopped**
- **2 teaspoons shortening**

1. In a double boiler or metal bowl over simmering water, heat chocolate and butter until melted, stirring frequently. Whisk a small amount of mixture into yolks. Return all to pan, whisking constantly. Cook and stir until mixture is thickened and coats the back of a spoon.
2. Remove from the heat; divide mixture among three small bowls. Into one bowl, stir rum and coffee granules until smooth. Stir raisins and Cognac into another; stir orange liqueur and peel into the third bowl.
3. Cool to room temperature, stirring occasionally. Refrigerate for 1 hour or until easy to handle. Shape into 1-in. balls.
4. Roll the coffee-flavored truffles in cocoa; roll the raisin-flavored truffles in grated chocolate.
5. In a microwave, melt bittersweet chocolate and shortening; stir until smooth. Dip orange-flavored truffles in melted chocolate; allow excess to drip off. Place on waxed paper-lined baking sheets.
6. Refrigerate truffles for 2 hours or until firm. Store in an airtight container in the refrigerator.

Trio of Chocolate Truffles

Easy Lemon Curd Bars

## Easy Lemon Curd Bars

A cup of tea looks lonely without something yummy beside it. These tangy bars are a wonderful accompaniment. I love the combination of the almond crust and tart lemon curd.
**—DONNA HARDIN** NEW VIRGINIA, IOWA

**PREP:** 30 MIN. **BAKE:** 20 MIN. + COOLING **MAKES:** 2 DOZEN

- **1 cup butter, softened**
- **1 cup sugar**
- **2 cups all-purpose flour**
- **½ teaspoon baking soda**
- **1 jar (10 ounces) lemon curd**
- **⅔ cup flaked coconut**
- **½ cup chopped almonds, toasted**

1. In a large bowl, cream butter and sugar until light and fluffy. Combine flour and baking soda; gradually add to creamed mixture and mix well.
2. Set aside 1 cup mixture for topping; press remaining mixture onto the bottom of a greased 13-in. x 9-in. baking dish. Bake at 350° for 12-15 minutes or until edges are lightly browned. Cool for 10 minutes.
3. Spread lemon curd over the crust. In a small bowl, combine the coconut, almonds and reserved topping mixture; sprinkle over lemon curd.
4. Bake for 18-22 minutes or until golden brown. Cool completely on a wire rack. Cut into bars.

## Saltine Toffee Bark

Get ready for a new family favorite! I think this sweet-salty bark is similar to brittle, but even better. For a special treat to give friends and neighbors at Christmastime, pack the pieces in embellished cardboard gift tubes or recycled oatmeal containers wrapped with decorative paper.
**—LAURA COX** BREWSTER, MASSACHUSETTS

**PREP:** 15 MIN. **BAKE:** 10 MIN. + CHILLING **MAKES:** 2 POUNDS

- **40 saltines**
- **1 cup butter, cubed**
- **¾ cup sugar**
- **2 cups (12 ounces) semisweet chocolate chips**
- **1 package (8 ounces) milk chocolate English toffee bits**

1. Line a 15-in. x 10-in. x 1-in. baking pan with heavy-duty foil. Arrange the saltines in a single layer on the foil; set aside.
2. In a heavy saucepan over medium heat, melt butter. Stir in the sugar. Bring to a boil; cook and stir for 1-2 minutes or until the sugar is dissolved. Pour evenly over the saltines.
3. Bake at 350° for 8-10 minutes or until bubbly. Immediately sprinkle with the semisweet chocolate chips. Allow the chocolate chips to soften for a few minutes, then spread over the top. Sprinkle with the toffee bits. Cool.
4. Cover and refrigerate for 1 hour or until set. Break into pieces. Store in an airtight container.

## Cognac Date Squares

If you're tired of the same old pan of bars, try these. Apple cider, Cognac and chopped pistachios add new flavors—and a little sophistication—to each golden-brown square.
**—LISA SPEER** PALM BEACH, FLORIDA

**PREP:** 30 MIN. **BAKE:** 25 MIN. + COOLING **MAKES:** 16 SERVINGS

- **1 pound chopped dates**
- **¾ cup apple cider or juice**
- **¼ cup Cognac or brandy**
- **1 teaspoon fine sea salt or kosher salt, divided**
- **2 teaspoons vanilla extract**
- **1½ cups all-purpose flour**
- **1 cup old-fashioned oats**
- **1 cup packed light brown sugar**
- **1 teaspoon ground cinnamon**
- **¾ teaspoon baking soda**
- **¾ cup butter, melted**
- **½ cup finely chopped pistachios**

1. In a large saucepan, combine the dates, apple cider, Cognac and 1/2 teaspoon salt. Bring to a boil. Reduce the heat; simmer, uncovered, for 8-10 minutes or until the liquid is almost evaporated, stirring occasionally. Remove from the heat; stir in the vanilla. Cool to room temperature.

White Chocolate Cran-Pecan Cookies

2. In a small bowl, combine flour, oats, brown sugar, cinnamon, baking soda and remaining salt. Add butter; mix well. Press 1 1/3 cups into a greased 9-in. square baking pan. Add the pistachios to the remaining oat mixture; set aside.
3. Spread the date mixture over the crust; top with the reserved pistachio mixture. Bake at 350° for 24-28 minutes or until golden brown. Cool on a wire rack. Cut into squares.

## White Chocolate Cran-Pecan Cookies

Sometimes I put orange zest in my white chocolate-pecan cookies. It really complements the cranberries.
**—BARB GARRETT** JACKSONVILLE, NORTH CAROLINA

**PREP:** 15 MIN. **BAKE:** 10 MIN./BATCH
**MAKES:** ABOUT 2½ DOZEN

- **½ cup butter, softened**
- **½ cup sugar**
- **½ cup packed brown sugar**
- **1 egg**
- **1½ teaspoons vanilla extract**
- **1½ cups all-purpose flour**
- **½ teaspoon baking soda**
- **1 cup dried cranberries**
- **¾ cup white baking chips**
- **½ cup chopped pecans**

1. In a large bowl, cream butter and sugars until light and fluffy. Beat in egg and vanilla. Combine flour and baking soda; gradually add to creamed mixture and mix well. Fold in cranberries, baking chips and pecans.
2. Drop by tablespoonfuls 2 in. apart onto ungreased baking sheets. Bake at 375° for 8-10 minutes or until lightly browned. Remove to wire racks.

# Cakes & Pies

For a little **slice of heaven**, just turn to this sweet-as-can-be chapter. It features a delightful variety of **decadent desserts** guaranteed to make any dinner one to remember.

"The homemade truffles—a little bit sweet and a little bit salty—will keep you coming back for another piece of this creamy, chocolaty dessert. You'll want to savor every indulgent bite."

—**BILLIE ISAACS** MIAMISBURG, OHIO

## Praline Ice Cream Cake

Melted vanilla ice cream is one of the key ingredients in the batter for this delectable golden cake. It's been a family favorite for years because we love the pecan praline flavor. Top off big pieces with whipped cream.

—**JOAN HALLFORD**
NORTH RICHLAND HILLS, TEXAS

**PREP:** 20 MIN.
**BAKE:** 25 MIN. + COOLING
**MAKES:** 15 SERVINGS

- **1 cup packed brown sugar**
- **½ cup sour cream**
- **2 tablespoons plus ½ cup butter, divided**
- **2 teaspoons cornstarch**
- **1 teaspoon vanilla extract, divided**
- **2 cups vanilla ice cream, softened**
- **2 eggs**
- **1½ cups all-purpose flour**
- **1 cup graham cracker crumbs**
- **⅔ cup sugar**
- **2½ teaspoons baking powder**
- **½ teaspoon salt**
- **½ cup chopped pecans, toasted**
- **Whipped cream, optional**

**1.** In a heavy saucepan, combine the brown sugar, sour cream, 2 tablespoons butter and cornstarch; bring to a boil over medium heat, stirring constantly. Remove from heat; stir in ½ teaspoon vanilla.

**2.** Melt the remaining butter; place in a large bowl. Add ice cream; stir to blend. Add eggs, one at a time, beating well after each addition; stir in the remaining vanilla. In another bowl, mix flour, graham cracker crumbs, sugar, baking powder and salt; gradually stir into the ice cream mixture.

**3.** Pour batter into a greased 13-in. x 9-in. baking pan. Drizzle with half of the sauce. Bake at 350° for 25-30 minutes or until a toothpick inserted in center comes out clean. Cool slightly in pan on a wire rack.

**4.** Add pecans to remaining sauce; spoon over warm cake (sauce will not cover cake completely). Cool cake in pan. Serve with whipped cream if desired.

Praline Ice Cream Cake

## Dulce de Leche Banana Cream Pie

Here's a sweet celebration of South America. Don't have a lot of time for baking? Use a store-bought crust and a dulce de leche product instead of making them from scratch.

—**LEISA MILLER**
SHELLBROOK, SASKATCHEWAN

**PREP:** 1¾ HOURS + CHILLING
**BAKE:** 15 MIN. + COOLING
**MAKES:** 8 SERVINGS

- **1 can (14 ounces) sweetened condensed milk**
- **1⅓ cups all-purpose flour**
- **½ teaspoon salt**
- **½ cup cold lard**
- **3 to 4 tablespoons cold water**

**FILLING**

- **½ cup sugar**
- **⅓ cup all-purpose flour**
- **¼ teaspoon salt**
- **1 cup whole milk**
- **⅓ cup half-and-half cream**
- **3 egg yolks**
- **¼ teaspoon vanilla extract**
- **2 medium bananas, sliced**
- **2 cups heavy whipping cream, whipped**

**1.** For dulce de leche, pour the sweetened condensed milk into a 9-in. deep-dish pie plate; cover with foil. Place pie plate in a large shallow pan; add 1 in. of hot water to larger pan. Bake at 425° for 1½ hours or until caramel-colored. Whisk dulce de leche to blend; transfer to a bowl. Cool for 1 hour; cover and refrigerate until chilled.

**2.** In a small bowl, mix the flour and salt; cut in the lard until crumbly. Gradually add the water, tossing with a fork until dough holds together when pressed. Form dough into a disk; wrap in plastic wrap. Refrigerate for 1 hour or until easy to handle.

**3.** For the filling, in a small heavy saucepan, combine the sugar, flour and salt. Whisk in the milk and half-and-half cream until smooth. Cook and stir over medium heat until thickened and bubbly; cook 2 minutes longer. Remove from the heat. In a small bowl, whisk a small amount of the hot mixture into the egg yolks; return all to pan, whisking constantly. Bring to a gentle boil; cook and stir 2 minutes.

**4.** Immediately transfer to a clean bowl; stir in the vanilla. Cool for 30 minutes. Press waxed paper onto surface of filling; refrigerate until chilled.

**5.** Roll out the dough on lightly floured surface to ⅛-in.-thick circle. Transfer to a 9-in. pie plate, trimming to ½ in. beyond edge of plate; flute edges. Line unpricked pastry with a double thickness of heavy-duty foil. Fill with uncooked rice, dried beans or pie weights.

**6.** Bake at 450° for 12-15 minutes or until lightly browned. Remove foil and weights; bake 3-5 minutes longer or until the crust is golden brown. Cool on a wire rack.

**7.** To serve, spoon dulce de leche into crust. Layer with bananas and filling; top with whipped cream.

**Editor's Note:** *Let pie weights cool before storing. Beans and rice may be reused for pie weights, but not for cooking.*

### Did you know?

Translated literally from Spanish, dulce de leche means "sweet of milk" or "candy from milk." It's a thick, milk-based caramel sauce that originated in South America and is still popular there.

## Real Deal Apple Pie

**PREP:** 35 MIN.
**BAKE:** 1¼ HOURS + COOLING
**MAKES:** 8 SERVINGS

- **2¼ cups all-purpose flour**
- **2 teaspoons sugar**
- **¾ teaspoon kosher salt**
- **1 cup cold unsalted butter, cubed**
- **6 to 8 tablespoons ice water**

**FILLING**

- **5 medium Braeburn apples (about 1½ pounds), peeled and cut into ¼-in. slices**
- **4 medium Granny Smith apples (about 1½ pounds), peeled and cut into ¼-in. slices**
- **½ cup sugar**
- **3 tablespoons lemon juice**
- **2 tablespoons all-purpose flour**
- **½ teaspoon kosher salt**
- **¾ teaspoon ground cinnamon**
- **Dash ground nutmeg**
- **3 tablespoons unsalted butter, cut into pieces**
- **1 egg, lightly beaten**
- **1 to 2 tablespoons superfine sugar**

**1.** In a large bowl, mix the flour, sugar and salt; cut in butter until crumbly. Gradually add the ice water, tossing with a fork until the dough holds together when pressed. Divide the dough into two portions so that one is slightly larger than the other; wrap each in plastic wrap. Refrigerate for 1 hour or until easy to handle.
**2.** In a large bowl, combine apples, sugar, lemon juice, flour, salt, cinnamon and nutmeg.
**3.** On a lightly floured surface, roll out the larger portion of dough to a ⅛-in.-thick circle. Transfer to a 9-in. pie plate, trimming even with edge. Fill with apple mixture, mounding in the center. Dot apples with butter. Lightly brush rim of pastry with some of the beaten egg.
**4.** Roll out the remaining dough to fit top of pie; place over filling. Trim, seal and flute the edges. Cut slits in pastry. Brush the top with egg; sprinkle with superfine sugar. Place on a foil-lined 15-in. x 10-in. x 1-in. baking pan.
**5.** Bake at 425° for 20 minutes. Reduce heat to 375°. Bake 50-60 minutes longer or until crust is golden brown and filling is bubbly. Cool on a wire rack for 2 hours before serving.

**Real Deal Apple Pie**

Everyone should know how to prepare apple pie in the classic style. Real Deal Apple Pie is the perfect example of why this traditional dessert has been a hit for hundreds of years. My recipe gets its impressive height from 3 pounds of apples, so stock up—you'll need them!
**—MARGO FERRICK** WESTFORD, MASSACHUSETTS

## Grasshopper Pie

My family looks forward to this fluffy dessert every year at Christmastime. No one can resist the combination of refreshing mint and rich chocolate. Plus, the pretty pastel green color is festive for the holiday season.
**—LINDSEY DORN**
NEW GLARUS, WISCONSIN

**PREP:** 30 MIN. + CHILLING
**MAKES:** 8 SERVINGS

- **1½ cups plus 1 tablespoon chocolate wafer crumbs, divided**
- **5 tablespoons butter, melted**
- **24 large marshmallows**
- **⅔ cup plus 1 cup heavy whipping cream, divided**
- **2 tablespoons clear creme de cacao**
- **2 tablespoons green creme de menthe**

**1.** Combine 1½ cups chocolate wafer crumbs and butter. Press into an ungreased 9-in. pie plate. Bake at 350° for 5-7 minutes or until set. Cool on a wire rack.
**2.** In a large heavy saucepan, combine marshmallows and ⅔ cup whipping cream; cook and stir over low heat until marshmallows are melted. Remove from the heat. Stir in creme de cacao and creme de menthe. Transfer to a small bowl; refrigerate for 1 hour or until slightly thickened.
**3.** In a large bowl, beat remaining whipping cream until stiff peaks form; fold into the marshmallow mixture. Pour into crust. Sprinkle with the remaining wafer crumbs. Refrigerate for several hours or overnight.

## Orange-Cranberry Pound Cake with Vanilla Glaze

This buttery delight combines the tangy flavors of orange and cranberry, then finishes off with a sweet glaze.

**—ANGELA SPENGLER**
CLOVIS, NEW MEXICO

**PREP:** 25 MIN. **BAKE:** 50 MIN. + COOLING
**MAKES:** 12 SERVINGS

- **1¼ cups butter, softened**
- **2¾ cups sugar**
- **5 eggs**
- **1 tablespoon grated orange peel**
- **1 teaspoon orange extract**
- **3 cups all-purpose flour**
- **1 teaspoon baking powder**
- **¼ teaspoon salt**
- **1 cup 2% milk**
- **½ cup fresh or frozen cranberries, halved**
- **½ cup chopped walnuts**

**GLAZE**

- **2 cups confectioners' sugar**
- **⅓ cup butter, melted**
- **2 teaspoons vanilla extract**
- **2 to 3 tablespoons hot water**

**1.** In a large bowl, cream butter and sugar until light and fluffy, about 5 minutes. Add eggs, one at a time, beating well after each addition. Beat in the orange peel and extract. Combine the flour, baking powder and salt; add to the creamed mixture alternately with milk. Beat just until combined. Fold in cranberries and walnuts.

**2.** Transfer to a greased and floured 10-in. fluted tube pan. Bake at 350° for 50-60 minutes or until a toothpick inserted near the center comes out clean. Cool for 10 minutes before removing from pan to a wire rack to cool completely.

**3.** For the glaze, in a small bowl, combine the confectioners' sugar, butter, vanilla and enough water to achieve the desired consistency. Drizzle over cake.

**ORANGE-CRANBERRY MINI POUND CAKES WITH VANILLA GLAZE**
Make the batter as directed; fill 16 greased and floured 4-in. fluted tube pans. Bake at 350° for 17-20 minutes or until a toothpick comes out clean.

Orange-Cranberry Pound Cake with Vanilla Glaze

## Greek Spice Cake

My dad and husband always request this spice cake as their birthday cake. The recipe has been in our family for as long as I can remember.

**—HEATHER ABEL** HALE CENTER, TEXAS

**PREP:** 25 MIN. **BAKE:** 50 MIN. + COOLING
**MAKES:** 12 SERVINGS

- **1 tablespoon shortening**
- **2 tablespoons plus 2½ cups all-purpose flour, divided**
- **1 cup sugar**
- **1 cup packed brown sugar**
- **1 cup canola oil**
- **1 cup buttermilk**
- **3 eggs**
- **1 tablespoon vanilla extract**
- **1½ teaspoons almond extract**
- **1½ teaspoons baking powder**
- **1 teaspoon salt**
- **1 teaspoon ground cinnamon**
- **½ teaspoon ground cloves**
- **½ teaspoon baking soda**
- **1 cup chopped pecans**
- **1 teaspoon confectioners' sugar**

**1.** Grease 10-in. fluted tube pan with shortening; lightly coat with 2 tablespoons flour. Set aside.

**2.** In a large bowl, beat the sugars, oil, buttermilk, eggs and extracts until well blended. Combine the remaining flour, baking powder, salt, cinnamon, cloves and baking soda; gradually beat into sugar mixture until blended. Stir in nuts.

**3.** Transfer to prepared pan. Bake at 325° for 50-60 minutes or until a toothpick inserted near the center comes out clean.

**4.** Cool cake for 10 minutes before removing from pan to wire rack to cool completely. Dust with confectioners' sugar.

## Honey & Spice Snack Cake

For happy snacking, the pros in the Taste of Home Test Kitchen blended honey, nutmeg, cloves and walnuts. If you like, add a chocolate ganache, too.

**PREP:** 15 MIN. **BAKE:** 15 MIN. + COOLING
**MAKES:** 12 SERVINGS

- **2 cups all-purpose flour**
- **Sugar substitute equivalent to ¾ cup sugar**
- **2½ teaspoons baking powder**
- **1½ teaspoons ground cinnamon**
- **½ teaspoon baking soda**
- **¼ teaspoon ground nutmeg**
- **¼ teaspoon ground cloves**
- **⅛ teaspoon salt**
- **¾ cup unsweetened applesauce**
- **2 eggs**
- **¼ cup canola oil**
- **¼ cup honey**
- **¼ cup finely chopped walnuts, toasted**

**OPTIONAL GANACHE**

- **¼ cup dark chocolate chips**
- **3 tablespoons heavy whipping cream**

**1.** In a large bowl, combine the first eight ingredients. Whisk the applesauce, eggs, oil and honey. Stir into the dry ingredients just until moistened. Fold in walnuts.
**2.** Pour into a 9-in. square baking pan coated with cooking spray. Bake at 350° for 15-20 minutes or until a toothpick inserted near the center comes out clean. Cool completely on a wire rack.
**3.** For the optional ganache, place the dark chocolate chips in a small bowl. In a microwave, heat the heavy whipping cream for 20-30 seconds or just until bubbly. Pour over the chocolate chips; whisk until smooth. Cool slightly; drizzle over the cake.
**Editor's Note:** *This recipe was tested with Splenda no-calorie sweetener.*

## Fresh Berry Shortcakes

I think fresh strawberries should have a place of honor on the plate because they're such a special seasonal treat. Show off the bounty of berries during late spring and early summer with the perfect foundation—golden, citrusy shortcakes sprinkled with a little bit of coarse sugar. Don't forget the dollop of whipped cream on top!

**—JENNIFER MASTNICK-COOK**
HARTVILLE, OHIO

**PREP:** 35 MIN. **BAKE:** 20 MIN.
**MAKES:** 10 SERVINGS

- **5 cups sliced fresh strawberries**
- **½ cup sugar**
- **¼ cup orange juice**

**SHORTCAKES**

- **3 cups all-purpose flour**
- **½ cup sugar**
- **1 tablespoon baking powder**
- **1 tablespoon grated orange peel**
- **½ teaspoon salt**
- **½ cup cold butter, cubed**
- **1½ cups plus 1 tablespoon heavy whipping cream, divided**
- **1 egg**
- **1 egg yolk**
- **1 teaspoon vanilla extract**
- **Coarse sugar, optional**

**WHIPPED CREAM**

- **2 cups heavy whipping cream**
- **¼ cup confectioners' sugar**
- **½ teaspoon vanilla extract**

**1.** In a small bowl, combine the strawberries, sugar and orange juice; set aside.
**2.** For shortcakes, combine flour, ½ cup sugar, baking powder, peel and salt; cut in butter until mixture resembles coarse crumbs. Whisk 1½ cups cream, egg, egg yolk and vanilla; add to flour mixture, stirring just until moistened. Turn onto a lightly floured surface; gently knead 8-10 times.
**3.** Pat or roll out to 1-in. thickness; cut with a floured 3-in. scalloped or round biscuit cutter. Place 2 in. apart on a parchment paper-lined baking sheet. Brush tops with 1 tablespoon cream; sprinkle with coarse sugar if desired. Bake at 400° for 15-18 minutes or until golden brown. Cool on a wire rack for 5 minutes.
**4.** For whipped cream, beat cream in a large bowl until it begins to thicken. Add confectioners' sugar and vanilla; beat until soft peaks form.
**5.** Just before serving, cut cakes in half horizontally. Place bottoms on dessert plates; top with strawberry mixture. Replace tops; dollop with whipped cream.

FAST FIX

## Molten Peppermint-Chocolate Cakes

With a warm chocolate sauce inside, these decadent desserts are so good on a chilly fall or winter night.

**—GENISE KRAUSE**
STURGEON BAY, WISCONSIN

**PREP/TOTAL TIME:** 25 MIN.
**MAKES:** 4 SERVINGS

- **½ cup butter, cubed**
- **4 ounces bittersweet chocolate, chopped**
- **2 eggs**
- **2 egg yolks**
- **⅓ cup sugar**
- **½ teaspoon peppermint extract**
- **¼ cup all-purpose flour**
- **⅛ teaspoon salt**
- **Confectioners' sugar**

**1.** In a small saucepan, melt butter and chocolate; transfer to a large bowl. Add the eggs, egg yolks and sugar; mix well. Stir in the extract. Add the flour and salt; stir until blended. Pour into four greased 6-oz. custard cups or ramekins.
**2.** Place the cups on a baking sheet. Bake at 425° for 10-12 minutes or until a thermometer inserted near the center reads 160° and the cake sides are set. Remove from oven and let stand for 1 minute. Run a knife around edge of cups; invert onto individual dessert plates. Garnish with confectioners' sugar. Serve immediately.

Fresh Berry Shortcakes

Molten Peppermint-Chocolate Cakes

## Sweet & Salty Truffle Pie

The homemade truffles—a little bit sweet and a little bit salty—will keep you coming back for another piece of this creamy, chocolaty dessert. You'll want to savor every indulgent bite.

**—SHIRLEY WARREN**
THIENSVILLE, WISCONSIN

**PREP:** 1 HOUR 10 MIN. + CHILLING
**BAKE:** 15 MIN.
**MAKES:** 8 SERVINGS (24 TRUFFLES)

- **1½ cups all-purpose flour**
- **¾ teaspoon salt**
- **½ cup shortening**
- **3 tablespoons cold water**
- **1½ teaspoons white vinegar**

**TRUFFLES**

- **2 cups (12 ounces) dark chocolate chips, divided**
- **⅓ cup heavy whipping cream**
- **½ cup crushed pretzels**
- **1 tablespoon shortening**
- **2 teaspoons coarse sugar**
- **½ teaspoon kosher salt**

**FILLING**

- **1⅓ cups semisweet chocolate chips, divided**
- **1¼ cups heavy whipping cream, divided**
- **¼ cup sugar**
- **2 egg yolks**
- **¼ cup butter, softened**
- **2 tablespoons vanilla extract**

**TOPPINGS**

- **1 cup heavy whipping cream**
- **3 tablespoons confectioners' sugar**
- **½ teaspoon vanilla extract**
- **Broken pretzels, optional**

Sweet & Salty Truffle Pie

**1.** In a small bowl, combine flour and salt; cut in the shortening until crumbly. Combine the water and vinegar; gradually add to flour mixture, tossing with a fork until dough forms a ball. Wrap in plastic wrap. Refrigerate for 1 hour or until easy to handle.

**2.** Roll out pastry to fit a 9-in. pie plate. Transfer pastry to plate. Trim pastry to ½ in. beyond edge of plate; flute edges. Line unpricked pastry with a double thickness of heavy-duty foil. Fill with uncooked rice, dried beans or pie weights.

**3.** Bake at 450° for 8 minutes. Remove foil and weights; bake 5-7 minutes longer or until golden brown. Cool on a wire rack.

**4.** For truffles, melt 1 cup dark chips in a microwave; stir until smooth. Gradually stir in the cream until blended. Add pretzels. Cool to room temperature, stirring occasionally. Refrigerate until firm. Divide into 24 portions; shape into balls.

**5.** In a microwave, melt shortening and remaining dark chips; stir until smooth. Combine coarse sugar and kosher salt. Dip truffles in chocolate mixture; allow excess to drip off. Place on waxed paper; sprinkle with sugar mixture. Refrigerate for 1 hour or until set.

**6.** For the filling, place ⅓ cup semisweet chips in a small bowl. In a small saucepan, bring ¼ cup cream just to a boil. Pour over chocolate; whisk until smooth. Pour into crust. Refrigerate for 15 minutes or until set.

**7.** Meanwhile, in a small heavy saucepan, cook and stir sugar and the remaining semisweet chips and cream over medium heat until smooth. Whisk a small amount of hot mixture into the egg yolks. Return all to the pan, stirring constantly. Cook and stir over low heat until mixture reaches 160°.

**8.** Pour into a large bowl; stir in butter and vanilla. Place bowl in ice-water bath, stirring frequently until cooled. Remove bowl from water. Beat mixture until stiff peaks form. Spread into crust; chill completely.

**9.** For topping, in a small bowl, beat cream until it begins to thicken. Add confectioners' sugar and vanilla; beat until soft peaks form. Spoon over filling. Garnish with truffles and pretzels if desired. Serve with any remaining truffles.

## Apple Upside-Down Cake

A nutty, caramelized topping makes apple cake extra special. Surprise your family on a cool fall day or anytime.

**—LINDA WETSCH**
MANDAN, NORTH DAKOTA

**PREP:** 25 MIN. **BAKE:** 30 MIN. + COOLING
**MAKES:** 8 SERVINGS

- **⅓ cup butter, melted**
- **1 cup packed brown sugar**
- **3 medium tart apples, peeled and sliced**
- **½ cup chopped walnuts**

**CAKE**

- **3 tablespoons butter, softened**
- **¾ cup sugar**
- **2 eggs**
- **1 cup all-purpose flour**
- **¾ teaspoon baking powder**
- **½ teaspoon baking soda**
- **¼ teaspoon salt**
- **¼ teaspoon ground cinnamon**
- **½ cup buttermilk**
- **3 tablespoons sour cream**
- **1 teaspoon apple brandy or rum, optional**

**1.** Pour butter into an ungreased 9-in. round baking pan; sprinkle with ½ cup brown sugar. Arrange apples in a single layer over brown sugar; layer with walnuts and remaining brown sugar.

**2.** In a large bowl, cream butter and sugar until light and fluffy. Add eggs, one at a time, beating well after each addition. Combine the flour, baking powder, baking soda, salt and cinnamon; add to creamed mixture alternately with buttermilk and sour cream, beating well after each addition. Beat in brandy if desired.

**3.** Spoon batter over sugar layer. Bake at 350° for 30-35 minutes or until a toothpick inserted near the center comes out clean. Cool for 10 minutes before inverting onto a serving plate. Serve warm.

## Lemon Pudding Cake Cups

Here's one of my favorite treats. The easy recipe yields two individual cake cups—perfect to share with a friend.

**—KATIE ANDERSON**
SPOKANE, WASHINGTON

**PREP:** 10 MIN.
**BAKE:** 35 MIN. + COOLING
**MAKES:** 2 SERVINGS

- **⅓ cup sugar**
- **2 tablespoons all-purpose flour**
- **1½ teaspoons grated lemon peel**
- **⅛ teaspoon salt**
- **½ cup 2% milk**
- **1 egg yolk, lightly beaten**
- **2 tablespoons lemon juice**
- **1 egg white**

**1.** In a small bowl, combine the first seven ingredients. In another small bowl, beat the egg white until stiff peaks form. Gently fold into lemon mixture.
**2.** Pour into two ungreased 6-oz. ramekins or custard cups. Place in a shallow baking dish; add 1 in. of hot water to dish.
**3.** Bake, uncovered, at 350° for 35-40 minutes or until a thermometer reaches 170°. Allow to cool in water bath for 10 minutes before carefully removing cups to a wire rack. Serve warm or refrigerate.

## Sweet Potato Coconut Pie with Marshmallow Meringue

My grandmother's wonderful sweet potato casserole contains coconut and marshmallows. I thought her side dish would be even better as a pie.

**—SIMONE BAZOS**
BALTIMORE, MARYLAND

**PREP:** 1 HOUR
**BAKE:** 1¼ HOURS + CHILLING
**MAKES:** 8 SERVINGS

- **1½ cups all-purpose flour**
- **¼ teaspoon salt**
- **¼ teaspoon ground ginger**
- **6 tablespoons cold butter**
- **2 tablespoons shortening**
- **3 to 4 tablespoons cold water**

**FILLING**

- **1 cup coconut milk**
- **¾ cup packed brown sugar**

Sweet Potato Coconut Pie with Marshmallow Meringue

- **¼ cup cream cheese, softened**
- **2 cups mashed sweet potatoes**
- **3 eggs, lightly beaten**
- **2 teaspoons lemon juice**
- **1½ teaspoons vanilla extract**
- **¼ teaspoon salt**
- **¼ teaspoon ground cinnamon**

**MERINGUE**

- **4 egg whites**
- **¼ teaspoon cream of tartar**
- **½ cup sugar**
- **1 jar (7 ounces) marshmallow creme**
- **½ cup miniature marshmallows**
- **¼ cup flaked coconut**

**1.** In a food processor, combine the flour, salt and ginger; cover and pulse to blend. Add butter and shortening; cover and pulse until mixture resembles coarse crumbs.
**2.** While processing, gradually add water just until moist crumbs form. Shape into a disk; wrap in plastic wrap and refrigerate for 30 minutes or until easy to handle.
**3.** Roll out the pastry to fit a 9-in. deep-dish pie plate. Transfer the pastry to pie plate. Trim pastry to ½ in. beyond edge of plate; flute the edges or decorate with pastry cutouts as desired. Line unpricked pastry with a double thickness of heavy-duty foil. Fill with uncooked rice, dried beans or pie weights.
**4.** Bake at 425° for 8 minutes. Remove the foil and weights; bake 5 minutes longer. Cool on a wire rack. Reduce heat to 325°.
**5.** For filling, in a small saucepan, combine the coconut milk, brown sugar and cream cheese. Cook and stir until smooth. Transfer to a large bowl; cool 5 minutes. Whisk in the sweet potatoes, eggs, lemon juice, vanilla, salt and cinnamon. Pour into crust.
**6.** Bake at 325° for 50-60 minutes or until a knife inserted near the center comes out clean. Cover edges with foil during the last 15 minutes to prevent overbrowning if necessary.
**7.** For meringue, in a large bowl, beat egg whites and cream of tartar on medium speed until soft peaks form. Gradually beat in the sugar, 1 tablespoon at a time, on high until stiff glossy peaks form and sugar is dissolved.
**8.** Place the marshmallow creme in a separate large bowl; fold in a third of the egg white mixture, then fold in the remaining mixture. Spread evenly over the hot filling, sealing edges to crust. Sprinkle with marshmallows and coconut.
**9.** Bake 12-15 minutes longer or until top is golden brown. Cool on a wire rack for 1 hour. Refrigerate for at least 3 hours before serving. Store leftovers in the refrigerator.

**Editor's Note:** *Let pie weights cool before storing. Beans and rice may be reused for pie weights, but not for cooking.*

# LAYERED WITH FLAVOR

What makes a chocolate cake even better? A luscious filling between the layers! These impossible-to-resist recipes give you three different ways to serve a decadent dessert.

## Heavenly Chocolate Cake

For a chocolate cake that's even more heavenly, spread on one of the yummy fillings featured on this page.

**—BILLIE ISAACS** MIAMISBURG, OHIO

**PREP:** 40 MIN. **BAKE:** 24 MIN.
**MAKES:** 12 SERVINGS

- **1 cup butter, softened**
- **2½ cups sugar**
- **5 eggs**
- **1½ teaspoons vanilla extract**
- **2¾ cups all-purpose flour**
- **1 cup baking cocoa**
- **2 teaspoons baking soda**
- **¾ teaspoon baking powder**
- **1 teaspoon salt**
- **1½ cups water**

**1.** In a large bowl, cream butter and sugar until light and fluffy. Add eggs, one at a time, beating well after each addition. Beat in vanilla. Combine the flour, cocoa, baking soda, baking powder and salt; add to the creamed mixture alternately with water, beating well after each addition.

**2.** Pour into three greased and floured 9-in. round baking pans. Bake at 350° for 24 to 28 minutes or until a toothpick inserted near the center comes out clean. Cool for 10 minutes; remove cakes from pans and transfer to wire racks to cool completely.

## Winter White Filling or Frosting

How versatile! Prepare this recipe for use as a filling, frosting or both.

**—SARAH THOMPSON**
GREENFIELD, WISCONSIN

**PREP:** 20 MIN. + COOLING
**MAKES:** 2 CUPS FILLING OR 6 CUPS FROSTING

**FOR USE AS A FILLING**
- **4 ounces white baking chocolate, chopped**
- **6 ounces cream cheese, softened**
- **1 tablespoon butter, softened**
- **1½ teaspoons lemon juice**

**FOR USE AS A FROSTING**
- **12 ounces white baking chocolate, chopped**
- **18 ounces cream cheese, softened**
- **3 tablespoons butter, softened**
- **4½ teaspoons lemon juice**

**1.** In a microwave, melt baking chocolate; stir until smooth. Cool to room temperature.

**2.** In a large bowl, beat the cream cheese and butter until light and fluffy. Beat in the cooled baking chocolate and lemon juice until smooth. Spread between the cake layers and/or over the top and sides of the cake.

## FAST FIX Raspberry Filling

Raspberry preserves will give your dessert a pretty touch of pastel pink color—and make every tall, layered slice absolutely irresistible.

**—LAURA MCDOWELL**
LAKE VILLA, ILLINOIS

**PREP/TOTAL TIME:** 10 MIN.
**MAKES:** 2 CUPS

- **¾ cup heavy whipping cream**
- **⅓ cup seedless raspberry preserves**
- **2¼ teaspoons sugar**
- **1½ teaspoons raspberry liqueur**

In a small bowl, beat cream until it begins to thicken. Add raspberry preserves, sugar and liqueur; beat until stiff peaks form. Spread between cake layers.

## FAST FIX Espresso Filling

Java lovers are sure to go crazy for a cake perked up with espresso powder.

**—MEGAN BYERS** WICHITA, KANSAS

**PREP/TOTAL TIME:** 15 MIN.
**MAKES:** 2¼ CUPS

- **2 tablespoons instant espresso powder**
- **1½ teaspoons hot water**
- **1½ cups mascarpone cheese**
- **¾ cup heavy whipping cream**
- **1 cup confectioners' sugar, sifted**
- **1½ teaspoons vanilla extract**

In a small bowl, mix espresso powder and hot water until smooth; cool. In a large bowl, beat the mascarpone cheese, cream, confectioners' sugar, vanilla and espresso mixture on medium speed until creamy and slightly thickened (do not overmix). Spread between cake layers.

Winter White Filling or Frosting
Raspberry Filling
Espresso Filling

## Spoon-Swirl Frosting Technique

To decorate your cake with graceful swirls of frosting, all you need is the tip of a spoon. Start by scooping a generous amount of frosting onto the back of the spoon. Place the spoon on the cake with its tip in the 12 o'clock position, then swirl the spoon in a half circle to the left, ending in the 6 o'clock position. Repeat until the cake is covered with swirls.

## Create Chocolate Ribbons

Combine 8 ounces melted white candy coating and 1 tablespoon oil. Using a small offset spatula, spread the mixture thinly in an 8-inch length on freezer paper. Dry it slightly; trim the edges to form a 1-inch-wide ribbon. Peel the ribbon from the freezer paper and fold the ribbon into a loop as shown. Repeat, making 13 loops. Secure the loops to the top of the frosted cake using a dab of frosting.

## Girolle Ruffle How-To

A special kitchen tool, a girolle allows you to create gorgeous ruffles. Mount a chocolate roll on the girolle according to the manufacturer's directions. Alternating between room temperature and the refrigerator as needed to bring the roll to the correct temperature, rotate the cutter over the roll lightly, releasing ruffles in 3- to 4-inch pieces. Refrigerate them until you are ready to decorate.

## Greek Honey Nut Pie

It's all about the walnuts in this treat dressed up with flaky, delicate phyllo dough. Look for phyllo in the frozen food section of your grocery store.

**—ROSALIND JACKSON**
STUART, FLORIDA

**PREP:** 30 MIN.
**BAKE:** 40 MIN. + COOLING
**MAKES:** 8 SERVINGS

- **4 cups chopped walnuts**
- **¼ cup packed brown sugar**
- **1 teaspoon ground cinnamon**
- **1 package (16 ounces, 14-inch x 9-inch sheet size) frozen phyllo dough, thawed**
- **1 cup butter, melted**

**SYRUP**

- **¾ cup sugar**
- **½ cup water**
- **½ cup honey**
- **1 teaspoon vanilla extract**

**1.** In a large bowl, combine nuts, brown sugar and cinnamon; set aside. Brush a 9-in. pie plate with some of the butter; set aside.
**2.** Unroll the phyllo dough; keep covered with plastic wrap and a damp towel to prevent it from drying out. Layer eight sheets of phyllo in prepared pan, brushing each layer with butter and rotating sheets to cover the pie plate. Let the edges of dough hang over sides. Sprinkle a third of the nut mixture onto the bottom.
**3.** Layer four sheets of phyllo over nut mixture in the same manner; sprinkle with a third of the nut mixture. Repeat these last two steps. Top with an additional eight sheets of phyllo, again brushing with butter and rotating sheets. Fold ends of phyllo up over top of pie; brush with butter.
**4.** Using a sharp knife, cut into eight wedges. Cut 1-2 additional sheets of phyllo into thin strips, rolling into rose shapes if desired; arrange decoratively over the top. (Save remaining phyllo for another use.) Bake at 350° for 40-45 minutes or until golden brown.
**5.** Meanwhile, in a saucepan, combine sugar, water and honey; bring to a boil. Reduce heat; simmer, uncovered, for 10 minutes. Add vanilla. Pour over warm pie. Cool on a wire rack. Refrigerate leftovers.

Greek Honey Nut Pie

## Sunny Peaches & Cream Pie

Here's a summery dessert you'll want to enjoy all year long. It's too good to reserve for just one season!

**—LORRAINE WRIGHT**
GRAND FORKS, BRITISH COLUMBIA

**PREP:** 25 MIN. **COOK:** 5 MIN. + CHILLING
**MAKES:** 8 SERVINGS

- **1¼ cups graham cracker crumbs**
- **¼ cup sugar**
- **6 tablespoons margarine, melted**

**FILLING**

- **4 ounces cream cheese, softened**
- **½ cup confectioners' sugar**
- **½ cup frozen whipped topping, thawed**

**TOPPING**

- **1 package (3 ounces) peach gelatin**
- **1 package (3 ounces) cook-and-serve vanilla pudding mix**
- **1¼ cups water**
- **2 cups sliced peeled fresh peaches or canned sliced peaches**

**1.** In a small bowl, mix cracker crumbs and sugar; stir in margarine. Press onto the bottom and up the sides of an ungreased 9-in. pie plate. Bake at 375° for 6-8 minutes or until lightly browned. Cool completely on a wire rack.
**2.** For filling, in a small bowl, mix cream cheese and confectioners' sugar until blended. Fold in the whipped topping. Carefully spread over crust; refrigerate until set.
**3.** For the topping, in a small saucepan, combine gelatin and pudding mix; stir in water. Bring just to a boil over medium-low heat, stirring constantly; remove from the heat. Cool 5 minutes.
**4.** Arrange peach slices over the filling. Spoon gelatin mixture over peaches. Refrigerate for 4 hours or until chilled.

## Mixed Nut 'n' Fig Pie

Can't decide on a favorite nut? This recipe settles the question by using mixed nuts, then makes things even more interesting with dried figs and a hint of orange marmalade.

**—BARBARA ESTABROOK**
RHINELANDER, WISCONSIN

**PREP:** 30 MIN. **BAKE:** 1 HOUR + COOLING
**MAKES:** 8 SERVINGS

- **Pastry for single-crust pie (9 inches)**
- **½ cup chopped dried Calimyrna figs**
- **3 tablespoons water**
- **2 tablespoons orange marmalade**
- **¾ cup packed brown sugar**
- **1 tablespoon cornstarch**
- **1 cup corn syrup**
- **3 eggs**
- **6 tablespoons unsalted butter, melted**
- **2 teaspoons vanilla extract**
- **1½ cups deluxe mixed nuts**

**TOPPING**

- **1 cup heavy whipping cream**
- **2 tablespoons sugar**
- **1 tablespoon orange marmalade**

**1.** Line a 9-in. pie plate with pastry; trim and flute edges. Line pastry with a double thickness of heavy-duty foil. Bake at 450° for 8 minutes. Remove foil; bake 5 minutes longer. Cool on a wire rack. Reduce heat to 300°.
**2.** In a small saucepan, combine the figs and water. Cook and stir over low heat until the water is absorbed. Remove from the heat;

stir in orange marmalade. In a large bowl, combine the brown sugar and cornstarch. Add corn syrup, eggs, butter, vanilla and fig mixture; stir in nuts. Pour into crust.

**3.** Bake at 300° for 1 to 1¼ hours or until set. Cover the edges with foil during the last 30 minutes to prevent overbrowning if necessary. Cool on a wire rack.

**4.** In a small bowl, beat the cream until it begins to thicken. Add the sugar and marmalade; beat until soft peaks form. Serve with pie. Refrigerate leftovers.

Crumb Topped Apple Pie

## Crumb Topped Apple Pie

**PREP:** 45 MIN. + CHILLING
**BAKE:** 1 HOUR **MAKES:** 8 SERVINGS

Everyone raves about Crumb Topped Apple Pie. If you're a beginner or just short on time, use a store-bought crust. You'll still get lots of compliments.

—**VIRGINIA OLSON** WEST DES MOINES, IOWA

- **1¼ cups all-purpose flour**
- **½ teaspoon salt**
- **½ cup shortening**
- **¼ cup cold water**

**FILLING**

- **5 large tart apples, peeled and thinly sliced**
- **⅔ cup sugar**
- **5 teaspoons all-purpose flour**
- **1¼ teaspoons ground cinnamon**

**TOPPING**

- **⅔ cup all-purpose flour**
- **½ cup sugar**
- **¼ cup cold butter**

**1.** In a large bowl, combine flour and salt; cut in the shortening until crumbly. Gradually add the water, tossing with a fork until the dough forms a ball. Wrap in plastic wrap. Refrigerate for 1 to 1½ hours or until easy to handle.

**2.** Roll out pastry to fit a 9-in. pie plate. Transfer pastry to pie plate. Trim pastry to ½ in. beyond edge of plate; flute edges.

**3.** For the filling, place apples in crust. Combine the sugar, flour and cinnamon; sprinkle over apples.

**4.** For the topping, combine flour and sugar in a small bowl; cut in butter until crumbly. Sprinkle over filling. Bake at 450° for 10 minutes. Reduce heat to 350°; bake 50-60 minutes longer or until topping is golden brown and filling is bubbly. Cool on a wire rack.

## Velvety Chocolate Butter Pecan Pie

Sweet tooths love this combo of two classic pies—pecan and chocolate.

—**HELEN FIELDS** SPRINGTOWN, TEXAS

**PREP:** 45 MIN. + CHILLING
**BAKE:** 55 MIN. **MAKES:** 8 SERVINGS

- **1¼ cups all-purpose flour**
- **1 tablespoon sugar**
- **½ teaspoon salt**
- **⅓ cup cold butter**
- **2 tablespoons butter-flavored shortening**
- **3 to 4 tablespoons ice water**
- **½ teaspoon white vinegar**
- **¼ teaspoon vanilla extract**

**EGG WASH**

- **1 egg**
- **1 tablespoon water**

**FILLING**

- **½ cup butter**
- **4 ounces bittersweet chocolate, chopped**
- **1¼ cups packed brown sugar**
- **¾ cup light corn syrup**
- **3 eggs, lightly beaten**
- **2 tablespoons molasses**
- **1 teaspoon vanilla extract**
- **½ teaspoon salt**
- **1½ cups finely chopped pecans**
- **½ cup pecan halves**

**1.** In a large bowl, combine the flour, sugar and salt; cut in the butter and shortening until crumbly. Combine water, vinegar and vanilla. Gradually add to the flour mixture, tossing with a fork until dough forms a ball. Wrap in plastic wrap; refrigerate for 8 hours or overnight.

**2.** Roll out pastry to fit a 9-in. pie plate. Transfer pastry to pie plate. Trim pastry to ½ in. beyond edge of plate; flute edges. Beat egg wash ingredients; brush over pastry.

**3.** For the filling, melt butter and chocolate in a microwave; stir until smooth. In a large bowl, combine the brown sugar, corn syrup, eggs, molasses, vanilla and salt. Stir in the chopped pecans and butter mixture. Pour into pastry. Arrange pecan halves over filling.

**4.** Bake at 350° for 55-65 minutes or until a knife inserted near the center comes out clean. Cover the edges with foil during the last 15 minutes to prevent overbrowning if necessary. Cool on a wire rack. Refrigerate leftovers.

# Just Desserts

A delicious meal just isn't complete without **something sweet** at the end. So **treat your family** with any of these tempting cheesecakes, puddings, freezer favorites and more!

"When I received a request for a turtle cheesecake, I couldn't find a recipe that appealed to me. So I came up with my own. It remains a popular item at the coffee shop where I work."

—**SUE GRONHOLZ** BEAVER DAM, WISCONSIN

MAKE AHEAD
## Island Crunch Cheesecake

I came up with this cheesecake after going on vacation. Featuring pineapple and coconut, the rich slices will remind you of a tropical island paradise.

**—ELLEN BATENHORST**
OMAHA, NEBRASKA

**PREP:** 45 MIN.
**BAKE:** 1 HOUR. + CHILLING
**MAKES:** 16 SERVINGS

- **1½ cups vanilla wafer crumbs (about 45 wafers)**
- **⅓ cup butter, melted**
- **4 packages (8 ounces each) cream cheese, softened**
- **2 cups sugar**
- **1 teaspoon vanilla extract**
- **¼ teaspoon salt**
- **5 eggs, lightly beaten**
- **1 can (8 ounces) crushed pineapple, drained**
- **½ cup flaked coconut**
- **2 ounces unsweetened chocolate, melted and cooled**
- **1 tablespoon creme de cacao**
- **¾ cup semisweet chocolate chunks**

**SOUR CREAM LAYER**

- **2 cups (16 ounces) sour cream**
- **¼ cup sugar**
- **1 teaspoon vanilla extract**
- **1 teaspoon orange liqueur (Grand Marnier)**

**TOPPINGS**

- **½ cup flaked coconut, toasted**
- **½ cup macadamia nuts, chopped**
- **¼ cup semisweet chocolate chips**
- **1 teaspoon shortening**

Island Crunch Cheesecake

**1.** Place a greased 10-in. springform pan on a double thickness of heavy-duty foil (about 18 in. square). Securely wrap foil around pan.
**2.** In a small bowl, combine wafer crumbs and butter. Press onto the bottom and 1 in. up the sides of the prepared pan; set aside.
**3.** In a large bowl, beat the cream cheese and sugar until smooth. Beat in the vanilla and salt. Add the eggs; beat on low speed just until combined.
**4.** Remove half of the mixture to a small bowl. Fold in the pineapple and coconut; pour into the crust. Stir cooled chocolate and creme de cacao into plain cream cheese mixture; fold in chocolate chunks. Carefully spoon over pineapple layer, spreading evenly.
**5.** Place springform pan in a large baking pan; add 1 in. of boiling water to larger pan. Bake at 325° for 50-60 minutes or until center is almost set. Let stand for 5 minutes. For the sour cream layer, combine all ingredients in a small bowl; spread over the cheesecake. Bake 5 minutes longer.
**6.** Remove springform pan from the water bath; remove foil. Cool the cheesecake on a wire rack for 10 minutes; loosen edges from pan with a knife. Cool 1 hour longer. Refrigerate overnight.
**7.** Remove rim from pan. Sprinkle coconut and nuts over cheesecake. In a microwave, melt the chocolate chips and shortening; stir until smooth. Drizzle over top.

**Editor's Note:** *To toast coconut, spread in a 15-in. x 10-in. x 1-in. baking pan. Bake at 350° for 5-10 minutes or until golden brown, stirring frequently.*

MAKE AHEAD
## Thomas Jefferson's Vanilla Ice Cream

The third U.S. president is credited with jotting down the first American recipe for vanilla ice cream. If you don't have a vanilla bean on hand for this version from the Taste of Home Test Kitchen, stir 1 tablespoon vanilla extract into the cream mixture after the ice-water bath.

**Thomas Jefferson's Vanilla Ice Cream**
**Easy Chocolate Sauce**

**PREP:** 15 MIN. + CHILLING
**PROCESS:** 20 MIN./BATCH + FREEZING
**MAKES:** 2¼ QUARTS

- **2 quarts heavy whipping cream**
- **1 cup sugar**
- **1 vanilla bean**
- **6 egg yolks**

**1.** In a large heavy saucepan, combine cream and sugar. Split vanilla bean in half lengthwise. With a sharp knife, scrape seeds into pan; add bean. Heat cream mixture over medium heat until bubbles form around side of pan, stirring to dissolve sugar.
**2.** In a small bowl, whisk a small amount of the hot mixture into the egg yolks; return all to the pan, whisking constantly.
**3.** Cook over low heat until the mixture is just thick enough to coat a metal spoon and temperature reaches 160°, stirring constantly. Do not allow to boil. Immediately transfer to a bowl.
**4.** Place bowl in a pan of ice water. Stir gently and occasionally for 2 minutes; discard vanilla bean. Press waxed paper onto surface of custard. Refrigerate several hours or overnight.
**5.** Fill cylinder of ice cream freezer two-thirds full; freeze according to the manufacturer's directions. (Refrigerate remaining mixture until ready to freeze.) Transfer ice cream to a freezer container; freeze for 4-6 hours or until firm. Repeat with remaining mixture.

## FAST FIX ▸ Easy Chocolate Sauce

The Taste of Home Test Kitchen experts share a sensational, 5-minute way to top ice cream—or coat ice cream bars.

**PREP/TOTAL TIME:** 5 MIN. **MAKES:** ⅔ CUP

- **1⅓ cups (8 ounces) semisweet chocolate chips**
- **1 tablespoon vegetable oil**

Place chocolate chips and oil in a microwave-safe bowl; microwave for 30 seconds. Give the mixture a stir, then finish in the microwave for another 30 seconds. Cool slightly and spoon the chocolate mixture over your favorite ice cream, or use for dipping ice cream bars.

## Homemade Butterscotch Pudding

With the essence of butterscotch, this homemade pudding is sure to stir fond memories of childhood treats.
—**TERESA WILKES** PEMBROKE, GEORGIA

**PREP:** 10 MIN. **COOK:** 10 MIN. + CHILLING **MAKES:** 6 SERVINGS

- **½ cup sugar**
- **½ cup packed dark brown sugar**
- **3 tablespoons cornstarch**
- **¼ teaspoon salt**
- **⅛ teaspoon ground nutmeg**
- **3 cups 2% milk**
- **3 egg yolks**
- **2 tablespoons butter, cubed**
- **2 teaspoons vanilla extract**
- **Whipped cream, optional**

**1.** In a large heavy saucepan, combine the first five ingredients. Stir in the milk until smooth. Cook and stir over medium-high heat until thickened and bubbly. Reduce heat to low; cook and stir 2 minutes longer. Remove from the heat.
**2.** Stir a small amount of the hot mixture into the egg yolks; return all to the pan. Bring to a gentle boil, stirring constantly; cook 2 minutes or until mixture is thickened and coats the back of a spoon. Remove from the heat.
**3.** Stir in the butter and vanilla. Cool for 15 minutes, stirring occasionally. Transfer to six dessert dishes. Cover and refrigerate until chilled. Garnish with whipped cream if desired.

Homemade Butterscotch Pudding

## Tempting Caramel Apple Pudding with Gingersnap Crust

Here's a wonderful fall dessert. The smooth layer of cream cheese and pudding is complemented by a crunchy apple topping and nicely spiced gingersnap crust.
—**MARGARET WILSON** SUN CITY, CALIFORNIA

**PREP:** 30 MIN. + CHILLING **MAKES:** 15 SERVINGS

- **2 cups crushed gingersnap cookies (about 40 cookies)**
- **⅓ cup butter, melted**
- **1 package (8 ounces) cream cheese, softened**
- **¼ cup sugar**
- **3¼ cups cold 2% milk, divided**
- **1 carton (8 ounces) frozen whipped topping, thawed, divided**
- **2 packages (3.4 ounces each) instant butterscotch pudding mix**
- **½ cup hot caramel ice cream topping, divided**
- **1 medium Red Delicious, Gala or Cortland apple, chopped**
- **1 medium Granny Smith apple, chopped**
- **⅓ cup dry roasted peanuts, chopped**

**1.** In a small bowl, mix the crushed cookies and butter until blended; press onto the bottom of a greased 13-in. x 9-in. baking dish. Refrigerate for at least 15 minutes.
**2.** Meanwhile, in a large bowl, beat cream cheese, sugar and 1/4 cup milk until smooth. Fold in 1 cup whipped topping; spread over crust.
**3.** In a large bowl, whisk remaining milk and pudding mixes for 2 minutes; let stand for 2 minutes or until soft-set. Stir in 1/4 cup caramel topping. Spoon over cream cheese layer. Cover and refrigerate for 15 minutes.
**4.** Spread remaining whipped topping over top. Cover and refrigerate for at least 4 hours or until filling is firm.
**5.** Just before serving, top with apples; drizzle with remaining caramel topping. Sprinkle with peanuts.

MAKE AHEAD

## 3D Chocolate Cheesecake

This chocolate sensation is deep, dark and decadent—so "3D" is the perfect name for it! Plus, the ganache coating conceals any cracks that sometimes appear on cheesecakes.

**—VANASSA HICKS** FLINT, MICHIGAN

**PREP:** 30 MIN.
**BAKE:** 55 MIN. + CHILLING
**MAKES:** 16 SERVINGS

- **1 cup chocolate graham cracker crumbs (about 5 whole crackers)**
- **1 tablespoon sugar**
- **¼ cup butter, melted**

**FILLING**

- **4 packages (8 ounces each) cream cheese, softened**
- **1⅓ cups sugar**
- **1 package (10 ounces) 60% cacao bittersweet chocolate baking chips, melted and cooled**
- **¼ cup baking cocoa**
- **4 eggs, lightly beaten**

**GANACHE**

- **⅔ cup (4 ounces) 60% cacao bittersweet chocolate baking chips**
- **½ cup heavy whipping cream**
- **1 tablespoon sugar**

**1.** Place a greased 9-in. springform pan on a double thickness of heavy-duty foil (about 18 in. square). Securely wrap foil around pan.
**2.** In a small bowl, combine the cracker crumbs and sugar; stir in butter. Press onto the bottom of prepared pan. Place pan on a baking sheet. Bake at 325° for 10 minutes. Cool on a wire rack.
**3.** In a large bowl, beat cream cheese and sugar until smooth. Beat in cooled chocolate and cocoa. Add eggs; beat on low speed just until combined. Pour over crust. Place springform pan in a large baking pan; add 1 in. of boiling water to larger pan.
**4.** Bake at 325° for 55-60 minutes or until center is just set and top appears dull. Remove springform pan from water bath; remove foil. Cool cheesecake on a wire rack for 10 minutes; loosen edges from pan with a knife. Cool 1 hour longer. Refrigerate overnight.
**5.** For ganache, place chocolate in a small bowl. In a small saucepan, bring the cream and sugar just to a boil. Pour over the chocolate; whisk until smooth. Cool to reach a spreading consistency, stirring occasionally.
**6.** Remove rim from pan. Spread ganache over cheesecake to within 1-in. of edge. Refrigerate for 1 hour or until set.

3D Chocolate Cheesecake

MAKE AHEAD

## Fudgy Almond Pops

Amaretto is the "surprise" ingredient that enhances the almond flavor.

**—SHARON GUINTA**
STAMFORD, CONNECTICUT

**PREP:** 10 MIN. + FREEZING
**MAKES:** 8 POPS

- **2 cups whole milk**
- **1 package (3.9 ounces) instant chocolate fudge pudding mix**
- **½ cup sugar**
- **½ cup amaretto-flavored refrigerated nondairy creamer**
- **⅛ teaspoon almond extract**
- **8 Popsicle molds or paper cups (3 ounces each) and Popsicle sticks**

In a bowl, whisk the milk, pudding mix, sugar, creamer and extract for 2 minutes or until creamy. Pour into Popsicle molds or cups; top molds with holders or insert wooden sticks into cups. Freeze.

Pistachio Cardamom Cheesecake

MAKE AHEAD

## Pistachio Cardamom Cheesecake

Cardamom makes me think of clove, allspice and pepper all wrapped up in one spice. Combine it with pistachios and add it to cheesecake for a dessert that has the exotic flair of India.

**—CAROLYN HARKONNEN**
LOOMIS, CALIFORNIA

**PREP:** 30 MIN.
**BAKE:** 35 MIN. + CHILLING
**MAKES:** 12 SERVINGS

- **1¼ cups finely crushed animal crackers**
- **3 tablespoons packed brown sugar**
- **¼ cup butter, melted**

**FILLING**

- **2 packages (8 ounces each) cream cheese, softened**
- **1 can (14 ounces) sweetened condensed milk**
- **1 tablespoon lemon juice**
- **1½ teaspoons ground cardamom**
- **1 drop green food coloring, optional**
- **3 eggs, lightly beaten**
- **½ cup pistachios, finely chopped**
- **Sweetened whipped cream, optional**
- **Additional chopped pistachios and animal cracker crumbs, optional**

**1.** Place a greased 9-in. springform pan on a double thickness of heavy-duty foil (about 18 in. square). Securely wrap foil around pan.

**2.** In a small bowl, combine the cracker crumbs and brown sugar; stir in butter. Press onto the bottom of prepared pan. Place pan on a baking sheet. Bake at 325° for 15 minutes. Cool on a wire rack.
**3.** In a large bowl, beat cream cheese until smooth. Beat in the milk, lemon juice, cardamom and, if desired, food coloring. Add eggs; beat on low speed just until combined. Fold in pistachios. Pour over crust. Place springform pan in a large baking pan; add 1 in. of boiling water to larger pan.
**4.** Bake at 325° for 35-40 minutes or until center is just set and top appears dull. Remove springform pan from water bath; remove foil. Cool cheesecake on a wire rack for 10 minutes; loosen edges from pan with a knife. Cool 1 hour longer. Refrigerate overnight.
**5.** Remove rim from pan. Top cheesecake with whipped cream and sprinkle with pistachios and cracker crumbs if desired.
**Editor's Note:** *To toast nuts, spread in a 15-in. x 10-in. x 1-in. baking pan. Bake at 350° for 5-10 minutes or until lightly browned, stirring occasionally. Or, spread in a dry nonstick skillet and heat over low heat until lightly browned, stirring occasionally.*

MAKE AHEAD

## Lemon & Cream Pops

Sweetened condensed milk ensures a creamy, dreamy freezer pop. Yummy!

**—SHARON GUINTA**
STAMFORD, CONNECTICUT

**PREP:** 10 MIN. + FREEZING
**MAKES:** 8 POPS

- **1 can (14 ounces) sweetened condensed milk**
- **1 cup whole milk**
- **½ cup fresh lemon juice**
- **⅓ cup sugar**
- **½ teaspoon grated lemon peel**
- **8 Popsicle molds or paper cups (3 ounces each) and Popsicle sticks**

In a large bowl, whisk the sweetened condensed milk, whole milk, lemon juice, sugar and grated lemon peel until sugar is dissolved. Pour into Popsicle molds or cups; top molds with holders or insert wooden sticks into cups. Freeze.

## Nectarine Plum Crisps

A fusion of late-summer fruits, these crisps are delightful after dinner—and leftovers can be enjoyed for breakfast. Look for apple crisp mix in the produce department of your grocery store.

**—NICOLE WERNER**
ANN ARBOR, MICHIGAN

**PREP:** 20 MIN. **BAKE:** 25 MIN.
**MAKES:** 4 SERVINGS

- **1 package (9 ounces) apple crisp mix**
- **6 tablespoons cold butter, cubed**
- **2 cups sliced fresh nectarines**
- **2 cups sliced fresh plums**
- **2 teaspoons cornstarch**
- **Vanilla ice cream, optional**

**1.** Place the crisp mix in a small bowl; cut in butter until crumbly. Spoon half of the mixture into four 10-oz. ramekins or custard cups coated with cooking spray; reserve remaining mixture for topping.
**2.** In another bowl, combine the nectarines, plums and cornstarch; toss to coat. Spoon over crumb layer. Sprinkle with topping.
**3.** Bake at 375° for 25-30 minutes or until filling is bubbly and topping is golden brown. Serve warm; top with ice cream if desired.
**Editor's Note:** *This recipe was tested with Marzetti apple crisp mix. Look for it in the produce section of your grocery store.*

Nectarine Plum Crisps

FAST FIX

## Warm Pineapple Sundaes with Rum Sauce

For my Warm Pineapple Sundaes with Rum Sauce, I add ginger and butter to a popular fruit-and-liquor combo, then turn up the heat. Try it—you'll love it!
**—JAMIE MILLER** MAPLE GROVE, MINNESOTA

**PREP/TOTAL TIME:** 25 MIN.
**MAKES:** 2 SERVINGS

- **4 fresh pineapple spears (about 8 ounces)**
- **½ cup packed brown sugar**
- **2 tablespoons dark rum**
- **¾ teaspoon ground ginger**
- **4 teaspoons butter, cut into small pieces**
- **2 scoops vanilla ice cream or low-fat frozen yogurt**
- **4 gingersnap cookies**

**1.** Place the pineapple spears in a 1-qt. baking dish. In a small bowl, combine the brown sugar, rum and ginger; spoon over the pineapple. Dot with butter.
**2.** Bake, uncovered, at 425° for 8-10 minutes or until the pineapple is lightly browned and the sauce is bubbly. Place ice cream in two dessert dishes; top with pineapple and sauce. Serve immediately with cookies.

MAKE AHEAD

## Nutty Caramel Ice Cream Cake

Store a sensational ice cream treat in the freezer for a spur-of-the-moment celebration—or any time you want to surprise your family. My butter pecan version is our favorite, but feel free to try other ice cream flavors.
**—TINA STELZL**
WAXHAW, NORTH CAROLINA

Nutty Caramel Ice Cream Cake

**PREP:** 30 MIN. + FREEZING
**MAKES:** 16 SERVINGS

- **4 cups crushed pecan shortbread cookies (about 52 cookies)**
- **¼ cup butter, melted**
- **6 cups butter pecan ice cream, softened**
- **1 carton (8 ounces) frozen whipped topping, thawed**
- **¾ cup slivered almonds, toasted**
- **¾ cup milk chocolate English toffee bits**
- **¼ cup caramel sundae syrup**

**1.** In a large bowl, combine the shortbread cookie crumbs and butter. Press 2 cups onto bottom of a greased 9-in. springform pan. Spoon half of the butter pecan ice cream into the prepared pan. Freeze for 20 minutes.
**2.** Repeat layers with remaining cookie crumbs and ice cream. Spread with whipped topping. Sprinkle with almonds and toffee bits. Cover and freeze overnight or until firm. May be frozen for up to 2 months.
**3. TO USE FROZEN CAKE:** Remove from the freezer 10 minutes before serving. Drizzle with syrup.

SLOW COOKER

## Butterscotch Pears

These delectable pears go in a 4-quart slow cooker and simmer while you eat dinner. Serve them by themselves or present each drizzled pear half with a slice of purchased pound cake and a scoop of vanilla ice cream.
**—THERESA KREYCHE**
TUSTIN, CALIFORNIA

**PREP:** 20 MIN. **COOK:** 2 HOURS
**MAKES:** 8 SERVINGS

- **4 large firm pears**
- **1 tablespoon lemon juice**
- **¼ cup packed brown sugar**
- **3 tablespoons butter, softened**
- **2 tablespoons all-purpose flour**
- **½ teaspoon ground cinnamon**
- **¼ teaspoon salt**
- **½ cup chopped pecans**
- **½ cup pear nectar**
- **2 tablespoons honey**

**1.** Cut pears in half lengthwise; remove the cores. Brush pears with lemon juice. In a small bowl, combine the brown sugar, butter, flour, cinnamon and salt; stir in pecans. Spoon into pears; place in 4-qt. slow cooker.
**2.** Combine the pear nectar and honey; drizzle over pears. Cover and cook on low for 2-3 hours or until heated through. Serve warm.

MAKE AHEAD

## Spiced Apple Cheesecake

I live in apple country and am always looking for ways to use our bountiful harvest. For a cheesecake topping, I combine tart Granny Smith apples with sugar, cinnamon and nutmeg. It makes a decadent dessert even better.
**—GRACE HUGHES**
OROVILLE, WASHINGTON

**PREP:** 35 MIN.
**BAKE:** 1 HOUR + CHILLING
**MAKES:** 12 SERVINGS

- **1⅔ cups crushed gingersnap cookies (about 45 cookies)**
- **¼ cup butter, melted**

**FILLING**

- **3 packages (8 ounces each) cream cheese, softened**
- **1 can (14 ounces) sweetened condensed milk**
- **2 tablespoons all-purpose flour**
- **2 teaspoons vanilla extract**
- **4 eggs, lightly beaten**
- **4 cups chopped peeled tart apples**
- **½ cup sugar**
- **2 teaspoons ground cinnamon**
- **1 teaspoon ground nutmeg**

**CINNAMON SAUCE**

- **½ cup water**
- **2 tablespoons red-hot candies**
- **1 tablespoon lemon juice**
- **2 teaspoons cornstarch**

**1.** In a small bowl, combine cookie crumbs and butter. Press onto the bottom of a greased 9-in. springform pan. Place the pan on a baking sheet. Bake at 350° for 10 minutes. Cool on a wire rack.
**2.** In a large bowl, beat the cream cheese until smooth. Beat in the milk, flour and vanilla. Add eggs; beat on low speed just until combined. Pour over the crust. In a large bowl, combine the apples, sugar, cinnamon and nutmeg; spoon over cream cheese mixture. Return pan to baking sheet.
**3.** Bake at 350° for 60-70 minutes or until the center is almost set. Cool on a wire rack for 10 minutes. Loosen edges of cheesecake from pan with a knife. Cool 1 hour longer. Refrigerate overnight.
**4.** In a small saucepan, combine the sauce ingredients. Bring to a boil; cook and stir for 2 minutes or until thickened; cool completely.
**5.** Remove the rim from the pan. Drizzle the sauce over the cheesecake.

Layered Turtle Cheesecake

## MAKE AHEAD Layered Turtle Cheesecake

When I received a request for a turtle cheesecake, I couldn't find a recipe that appealed to me. So I came up with my own. It remains a popular item at the coffee shop where I work.
**—SUE GRONHOLZ** BEAVER DAM, WISCONSIN

**PREP:** 40 MIN. **BAKE:** 1¼ HOURS + CHILLING
**MAKES:** 12 SERVINGS

- **1 cup all-purpose flour**
- **⅓ cup packed brown sugar**
- **¼ cup finely chopped pecans**
- **6 tablespoons cold butter, cubed**

**FILLING**

- **4 packages (8 ounces each) cream cheese, softened**
- **1 cup sugar**
- **⅓ cup packed brown sugar**
- **¼ cup plus 1 teaspoon all-purpose flour, divided**
- **2 tablespoons heavy whipping cream**
- **1½ teaspoons vanilla extract**
- **4 eggs, lightly beaten**
- **½ cup milk chocolate chips, melted and cooled**
- **¼ cup caramel ice cream topping**
- **⅓ cup chopped pecans**

**GANACHE**

- **½ cup milk chocolate chips**
- **¼ cup heavy whipping cream**
- **2 tablespoons chopped pecans**
- **Additional caramel ice cream topping, optional**

**1.** Place a greased 9-in. springform pan on a double thickness of heavy-duty foil (about 18 in. square). Securely wrap foil around pan.
**2.** In a small bowl, combine the flour, brown sugar and pecans; cut in the butter until crumbly. Press onto the bottom of the prepared pan. Place the pan on a baking sheet. Bake at 325° for 12-15 minutes or until set. Cool on a wire rack.
**3.** In a large bowl, beat the cream cheese and sugars until smooth. Beat in 1/4 cup flour, cream and vanilla. Add eggs; beat on low speed just until blended. Remove 1 cup batter to a small bowl; stir in melted chocolate. Spread over crust.
**4.** In another bowl, mix caramel topping and remaining flour; stir in pecans. Drop by tablespoonfuls over the chocolate batter. Top with the remaining batter. Place springform pan in a large baking pan; add 1 in. of hot water to larger pan.
**5.** Bake at 325° for 1 1/4 to 1 1/2 hours or until center is just set and top appears dull. Remove springform pan from water bath; remove foil. Cool cheesecake on a wire rack for 10 minutes. Loosen sides from pan with a knife; cool 1 hour longer. Refrigerate overnight.
**6.** For ganache, place chips in a small bowl. In a small saucepan, bring cream just to a boil. Pour over chips; whisk until smooth. Cool slightly, stirring occasionally.
**7.** Remove the sides of springform pan. Spread ganache over the cheesecake; sprinkle with pecans. Refrigerate until set. If desired, drizzle with additional caramel topping before serving.

## Chocolate & Peanut Butter Mousse Cheesecake

**PREP:** 50 MIN. + CHILLING
**MAKES:** 16 SERVINGS

- **1½ cups chocolate wafer crumbs**
- **¼ cup butter, melted**

**MOUSSE LAYERS:**

- **1¼ cups heavy whipping cream**
- **¾ cup creamy peanut butter**
- **5 ounces cream cheese, softened**
- **2 tablespoons butter, softened**
- **1¼ cups confectioners' sugar**
- **5 ounces bittersweet chocolate, chopped**
- **1 milk chocolate candy bar (3½ ounces), chopped**
- **⅓ cup sugar**
- **¼ cup 2% milk**
- **1 teaspoon vanilla extract**

**GANACHE**

- **6 ounces bittersweet chocolate, chopped**
- **⅔ cup heavy whipping cream**
- **1 teaspoon vanilla extract**
- **Shaved chocolate, optional**

**1.** In a small bowl, combine wafer crumbs and butter. Press onto the bottom of a greased 9-in. springform pan; set aside.
**2.** In a large bowl, beat cream until stiff peaks form. In another bowl, beat the peanut butter, cream cheese and butter until smooth. Beat in confectioners' sugar. Fold in half of the whipped cream. Spread over crust.
**3.** Place bittersweet and milk chocolates in a small bowl. In a small saucepan, combine sugar and milk; bring just to a boil. Pour over chocolate and whisk until smooth. Stir in the vanilla. Cool to room temperature, stirring occasionally. Fold in remaining whipped cream. Spread over peanut butter layer. Freeze for 2 hours or until firm.
**4.** For ganache, place bittersweet chocolate in a small bowl. In a small saucepan, bring cream just to a boil. Pour over chocolate; whisk until smooth. Stir in the vanilla. Cool, stirring occasionally, to room temperature or until the ganache reaches a spreading consistency. Spread over the cheesecake. Refrigerate for 1 hour or until set.
**5.** Just before serving, remove sides of pan and garnish with shaved chocolate if desired.

With a rich ganache on top, Chocolate & Peanut Butter Mousse Cheesecake is a wonderful no-bake option. It takes a little extra time to assemble, but I know it's worth the effort when I see the smiles at the table. For an extra-special finish, use shaved chocolate as a garnish.
—**JANON FURRER,** PRESCOTT, ARIZONA

## Baked Sweet Potato Pudding

When I put my leftover sweet potatoes in this yummy dessert, they're gone faster than you can say "Thanksgiving!" I think the baked pudding is best served warm with a scoop of vanilla ice cream.
—**JOYCE WELLING** SWANTON, OHIO

**PREP:** 25 MIN. **BAKE:** 50 MIN.
**MAKES:** 8 SERVINGS

- **4 cups mashed sweet potatoes**
- **½ cup heavy whipping cream**
- **3 eggs, separated**
- **2 tablespoons lemon juice**
- **1 teaspoon grated lemon peel**
- **½ teaspoon ground cinnamon**
- **½ teaspoon ground ginger**
- **¼ teaspoon ground cloves**
- **1 cup flaked coconut, divided**
- **⅓ cup packed brown sugar**
- **⅓ cup slivered almonds**
- **Vanilla ice cream, optional**

**1.** In a large bowl, beat the sweet potatoes, heavy whipping cream, egg yolks, lemon juice, lemon peel and spices until smooth. Fold in 2/3 cup coconut.
**2.** In a large bowl with clean beaters, beat the egg whites on medium speed until soft peaks form. Gradually beat in brown sugar, 1 tablespoon at a time, on high until stiff glossy peaks form and sugar is dissolved.
**3.** With a spatula, stir a fourth of the egg whites into sweet potato mixture until no white streaks remain. Fold in remaining egg whites until combined.
**4.** Transfer to a greased 11-in. x 7-in. baking dish. Sprinkle with almonds and remaining coconut. Bake at 325° for 50-55 minutes or until a knife inserted near the center comes out clean. Serve warm with ice cream if desired.

## *MAKE AHEAD* Chocolate-Glazed Coconut Almond Cheesecake

I came up with a cheesecake that tastes like my favorite candy bar. My creation also works in "bite size" — just like the candy bar! Use a mini muffin pan with muffin liners, filling each one about ¾ full. Bake for 15-17 minutes, then allow them to cool completely before adding toppings.
—**KERI BRAMMER**
LAWTON, OKLAHOMA

**PREP:** 25 MIN. **BAKE:** 45 MIN. + CHILLING
**MAKES:** 12 SERVINGS

- **1¼ cups graham cracker crumbs**
- **⅓ cup flaked coconut**
- **⅓ cup finely chopped almonds**
- **⅓ cup butter, melted**

**FILLING**

- **3 packages (8 ounces each) cream cheese, softened**
- **¾ cup sugar**
- **1 tablespoon coconut extract**
- **3 eggs, lightly beaten**
- **1 cup flaked coconut**

**GLAZE**

- **1 cup (6 ounces) semisweet chocolate chips**
- **¾ cup heavy whipping cream**
- **1½ teaspoons vanilla extract**
- **Toasted shaved coconut and chopped almonds, optional**

**1.** Place a greased 9-in. springform pan on a double thickness of heavy-duty foil (about 18 in. square). Securely wrap foil around pan.
**2.** In a small bowl, combine the cracker crumbs, coconut and almonds; stir in butter. Press onto the bottom and 1 in. up the sides of prepared pan. Place pan on a baking sheet. Bake at 350° for 12 minutes. Cool on a wire rack.
**3.** In a large bowl, beat cream cheese and sugar until smooth. Beat in coconut extract. Add the eggs; beat on low speed just until combined. Fold in coconut. Pour into crust. Place springform pan in a large baking pan; add 1 in. of boiling water to larger pan.
**4.** Bake at 325° for 45-55 minutes or until center is just set and top appears dull. Remove springform pan from water bath; remove foil. Cool cheesecake on a wire rack for 10 minutes; loosen edges from pan with a knife. Cool 1 hour longer. Refrigerate overnight.
**5.** For the glaze, place chocolate chips in a small bowl. In a small saucepan, bring cream just to a boil. Pour over chocolate; whisk until smooth. Stir in vanilla. Cool slightly to reach a spreading consistency, stirring occasionally.
**6.** Remove rim from pan. Spread glaze over cheesecake. Refrigerate for 1 hour or until set. Top with toasted coconut and almonds if desired.

**Editor's Note:** *To toast coconut, spread in a 15-in. x 10-in. x 1-in. baking pan. Bake at 350° for 5-10 minutes or until golden brown, stirring frequently.*

## MAKE AHEAD Swirled Raspberry & Chocolate Cheesecake

Here's my secret to a lighter, fluffier cheesecake—the foaming power of eggs. When you beat egg whites to stiff peaks and gently fold them into the cream cheese mixture, the eggs give it greater volume and lightness because of the trapped air. Try this berry-chocolate treat and see!

**—BRITTNEY SEGOBIANO**
GENESEO, ILLINOIS

**PREP:** 40 MIN.
**BAKE:** 55 MIN. + CHILLING
**MAKES:** 12 SERVINGS

- **4 eggs**
- **1½ cups graham cracker crumbs**
- **¼ cup confectioners' sugar**
- **⅓ cup butter, melted**

**FILLING**

- **1 cup fresh raspberries**
- **½ teaspoon sugar**
- **3 packages (8 ounces each) cream cheese, softened**
- **1 can (14 ounces) sweetened condensed milk**
- **1 teaspoon vanilla extract**
- **1 cup (6 ounces) semisweet chocolate chips, melted and cooled**
- **Additional fresh raspberries, optional**

**1.** Separate eggs; let stand at room temperature for 30 minutes. Place a greased 9-in. springform pan on a double thickness of heavy-duty foil (about 18 in. square). Securely wrap foil around pan.
**2.** In a small bowl, combine the cracker crumbs and confectioners' sugar; stir in butter. Press onto the bottom of prepared pan. Place raspberries and sugar in a blender; cover and process until smooth. Strain and discard seeds.
**3.** In a large bowl, beat cream cheese until smooth. Beat in milk and vanilla. Add egg yolks; beat on low speed just until combined. Remove 1 tablespoon; stir into raspberry puree. Remove half of the remaining mixture to another bowl; stir in cooled chocolate.
**4.** In a large bowl with clean beaters, beat egg whites until stiff peaks form. With a spatula, fold half of the egg whites into chocolate mixture until no white streaks remain. Pour over crust.
**5.** Fold the remaining egg whites into plain cream cheese mixture; spread over chocolate layer. Drop raspberry mixture by tablespoonfuls over top; cut through filling with a knife to swirl.
**6.** Place springform pan in a large baking pan; add 1 in. of boiling water to larger pan.
**7.** Bake at 325° for 55-65 minutes or until center is just set and top appears dull. Remove springform pan from water bath; remove foil. Cool cheesecake on a wire rack for 10 minutes; loosen edges from pan with a knife. Cool 1 hour longer. Refrigerate overnight.
**8.** Remove the rim from the pan. Serve cheesecake with additional raspberries if desired.

## MAKE AHEAD Salted Caramel Cappuccino Cheesecake

I spent 16 years living in Seattle and became a coffee junkie! When I had to relocate across the country, I created this cheesecake as a sweet reminder of my former home. The flavors of salted caramel, espresso and coffee are a real pick-me-up anytime and go over well with guests, too.

—JULIE MERRIMAN
COLD BROOK, NEW YORK

**PREP:** 30 MIN. **BAKE:** 55 MIN. + CHILLING
**MAKES:** 12 SERVINGS

**1 package (9 ounces) chocolate wafers**
**1 cup (6 ounces) semisweet chocolate chips**
**½ cup packed brown sugar**
**2 tablespoons instant espresso powder**
**⅛ teaspoon ground nutmeg**
**½ cup butter, melted**

**FILLING**

**3 packages (8 ounces each) cream cheese, softened**
**1 cup packed brown sugar**
**½ cup sour cream**
**¼ cup Kahlua (coffee liqueur)**
**2 tablespoons all-purpose flour**
**2 tablespoons instant espresso powder**
**4 eggs, lightly beaten**

Salted Caramel Cappuccino Cheesecake

**TOPPING**

**½ cup hot caramel ice cream topping**
**½ teaspoon coarse sea salt**

**1.** Place a greased 9-in. springform pan on a double thickness of heavy-duty foil (about 18 in. square). Securely wrap foil around pan.
**2.** Place the first five ingredients in a food processor; cover and pulse until fine crumbs form. Gradually add butter, pulsing until combined. Press onto the bottom and 2-in. up the sides of prepared pan; set aside.
**3.** In a large bowl, beat cream cheese and brown sugar until smooth. Beat in the sour cream, Kahlua, flour and espresso powder. Add eggs; beat on low speed just until combined. Pour into crust. Place springform pan in a large baking pan; add 1 in. of boiling water to larger pan.
**4.** Bake at 350° for 55-65 minutes or until center is just set and top appears dull. Remove springform pan from water bath; remove foil. Cool cheesecake on a wire rack for 10 minutes; loosen edges from pan with a knife. Cool 1 hour longer. Refrigerate overnight.
**5.** Pour caramel topping over the cheesecake. Refrigerate for at least 15 minutes. Remove rim from pan. Just before serving, sprinkle sea salt over caramel.

## MAKE AHEAD Berry White Ice Pops

Speckled with tangy mixed berries, these treats require just three other ingredients—milk, honey and vanilla.

—SHARON GUINTA
STAMFORD, CONNECTICUT

**PREP:** 10 MIN. + FREEZING
**MAKES:** 10 POPS

**1¾ cups whole milk**
**1 tablespoon honey**
**¼ teaspoon vanilla extract**
**1 package (12 ounces) frozen unsweetened mixed berries, thawed and drained**
**10 Popsicle molds or paper cups (3 ounces each) and Popsicle sticks**

In a small bowl, whisk the milk, honey and vanilla. Evenly divide berries among Popsicle molds or cups. Pour milk mixture over berries. Top molds with holders or insert wooden sticks into cups. Freeze.

New York-Style Cheesecake Mousse

## New York-Style Cheesecake Mousse

As good as this mousse is the day you make it, I think it tastes even better after chilling overnight. Once chilled, it can be covered with plastic wrap and refrigerated for up to three days. Sliced strawberries are a refreshing, colorful finishing touch.

—CAROLINE WAMELINK
CLEVELAND HEIGHTS, OHIO

**PREP:** 20 MIN. + CHILLING
**MAKES:** 12 SERVINGS

**1 package (8 ounces) cream cheese, softened**
**½ cup confectioners' sugar**
**1½ teaspoons vanilla extract**
**½ teaspoon grated lemon peel**
**¾ cup heavy whipping cream, whipped**
**½ cup graham cracker crumbs**
**4 teaspoons sugar**
**2 tablespoons butter, melted**
**Sliced fresh strawberries, optional**

**1.** In a large bowl, beat cream cheese, confectioners' sugar, vanilla and lemon peel until fluffy. Fold in the whipped cream. Divide among 12 dessert dishes. Cover and refrigerate for at least 2 hours.

**2.** Meanwhile, combine cracker crumbs and sugar in a small bowl; add butter and mix well. Press to a 1/4-in. thickness on an ungreased baking sheet. Bake at 375° for 10-12 minutes or until lightly browned. Cool completely.
**3.** Just before serving, crumble graham cracker mixture; sprinkle over mousse. Top with berries if desired.

## MAKE AHEAD Creamy Tiramisu Cheesecake

What do you get when you combine classic Italian tiramisu with a rich, decadent cheesecake? Double the delight!
**—PRISCILLA GILBERT** INDIAN HARBOUR BEACH, FLORIDA

**PREP:** 30 MIN. **BAKE:** 70 MIN. + CHILLING **MAKES:** 12 SERVINGS

- **1 tablespoon butter, melted**
- **1/3 cup chocolate graham cracker crumbs (about 2 whole crackers)**
- **2 tablespoons plus 2 teaspoons instant coffee granules**
- **1 tablespoon hot water**
- **1/3 cup strong brewed coffee**
- **1 teaspoon rum extract**
- **1 package (3 ounces) ladyfingers, split**
- **4 packages (8 ounces each) cream cheese, softened**
- **1 1/3 cups sugar**
- **1/3 cup heavy whipping cream**
- **1/3 cup sour cream**
- **2 teaspoons vanilla extract**
- **4 eggs, lightly beaten**
- **Baking cocoa**

**1.** Brush bottom of a 9-in. springform pan with butter; sprinkle evenly with cracker crumbs. Place pan on a double thickness of heavy-duty foil (about 18 in. square). Securely wrap foil around pan.
**2.** Dissolve coffee granules in hot water; cool and set aside for filling. Combine brewed coffee and rum extract; brush over flat sides of split ladyfingers. Arrange ladyfingers, rounded sides out, along sides of prepared pan.
**3.** In a large bowl, beat cream cheese and sugar until smooth. Beat in the cream, sour cream, vanilla and dissolved coffee. Add eggs; beat on low speed just until combined. Pour into prepared pan. Place springform pan in a large baking pan; add 1 in. of boiling water to larger pan.
**4.** Bake at 325° for 70-80 minutes or until center is just set and top appears dull. Remove springform pan from water bath; remove foil. Cool cheesecake on a wire rack for 10 minutes; loosen edges from pan with a knife. Cool 1 hour longer. Refrigerate overnight.
**5.** Remove the rim from pan. Just before serving, dust cheesecake with cocoa.

Creamy Tiramisu Cheesecake

## FAST FIX Grilled Apple Pizza

Start with this basic apple pizza, then dress it up any way you like using the creative ideas at the end of the recipe.
**—R. SANDLIN** PRESCOTT VALLEY, ARIZONA

**PREP/TOTAL TIME:** 25 MIN. **MAKES:** 2 PIZZAS (4 PIECES EACH)

- **5 medium tart apples, peeled and sliced**
- **4 tablespoons butter, divided**
- **1/2 cup packed brown sugar**
- **1 teaspoon ground cinnamon**
- **1 tube (13.8 ounces) refrigerated pizza crust**

**1.** In a large skillet, saute apples in 3 tablespoons butter until crisp-tender. Stir in brown sugar and cinnamon; keep warm.
**2.** Unroll the pizza crust and cut lengthwise in half. In a microwave, melt remaining butter; brush onto both sides of crust.
**3.** Grill, covered, over medium heat for 1-3 minutes on each side or until lightly browned, rotating halfway through cooking to ensure an evenly browned crust. Remove from the grill. Top pizza with the apples and desired topping ingredients.

**AMERICAN WAY**
Sprinkle with arugula, cooked chopped bacon and shredded cheddar cheese.

**FRUIT AND CREAMY**
Sprinkle with dried cranberries; drizzle with cream cheese frosting.

**FRENCH**
Top with sliced Brie cheese and fresh thyme.

**TURTLE-STYLE**
Sprinkle with chopped toasted pecans; drizzle with caramel sauce.

# Breakfast & Brunch

**Rise and shine** in the morning with sunrise delights such as Upside-Down Bacon Pancake, Flaky Egg Bake and Chai Tea Mix. You'll start off the day in an **especially scrumptious** way.

"The Italian word "frittata" refers to frying the egg-based dish in a skillet. My Individual Italian Frittatas bake in a ramekin, but the result is the same—a great menu item day or night."

—**NANCY ELLIOTT** HOUSTON, TEXAS

## Dutch Letters

These "S"-shaped, super-flaky butter pastries topped with crunchy sugar and filled with almond paste are popular in both Iowa and Holland during the Christmas season. With this basic recipe, you'll want to enjoy them year-round.
**—SHIRLEY DE LANGE** BYRON CENTER, MICHIGAN

**PREP:** 50 MIN. **BAKE:** 30 MIN. + COOLING **MAKES:** 28 PASTRIES

- **1 can (8 ounces) almond paste**
- **1 cup sugar**
- **1 egg**
- **½ teaspoon lemon extract**

**DOUGH**

- **4 cups all-purpose flour**
- **1 teaspoon salt**
- **2 cups cold butter**
- **1 cup ice water**
- **1 egg white**
- **2 teaspoons water**

**1.** In a large bowl, beat the almond paste, sugar, egg and extract until smooth. Divide into four portions. On lightly floured waxed paper, roll each portion into a 12-in. x ½-in. rope; set aside.
**2.** In a large bowl, combine the flour and salt; cut in the butter until crumbly. Gradually add the ice water, tossing with a fork until the dough forms a ball. Divide into four portions.

Dutch Letters

Hungry Fruit Caterpillar

**3.** On a lightly floured surface, roll out each portion into a 14-in. x 6-in. rectangle. Place one almond paste rope in the center of each rectangle. Moisten the long edges of the dough; fold over the filling. Press the seam to seal; tuck in the ends.
**4.** Transfer seam side down to greased baking sheets; form each into an S-shape. Whisk egg white and water; brush over dough. Using a fork, prick the tops at 1-in. intervals to vent.
**5.** Bake at 350° for 30-35 minutes or until golden brown. Cool on wire racks. To serve, cut into 2-in. pieces.

## FAST FIX Hungry Fruit Caterpillar

Hungry caterpillars make good children's stories as well as a wholesome treat featuring apples, strawberries, clementines and other fruits. Add sprigs of mint to create "antennae."
**—KIM MORDECAI** LITTLE ROCK, ARKANSAS

**PREP:** 20 MIN. **MAKES:** 4 SERVINGS

- **1 cup confectioners' sugar**
- **2 tablespoons milk**
- **⅛ teaspoon almond extract**
- **1 medium apple, sliced**
- **3 tablespoons orange juice**
- **1 medium plum plus ½ small plum**
- **1 teaspoon creamy peanut butter**
- **2 green grapes**
- **1 small lemon slice**
- **2 flowering sprigs of mint, optional**
- **6 fresh strawberries**
- **2 clementines, peeled**
- **1 medium kiwifruit, peeled and halved**
- **¼ cup hot caramel ice cream topping**

**1.** In a small bowl, whisk the confectioners' sugar, milk and extract until smooth; set aside. In another bowl, combine apple and orange juice; toss to coat.

**2.** Place whole plum on a serving platter. Using peanut butter, attach grapes for eyes and lemon for mouth. Attach mint sprigs for antennae if desired. Arrange apple and remaining fruit in a zigzag pattern to form caterpillar body. Drizzle caramel topping for legs; spoon almond glaze over fruit.

## Sausage Breakfast Pockets

A satisfying breakfast doesn't get much quicker and easier. Just grab one of these cheesy, sausage-stuffed rolls, and you'll be on your way.
**—CHERI HARRISON** CAIRO, GEORGIA

**PREP:** 25 MIN. **BAKE:** 15 MIN.
**MAKES:** 4 SERVINGS

- **¼ pound bulk pork sausage, cooked and drained**
- **½ cup shredded cheddar cheese**
- **2 ounces cream cheese, softened**
- **1 tablespoon dried parsley flakes**
- **1 tube (8 ounces) refrigerated crescent rolls**

**1.** In a small bowl, combine the sausage, cheddar cheese, cream cheese and parsley.
**2.** Unroll the crescent roll dough and separate into four rectangles; seal the perforations. Transfer to a foil-lined baking sheet. Place 3 tablespoons sausage mixture in the center of each rectangle. Bring four corners of dough over filling and twist; pinch to seal.
**3.** Bake at 375° for 14-16 minutes or until golden brown. Serve warm. Refrigerate leftovers.

### Did you know?

If you want to perk up in the morning without relying on caffeine, try a cup of eye-opening Winter Herb Tea Mix. The soothing, caffeine-free drink contains a built-in boost—mint. The aroma of mint has been shown to increase feelings of alertness.

**Winter Herb Tea Mix**

Melt away chilly-morning blahs with Winter Herb Tea Mix. The sweet-spicy, caffeine-free blend of mint, thyme, sage and rosemary makes a great gift, too.
**—SUE GRONHOLZ** BEAVER DAM, WISCONSIN

FAST FIX | MAKE AHEAD

## Winter Herb Tea Mix

**PREP/TOTAL TIME:** 10 MIN.
**MAKES:** 18 SERVINGS (9 TABLESPOONS TEA MIX)

- **6 tablespoons dried mint**
- **1 tablespoon dried sage leaves**
- **1 tablespoon dried rosemary, crushed**
- **1 tablespoon dried thyme**

**ADDITIONAL INGREDIENTS (for each serving)**

- **1 cup boiling water**
- **1 teaspoon honey**
- **1 lemon wedge**

**1.** In a small airtight container, combine the herbs. Store in a cool dry place for up to 6 months.
**2. TO PREPARE TEA:** Place 1½ teaspoons tea mix in a glass measuring cup. With the end of a wooden spoon handle, crush mixture until aromas are released. Add boiling water. Cover and steep for 10 minutes. Strain tea into a mug, discarding herbs. Stir in honey; serve with lemon.

## FAST FIX Chai Tea Mix

I received a wonderful tea recipe from my sister, who got it from a friend of hers in Alaska. The warm-you-up chai makes a fun gift. Try pouring the mix into a glass sugar shaker trimmed with self-adhesive ribbon, then place it in a stamped paper lunch bag clipped shut with a ribbon-trimmed clothespin.

**—DONNA GISH**
BLUE SPRINGS, MISSOURI

**PREP/TOTAL TIME:** 20 MIN.
**MAKES:** 32 SERVINGS (8 CUPS TEA MIX)

- **2 cups sugar**
- **2 cups unsweetened instant tea**
- **1½ cups powdered French vanilla nondairy creamer**
- **1¼ cups powdered nondairy creamer**
- **1¼ cups packed brown sugar**
- **¾ cup nonfat dry milk powder**
- **2½ teaspoons ground cinnamon**
- **1½ teaspoons ground nutmeg**
- **1¼ teaspoons ground cardamom**
- **1¼ teaspoons ground cloves**
- **1 teaspoon ground allspice**
- **¼ teaspoon white pepper**

**EACH SERVING**

- **1 cup hot 2% milk**

**1.** In a large bowl, combine the first 12 ingredients. In a blender, cover and process tea mixture in batches until powdery. Store in an airtight container in a cool dry place for up to 6 months.
**2. TO PREPARE CHAI TEA:** Place 1/4 cup mix in a mug. Add hot milk; stir until combined.

## FAST FIX Grape Melon Medley

No cantaloupe? Round out this fruit bowl with pears, mango or bananas.

**—DORIS RUSSELL**
FALLSTON, MARYLAND

**PREP/TOTAL TIME:** 15 MIN.
**MAKES:** 8 SERVINGS

- **2 cups cubed cantaloupe**
- **1½ cups green grapes, halved**
- **1½ cups seedless red grapes, halved**
- **1 can (11 ounces) mandarin oranges, drained**
- **½ cup pineapple preserves**

In a large bowl, combine the cantaloupe, grapes and oranges. Whisk preserves; pour over fruit and toss to coat. Chill until serving.

Chai Tea Mix

## Twice-Baked Breakfast Potatoes

Leftover baked potatoes were the inspiration for my twice-baked recipe. Serve the meaty, cheesy spuds as a hearty breakfast dish—or even as a satisfying lunch or dinner.

**—WILLIAM BROCK** AMELIA, OHIO

**PREP:** 30 MIN. **BAKE:** 15 MIN.
**MAKES:** 8 SERVINGS

- **4 large baking potatoes**
- **1 tablespoon butter**
- **4 eggs, beaten**
- **10 ounces bulk sausage**
- **¼ cup sour cream**
- **8 bacon strips, cooked and crumbled**
- **¾ cup shredded cheddar cheese, divided**
- **½ cup minced chives, divided**
- **1 tablespoon minced fresh parsley**
- **½ teaspoon salt**
- **½ teaspoon pepper**
- **Additional sour cream, optional**

**1.** Scrub and pierce potatoes; place on a microwave-safe plate. Microwave, uncovered, on high for 15-17 minutes or until tender, turning once.
**2.** Meanwhile, in a large skillet, melt butter over medium-high heat. Add the eggs; cook and stir until set. Remove and set aside. In the same skillet, cook sausage over medium heat until no longer pink; drain and set aside.
**3.** When the potatoes are cool enough to handle, cut each in half lengthwise. Scoop out pulp, leaving thin shells. In a large bowl, mash the pulp with sour cream. Stir in the bacon, 1/2 cup cheese, 1/4 cup chives, parsley, salt, pepper, eggs and sausage. Spoon into the potato shells.
**4.** Place on a baking sheet. Bake, uncovered, at 375° for 12-15 minutes or until heated through. Sprinkle with remaining cheese and chives. Serve with additional sour cream if desired.

Grape Melon Medley

Twice-Baked Breakfast Potatoes

# LOTS OF LATKES

Crunchy on the outside but moist on the inside, latkes are a traditional treat. To savor these golden-brown, aromatic delights yourself, try any of the taste-tempting variations here.

## Cheese & Red Pepper Latkes

These zesty cakes feature a colorful burst of red peppers, three cheeses and a handful of garlic. I like to shred the potatoes the night before for less prep work on the day of the meal.

**—CHRISTINE MONTALVO**
WINDSOR HEIGHTS, IOWA

**PREP:** 30 MIN. **COOK:** 5 MIN./BATCH
**MAKES:** 3 DOZEN

- **3 large onions, finely chopped**
- **3 medium sweet red peppers, finely chopped**
- **⅓ cup butter, cubed**
- **18 medium garlic cloves, minced, divided**
- **1 tablespoon celery salt**
- **1 tablespoon coarsely ground pepper**
- **3 pounds russet potatoes, peeled and shredded**
- **1½ cups grated Parmesan cheese**
- **1½ cups (6 ounces) shredded cheddar cheese**
- **1 cup (4 ounces) shredded part-skim mozzarella cheese**
- **1 cup all-purpose flour**
- **¾ cup sour cream**
- **¾ cup canola oil**
- **Minced fresh parsley**

**1.** In a large skillet, saute onions and red peppers in butter until tender. Add 1/4 cup garlic, celery salt and pepper; cook 1 minute longer.
**2.** Transfer to a large bowl. Add the potatoes, cheeses, flour, sour cream and remaining garlic; mix well.
**3.** Heat 2 tablespoons oil in a large nonstick skillet over medium heat. Drop the batter by 1/4 cupfuls into oil; press lightly to flatten. Fry in batches until golden brown on both sides, using remaining oil as needed. Drain on paper towels. Sprinkle with parsley.

Cheese & Red Pepper Latkes

Vanilla & Cinnamon-Kissed Apple Latkes

## Vanilla & Cinnamon-Kissed Apple Latkes

Apples replace spuds—and combine with sugar, vanilla and cinnamon—to take latkes into the dessert realm.

**—CANDY MCMENAMIN**
LEXINGTON, SOUTH CAROLINA

**PREP:** 20 MIN. **COOK:** 5 MIN./BATCH
**MAKES**: 3 DOZEN

- **2 tablespoons confectioners' sugar**
- **2 tablespoons ground cinnamon**
- **4 cups all-purpose flour**
- **⅔ cup sugar**
- **2 teaspoons baking powder**
- **½ teaspoon salt**
- **2 cups orange juice**
- **1 cup 2% milk**
- **4 eggs, lightly beaten**
- **1 teaspoon vanilla extract**
- **2¾ pounds apples (about 6 large apples), peeled and shredded**
- **¾ cup canola oil**

**1.** In a small bowl, combine the confectioners' sugar and cinnamon; set aside.
**2.** In a large bowl, combine the flour, sugar, baking powder and salt. Stir in the orange juice, milk, eggs and vanilla until blended; fold in apples.
**3.** Heat 2 tablespoons oil in a large nonstick skillet over medium heat. Drop batter by 1/4 cupfuls into oil; press lightly to flatten. Fry in batches until golden brown on both sides, using remaining oil as needed. Drain on paper towels. Sprinkle with cinnamon-sugar.

## Sauerkraut Latkes

Really? Sauerkraut in potato pancakes? Oh yes, when the apples mellow the sauerkraut's tang so very nicely.
**—AYSHA SCHURMAN** AMMON, IDAHO

**PREP:** 20 MIN. **COOK:** 5 MIN./BATCH
**MAKES:** 2½ DOZEN

- **3 pounds russet potatoes, peeled and shredded**
- **1½ cups shredded peeled apples**
- **1½ cups sauerkraut, rinsed and well drained**
- **6 eggs, lightly beaten**
- **6 tablespoons all-purpose flour**
- **2 teaspoons salt**
- **1½ teaspoons pepper**
- **¾ cup canola oil**
- **Sour cream and chopped green onions, optional**

**1.** In a large bowl, combine the potatoes, apples, sauerkraut and eggs. Combine the flour, salt and pepper; stir into potato mixture.
**2.** Heat 2 tablespoons oil in a large nonstick skillet over medium heat. Drop batter by 1/4 cupfuls into oil; press lightly to flatten. Fry in batches until golden brown on both sides, using remaining oil as needed. Drain on paper towels. Top with sour cream and green onions if desired.

Sauerkraut Latkes

Latkes with Lox

## Latkes with Lox

Inspired by a recipe showcased in the *Jewish Journal*, the Taste of Home Test Kitchen experts used lox as a topping. If you like, add fresh chives and a dollop of sour cream, too.

**PREP:** 20 MIN. **COOK:** 5 MIN./BATCH
**MAKES:** 3 DOZEN

- **2 cups finely chopped onion**
- **¼ cup all-purpose flour**
- **6 garlic cloves, minced**
- **2 teaspoons salt**
- **1 teaspoon coarsely ground pepper**
- **4 eggs, lightly beaten**
- **4 pounds russet potatoes, peeled and shredded**
- **¾ cup canola oil**

**TOPPINGS**

- **4 ounces lox**
- **Sour cream and minced fresh chives, optional**

**1.** In a large bowl, combine the first five ingredients. Stir in eggs until blended. Add potatoes; toss to coat.
**2.** Heat 2 tablespoons oil in a large nonstick skillet over medium heat. Drop the batter by 1/4 cupfuls into oil; press lightly to flatten. Fry in batches until golden brown on both sides, using remaining oil as needed. Drain on paper towels. Serve with lox; top with sour cream and chives if desired.

### Did you know?

Enjoyed in Jewish households during Hanukkah, a traditional latke is made with freshly grated or shredded potatoes (using a food processor isn't cheating) plus eggs, grated onion, salt, pepper and either flour or matzo meal. The usual topping is sour cream or applesauce, though some prefer just a sprinkling of sugar.

## FAST FIX Upside-Down Bacon Pancake

You'll make a big impression when you put this family-size pancake on the breakfast table. The sweetness of the brown sugar complements the salty bacon. If you can fit more bacon in the skillet and want to add more, go for it!

**—MINDIE HILTON**
SUSANVILLE, CALIFORNIA

**PREP/TOTAL TIME:** 30 MIN.
**MAKES:** 6 SERVINGS

- **6 bacon strips, coarsely chopped**
- **¼ cup packed brown sugar**
- **2 cups complete buttermilk pancake mix**
- **1½ cups water**
- **Maple syrup and butter, optional**

**1.** In a large ovenproof skillet, cook the bacon over medium heat until crisp. Remove the bacon to paper towels with a slotted spoon. Remove the drippings, reserving 2 tablespoons. Return bacon to pan with reserved drippings; sprinkle with brown sugar.
**2.** In a small bowl, combine pancake mix and water just until moistened. Pour into pan.
**3.** Bake at 350° for 18-20 minutes or until a toothpick inserted near the center comes out clean. Cool for 10 minutes before inverting onto a serving plate. Serve warm with maple syrup and butter if desired.

Upside-Down Bacon Pancake

## FAST FIX Brittany's Breakfast Bites

Crescent rolls stuffed with eggs, ham and other morning staples will start your day off in a satisfying way. Thanks to convenient refrigerated dough, the prep work is quick and easy.

**—BRITTANY WHITWORTH**
COLORADO SPRINGS, COLORADO

**PREP/TOTAL TIME:** 30 MIN.
**MAKES:** 8 ROLLS

- **1 tablespoon butter**
- **2 eggs**
- **3 tablespoons crumbled cooked bacon**
- **3 tablespoons finely chopped deli ham**
- **3 tablespoons shredded cheddar cheese**
- **1 tube (8 ounces) refrigerated crescent rolls**

**1.** In a large skillet, melt butter over medium-high heat. Whisk eggs; add to skillet. Cook and stir until set. Remove from the heat; add the bacon, ham and cheese.
**2.** Unroll the crescent dough; separate into triangles. Place 2 tablespoons egg mixture at the wide end of each triangle; roll up and seal the edges. Place point side down 2 in. apart on a foil-lined baking sheet; curve the ends to form a crescent.
**3.** Bake at 375° for 11-13 minutes or until golden brown. Serve immediately. Refrigerate leftovers.

## Sweet Potato Pancakes with Caramel Sauce

Have leftover sweet potatoes from a holiday dinner or other meal? They work wonderfully in pancake batter. Top them off with caramel sauce, butter and toasted cashews for a treat that looks nothing like yesterday's dish. If you don't have leftover sweet potatoes, use the canned variety.

**—SHERYL LITTLE**
SHERWOOD, ARKANSAS

**PREP:** 25 MIN. **COOK:** 10 MIN./BATCH
**MAKES:** 7 SERVINGS

- **2 cups all-purpose flour**
- **2 tablespoons packed brown sugar**
- **3 teaspoons baking powder**
- **½ teaspoon salt**
- **½ teaspoon ground ginger**
- **¼ teaspoon ground allspice**
- **¼ teaspoon ground cinnamon**
- **¼ teaspoon ground nutmeg**
- **1 egg**
- **1¾ cups 2% milk**
- **½ cup canned sweet potatoes, mashed**
- **2 tablespoons butter, melted**
- **1 jar (12 ounces) hot caramel ice cream topping, warmed**
- **¾ cup coarsely chopped unsalted cashews, toasted**
- **Whipped butter, optional**

**1.** In a small bowl, combine the first eight ingredients. In another bowl, whisk the egg, milk, sweet potatoes and melted butter. Stir into the dry ingredients just until moistened.

Blackberry Smoothies

2. Pour batter by 1/4 cupfuls onto a greased hot griddle; turn when bubbles form on top. Cook until the second side is golden brown.
3. Drizzle with caramel topping; sprinkle with nuts. Serve with whipped butter if desired.

## FAST FIX Blackberry Smoothies

Wholesome and creamy, smoothies will get you going no matter how early it is. I like to combine blackberries, mixed berries, yogurt, orange juice and honey in the blender for a 10-minute refresher. Try it as an afternoon snack, too.
**—VALERIE BELLEY** ST. LOUIS, MISSOURI

**PREP/TOTAL TIME:** 10 MIN. **MAKES:** 4 SERVINGS

- **1 cup orange juice**
- **1 cup (8 ounces) plain yogurt**
- **2 to 3 tablespoons honey**
- **1½ cups fresh or frozen blackberries**
- **½ cup frozen unsweetened mixed berries**
- **Additional blackberries and yogurt, optional**

In a blender, combine the first five ingredients; cover and process for about 15 seconds or until smooth. Pour into chilled glasses; serve immediately. Top with additional blackberries and yogurt if desired.

My mom and grandma made Nutmeg Spiced Milk—wonderful on apple crisp and oatmeal. Add 1/4 teaspoon nutmeg to 1/2 cup milk and gently warm it on the stove while stirring.
—TERESA HEANEY BELFAST, NEW YORK

## FAST FIX Soul-Satisfying Oatmeal Waffles

These homemade waffles freeze well, so feel free to toast and enjoy them all week long. For a fall-flavored version, just substitute 1/2 cup pumpkin puree for 1/2 cup of milk.
**—JEANNE STICKELL** TUCSON, ARIZONA

**PREP/TOTAL TIME:** 25 MIN. **MAKES:** 10 WAFFLES

- **1 cup all-purpose flour**
- **½ cup whole wheat flour**
- **2 packets instant maple and brown sugar oatmeal or apple cinnamon oatmeal**
- **1 tablespoon baking powder**
- **1 teaspoon ground cinnamon**
- **¼ teaspoon salt**
- **1½ cups 2% milk**
- **2 eggs**
- **⅓ cup butter, melted**
- **½ cup chopped pecans or walnuts**
- **Maple syrup**

1. In a large bowl, mix the first six ingredients. In another bowl, whisk the milk, eggs and butter. Stir into dry ingredients just until moistened. Fold in pecans.
2. Bake in a preheated waffle iron according to the manufacturer's directions until golden brown. Serve with maple syrup.

Soul-Satisfying Oatmeal Waffles

## MAKE AHEAD Flaky Egg Bake

Delicate phyllo dough brings a touch of elegance and layers of flaky, buttery crispness to this morning casserole. Loaded with Italian sausage, vegetables and three kinds of cheese, it's special enough to serve guests. Plus, you can assemble it ahead of time and freeze it for up to 3 months.
**—CRYSTAL BRUNS** ILIFF, COLORADO

**PREP:** 40 MIN. + FREEZING **BAKE:** 40 MIN. **MAKES:** 12 SERVINGS

- **¾ pound bulk Italian sausage**
- **1 cup sliced fresh mushrooms**
- **1 medium onion, finely chopped**
- **1 medium sweet red pepper, chopped**
- **1 medium green pepper, chopped**
- **6 eggs, divided**
- **1½ cups (6 ounces) shredded Havarti cheese**
- **1 package (10 ounces) frozen chopped spinach, thawed and squeezed dry**
- **1 cup ricotta cheese**
- **⅓ cup grated Parmesan cheese**
- **2 tablespoons minced fresh basil or 2 teaspoons dried basil**
- **1 cup butter, melted**
- **30 sheets phyllo dough (14 inches x 9 inches)**

**1.** In a large skillet, cook sausage, mushrooms, onion and peppers over medium heat until meat is no longer pink and vegetables are tender; drain. Return sausage mixture to skillet. Whisk 5 eggs; add to skillet. Cook and stir over medium-high heat until set; stir in Havarti cheese. Set aside.
**2.** In a small bowl, combine the spinach, ricotta cheese, Parmesan cheese, basil and remaining egg. Brush a 13-in. x 9-in. baking pan with butter. Unroll the phyllo dough; trim to fit into the pan.
**3.** Layer 10 sheets in the prepared pan, brushing each sheet with butter. (Keep remaining phyllo covered with plastic wrap and a damp towel to prevent it from drying out.) Top with half of the sausage mixture.
**4.** Layer with 10 additional phyllo sheets, brushing each with butter; spread with ricotta mixture. Layer with five phyllo sheets, brushing again with butter; top with the remaining sausage mixture. Layer with the remaining phyllo and butter. Using a sharp knife, cut into 12 rectangles. Cover and freeze the casserole for up to 3 months.
**5. TO USE FROZEN CASSEROLE:** Thaw in refrigerator overnight. Remove from refrigerator 30 minutes before baking. Cover and bake at 350° for 40-50 minutes or until golden brown and heated through.
**Editor's Note:** *Look for phyllo dough in the frozen pastry section.*

Flaky Egg Bake

## Great Granola

Here's a crunchy mix to enjoy as a topping on oatmeal or to gobble up by the handful as a snack. Want a made-from-scratch gift for Christmas? Put the granola in a see-through container decked with tinsel and tie on mini ornaments as trims.
**—JOHNNA JOHNSON** SCOTTSDALE, ARIZONA

**PREP:** 25 MIN. **BAKE:** 25 MIN. + COOLING **MAKES:** 7 CUPS

- **2 cups old-fashioned oats**
- **½ cup chopped almonds**
- **½ cup salted pumpkin seeds or pepitas**
- **½ cup chopped walnuts**
- **¼ cup chopped pecans**
- **¼ cup sesame seeds**
- **¼ cup sunflower kernels**
- **⅓ cup honey**
- **¼ cup packed brown sugar**
- **¼ cup maple syrup**
- **2 tablespoons toasted wheat germ**
- **2 tablespoons canola oil**
- **1 teaspoon ground cinnamon**
- **1 teaspoon vanilla extract**
- **1 package (7 ounces) dried fruit bits**

**1.** In a large bowl, combine the first seven ingredients; set aside.
**2.** In a small saucepan, combine the honey, brown sugar, syrup, wheat germ, oil and cinnamon. Cook and stir over medium heat for 4-5 minutes or until smooth. Remove from the heat; stir in vanilla. Pour over the oat mixture and toss to coat.
**3.** Transfer to a greased 15-in. x 10-in. x 1-in. baking pan. Bake at 350° for 22-27 minutes or until golden brown, stirring occasionally. Cool completely on a wire rack. Stir in fruit bits. Store in an airtight container.

## Individual Italian Frittatas

**PREP:** 25 MIN. **BAKE:** 20 MIN.
**MAKES:** 2 SERVINGS

- **¼ cup finely chopped onion**
- **2 teaspoons olive oil**
- **4 medium fresh mushrooms, chopped**
- **4 thinly sliced hard salami, julienned**
- **2 tablespoons finely chopped roasted sweet red pepper**
- **4 eggs**
- **1 tablespoon 2% milk**
- **1 tablespoon grated Parmesan cheese**
- **2 teaspoons minced fresh parsley**
- **1 teaspoon minced fresh chives**
- **Dash pepper**
- **¼ cup shredded part-skim mozzarella cheese**
- **Chopped fresh chives, optional**

**1.** In a small skillet, cook and stir onion in oil over medium heat until tender. Add mushrooms; cook 2-4 minutes longer or until tender. Divide between two greased 8-oz. ramekins. Top with the salami and red pepper.

**2.** In a small bowl, whisk the eggs, milk, Parmesan cheese, parsley, minced chives and pepper; pour into ramekins. Bake at 400° for 10 minutes.

**3.** Sprinkle with mozzarella cheese; bake 8-10 minutes longer or until eggs are set. Sprinkle with chopped chives if desired.

**Individual Italian Frittatas**

**Raspberry-Lime Yogurt Dip for Fresh Fruit**

The Italian word "frittata" refers to frying the egg-based dish in a skillet. My Individual Italian Frittatas bake in a ramekin, but the result is the same—a great menu item day or night.

**—NANCY ELLIOTT** HOUSTON, TEXAS

## FAST FIX Raspberry-Lime Yogurt Dip for Fresh Fruit

A bowl of fresh, seasonal fruit is always a welcome sight on breakfast tables and brunch buffets. To make a good thing even better, include a creamy, sweet-tangy dip.

**—CLARA COULSON MINNEY**
WASHINGTON COURT HOUSE, OHIO

**PREP:** 15 MIN. **MAKES:** 1¾ CUPS

- **1 cup fresh or frozen unsweetened raspberries, thawed and drained**
- **1¼ cups reduced-fat plain Greek yogurt**
- **⅓ cup packed brown sugar**
- **1 tablespoon lime juice**
- **½ teaspoon grated lime peel**
- **Assorted fresh fruit**

Place raspberries in a blender; cover and process until smooth. Strain and discard seeds. In a large bowl, whisk yogurt, brown sugar, lime juice, peel and raspberry puree until blended. Chill until serving. Serve with fruit.

## FAST FIX Cinnamon-Toast Blueberry Bakes

What a treat! These little toast cups dotted with blueberries are so yummy served warm from the oven.

**—CLAIRE WATSON**
CAPE GIRARDEU, MISSOURI

**PREP/TOTAL TIME:** 30 MIN.
**MAKES:** 4 SERVINGS

- **6 tablespoons butter, melted**
- **3 tablespoons sugar**
- **½ teaspoon ground cinnamon**
- **4 slices whole wheat bread, cut into ½-inch cubes**
- **1 cup fresh or frozen blueberries**
- **¼ cup packed brown sugar**
- **2 teaspoons lemon juice**

**1.** In a large bowl, combine the butter, sugar and cinnamon. Add bread cubes; toss to coat. In a small bowl, combine the remaining ingredients; toss to coat.

**2.** Place half of bread mixture in four 8-oz. ramekins. Layer with blueberry mixture and remaining bread mixture. Bake, uncovered, at 350° for 15-20 minutes or until crisp and heated through.

# Potluck Pleasers

**Wow the crowd** at a neighborhood block party, church social or other get-together with the **large-yield dishes** in this chapter. Everyone will line up for a helping—and go back for seconds!

"Instead of bringing the usual spinach or artichoke dip to your next event, add a Southern touch using collard greens. If you like, replace the wedges of flatbread with tortilla chips."

—**BILLIE WILLIAMS-HENDERSON** BOWIE, MARYLAND

## Buffalo Chicken Wings

Hot wings got their start in a kitchen in Buffalo, New York. Although there was no sporting event on TV at the time, zippy wings and cool sauces are now traditional game-day fare across the country. Cayenne, red sauce and spices keep these wings nice and hot, just like the originals.
—**NANCY CHAPMAN** CENTER HARBOR, NEW HAMPSHIRE

**PREP:** 10 MIN. **COOK:** 10 MIN./BATCH **MAKES:** ABOUT 4 DOZEN

- **25 whole chicken wings (5 pounds)**
- **Oil for frying**
- **1 cup butter, cubed**
- **¼ cup Louisiana-style hot sauce**
- **¾ teaspoon cayenne pepper**
- **¾ teaspoon celery salt**
- **½ teaspoon onion powder**
- **½ teaspoon garlic powder**
- **Celery ribs and ranch salad dressing, optional**

1. Cut chicken wings into three sections; discard wing tip sections. In an electric skillet, heat 1 in. of oil to 375°. Fry wings in oil, a few at a time, for 3-4 minutes on each side or until chicken juices run clear. Drain on paper towels.
2. Meanwhile, in a small saucepan, melt butter. Stir in the hot sauce and spices. Place chicken in a large bowl; add sauce and toss to coat. Remove to a serving plate with a slotted spoon. Serve with celery and ranch dressing if desired.

**Editor's Note:** *Uncooked chicken wing sections (wingettes) may be substituted for whole chicken wings.*

Buffalo Chicken Wings

Jalapeno Popper Spread

## Jalapeno Popper Spread

My cheese spread is great for busy days because it goes together without a lot of fuss. I've been told by party-goers that it tastes exactly like a jalapeno popper.
—**ARIANE MCALPINE** PENTICTON, BRITISH COLUMBIA

**PREP:** 10 MIN. **BAKE:** 25 MIN. **MAKES:** 16 SERVINGS

- **2 packages (8 ounces each) cream cheese, softened**
- **1 cup mayonnaise**
- **½ cup shredded Monterey Jack cheese**
- **¼ cup canned chopped green chilies**
- **¼ cup canned diced jalapeno peppers**
- **1 cup shredded Parmesan cheese**
- **½ cup panko (Japanese) bread crumbs**
- **Sweet red and yellow pepper pieces and corn chips**

In a large bowl, beat the first five ingredients until blended; spread into an ungreased 9-in. pie plate. Sprinkle with Parmesan cheese; top with bread crumbs. Bake at 400° for 25-30 minutes or until lightly browned. Serve with peppers and chips.

## FAST FIX Speedy Salsa

Skip the usual store-bought salsa and savor the flavor of a homemade version. For a smaller batch, simply cut the recipe in half...or share jars with family and friends.
—**DANA SAPP** SCOTTSVILLE, KENTUCKY

**PREP/TOTAL TIME:** 20 MIN. **MAKES:** 7 CUPS

- **4 cans (14½ ounces each) diced tomatoes, drained**
- **2 medium onions, chopped**
- **½ cup minced fresh cilantro**
- **2 jalapeno peppers, seeded and minced**
- **2 tablespoons sugar**
- **1 teaspoon salt**
- **Tortilla chips**

In a large bowl, combine the first six ingredients. Cover and chill until serving. Serve with tortilla chips.

**Editor's Note:** *Wear disposable gloves when cutting hot peppers; the oils can burn skin. Avoid touching your face.*

## Garden Veggie Lasagna

Ever stroll the farmers market and find vegetables you don't know what to do with? Combine them into one harmonious harvest and assemble a wonderfully cheesy, saucy lasagna. It's so good, you won't miss the meat.

**—SAMANTHA NEAL**
MORGANTOWN, WEST VIRGINIA

**PREP:** 50 MIN.
**BAKE:** 35 MIN. + STANDING
**MAKES:** 12 SERVINGS

- **2 medium zucchini, sliced diagonally ¼-in. thick**
- **2 cups fresh broccoli florets**
- **2 large carrots, julienned**
- **2 medium sweet red peppers, julienned**
- **¼ cup olive oil**
- **2 garlic cloves, minced**
- **¾ teaspoon dried thyme**
- **½ teaspoon salt**
- **½ teaspoon pepper**

**SAUCE**

- **2 cups finely chopped baby portobello mushrooms**
- **1 large onion, finely chopped**
- **2 garlic cloves, minced**
- **2 tablespoons olive oil**
- **2 cans (28 ounces each) crushed tomatoes**
- **3 teaspoons Italian seasoning**
- **¾ teaspoon salt**
- **¾ teaspoon pepper**

**FILLING**

- **1¼ cups ricotta cheese**
- **1 package (8 ounces) cream cheese, softened**
- **¾ cup grated Parmesan cheese**
- **1 egg, lightly beaten**
- **2 teaspoons dried basil**

**ASSEMBLY**

- **12 no-cook lasagna noodles**
- **3 cups (12 ounces) shredded Italian cheese blend**

1. Place the first nine ingredients in a large bowl; toss to coat. Arrange on two greased 15-in. x 10-in. x 1-in. baking pans. Bake at 425° for 10-15 minutes or until tender, stirring occasionally.
2. Meanwhile, in a Dutch oven, saute the mushrooms, onion and garlic in oil until tender. Stir in the remaining sauce ingredients; bring to a boil. Reduce the heat; simmer, uncovered, for 10-12 minutes, stirring occasionally.
3. In a large bowl, combine the filling ingredients. Spread 1 cup tomato sauce into a greased 13-in. x 9-in. baking dish. Layer a third of the lasagna noodles, a third of the ricotta cheese mixture, half of the vegetables, a third of the remaining tomato sauce and a third of the Italian cheese blend; repeat. Top with the remaining lasagna noodles, ricotta mixture, tomato sauce and Italian cheese blend.
4. Cover and bake at 350° for 35-40 minutes or until bubbly. Let lasagna stand for 15 minutes before cutting.

Garden Veggie Lasagna

Don't let the length of the ingredient list stop you from preparing a pan of mouthwatering Garden Veggie Lasagna. Many of the items are pantry staples you probably already have in your kitchen—and the end result is well worth it!

**—SAMANTHA NEAL**
MORGANTOWN, WEST VIRGINIA

When reheating a piece of lasagna in the microwave, I stick a toothpick into the center of the piece partway down and then "tent" a microwave-safe paper towel over the top. After reheating, I have very little splatter in my microwave, and the cheese isn't stuck to the paper towel.

—CYNTHIA WOODROW
MORENO VALLEY, CALIFORNIA

## Coconut-Bourbon Sweet Potatoes

**PREP:** 25 MIN. **BAKE:** 35 MIN.
**MAKES:** 14 SERVINGS

- **8 cups mashed sweet potatoes**
- **¾ cup half-and-half cream**
- **½ cup packed brown sugar**
- **½ cup bourbon**
- **2 eggs**
- **¼ cup honey**
- **3 teaspoons vanilla extract**
- **1¼ teaspoons ground cinnamon**
- **¼ teaspoon salt**
- **1 tablespoon molasses, optional**
- **½ teaspoon ground cardamom, optional**
- **1 cup flaked coconut**
- **¾ cup golden raisins**
- **1½ cups miniature marshmallows**

**TOPPING**

- **½ cup all-purpose flour**
- **½ cup packed brown sugar**
- **1 teaspoon ground cinnamon**
- **⅓ cup butter, melted**
- **1 cup chopped pecans**

1. In a large bowl, combine the first nine ingredients; add molasses and cardamom if desired. Stir in coconut and raisins. Transfer to a greased 13-in. x 9-in. baking dish; sprinkle with marshmallows.

Have family members or friends who refuse to eat sweet potatoes? Try my Coconut-Bourbon Sweet Potatoes, and you just might win them over. The rich addition of coconut, spices and bourbon results in an extra-special treat.
—**REBECCA ANDERSON** DRIFTWOOD, TEXAS

2. In a small bowl, combine the flour, brown sugar and cinnamon. Add butter; mix until crumbly. Stir in pecans; sprinkle over marshmallows.
3. Bake, uncovered, at 350° for 35-40 minutes or until heated through and topping is golden brown.

**Coconut-Bourbon Sweet Potatoes**

## Two-Cheese Mac 'n' Cheese

Different stories claim that macaroni and cheese was invented by everyone from Thomas Jefferson to an Italian housewife. All I know is that the two cheeses—cheddar and Asiago—in this version make it doubly delightful.
—**STEPHANIE SORBIE**
GLENDALE, ARIZONA

**PREP:** 35 MIN. **BAKE:** 35 MIN.
**MAKES:** 15 SERVINGS

- **1 package (16 ounces) spiral pasta**
- **3 tablespoons butter**
- **3 garlic cloves, minced, optional**
- **3 tablespoons all-purpose flour**
- **⅛ teaspoon pepper**
- **Dash salt**
- **4 cups 2% milk**
- **5 cups (20 ounces) shredded sharp cheddar cheese, divided**
- **1 cup shredded Asiago cheese**

1. In a Dutch oven, cook pasta according to package directions.
2. Meanwhile, in a large saucepan, melt butter over medium heat. Add garlic if desired; cook and stir until tender. Stir in the flour, pepper and salt until blended; cook and stir until golden brown, about 5 minutes. Gradually whisk in milk, stirring until smooth. Bring to a boil; cook 2 minutes longer or until thickened.
3. Remove from the heat. Stir in 4 cups cheddar cheese and Asiago cheese until melted. Mixture will thicken.
4. Drain pasta and return to the pan; stir in cheese sauce. Transfer to a greased 13-in. x 9-in. baking dish. Sprinkle with remaining cheddar cheese.
5. Bake, uncovered, at 350° for 35-40 minutes or until golden brown. Let stand for 5 minutes before serving.

## Cowabunga Root Beer Cupcakes

I whipped up a batch of these root beer-flavored cakes for my daughter's first birthday party. They're so easy to create using a purchased mix.
—**MINDY CARSWELL**
WALKER, MICHIGAN

**PREP:** 10 MIN.
**BAKE:** 15 MIN. + COOLING
**MAKES:** 24 SERVINGS

- **1 package (18½ ounces) butter recipe golden cake mix**
- **4 teaspoons root beer concentrate, divided**
- **1 carton (12 ounces) frozen whipped topping, thawed**
- **Vanilla ice cream**

1. Prepare and bake cupcakes according to package directions, adding 2 teaspoons root beer concentrate when mixing batter. Remove to wire racks to cool completely.
2. In a small bowl, mix whipped topping and remaining root beer concentrate until blended; spread over cupcakes. Serve with ice cream.

SLOW COOKER | MAKE AHEAD

## Mom's Italian Beef Sandwiches

My mother made the best Italian beef. I've added to the recipe a bit over the years, but it's still hers. She liked to fix it for family reunions, and there were never any leftovers. Now I prepare it for myself and freeze individual-size portions for a quick, meaty dinner served on a bun or over noodles.

—MARY MCVEY
COLFAX, NORTH CAROLINA

**PREP:** 20 MIN. **COOK:** 8 HOURS
**MAKES:** 16 SERVINGS

- **1 boneless beef rump roast or bottom round roast (2 pounds), halved**
- **1 boneless beef chuck roast (2 pounds), halved**
- **1 beef sirloin tip roast (1 pound)**
- **2 tablespoons canola oil**
- **2 cups water**
- **1 medium onion, chopped**
- **4 garlic cloves, minced**
- **2 envelopes Italian salad dressing mix**
- **1 envelope zesty Italian salad dressing mix**
- **1 envelope (0.87 ounce) brown gravy mix**
- **2 tablespoons crushed red pepper flakes**
- **1 tablespoon Italian seasoning**
- **2 teaspoons Worcestershire sauce**
- **16 hoagie buns, split**
- **Sliced provolone cheese, optional**
- **Giardiniera, optional**

1. In a large skillet, brown each roast in oil on all sides. Drain. Transfer meat to a 7-qt. slow cooker. Combine the water, onion, garlic, salad dressing and gravy mixes, pepper flakes, Italian seasoning and Worcestershire sauce; pour over beef. Cover and cook on low for 8-10 hours or until meat is tender.
2. Remove beef; cool slightly. Skim fat from cooking juices. Pour juices into a large bowl. Shred beef with two forks; add to bowl. Cool. Transfer to freezer containers. Freeze for up to 3 months.
3. TO USE FROZEN MEAT: Thaw in the refrigerator overnight. Place in a Dutch oven; heat through. Using a slotted spoon, place ½ cup on each bun. Top with cheese and giardiniera if desired.

Mom's Italian Beef Sandwiches

Baked Reuben Dip

## Baked Reuben Dip

I love the traditional Reuben sandwich, and this dip combines its distinctive ingredients—from corned beef to sauerkraut—into a baked appetizer. Pair it with a basket of rye crackers, and you'll have a winner every time.

—JEFFREY METZLER
CHILLICOTHE, OHIO

**PREP:** 10 MIN. **BAKE:** 25 MIN.
**MAKES:** 8 CUPS

- **1 jar (32 ounces) sauerkraut, rinsed and well drained**
- **10 ounces sliced deli corned beef, chopped**
- **2 cups (8 ounces) shredded sharp cheddar cheese**
- **2 cups (8 ounces) shredded Swiss cheese**
- **1 cup mayonnaise**
- **¼ cup Russian salad dressing**
- **1 teaspoon caraway seeds, optional**
- **Rye crackers**

In a large bowl, mix the first six ingredients; stir in caraway seeds if desired. Transfer to a greased 13-in. x 9-in. baking dish. Bake at 350° for 25-30 minutes or until bubbly. Serve with crackers.

## Hot Collards & Artichoke Dip

Instead of bringing the usual spinach or artichoke dip to your next event, add a Southern touch using collard greens. If you like, replace the wedges of flatbread with tortilla chips.

**—BILLIE WILLIAMS-HENDERSON**
BOWIE, MARYLAND

**PREP:** 20 MIN. **BAKE:** 25 MIN.
**MAKES:** 24 SERVINGS (¼ CUP EACH)

- **12 ounces frozen chopped collard greens (about 4 cups), thawed and squeezed dry**
- **2 jars (7½ ounces each) marinated quartered artichoke hearts, drained and chopped**
- **1 cup (8 ounces) sour cream**
- **1 package (6½ ounces) garlic-herb cheese spread**
- **1 cup grated Parmesan cheese**
- **10 thick-sliced peppered bacon strips, cooked and crumbled**
- **¾ cup mayonnaise**
- **1½ cups (6 ounces) shredded part-skim mozzarella cheese, divided**
- **Garlic naan flatbreads, warmed and cut into wedges**

1. In a large bowl, mix the first seven ingredients and 1 cup mozzarella cheese until blended. Transfer to a greased 11-in. x 7-in. baking dish. Sprinkle with remaining mozzarella cheese.
2. Bake, uncovered, at 350° for 20-25 minutes or until heated through and mozzarella cheese is melted. Serve with garlic naan flatbread wedges.

## MAKE AHEAD Savory BLT Cheesecake

Did you know that cheesecake can be savory instead of sweet? Served on lettuce, this BLT version is great on its own, but it's also fantastic as a spread with crackers. Feel free to substitute another cheese for the Gruyere and to toss in olives, cooked mushrooms, crab—whatever strikes your fancy.

**—JONI HILTON** ROCKLIN, CALIFORNIA

**PREP:** 35 MIN.
**BAKE:** 45 MIN. + CHILLING
**MAKES:** 24 SERVINGS

- **¾ cup dry bread crumbs**
- **½ cup grated Parmesan cheese**
- **3 tablespoons butter, melted**

**FILLING**

- **4 packages (8 ounces each) cream cheese, softened**
- **½ cup heavy whipping cream**
- **1½ cups crumbled cooked bacon**
- **1 cup oil-packed sun-dried tomatoes, patted dry and chopped**
- **1 cup (4 ounces) shredded Gruyere or Swiss cheese**
- **2 green onions, sliced**
- **1 teaspoon freshly ground pepper**
- **4 eggs, lightly beaten**
- **Optional toppings: shredded iceberg lettuce, chopped cherry tomatoes and additional crumbled cooked bacon**
- **Assorted crackers**

1. Place a greased 9-in. springform pan on a double thickness of heavy-duty foil (about 18 in. square). Securely wrap foil around pan.
2. In a small bowl, combine the bread crumbs, Parmesan cheese and butter. Press onto the bottom of prepared pan. Place pan on a baking sheet. Bake at 325° for 12 minutes. Cool on a wire rack.
3. In a large bowl, beat cream cheese and cream until smooth. Beat in the bacon, tomatoes, Gruyere cheese, onions and pepper. Add eggs; beat on low speed just until combined. Pour over crust. Place springform pan in a large baking pan; add 1 in. of boiling water to larger pan.
4. Bake at 325° for 45-55 minutes or until center is just set and top appears dull. Remove springform pan from water bath; remove foil. Cool cheesecake on a wire rack for 10 minutes; loosen edges from pan with a knife. Cool 1 hour longer. Refrigerate overnight.
5. Remove rim from pan. Serve cheesecake with toppings and crackers if desired.

Hot Collards & Artichoke Dip

SLOW COOKER

## Black Bean, Chorizo & Sweet Potato Chili

**PREP:** 20 MIN. **COOK:** 6 HOURS
**MAKES:** 16 SERVINGS (4 QT.)

- **1 pound uncooked chorizo, casings removed, or spicy bulk pork sausage**
- **1 large onion, chopped**
- **2 poblano peppers, finely chopped**
- **2 jalapeno peppers, seeded and finely chopped**
- **3 tablespoons tomato paste**
- **3 large sweet potatoes, peeled and cut into ½-in. cubes**
- **4 cans (14½ oz. each) fire-roasted diced tomatoes, undrained**
- **2 cans (15 oz. each) black beans, rinsed and drained**
- **2 cups beef stock**
- **2 tablespoons chili powder**
- **1 tablespoon dried oregano**
- **1 tablespoon ground coriander**
- **1 tablespoon ground cumin**
- **1 tablespoon smoked paprika**
- **¼ cup lime juice**

1. In a large skillet, cook and stir the chorizo, onion, poblanos and jalapenos over medium heat for 8-10 minutes or until chorizo is cooked. Using a slotted spoon, transfer to a 6-qt. slow cooker.
2. Stir in paste. Add the potatoes, tomatoes, beans, stock and spices; stir to combine. Cover and cook on low for 6-7 hours or until potatoes are tender. Stir in lime juice.

Black Bean, Chorizo & Sweet Potato Chili

Cheese-Stuffed Meatball Sliders

Garden Veg Salsa

Chili is one of my all-time favorites. Black Bean, Chorizo & Sweet Potato Chili takes it to the next level with the addition of surprisingly different flavors.
**—JULIE MERRIMAN** COLD BROOK, NEW YORK

## Cheese-Stuffed Meatball Sliders

Tailgating? Fix these in advance and warm them up on the grill at the game.
**—HILARY BREINHOLT**
GLENWOOD, UTAH

**PREP:** 15 MIN. **BAKE:** 25 MIN.
**MAKES:** 16 SERVINGS

- **1½ pounds bulk Italian sausage**
- **16 cubes part-skim mozzarella cheese**
- **1 jar (24 oz.) spaghetti sauce**
- **1 jar (8.1 oz.) prepared pesto**
- **16 dinner rolls, split and toasted**

1. Divide sausage into 16 portions. Shape each portion around a cube of cheese. Place on a greased rack in a shallow baking pan. Bake at 350° for 25-30 minutes or until meat is no longer pink. Remove to paper towels to drain.
2. Meanwhile, in a large saucepan, combine spaghetti sauce and pesto; bring just to a boil over medium heat, stirring occasionally. Add meatballs; heat through, stirring gently. Serve on rolls.

FAST FIX

## Garden Veg Salsa

We love this zippy, chunky salsa made mostly with fresh-picked tomatoes, peppers and other garden vegetables. You can easily adjust the ingredients to suit your family's tastes.
**—DAWN GILSON**
DENMARK, WISCONSIN

**PREP/TOTAL TIME:** 20 MIN.
**MAKES:** 6 CUPS

- **3 large tomatoes, chopped**
- **1 cup chopped cucumber**
- **1 medium sweet yellow or red pepper, chopped**
- **¾ cup chopped zucchini**
- **1 small red onion, finely chopped**
- **½ cup chopped fresh cilantro**
- **1 jalapeno pepper, seeded and finely chopped**
- **2 tablespoons olive oil**
- **1 tablespoon white vinegar**
- **¾ teaspoon pepper**
- **½ teaspoon salt**
- **½ teaspoon ground cumin**
- **Tortilla chips**

In a large bowl, combine all ingredients; toss to combine. Refrigerate, covered, until serving. Serve with chips.

**Editor's Note:** *Wear disposable gloves when cutting hot peppers; the oils can burn skin. Avoid touching your face.*

## Chive & Onion Hash Brown Potatoes

Have potatoes in your pantry but don't know what to do with them? Peel and shred enough to measure 8 cups, and you'll have just the right amount to whip up a big pan of hash browns. To quickly and easily prepare the potatoes, use a food processor fitted with a shredding disk.

**—BARB TEMPLIN**
NORWOOD, MINNESOTA

**PREP:** 15 MIN.
**BAKE:** 45 MIN. + STANDING
**MAKES:** 12 SERVINGS

- **1½ cups half-and-half cream**
- **1 cup spreadable chive and onion cream cheese**
- **2 tablespoons dried minced onion**
- **1 teaspoon salt**
- **½ teaspoon pepper**
- **2 packages (20 ounces each) refrigerated shredded hash brown potatoes**
- **2 cups shredded Swiss cheese**
- **3 tablespoons minced fresh chives, divided**
- **2 tablespoons butter, cubed**

**1.** In a small saucepan, combine the first five ingredients. Cook and stir over medium heat until blended; transfer to a large bowl. Add potatoes; mix well.
**2.** In a greased 13-in. x 9-in. or 3-qt. baking dish, layer a third of the hash brown mixture and a third of the cheese; sprinkle with 1 tablespoon chives. Repeat layers. Top with remaining hash brown mixture and cheese; dot with butter.
**3.** Cover and bake at 375° for 35 minutes. Uncover; bake 10-20 minutes longer or until edges begin to brown. Let stand for 10 minutes before cutting. Sprinkle with remaining chives.

## MAKE AHEAD Cheese & Crab Brunch Bake

Your family and friends are sure to love this seafood casserole. It can be assembled in half an hour, popped in the fridge overnight and ready for its baked debut the next day.

**—JOYCE CONWAY**
WESTERVILLE, OHIO

**PREP:** 30 MIN. + CHILLING
**BAKE:** 50 MIN. **MAKES:** 12 SERVINGS

- **2 tablespoons Dijon mustard**
- **6 English muffins, split**
- **8 ounces lump crabmeat, drained**
- **2 tablespoons lemon juice**
- **2 teaspoons grated lemon peel**
- **2 cups (8 ounces) shredded white cheddar cheese**
- **12 eggs**
- **1 cup half-and-half cream**
- **1 cup 2% milk**
- **½ cup mayonnaise**
- **1 teaspoon salt**
- **½ teaspoon cayenne pepper**
- **½ teaspoon pepper**
- **2 cups (8 ounces) shredded Swiss cheese**
- **1 cup grated Parmesan cheese**
- **4 green onions, chopped**
- **¼ cup finely chopped sweet red pepper**
- **¼ cup finely chopped sweet yellow pepper**

**1.** Spread mustard over bottom half of muffins. Place in a greased 13-in. x 9-in. baking dish. Top with crab, lemon juice and peel. Sprinkle with cheddar cheese. Top with muffin tops; set aside.
**2.** In a large bowl, whisk the eggs, cream, milk, mayonnaise, salt, cayenne and pepper. Pour over muffins; sprinkle with Swiss cheese, Parmesan cheese, onions and peppers. Cover and refrigerate overnight.
**3.** Remove from the refrigerator 30 minutes before baking. Cover and bake at 375° for 30 minutes. Uncover; bake 20-25 minutes longer or until set. Let stand for 5 minutes before serving.

Plan on serving Gingerbread Pancakes with Banana Cream—or another flapjack recipe—at a family gathering or kids' party? Bring a bit of extra fun to the meal with pancakes of different shapes. Simply cook the cakes on the griddle using cookie cutters or pancake molds to form whatever shapes you like. For example, choose a gingerbread man for Christmastime, a bunny for Easter Sunday brunch, a dog or cat for pet lovers...the possibilities are endless!

## Gingerbread Pancakes with Banana Cream

To save time during the busy holiday season, I make and refrigerate the batter for my gingerbread pancakes two hours before cooking. That way, I don't have to fuss with measuring ingredients while my guests mill about the kitchen awaiting brunch.

**—BARBARA BRITTAIN**
SANTEE, CALIFORNIA

**PREP:** 25 MIN. **COOK:** 5 MIN./BATCH
**MAKES:** 42 PANCAKES (4⅔ CUPS TOPPING)

- **2 cups heavy whipping cream**
- **⅓ cup confectioners' sugar**
- **2 medium bananas, chopped**
- **¾ cup butter, softened**
- **1½ cups packed brown sugar**
- **6 eggs**
- **1½ cups molasses**
- **6 cups all-purpose flour**
- **4½ teaspoons baking powder**
- **1 tablespoon ground ginger**
- **1 tablespoon ground cinnamon**
- **2¼ teaspoons salt**
- **¾ teaspoon ground allspice**
- **4 cups 2% milk**

**1.** In a large bowl, beat cream until it begins to thicken. Add confectioners' sugar; beat until soft peaks form. Fold in bananas. Cover and chill until serving.
**2.** In a very large bowl, cream butter and brown sugar until light and fluffy. Add eggs, one at a time, beating well after each addition. Beat in molasses. Combine the flour, baking powder, ginger, cinnamon, salt and allspice; add to the creamed mixture alternately with milk, beating well after each addition.
**3.** Pour batter by ¼ cupfuls onto a greased hot griddle; turn when bubbles form on top. Cook until the second side is golden brown. Serve with banana cream.

Cheese & Crab Brunch Bake
Chive & Onion Hash Brown Potatoes
Gingerbread Pancakes with Banana Cream
taste of home COOKBOOK
BAKING

## Bite-Size Apple Pies

These little bites from the Taste of Home Test Kitchen are fun for kids to help with. Simply wrap strips of pastry around apple wedges and shake on some cinnamon-sugar. Then just bake and watch them disappear!

**PREP:** 20 MIN. **BAKE:** 15 MIN.
**MAKES:** 16 SERVINGS

- **½ cup sugar**
- **2 teaspoons ground cinnamon**
- **1 package (14.1 ounces) refrigerated pie pastry**
- **3 tablespoons butter, melted, divided**
- **2 medium tart apples, each cut into 8 wedges**

1. In a small bowl, combine the sugar and cinnamon; set aside 1 tablespoon. On a lightly floured surface, unroll pastry. Brush with 2 tablespoons butter; sprinkle with remaining sugar mixture.
2. Cut each sheet into eight 1-in. strips, about 8 inches long. Wrap one strip around each apple wedge, placing the sugared side of the pastry against the apple.
3. Place on parchment paper-lined baking sheet. Brush tops with remaining butter; sprinkle with the reserved sugar mixture. Bake at 425° for 13-15 minutes or until pastry is golden brown. Serve warm.

Bite-Size Apple Pies

## MAKE AHEAD Make-Ahead Hearty Six-Layer Salad

Here's one of our all-time favorite recipes. I reach for it whenever I need a potluck contribution because I can do the prep work the day before.

**—NOREEN MEYER**
MADISON, WISCONSIN

**PREP:** 20 MIN. + CHILLING
**MAKES:** 12 SERVINGS

- **1½ cups uncooked small pasta shells**
- **1 tablespoon vegetable oil**
- **3 cups shredded lettuce**
- **3 hard-cooked eggs, sliced**
- **¼ teaspoon salt**
- **⅛ teaspoon pepper**
- **2 cups shredded cooked chicken breast**
- **1 package (10 ounces) frozen peas, thawed**

**DRESSING**

- **1 cup mayonnaise**
- **¼ cup sour cream**
- **2 green onions, chopped**
- **2 teaspoons Dijon mustard**

**TOPPINGS**

- **1 cup (4 ounces) shredded Colby or Monterey Jack cheese**
- **2 tablespoons minced fresh parsley**

1. Cook pasta according to the package directions; drain and rinse with cold water. Drizzle with oil and toss to coat.
2. Place the lettuce in a 2½-qt. glass serving bowl; top with pasta and eggs. Sprinkle with salt and pepper. Layer with chicken and peas. In a small bowl, mix dressing ingredients until blended; spread over top. Refrigerate, covered, for several hours or overnight.
3. Just before serving, sprinkle with cheese and parsley.

Marinated Fresh Vegetable Salad

## MAKE AHEAD Marinated Fresh Vegetable Salad

My veggie bowl is full of the goodness of the garden, and the light marinade allows the just-picked flavor to shine through. When I feel like a change of pace and have some zucchini, I use that in place of the cucumber.

**—HARRIET STICHTER**
MILFORD, INDIANA

**PREP:** 25 MIN. + CHILLING
**MAKES:** 12 SERVINGS (¾ CUP EACH)

- **2 cups sliced celery**
- **2 cups thinly sliced cauliflower**
- **2 cups halved cherry tomatoes**
- **2 cups thinly sliced carrots**
- **2 cups sliced cucumber**
- **1 medium onion, thinly sliced and separated into rings**

**DRESSING**

- **¾ cup olive oil**
- **½ cup minced fresh parsley**
- **3 tablespoons white wine vinegar**
- **1 garlic clove, minced**
- **1 teaspoon salt**
- **1 teaspoon ground mustard**
- **⅛ teaspoon pepper**

In a large serving bowl, combine the vegetables. In a small bowl, whisk the dressing ingredients. Pour over vegetables; gently toss to coat. Cover and refrigerate for at least 2 hours or overnight. Serve with a slotted spoon.

## FAST FIX Crunchy Cool Coleslaw

**PREP/TOTAL TIME:** 30 MIN.
**MAKES:** 16 SERVINGS

- **2 packages (16 ounces each) coleslaw mix**
- **2 medium Honey Crisp apples, julienned**
- **1 large carrot, shredded**
- **¾ cup chopped red onion**
- **½ cup chopped green pepper**
- **½ cup cider vinegar**
- **⅓ cup canola oil**
- **1½ teaspoons sugar**
- **½ teaspoon celery seed**
- **½ teaspoon salt**
- **½ cup coarsely chopped dry roasted peanuts or cashews**

1. In a large bowl, combine the first five ingredients. In a small bowl, whisk the vinegar, oil, sugar, celery seed and salt.
2. Just before serving, pour dressing over salad; toss to coat. Sprinkle with peanuts.

Crunchy Cool Coleslaw

After having a peanutty slaw at a popular restaurant, I experimented at home and came up with Crunchy Cool Coleslaw. I think it's a pretty close match!
—ELAINE HOFFMANN SANTA ANA, CALIFORNIA

## Lemon Vinaigrette Potato Salad

I created this for a friend who needed a potato salad that could withstand sitting outdoors in typical Fourth of July heat. The lemony vinaigrette is a safe yet crowd-pleasing alternative to the usual mayonnaise-based versions. For variety, substitute fresh thyme or other fresh herbs for the basil.
—MELANIE CLOYD
MULLICA HILL, NEW JERSEY

**PREP:** 25 MIN. **COOK:** 15 MIN.
**MAKES:** 12 SERVINGS

- **3 pounds red potatoes, cut into 1-inch cubes**
- **½ cup olive oil**
- **3 tablespoons lemon juice**
- **2 tablespoons minced fresh basil**
- **2 tablespoons minced fresh parsley**
- **1 tablespoon red wine vinegar**
- **1 teaspoon grated lemon peel**
- **¾ teaspoon salt**
- **½ teaspoon pepper**
- **1 small onion, finely chopped**

1. Place the potatoes in a large saucepan and cover with water. Bring to a boil. Reduce heat; cover and simmer for 10-15 minutes or until tender. Meanwhile, in a small bowl, whisk the oil, lemon juice, herbs, vinegar, lemon peel, salt and pepper.
2. Drain potatoes. Place in a large bowl; add onion. Drizzle with vinaigrette; toss to coat. Serve warm or chill until serving.

## Fennel-Bacon Pasta Salad

Enjoy a substantial side dish that's a breeze to prepare but elegant enough to include at a special dinner party. The pasta is best served warm, but chilling it is another delicious option.
—JULIAN WONG
LA JOLLA, CALIFORNIA

**PREP:** 15 MIN. **COOK:** 20 MIN.
**MAKES:** 16 SERVINGS

- **1 package (16 ounces) spiral pasta**
- **6 thick-sliced bacon strips, chopped**
- **3 small fennel bulbs, thinly sliced**
- **1½ cups walnut halves**
- **1¼ cups (5 ounces) crumbled Stilton cheese, divided**
- **1 teaspoon coarsely ground pepper**
- **¾ teaspoon salt**

1. Cook pasta according to the package directions.
2. Meanwhile, in a large skillet, cook the bacon over medium heat until crisp. Remove bacon with a slotted spoon; drain on paper towels. Remove drippings, reserving 3 tablespoons. Saute fennel in reserved drippings for 4-6 minutes or until crisp-tender. Add walnuts; cook 3-4 minutes longer or until toasted.
3. Drain pasta, reserving ⅓ cup pasta water. Add pasta, bacon and ¾ cup cheese to the fennel mixture; sprinkle with pepper and salt. Toss lightly until cheese is melted, adding enough reserved pasta water to coat pasta. Serve warm with remaining cheese. Refrigerate leftovers.

# Weeknight Solutions

Enjoy **over a month's worth** of Monday-through-Friday dinners, each with a main dish and a side. These **easy meals** serve up something for the whole family—in a flash!

"We're always searching for quick ways to use the harvest from our garden. These mouthwatering grape tomatoes require mere minutes to dress up before you pop them in the oven."

—**LINDA GREEN** ARDMORE, OKLAHOMA

## Chicken Creole

I like to ladle this vegetable-packed main dish over jasmine rice. It's a long-grain rice that's not as sticky as most, but any cooked rice, including brown, would work well here.
—VIRGINIA CROWELL
LYONS, OREGON

**PREP:** 20 MIN. **COOK:** 30 MIN.
**MAKES:** 8 SERVINGS

- **2 medium green peppers, chopped**
- **1 large onion, thinly sliced**
- **2 celery ribs, chopped**
- **4 garlic cloves, minced**
- **4 teaspoons canola oil, divided**
- **½ pound fresh mushrooms, sliced**
- **2 cans (14½ ounces each) diced tomatoes, undrained**
- **½ cup chicken broth**
- **2 tablespoons minced fresh oregano or 2 teaspoons dried oregano**
- **2 tablespoons lemon juice**
- **1 tablespoon minced fresh basil or 1 teaspoon dried basil**
- **½ teaspoon salt**
- **½ teaspoon pepper**
- **½ teaspoon crushed red pepper flakes**
- **2 pounds boneless skinless chicken breasts, cubed**
- **Hot cooked rice**
- **Minced fresh parsley, optional**

**1.** In a large saucepan, saute the green peppers, onion, celery and garlic in 2 teaspoons oil until tender. Add mushrooms; cook until liquid has evaporated. Stir in the tomatoes, broth, oregano, lemon juice, basil and spices. Bring to a boil. Reduce heat; cover and simmer 5-10 minutes or until slightly thickened and flavors are blended.
**2.** Meanwhile, in a Dutch oven, saute chicken in remaining oil in batches until no longer pink. Return chicken to pan; stir in sauce. Heat through, stirring to loosen browned bits from pan. Serve over rice; garnish with parsley if desired.

Chicken Creole

Chili Corn Bread Wedges

## FAST FIX Chili Corn Bread Wedges

To trim the baking time for this Taste of Home Test Kitchen recipe, spoon the batter into greased muffin cups until they're about half-full and bake 15-20 minutes until golden brown.

**PREP/TOTAL TIME:** 30 MIN.
**MAKES:** 8 SERVINGS

- **1 package (8½ ounces) corn bread/muffin mix**
- **⅓ cup milk**
- **1 egg, lightly beaten**
- **1 can (4 ounces) chopped green chilies**
- **2 tablespoons sugar**
- **¾ cup frozen corn, thawed**

**1.** Place corn bread mix in a large bowl. Combine the milk, egg, chilies and sugar; stir into corn bread mix just until moistened. Fold in corn.
**2.** Pour into a greased 9-in. round baking pan. Bake at 400° for 20-25 minutes or until a toothpick inserted near the center comes out clean. Cool on a wire rack for 5 minutes. Cut into wedges; serve warm.

## Crispy Baked Chicken

Combine mashed potato flakes with Parmesan to make an ultra-crunchy coating for oven-baked chicken. It's oh-so-tender and perfectly moist.

**—JUNE BROWN** VENETA, OREGON

**PREP:** 15 MIN. **BAKE:** 50 MIN.
**MAKES:** 4 SERVINGS

- **2 cups mashed potato flakes**
- **2 tablespoons grated Parmesan cheese**
- **2 to 3 teaspoons poultry seasoning**
- **½ to 1 teaspoon pepper**
- **½ cup butter, melted**
- **1 broiler/fryer chicken (3½ to 4½ pounds), cut up**

**1.** In a shallow dish, combine the potato flakes, Parmesan cheese, poultry seasoning and pepper. Place butter in another shallow dish. Dip chicken in butter, then coat with potato flake mixture.
**2.** Place on a lightly greased 15-in. x 10-in. x 1-in. baking pan. Bake, uncovered, at 375° for 50-65 minutes or until juices run clear.

## Creamy Chive Mashed Potatoes

Rich and creamy spuds dotted with fresh chives...what's not to love?

**—BONNIE THOMPSON**
RATHDRUM, IDAHO

**PREP:** 15 MIN. **COOK:** 25 MIN.
**MAKES:** 4 SERVINGS

- **5 medium potatoes, peeled**
- **1½ teaspoons salt, divided**
- **4 ounces cream cheese, softened**
- **2 tablespoons butter, softened**
- **2 tablespoons minced fresh chives**
- **¼ teaspoon pepper**
- **¼ to ½ cup buttermilk**

**1.** Place the potatoes in a large saucepan and cover with water; add 1 teaspoon salt. Bring to a boil. Reduce heat; cover and cook for 15- 20 minutes or until tender. Drain.
**2.** In a large bowl, mash the potatoes with the cream cheese, butter, chives, pepper and remaining salt; gradually beat in enough buttermilk to achieve desired consistency.

Creamy Chive Mashed Potatoes

Crispy Baked Chicken

### Cream Cheese Clue

Soften cream cheese quickly by heating it on a microwave-safe plate on high for 15 seconds or until softened.

## Caramelized Onion & Garlic Pasta

This full-flavored recipe is the result of my mom's love of pasta and our love of cooking together. With a little bit of pepper heat and some smoky bacon, this entree is excellent alone or paired with grilled chicken for a heartier meal.
**—LACY JO MATHESON** SAULT SAINTE MARIE, MICHIGAN

**PREP:** 20 MIN. **COOK:** 35 MIN. **MAKES:** 6 SERVINGS

- **¼ cup butter, cubed**
- **2 large sweet onions, thinly sliced**
- **¼ teaspoon crushed red pepper flakes**
- **⅛ teaspoon salt**
- **8 garlic cloves, minced**
- **2 cups grape tomatoes, halved**
- **¼ cup balsamic vinegar**
- **¼ cup olive oil, divided**
- **1 package (16 ounces) uncooked angel hair pasta**
- **9 bacon strips, cooked and crumbled**
- **⅔ cup shredded Parmesan cheese**
- **½ teaspoon coarsely ground pepper**
- **Fresh basil leaves, optional**

**1.** In a large skillet over medium-high heat, melt butter. Add the onions, pepper flakes and salt; saute until onions are tender. Stir in garlic. Reduce heat to medium-low; cook, stirring occasionally, for 30-40 minutes or until onions are deep golden brown.
**2.** Add the tomatoes, vinegar and 2 tablespoons oil to the skillet. Cook pasta according to package directions. Drain pasta; toss with onion mixture.
**3.** Drizzle with remaining olive oil. Sprinkle with bacon, cheese and pepper; heat through. Garnish with basil if desired.

## FAST FIX Savory Romano Sticks

It's hard to munch just one fresh-from-the-oven breadstick. I can make a batch quickly using purchased puff pastry.
**—TIM AILPORT** WEST LAKELAND, MINNESOTA

**PREP/TOTAL TIME:** 20 MIN. **MAKES:** 20 PASTRY STICKS

- **1 package (17.3 ounces) frozen puff pastry, thawed**
- **1 egg, lightly beaten**
- **1½ cups grated Romano cheese**
- **1 tablespoon dried basil**

**1.** Brush one side of each puff pastry sheet with egg; sprinkle with cheese and basil. Cut each sheet into ten 1-in. strips. Place 1 in. apart on greased baking sheets.
**2.** Bake at 400° for 10-13 minutes or until golden brown.

Caramelized Onion & Garlic Pasta
Savory Romano Sticks

## FAST FIX Presto Pizza Patties

Have a taste for both beef and pizza? These patties let you satisfy your cravings with a hot, open-faced sandwich.
—**BARBARA SCHINDLER** NAPOLEON, OHIO

**PREP/TOTAL TIME:** 30 MIN. **MAKES:** 6 SERVINGS

- **2 egg whites**
- **½ cup seasoned bread crumbs**
- **½ cup finely chopped green pepper**
- **1 can (8 ounces) pizza sauce, divided**
- **¼ cup finely chopped onion**
- **1 garlic clove, minced**
- **1 pound lean ground beef (90% lean)**
- **6 slices Italian bread (½ inch thick)**
- **2 teaspoons olive oil**
- **1½ teaspoons Italian seasoning**
- **½ cup shredded part-skim mozzarella cheese**

**1.** In a large bowl, combine the egg whites, bread crumbs, green pepper, ⅓ cup pizza sauce, onion and garlic. Crumble beef over mixture and mix well. Shape into six oval patties.
**2.** In a large nonstick skillet, cook patties over medium heat for 4-5 minutes on each side or until a meat thermometer reads 160° and juices run clear.
**3.** Meanwhile, place bread on an ungreased baking sheet. Brush tops with oil; sprinkle with Italian seasoning. Broil 4 in. from the heat for 2-3 minutes or until lightly toasted.
**4.** Microwave remaining pizza sauce, covered, on high for 10-20 seconds or until heated through. Place patties on toast; top with cheese and sauce.

Chili-Spiced Sweet Potato Wedges
Presto Pizza Patties

## FAST FIX Chili-Spiced Sweet Potato Wedges

Here's a fantastic, restaurant-worthy plate-filler to go with your favorite burgers, hot dogs...you name it. The recipe couldn't be much easier to fix—it calls for sweet potatoes and just five other ingredients you likely have on hand.
—**TONI CORDOVA** PUEBLO, COLORADO

**PREP/TOTAL TIME:** 30 MIN. **MAKES:** 6 SERVINGS

- **3 medium sweet potatoes (about 1½ pounds), peeled**
- **2 tablespoons olive oil**
- **1 tablespoon sugar**
- **1 teaspoon chili powder**
- **¼ teaspoon salt**
- **¼ teaspoon pepper**

Cut each sweet potato lengthwise into eight wedges. In a large bowl, combine sweet potatoes and the remaining ingredients; toss to coat. Transfer to a greased 15-in. x 10-in. x 1-in. baking pan. Bake at 425° for 20-25 minutes or until tender, turning once.

### Sweet Spuds

The sweet potato is a member of the morning glory family and native to Central America. Two varieties are readily available. One has a pale skin with a light yellow flesh and a dry mealy texture. The other has dark skin with a dark orange flesh that cooks to a moist texture.

The darker-skinned variety is often referred to as a yam. True yams, though, are not readily available in the United States and are seldom grown here.

Select sweet potatoes that are firm and have no cracks or bruises. If stored in a cool (below 60°), dark, well-ventilated place, they'll remain fresh for about 2 weeks.

### Garlic Galore

Depending on how it is prepared, garlic can add zip or mellow undertones to your dishes. Select heads that are firm and plump, avoiding those that are shriveled, soft or showing signs of sprouting.

To peel fresh garlic, use the blade of a chef's knife to crush the garlic clove. Peel away the skin, then chop or mince as directed in the recipe.

Minced garlic that you can buy, garlic that's been finely chopped by hand and garlic that's been put through a press can all be used interchangeably in recipes. Choose whichever is easiest and most convenient for you.

## Spinach Mushroom Enchiladas

In these satisfying enchiladas, baby portobello mushrooms take the place of meat. You won't miss it!

**—EVANGELINE BRADFORD**
ERLANGER, KENTUCKY

**PREP:** 35 MIN. **BAKE:** 15 MIN.
**MAKES:** 6 SERVINGS

- **1 pound baby portobello mushrooms, chopped**
- **1 small onion, finely chopped**
- **2 tablespoons butter**
- **3 garlic cloves, minced**
- **¼ cup white wine or chicken broth**
- **12 ounces chopped fresh spinach, coarsely chopped**
- **½ teaspoon seasoned salt, divided**
- **¾ cup water**
- **¼ cup lime juice**
- **1 tablespoon chicken bouillon granules**
- **1 tablespoon garlic powder**
- **1½ cups (12 ounces) sour cream**
- **½ cup minced fresh cilantro**
- **12 corn tortillas (6 inches), warmed**
- **1½ cups (6 ounces) shredded Monterey Jack cheese**
- **Crushed red pepper flakes, optional**

**1.** In a large skillet, saute mushrooms and onion in butter until tender; add garlic, cook 1 minute longer. Set aside half of the mushroom mixture for sauce.
**2.** Add wine to remaining mixture; cook and stir for 2 minutes. Add spinach and 1/4 teaspoon seasoned salt; cook until spinach is wilted and liquid is evaporated.
**3.** In a large saucepan, bring the water, lime juice, chicken bouillon, garlic powder and remaining seasoned salt to a boil, stirring to dissolve bouillon. Stir in the sour cream, cilantro and reserved mushroom mixture; heat through.
**4.** Place a scant 3 tablespoons spinach mixture down the center of each tortilla; roll up and place seam side down in a greased 13-in. x 9-in. baking dish. Spoon sauce over top; sprinkle with cheese. Bake, uncovered, at 350° for 14-18 minutes or until heated through. Sprinkle with red pepper flakes if desired.

Spinach Mushroom Enchiladas

Harvest Salads with Pear Vinaigrette

FAST FIX

## Harvest Salads with Pear Vinaigrette

Savor fresh-picked autumn pears in a simple but elegant salad topped with a subtly tart dressing. Sliced almonds add a nice crunch, too. If you don't have Gouda cheese, try Swiss instead.

**—CHERYL PERRY**
HERTFORD, NORTH CAROLINA

**PREP/TOTAL TIME:** 15 MIN.
**MAKES:** 6 SERVINGS

- **3 medium pears**
- **⅓ cup oil and vinegar salad dressing**
- **1 package (5 ounces) spring mix salad greens**
- **6 ounces Gouda cheese, shaved**
- **¾ cup honey-roasted sliced almonds**

**1.** Peel and core one pear; coarsely chop. Place in a small food processor; cover and process until smooth. While processing, gradually add salad dressing in a steady stream. Set aside.
**2.** Divide salad greens among six salad plates. Slice remaining pears. Arrange pears and cheese over salads. Sprinkle with almonds; drizzle with dressing.

SLOW COOKER

## Easy Ropa Vieja Stew

I use my slow cooker to serve a Cuban classic. It offers bold flavors without requiring lots of hands-on time.

**—DENISE NYLAND**
PANAMA CITY, FLORIDA

**PREP:** 25 MIN. **COOK:** 6 HOURS
**MAKES:** 8 SERVINGS

- **2 pounds boneless beef chuck roast, cut in half**
- **2 tablespoons olive oil**
- **2 large onions, coarsely chopped**
- **2 large green peppers, coarsely chopped**
- **4 jalapeno peppers, seeded and minced**
- **1 habanero pepper, seeded and minced**
- **3 cans (14½ ounces each) diced tomatoes, undrained**
- **½ cup water**
- **6 garlic cloves, minced**
- **2 tablespoons minced fresh cilantro**
- **4 teaspoons beef bouillon granules**
- **2 teaspoons pepper**
- **1½ teaspoons ground cumin**
- **1 teaspoon dried oregano**
- **½ cup pimiento-stuffed olives, coarsely chopped**
- **Hot cooked rice, optional**

**1.** In a large skillet, brown beef in oil on all sides. Transfer meat to a 5-qt. slow cooker. Add onions and peppers. Combine tomatoes, water, garlic, cilantro, beef bouillon, pepper, cumin and oregano; pour over vegetables.

**2.** Cover and cook on low for 6-8 hours or until meat is tender. Remove beef; cool slightly. Skim fat from cooking juices; stir in olives. Shred beef with two forks and return to slow cooker; heat through. Serve with rice if desired.

**Editor's Note:** *Wear disposable gloves when cutting hot peppers; the oils can burn skin. Avoid touching your face.*

Easy Ropa Vieja Stew
Cumin Roasted Tortillas

FAST FIX

## Cumin Roasted Tortillas

You'll want to fiesta when you munch these simple but zesty tortillas.

**—EMILY SEEFELDT**
RED WING, MINNESOTA

**PREP/TOTAL TIME:** 15 MIN.
**MAKES:** 8 SERVINGS

- **¼ cup olive oil**
- **1 teaspoon dried oregano**
- **1 teaspoon ground cumin**
- **¼ teaspoon salt**
- **8 flour tortillas (8 inches)**

In a small bowl, combine the oil, oregano, cumin and salt; brush over both sides of tortillas. Fold tortillas into quarters; place on an ungreased baking sheet. Bake at 425° for 4-5 minutes or until heated through. Serve immediately.

## Chicken Stuffed with Broccolini & Cheese

I experimented to come up with a twist on classic Chicken Cordon Bleu using Broccolini. It resembles small broccoli, but we think it's a little sweeter and more tender.
**—CHER SCHWARTZ** ELLISVILLE, MISSOURI

**PREP:** 20 MIN. **BAKE:** 15 MIN. **MAKES:** 4 SERVINGS

- **4 boneless skinless chicken breast halves (6 ounces each)**
- **8 Broccolini stalks or ⅔ cup chopped fresh broccoli**
- **½ cup shredded Italian cheese blend**
- **3 tablespoons all-purpose flour**
- **¼ teaspoon salt**
- **¼ teaspoon garlic powder**
- **¼ teaspoon pepper**
- **⅛ teaspoon paprika**
- **2 egg whites**
- **1 tablespoon fat-free milk**
- **¾ cup panko (Japanese) bread crumbs**
- **1 teaspoon dried parsley flakes**
- **Olive oil-flavored cooking spray**

**1.** Flatten chicken to ½-in. thickness. Place two stalks of Broccolini lengthwise down the center of each chicken breast; sprinkle with 2 tablespoons cheese. Fold over and secure with toothpicks.
**2.** Combine the flour, salt, garlic powder, pepper and paprika in a shallow bowl. In a separate shallow bowl, whisk egg whites and milk. In another shallow bowl, combine bread crumbs and parsley. Coat chicken with flour mixture, dip in egg white mixture, then coat with crumb mixture.
**3.** Place on a baking sheet coated with cooking spray. Spritz tops of chicken with cooking spray. Bake, uncovered, at 450° for 15-20 minutes or until a meat thermometer reads 170°. Discard toothpicks.

## FAST FIX Rosemary Polenta

Bring a taste of Italy to your dinner by dressing up polenta. Using the purchased kind gets this dish to the table pronto.
**—CASANDRA RITTENHOUSE**
NORTH HOLLYWOOD, CALIFORNIA

**PREP/TOTAL TIME:** 10 MIN. **MAKES:** 4 SERVINGS

- **1 tube (1 pound) polenta**
- **½ cup grated Parmesan cheese**
- **¼ teaspoon dried rosemary, crushed**
- **⅓ to ½ cup water**
- **Butter, minced fresh parsley and coarsely ground pepper, optional**

Prepare polenta according to package directions for soft polenta, stirring in cheese, rosemary and enough water to achieve desired consistency. Top with butter, parsley and pepper if desired.
**Editor's Note:** *This recipe was tested in a 1,100-watt microwave.*

Rosemary Polenta
Chicken Stuffed with Broccolini & Cheese

## SLOW COOKER Pulled Brisket Sandwiches

The sauce is what makes these hearty sandwiches special. What's not to like about ketchup, brown sugar and butter drizzled over beef brisket? The ingredients are pantry staples, so I usually have most of them on hand.

**—JANE GUILBEAU**
NEW ORLEANS, LOUISIANA

**PREP:** 25 MIN. **COOK:** 8 HOURS
**MAKES:** 12 SERVINGS

- **1 fresh beef brisket (4 to 5 pounds)**
- **1½ cups water**
- **½ cup Worcestershire sauce**
- **2 tablespoons cider vinegar**
- **2 garlic cloves, minced**
- **1½ teaspoons beef bouillon granules**
- **1½ teaspoons chili powder**
- **1 teaspoon ground mustard**
- **½ teaspoon cayenne pepper**
- **¼ teaspoon garlic salt**
- **½ cup ketchup**
- **2 tablespoons brown sugar**
- **2 tablespoons butter**
- **½ teaspoon hot pepper sauce**
- **12 kaiser rolls, split**

**1.** Cut brisket in half; place in a 5-qt. slow cooker. In a small bowl, combine the water, Worcestershire sauce, vinegar, garlic, bouillon, chili powder, mustard, cayenne and garlic salt. Cover and refrigerate ½ cup mixture for sauce; pour remaining mixture over beef. Cover and cook on low for 8-10 hours or until meat is tender.

**2.** Remove beef; cool slightly. Skim fat from cooking juices. Shred meat with two forks and return to the slow cooker; heat through.

**3.** In a small saucepan, combine the ketchup, brown sugar, butter, pepper sauce and reserved water mixture. Bring to a boil; reduce heat. Simmer, uncovered, for 2-3 minutes to allow flavors to blend. Using a slotted spoon, place beef on rolls; drizzle with sauce.

**Editor's Note:** *This is a fresh beef brisket, not corned beef.*

Zippy Tortilla Chips
Pulled Brisket Sandwiches

## FAST FIX Zippy Tortilla Chips

If you find store-bought chips to be too salty, give these a try. You're sure to get a (spicy) kick out of them!
**—KIM SUMRALL** APTOS, CALIFORNIA

**PREP/TOTAL TIME:** 20 MIN.
**MAKES:** 2 SERVINGS

- **½ teaspoon brown sugar**
- **¼ teaspoon garlic powder**
- **¼ teaspoon onion powder**
- **¼ teaspoon ground cumin**
- **¼ teaspoon paprika**
- **⅛ teaspoon cayenne pepper**
- **4 corn tortillas (6 inches)**
- **Cooking spray**

**1.** In a small bowl, combine the first six ingredients. Stack the tortillas; cut into six wedges. Arrange in a single layer on a baking sheet coated with cooking spray.

**2.** Spritz the wedges with cooking spray; sprinkle with seasoning mixture. Bake at 375° for 9-10 minutes or until lightly browned. Cool for 5 minutes.

## Chicken Caesar Florentine

I adapted this flavorful main course from my favorite chicken Caesar salad. The entree has many of the same ingredients the salad has—croutons, grated Parmesan and creamy Caesar dressing. I simply stuffed them into bone-in chicken breasts and baked.

**—JOYCE CONWAY**
WESTERVILLE, OHIO

**PREP:** 15 MIN. **BAKE:** 40 MIN.
**MAKES:** 4 SERVINGS

- **2 cups grated Parmesan cheese, divided**
- **2 cups Caesar salad croutons, coarsely crushed, divided**
- **1 cup fresh baby spinach**
- **1 cup creamy Caesar salad dressing, divided**
- **4 bone-in chicken breast halves, skin removed (8 ounces each)**

**1.** In a large bowl, combine 1 cup cheese, 1 cup crushed croutons, spinach and 1/2 cup salad dressing. Cut a pocket in the thickest part of each chicken breast; fill with cheese mixture.

**2.** Place remaining dressing and crushed croutons in separate shallow bowls. Dip chicken in dressing, then roll in croutons.

**3.** Transfer to a greased 13-in. x 9-in. baking dish. Bake, uncovered, at 375° for 30 minutes. Sprinkle with remaining cheese; bake 10-15 minutes longer or until a meat thermometer reads 170°.

## FAST FIX Sweet-Sour Green Beans

Here's a no-fuss side my mother often prepared for family and friends. The beans can be served warm or cold and are yummy either way. I like to bring them to picnics and church dinners.

**—CLAIRE MOSER**
MIDDLETOWN, MARYLAND

**PREP/TOTAL TIME:** 15 MIN.
**MAKES:** 2 SERVINGS

- **2 cups cut fresh green beans (2-inch pieces)**
- **2 bacon strips, diced**
- **¼ cup chopped onion**
- **4 teaspoons brown sugar**
- **4 teaspoons cider vinegar**

**1.** Place green beans in a small saucepan and cover with water. Bring to a boil; cook, uncovered, for 8-10 minutes or until crisp-tender.

**2.** Meanwhile, in a small skillet, cook bacon over medium heat until crisp. Using a slotted spoon, remove to paper towels. Drain, reserving 2 teaspoons drippings; saute onion in the drippings until tender. Stir in brown sugar and vinegar; heat through. Drain beans and place in a bowl; stir in onion mixture. Top with bacon.

Sweet-Sour Green Beans
Chicken Caesar Florentine

## Rosemary-Apricot Pork Tenderloin

You'll be surprised at how quickly this home-style recipe comes together for a weeknight meal. Be happy if there are leftovers—you'll have tender, juicy meat that just begs to be added to a salad or sandwich the next day.
**—MARIE RIZZIO** INTERLOCHEN, MICHIGAN

**PREP:** 15 MIN. **BAKE:** 25 MIN. **MAKES:** 8 SERVINGS

- **3 tablespoons minced fresh rosemary or 1 tablespoon dried rosemary, crushed**
- **3 tablespoons olive oil, divided**
- **4 garlic cloves, minced**
- **1 teaspoon salt**
- **½ teaspoon pepper**
- **2 pork tenderloins (1 pound each)**

**GLAZE**

- **1 cup apricot preserves**
- **3 tablespoons lemon juice**
- **2 garlic cloves, minced**

**1.** In a small bowl, combine the rosemary, 1 tablespoon oil, garlic, salt and pepper; brush over pork.
**2.** In a large ovenproof skillet, brown pork in remaining oil on all sides. Bake at 425° for 15 minutes.
**3.** In a small bowl, combine the glaze ingredients; brush over pork. Bake 10-15 minutes longer or until a meat thermometer reads 160°, basting occasionally with pan juices. Let stand for 5 minutes before slicing.

## FAST FIX Curried Apricot Couscous

As a single working mom, I don't have a lot of time to spend cooking. This colorful couscous is fast, easy and delicious. It tastes a lot like one I tried when I was in Israel.
**—JESSICA GRETTIE** DEERFIELD, WISCONSIN

**PREP/TOTAL TIME:** 20 MIN. **MAKES:** 5 SERVINGS

- **⅓ cup chopped onion**
- **3 tablespoons butter**
- **1½ cups chicken broth**
- **1 cup chopped dried apricots**
- **¼ teaspoon curry powder**
- **1 cup uncooked couscous**

**1.** In a small saucepan, saute onion in butter. Stir in the broth, apricots and curry powder. Bring to a boil. Stir in couscous.
**2.** Cover and remove from the heat; let stand for 5-10 minutes or until liquid is absorbed. Fluff with a fork.

To save time in the kitchen during the week, I slice and dice all of my vegetables on Sunday. That way, I don't have to get out the cutting board as often on my busiest days.
—**JESS BROWN BOHRER** MADISON, WISCONSIN

## FAST FIX Roasted Grape Tomatoes

We're always searching for quick ways to use the harvest from our garden. These mouthwatering grape tomatoes require mere minutes to dress up before you pop them in the oven.

**—LINDA GREEN**
ARDMORE, OKLAHOMA

**PREP/TOTAL TIME:** 25 MIN.
**MAKES:** 4 CUPS

- **½ cup cider vinegar**
- **¼ cup packed brown sugar**
- **2 tablespoons canola oil**
- **4 garlic cloves, minced**
- **½ teaspoon salt**
- **½ teaspoon pepper**
- **1 pound grape tomatoes**
- **1 tablespoon minced fresh parsley**
- **Assorted crackers and Gouda cheese slices**

**1.** In a large bowl, whisk the first six ingredients. Add tomatoes; toss to coat. Transfer to a greased 15-in. x 10-in. x 1-in. baking pan. Sprinkle with parsley.

**2.** Bake, uncovered, at 375° for 12-14 minutes or until softened, stirring occasionally. Serve with crackers and cheese.

Roasted Grape Tomatoes

Peas and Pasta Carbonara

## FAST FIX Peas and Pasta Carbonara

Here's my take on classic carbonara. Using cream cheese to fortify the sauce speeds up cooking time and will have you eating in just half an hour.

**—CELESTE BRANTOLINO**
LENOIR, NORTH CAROLINA

**PREP/TOTAL TIME:** 30 MIN.
**MAKES:** 6 SERVINGS

- **1 package (16 ounces) fettuccine**
- **2 cups frozen peas**
- **2 tablespoons butter**
- **1 garlic clove, minced**
- **1½ cups 2% milk**
- **1 package (8 ounces) cream cheese, cubed**
- **4 ounces thinly sliced prosciutto or deli ham, cut into thin strips**
- **⅓ cup grated Parmesan cheese**
- **Coarsely ground pepper**

**1.** In a Dutch oven, cook fettuccine according to package directions, adding the peas during the last 3 minutes of cooking.

**2.** In a large skillet, melt butter over medium heat. Add garlic; cook 1 minute. Add milk and cream cheese; cook and stir until blended. Remove from the heat; stir in prosciutto and Parmesan cheese.

**3.** Drain fettuccine and peas; toss with sauce. Sprinkle with pepper.

### Did you know?

Prosciutto is a thinly sliced Italian-style ham that is salt-cured and air-dried for 10 months to 2 years. In many recipes, deli ham can be used in place of prosciutto with good results.

## FAST FIX Hearty Sausage 'n' Beans

Our son cooked a medley of smoked sausage, pinto beans, tomatoes and rice when we came to visit. The beauty of his dish is the simplicity: Toss the ingredients in one pan, simmer, and you have a terrific dinner.

**—WILL OWEN** WACO, TEXAS

**PREP/TOTAL TIME:** 25 MIN.
**MAKES:** 6 SERVINGS

- **1 pound smoked sausage, sliced**
- **1 medium onion, chopped**
- **2 tablespoons canola oil**
- **2 cans (15 ounces each) pinto beans, rinsed and drained**
- **1½ cups water**
- **1 can (14½ ounces) diced tomatoes with mild green chilies, undrained**
- **1 tablespoon ranch salad dressing mix**
- **2 cups uncooked instant rice**

In a Dutch oven, cook sausage and onion in oil over medium heat until onion is tender. Add the beans, water, tomatoes and salad dressing mix. Bring to a boil; stir in rice. Reduce heat; cover and simmer for 5 minutes or until rice is tender.

## FAST FIX Sauteed Spinach

My dad has grown spinach for years. We've developed a number of recipes for it, but this one beats them all.

**—TERRA FONDRIEST**
ST. JOE, ARKANSAS

**PREP/TOTAL TIME:** 15 MIN.
**MAKES:** 4 SERVINGS

- **3 garlic cloves, minced**
- **2 tablespoons olive oil**
- **2 tablespoons white wine or chicken broth**
- **2 packages (9 ounces each) fresh spinach**
- **¾ teaspoon salt**

**1.** In a large skillet, saute the garlic in oil for 1 minute. Add wine. Bring to a boil; cook until liquid is reduced by half.
**2.** Add spinach and salt; cook and stir for 2 minutes or just until spinach is wilted. Serve with a slotted spoon.

Sauteed Spinach
Hearty Sausage 'n' Beans

## Stacked Enchilada

This stacked version of a traditional Tex-Mex casserole shows just how simple a delicious dinner can be.

**—REBECCA PEPSIN**
LONGMONT, COLORADO

**PREP:** 20 MIN. **BAKE:** 20 MIN.
**MAKES:** 4 SERVINGS

- **⅔ cup chopped green pepper**
- **2 teaspoons canola oil**
- **1 garlic clove, minced**
- **1 cup shredded cooked chicken**
- **1 cup canned black beans, rinsed and drained**
- **⅓ cup thinly sliced green onions**
- **½ cup enchilada sauce**
- **½ cup picante sauce**
- **4 corn tortillas (6 inches)**
- **1 cup shredded cheddar cheese**
- **Sour cream and shredded lettuce, optional**

**1.** In a large skillet, saute pepper in oil for 3 minutes. Add garlic and cook 2 minutes longer or until pepper is crisp-tender. Stir in the chicken, beans and onions; heat through. Transfer to a bowl and keep warm.

**2.** In the same skillet, combine enchilada and picante sauces. Coat both sides of one tortilla with sauce mixture; place in a greased 9-in. pie plate. Top with a third of the chicken mixture and ¼ cup cheese. Repeat layers twice. Top with remaining tortilla, sauce and cheese.

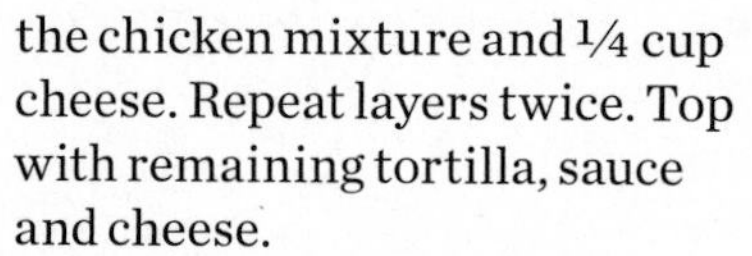

**3.** Cover and bake at 350° for 18-22 minutes or until heated through. Remove to a serving plate and cut into wedges. Serve with sour cream and lettuce if desired.

Colorful Avocado Salad
Stacked Enchilada

## FAST FIX Colorful Avocado Salad

I love the crisp, fresh vegetables and bright colors in this nutritious salad.

**—BEV LEHRMAN** GIJOCA, BRAZIL

**PREP/TOTAL TIME:** 20 MIN.
**MAKES:** 2 SERVINGS

- **1 medium tomato, cut into eighths**
- **½ small cucumber, peeled and thinly sliced**
- **1 small red onion, halved and thinly sliced**
- **⅓ cup julienned green pepper**
- **2 tablespoons Italian salad dressing**
- **1 medium ripe avocado, peeled and cubed**

In a small bowl, combine the first four ingredients. Add dressing and toss to coat. Chill until serving. Just before serving, add avocado and toss gently.

## Beef & Mushroom Potpies

Just about everyone likes a good potpie, with its flaky crust draped over a hearty blend of vegetables, meat and gravy. Skip the homemade dough and let a package of crescent rolls fill in.

**—MACEY ALLEN**
GREEN FOREST, ARKANSAS

**PREP:** 40 MIN. **BAKE:** 20 MIN.
**MAKES:** 4 SERVINGS

- **1½ cups cubed peeled potatoes**
- **1 pound beef top sirloin steak, cut into ¼-inch pieces**
- **2 tablespoons olive oil, divided**
- **1 large red onion, chopped**
- **2 cups sliced fresh mushrooms**
- **1 cup frozen sliced carrots**
- **1 cup frozen peas**
- **2 tablespoons ketchup**
- **1 teaspoon pepper**
- **1 tablespoon cornstarch**
- **1 cup sour cream**
- **1 cup beef gravy**
- **1 tube (8 ounces) refrigerated crescent rolls**

**1.** Place potatoes in a microwave-safe dish; cover with water. Cover and microwave on high for 7-8 minutes or until tender; drain and set aside.

**2.** In a skillet, saute beef in 1 tablespoon oil in batches until no longer pink. Remove and set aside.

**3.** In the same pan, saute onion and mushrooms in remaining oil until tender; add the carrots, peas, ketchup and pepper. Combine the cornstarch, sour cream and gravy until blended; stir into pan and heat through. Stir in potatoes and beef. Divide mixture among four greased 16-oz. ramekins.

**4.** Remove crescent roll dough from tube, but do not unroll; cut dough into 16 slices. Cut each slice in half. Arrange seven pieces, curved sides out, around the edge of each ramekin. Press dough slightly to secure in place. Place remaining pieces in the center of each. Place ramekins on a baking sheet.

**5.** Bake at 375° for 17-20 minutes or until filling is bubbly and crusts are golden brown.

## Onion Veggie Dip

With just four ingredients and only 10 minutes of prep, this creamy dip is perfect with veggies or crackers.

**—RUTHIE POMEROY**
MT. ANGEL, OREGON

**PREP:** 10 MIN. + CHILLING
**MAKES:** 2 CUPS

- **2 cups (16 ounces) sour cream**
- **3 tablespoons dried minced onion**
- **3 tablespoons dried parsley flakes**
- **1 teaspoon seasoned salt**
- **Assorted fresh vegetables or crackers**

In a small bowl, combine the sour cream, minced onion, parsley flakes and seasoned salt. Cover and refrigerate for at least 1 hour. Serve with vegetables.

Onion Veggie Dip
Beef & Mushroom Potpies

## Parm-Breaded Pork Chops

That Italian favorite, Parmesan cheese, brings a buttery, sweet and nutty essence to the crumb coating for breaded pork loin chops. Combined with crushed butter-flavored crackers, it makes a standard dinner special.
**—MELANIE HOGAN** BIRMINGHAM, ALABAMA

**PREP:** 10 MIN. **BAKE:** 35 MIN. **MAKES:** 6 SERVINGS

- **¼ cup all-purpose flour**
- **1 egg**
- **2 tablespoons 2% milk**
- **1 cup crushed butter-flavored crackers**
- **3 tablespoons grated Parmesan cheese**
- **½ teaspoon salt**
- **⅛ teaspoon pepper**
- **¼ cup butter, melted**
- **6 boneless pork loin chops (4 ounces each)**

**1.** Place flour in a shallow bowl. In a separate shallow bowl, whisk egg and milk. In a third shallow bowl, combine the crackers, cheese, salt and pepper. Dip pork chops in the flour, egg mixture, then cracker mixture.
**2.** Place butter in a 13-in. x 9-in. baking dish; add pork chops. Bake, uncovered, at 350° for 25-30 minutes or until a thermometer reads 145°. Let stand for 5 minutes before serving.

## FAST FIX Lemon-Butter New Potatoes

We just love the flavorful blend of fresh parsley, spices and a lemony butter sauce in these classic potatoes.
**—SANDY MCKENZIE** BRAHAM, MINNESOTA

**PREP/TOTAL TIME:** 30 MIN. **MAKES:** 4 SERVINGS

- **12 small red potatoes**
- **⅓ cup butter, cubed**
- **3 tablespoons lemon juice**
- **1 teaspoon salt**
- **1 teaspoon grated lemon peel**
- **¼ teaspoon pepper**
- **⅛ teaspoon ground nutmeg**
- **2 tablespoons minced fresh parsley**

**1.** Peel a strip from around each potato. Place potatoes in a large saucepan and cover with water. Bring to a boil. Reduce heat; cover and cook for 15-20 minutes or just until tender.
**2.** Meanwhile, in small saucepan, melt butter. Stir in the lemon juice, salt, lemon peel, pepper and nutmeg. Drain potatoes and place in a serving bowl. Pour butter mixture over potatoes; toss gently to coat. Sprinkle with parsley.

Lemon-Butter New Potatoes
Parm-Breaded Pork Chops

## Easy Chicken Cordon Bleu

Cordon Bleu is of French origin and means "blue ribbon"—given as a prize for culinary excellence. The term also refers to a signature dish of chicken topped with ham and Swiss cheese. Here, it's wrapped in convenient puff pastry for a quick and easy finish.

**—SHARON LAABS**
HARTFORD, WISCONSIN

**PREP:** 20 MIN. **BAKE:** 30 MIN.
**MAKES:** 8 SERVINGS

- **8 boneless skinless chicken breast halves (4 ounces each)**
- **¼ teaspoon salt**
- **⅛ teaspoon pepper**
- **3 tablespoons butter**
- **1 package (17.3 ounces) frozen puff pastry, thawed**
- **8 slices Swiss cheese**
- **8 slices fully cooked ham**
- **1 egg**
- **1 tablespoon water**

**1.** Sprinkle chicken with salt and pepper. In a large skillet, brown chicken in butter for 1-2 minutes on each side. Remove to paper towels to drain.

**2.** On a lightly floured surface, roll each pastry sheet into a 12-in. square. Cut into four 6-in. squares (discard scraps). Place a chicken breast in the center of each square; top with a cheese and ham slice.

**3.** Whisk egg and water; lightly brush over pastry edges. Bring two sides of pastry over chicken, overlapping one over the other; press seams to seal. Pinch together ends and fold under.

**4.** Transfer to a greased 15-in. x 10-in. x 1-in. baking pan; brush tops with egg mixture. Bake at 400° for 30-35 minutes or until chicken juices run clear.

Broccoli Mushroom Salad

Easy Chicken Cordon Bleu

## FAST FIX Broccoli Mushroom Salad

Packed with broccoli, mushrooms, bacon and cheddar cheese, this simple salad makes a perfect partner for all kinds of entrees. It's a fresh-tasting, pretty addition to menus.

**—DEB WILLIAMS** PEORIA, ARIZONA

**PREP/TOTAL TIME:** 20 MIN.
**MAKES:** 8 SERVINGS

- **7 cups fresh broccoli florets**
- **1 cup sliced fresh mushrooms**
- **½ cup shredded cheddar cheese**
- **⅓ cup prepared honey Dijon salad dressing**
- **4 bacon strips, cooked and crumbled**

**1.** In a large saucepan, bring 3 cups water to a boil. Add broccoli; cover and cook for 2-3 minutes or until crisp-tender. Drain and immediately place broccoli in ice water. Drain and pat dry.

**2.** Transfer broccoli to a large bowl; toss with remaining ingredients.

## SLOW COOKER Satay-Style Pork Stew

Thai cuisine features flavors that are hot, sour, salty and sweet. This one-dish pork satay balances all of them using ginger, red pepper flakes, rice vinegar, garlic, lime juice and creamy peanut butter. It's a restaurant-worthy treat.

**—NICOLE WERNER**
ANN ARBOR, MICHIGAN

**PREP:** 25 MIN. **COOK:** 8 HOURS
**MAKES:** 6 SERVINGS

- **1 boneless pork shoulder butt roast (3 to 4 pounds), cut into 1½ inch cubes**
- **2 medium parsnips, peeled and sliced**
- **1 small sweet red pepper, thinly sliced**
- **1 cup chicken broth**
- **¼ cup reduced-sodium teriyaki sauce**
- **2 tablespoons rice vinegar**
- **1 tablespoon minced fresh gingerroot**
- **1 tablespoon honey**
- **2 garlic cloves, minced**
- **½ teaspoon crushed red pepper flakes**
- **¼ cup creamy peanut butter**
- **Hot cooked rice, optional**
- **2 green onions, chopped**
- **2 tablespoons chopped dry roasted peanuts**

In a 3-qt. slow cooker, combine the first ten ingredients. Cover and cook on low for 8-10 hours or until pork is tender. Skim fat; stir in peanut butter. Serve with rice if desired; top with onions and peanuts.

## FAST FIX Pear Salad with Sesame Vinaigrette

I tossed together some leftover foods from a party—fresh pears, mozzarella cheese and salad greens. The result was colorful, a nice blend of textures and so simple to fix.

**—SHIRLEE BODFIELD**
TUCSON, ARIZONA

**PREP/TOTAL TIME:** 15 MIN.
**MAKES:** 6 SERVINGS

- **1 package (10 ounces) hearts of romaine salad mix**
- **3 medium pears, sliced**
- **8 ounces fresh mozzarella cheese, sliced**
- **¾ cup sesame ginger vinaigrette**
- **1 package (3¾ ounces) oven-roasted sliced almonds**

Divide salad mix among six plates. Top with pears and cheese; drizzle with vinaigrette. Sprinkle with almonds.

**Satay-Style Pork Stew**

**Pear Salad with Sesame Vinaigrette**

## FAST FIX Sizzle & Smoke Flat Iron Steaks

What a great entree when your family is craving steak. Pair it with a cool, refreshing salad, and you'll have a hit.

**—DENISE POUNDS**
HUTCHINSON, KANSAS

**PREP/TOTAL TIME:** 20 MIN.
**MAKES:** 4 SERVINGS

- **1½ teaspoons smoked paprika**
- **1 teaspoon salt**
- **1 teaspoon ground chipotle pepper**
- **½ teaspoon pepper**
- **1¼ pounds beef flat iron steaks or top sirloin steak (¾ inch thick)**
- **2 tablespoons butter**
- **Lime wedges, optional**

**1.** Combine seasonings; rub over steaks. In a large skillet, cook beef in butter over medium-high heat for 30 seconds on each side. Reduce heat to medium; cook steaks for 5-7 minutes on each side or until meat reaches desired doneness (for medium-rare, a thermometer should read 145°; medium, 160°; well-done, 170°).
**2.** Cut into slices; serve with lime wedges if desired.

## FAST FIX Minted Cucumber Salad

Fresh herbs and a light vinaigrette season the chopped cucumbers and tomatoes in this easy medley.

**—DEBBIE PURDUE**
WESTLAND, MICHIGAN

**PREP/TOTAL TIME:** 20 MIN.
**MAKES:** 6 SERVINGS

- **2 large cucumbers, chopped**
- **2 cups seeded chopped tomatoes**
- **½ cup chopped fresh mint**
- **½ cup chopped fresh parsley**
- **½ cup thinly sliced green onions**
- **¼ cup lemon juice**
- **¼ cup olive oil**
- **1 teaspoon salt**
- **¼ teaspoon pepper**

In a large bowl, combine the first five ingredients. In a small bowl, whisk the lemon juice, oil, salt and pepper. Add to cucumber mixture; toss to coat.

**Sizzle & Smoke Flat Iron Steaks**

**Minted Cucumber Salad**

Smoked paprika and chipotle pepper give Sizzle & Smoke Flat Iron Steaks a spicy, Southwestern flair bound to go over big with everyone at the table. To jazz up the juicy meat, you'll need just a handful of basic ingredients. If you like, finish off each plate with a lime wedge for a tangy burst of citrus.
**—DENISE POUNDS** HUTCHINSON, KANSAS

## FAST FIX Roasted Fish with Light Herb Sauce

**PREP/TOTAL TIME:** 25 MIN.
**MAKES:** 4 SERVINGS

- **4 haddock fillets (6 ounces each)**
- **2 teaspoons olive oil**
- **½ teaspoon salt**
- **½ teaspoon pepper**
- **1 shallot, thinly sliced**
- **½ teaspoon herbes de Provence or dried rosemary, crushed**
- **1 tablespoon butter**
- **¼ cup marinade for chicken**
- **2 tablespoons half-and-half cream**

**1.** Place the fillets in a greased 15-in. x 10-in. x 1-in. baking pan. Brush with oil; sprinkle with salt and pepper. Bake at 450° for 14-18 minutes or until fish flakes easily with a fork.

**2.** Meanwhile, in a small saucepan over medium heat, cook and stir shallot and herbes de Provence in butter until shallot is tender. Stir in marinade for chicken; cook and stir for 1 minute. Add cream; cook and stir 1 minute longer. Spoon over fish.

I love a fast supper featuring Roasted Fish with Light Herb Sauce. The recipe works with many types of fish.
—SUZANNE BANFIELD
BASKING RIDGE, NEW JERSEY

**Editor's Note:** *Look for herbes de Provence in the spice aisle. This recipe was tested with Lea & Perrins Marinade for Chicken.*

## FAST FIX Colorful Couscous

Side dishes add even more to a meal when they pop with color. Bits of red and green pepper brighten up this light and fluffy couscous from the Taste of Home Test Kitchen.

**PREP/TOTAL TIME:** 25 MIN.
**MAKES:** 6 SERVINGS

- **⅓ cup each finely chopped onion, green pepper and sweet red pepper**
- **2 garlic cloves, minced**
- **2 tablespoons olive oil**
- **1 can (14½ ounces) chicken broth**
- **¼ cup water**
- **½ teaspoon salt**
- **¼ teaspoon pepper**
- **1 package (10 ounces) couscous**

In a large saucepan, saute the onion, peppers and garlic in oil for 2-3 minutes or until tender. Stir in the chicken broth, water, salt and pepper. Bring to a boil. Stir in the couscous. Cover and remove from the heat; let stand for 5 minutes. Fluff with a fork.

Colorful Couscous

Roasted Fish with Light Herb Sauce

# All-American Sausage & Pepper Sliders

Give dinnertime ballpark appeal by transforming sausage and pepper hero sandwiches into sliders.

**—VERONICA CALLAGHAN**
GLASTONBURY, CONNECTICUT

**PREP:** 15 MIN. **COOK:** 30 MIN.
**MAKES:** 4 SERVINGS

- **4 uncooked Italian sausage links**
- **⅓ cup water**
- **2 teaspoons canola oil**
- **2 large sweet red peppers, thinly sliced**
- **2 large red onions, thinly sliced**
- **¼ cup packed brown sugar**
- **2 tablespoons balsamic vinegar**
- **2 tablespoons Worcestershire sauce**
- **½ teaspoon pepper**
- **8 dinner rolls, split**

**1.** In a large skillet, brown sausages on all sides, about 5 minutes. Reduce heat to medium-low; add water. Cover and cook 10-15 minutes or until a thermometer reads 160°. Remove from pan; keep warm.
**2.** In the same pan, heat oil over medium-high heat. Add peppers and onions; cook and stir until tender. Add brown sugar, vinegar, Worcestershire sauce and pepper; cook 5 minutes longer or until vegetables are coated.
**3.** Cut each sausage lengthwise in half, then crosswise in half. Serve in rolls with pepper mixture.

# FAST FIX Toasted Cheese Ravioli

Here's a great use for refrigerated ravioli. Jazzed up with Italian dressing and bread crumbs, the baked bites are so good dipped in marinara sauce.

**—KATHY MORGAN**
TEMECULA, CALIFORNIA

**PREP/TOTAL TIME:** 20 MIN.
**MAKES:** 4 SERVINGS

- **24 refrigerated small cheese ravioli (about 5 ounces)**
- **1 tablespoon Italian salad dressing**
- **1 tablespoon seasoned bread crumbs**
- **½ cup marinara sauce, warmed**

**1.** Cook ravioli according to package directions; drain. Place on a greased baking sheet. Brush tops with salad dressing; sprinkle with bread crumbs.
**2.** Bake at 400° for 6-8 minutes or until golden brown. Serve with marinara sauce.

**All-American Sausage & Pepper Sliders**

**Toasted Cheese Ravioli**

## Did you know?

Balsamic vinegar is made from sweet white grapes and aged in wooden barrels for at least 10 years. Feel free to substitute cider vinegar or a mild red wine vinegar.

## Deep-Fried Cheese Bites

These yummy cheese bites lack only a good supply of crinkly toothpicks to turn them into a vanishing act.

—KATIE ROSE PEWAUKEE, WISCONSIN

**PREP:** 10 MIN. **COOK:** 5 MIN./BATCH
**MAKES:** 12 SERVINGS

- **1¼ cups all-purpose flour, divided**
- **1 pound cheese curds or cubed cheddar cheese**
- **Oil for deep-fat frying**
- **1 cup beer**

**1.** Place 1/4 cup flour in a large resealable plastic bag. Add cheese curds, a few pieces at a time, and shake to coat.

**2.** In an electric skillet or deep fryer, heat oil to 375°. Meanwhile, in a large bowl, whisk beer and remaining flour. Dip cheese curds, a few at a time, into batter and fry for 2-3 minutes on each side or until golden brown. Drain on paper towels.

## Cuban Panini

Trade in the usual ham-and-cheese for a Cuban sandwich. It typically features ham, Swiss, condiments, pickles and, in this version, smoked turkey.

—JANET SANDERS
PINE MOUNTAIN, GEORGIA

**PREP:** 20 MIN. **COOK:** 5 MIN./BATCH
**MAKES:** 4 SERVINGS

- **2 garlic cloves, minced**
- **½ teaspoon olive oil**
- **½ cup reduced-fat mayonnaise**
- **8 slices artisan bread**
- **8 thick slices deli smoked turkey**
- **4 slices deli ham**
- **8 slices Swiss cheese**
- **12 dill pickle slices**
- **1 cup fresh baby spinach**

**1.** In a small skillet, cook and stir garlic in oil over medium-high heat until tender. Cool.

**2.** Stir garlic into mayonnaise; spread over bread slices. Layer 4 slices of bread with turkey, ham, cheese, pickles and spinach; close sandwiches.

**3.** Cook on a panini maker or indoor grill for 2-3 minutes or until browned and cheese is melted.

## FAST FIX Peanut Butter Milk Shakes

Nearly every kitchen contains some peanut butter, milk and sugar. Simply combine them with vanilla ice cream to whip up a creamy treat in seconds.

—JOYCE TURLEY
SLAUGHTERS, KENTUCKY

**PREP/TOTAL TIME:** 5 MIN.
**MAKES:** 3 SERVINGS

- **1 cup milk**
- **2 cups vanilla ice cream**
- **½ cup peanut butter**
- **2 tablespoons sugar**

In a blender, combine all ingredients; cover and process for 30 seconds or until smooth. Stir if necessary. Pour into chilled glasses; serve immediately.

## Sloppy Joe Dogs

You've seen variations on the loose meat sandwich, such as the Manwich, Dynamite, even Sloppy Jane. This one teams Joe with a hot dog.

—KIM WALLACE DENNISON, OHIO

**PREP:** 20 MIN. **COOK:** 15 MIN.
**MAKES:** 16 SERVINGS

**SLOPPY JOE TOPPING**

- **2 pounds ground beef**
- **2 celery ribs, chopped**
- **1 small green pepper, finely chopped**
- **1 small onion, chopped**
- **1 can (10¾ ounces) condensed tomato soup, undiluted**
- **¼ cup packed brown sugar**
- **¼ cup ketchup**
- **1 tablespoon cider vinegar**
- **1 tablespoon prepared mustard**
- **1½ teaspoons Worcestershire sauce**
- **1 teaspoon pepper**
- **½ teaspoon salt**
- **¼ teaspoon garlic powder**

**DOGS**

- **16 hot dogs**
- **16 hot dog buns, split**
- **Warmed process cheese sauce and grilled onions, optional**

**1.** In a Dutch oven, cook the beef, celery, green pepper and onion over medium heat until meat is no longer pink; drain. Stir in the tomato soup, brown sugar, ketchup, vinegar, mustard, Worcestershire sauce, pepper, salt and garlic powder; heat through.

**2.** Grill hot dogs, covered, over medium heat for 6-10 minutes or until heated through, turning occasionally. Serve on buns. Top each with 1/4 cup beef mixture. Top with warmed process cheese sauce and grilled onions if desired.

Cuban Panini

Deep-Fried Cheese Bites

Peanut Butter Milk Shakes

Sloppy Joe Dogs

## FAST FIX Chicken Nachos

Everyone needs a go-to nacho recipe. If you like, change this chicken version by using leftover shredded pork or brisket and substitute barbecue sauce for the salsa.
**—CRYSTAL BRUNS** ILIFF, COLORADO

**PREP/TOTAL TIME:** 30 MIN. **MAKES:** 8 SERVINGS

- **6 cups nacho tortilla chips**
- **¼ cup finely chopped onion**
- **3 garlic cloves, minced**
- **1 tablespoon canola oil**
- **3 cups shredded cooked chicken breasts**
- **2 tablespoons taco seasoning**
- **1 cup salsa**
- **1 cup (4 ounces) shredded Colby-Monterey Jack cheese**
- **1 plum tomato, seeded and diced**
- **2 green onions, chopped**

Arrange tortilla chips on a 12-in. pizza pan coated with cooking spray. In a large skillet, cook and stir onion and garlic in oil until tender. Add chicken and taco seasoning. Stir in salsa; heat through. Spoon over chips; sprinkle with cheese. Bake at 350° for 10-14 minutes or until cheese is melted. Top with tomato and green onions; serve immediately.

## Spicy Corn Kabobs

Corn transforms from so-so kernels to a tangy sensation when grilled, spread with sour cream, sprinkled with cheese and splashed with lime. Just try it and see!
**—LEAH LENZ** LOS ANGELES, CALIFORNIA

**PREP:** 10 MIN. **GRILL:** 25 MIN. **MAKES:** 6 SERVINGS

- **6 medium ears sweet corn, husks removed and halved**
- **¼ cup sour cream**
- **¼ cup mayonnaise**
- **½ cup grated cotija cheese or Parmesan cheese**
- **2 teaspoons chili powder**
- **¼ teaspoon cayenne pepper, optional**
- **6 lime wedges**

**1.** Insert a metal or soaked wooden skewer into the cut end of each piece of corn. Grill, covered, over medium heat for 25-30 minutes or until tender, turning often.
**2.** In a small bowl, combine sour cream and mayonnaise; spread over corn. Sprinkle with cheese, chili powder and, if desired, cayenne. Serve with lime wedges.

Spicy Corn Kabobs
Chicken Nachos

## FAST FIX Batter-Up Walleye

Celebrate the day's catch or enjoy a special dinner anytime with this fresh-tasting entree. It gets a tongue-tingling kick from onion powder, garlic powder and Cajun seasoning.
**—ALESHA OSTER** WILLISTON, NORTH DAKOTA

**PREP/TOTAL TIME:** 30 MIN. **MAKES:** 4 SERVINGS

- **1 cup biscuit/baking mix**
- **1 tablespoon garlic powder**
- **1 tablespoon onion powder**
- **1 tablespoon Cajun seasoning**
- **1½ teaspoons pepper**
- **1 teaspoon salt**
- **½ cup 2% milk**
- **Oil for frying**
- **1 pound walleye fillets, skin removed**
- **Lemon wedges**

**1.** In a shallow bowl, mix the first six ingredients. Place milk in a separate shallow bowl. In an electric skillet, heat ¼ in. of oil to 375°.
**2.** In batches, dip fish in milk, then coat with baking mix mixture; fry for 5 minutes on each side or until golden brown and fish flakes easily with a fork. Serve immediately with lemon wedges.

## Garlic-Chive Baked Fries

Yes, you DO want fries with that—especially when they're these baked, golden-brown bites featuring garlic flavor and a little peppery punch. Your family will love them!
**—STEVE WESTPHAL** WIND LAKE, WISCONSIN

**PREP:** 15 MIN. **BAKE:** 20 MIN. **MAKES:** 4 SERVINGS

- **4 medium russet potatoes**
- **1 tablespoon olive oil**
- **4 teaspoons dried minced chives**
- **½ teaspoon salt**
- **½ teaspoon garlic powder**
- **¼ teaspoon pepper**

**1.** Cut potatoes into ¼-in. julienne strips. Rinse well and pat dry.
**2.** Transfer potatoes to a large bowl. Drizzle with oil; sprinkle with the remaining ingredients. Toss to coat. Arrange in a single layer on two 15-in. x 10-in. x 1-in. baking pans coated with cooking spray.
**3.** Bake at 450° for 20-25 minutes or until lightly browned, turning once.

# Holiday & Seasonal Celebrations

On those **extra-special occasions**, rely on favorites such as Tangerine-Glazed Turkey, Thin Mint Wreaths and Sweet Holiday Carrots. These **festive dishes** are reason enough to celebrate!

"Banana Split Icebox Cake transforms a favorite summertime treat into a dessert that feeds a crowd. Plus, I can finish most of the prep work the day before."

—**SHELLY FLYE** ALBION, MAINE

# HAPPY VALENTINE'S DAY

One glance at these treats, and there will be instant attraction! Surprise that special someone on February 14 with hand-held sweets, a sparkling beverage or even a luscious cheesecake.

Chocolate-Dipped Anise Biscotti

## Chocolate-Dipped Anise Biscotti

Classic Italian biscotti takes on a whole new level of delightfulness with the licorice flavor of aniseed. Serve a plate of these biscuitlike, chocolate-dipped cookies alongside steaming cups of coffee or cocoa for dunking.

**—LESLIE KELLEY**
KLAMATH FALLS, OREGON

**PREP:** 35 MIN. **BAKE:** 40 MIN. + COOLING
**MAKES:** 3 DOZEN

- **½ cup butter, softened**
- **1 cup sugar**
- **2 eggs**
- **2 teaspoons anise extract**
- **2½ cups all-purpose flour**
- **1½ teaspoons baking powder**
- **½ teaspoon salt**
- **1½ cups sliced almonds, toasted**
- **2 tablespoons aniseed**
- **10 ounces milk chocolate candy coating, melted**

**1.** In a large bowl, cream butter and sugar until light and fluffy. Beat in eggs and extract. Combine the flour, baking powder and salt; gradually add to creamed mixture and mix well. Stir in the almonds and aniseed.

**2.** Divide the dough in half. On a parchment paper-lined baking sheet, shape each portion into a 12-in. x 2-in. rectangle. Bake at 325° for 25-30 minutes or until firm to the touch and the edges are golden brown.

**3.** Cool on the pans on wire racks. When cool enough to handle, transfer to a cutting board; cut diagonally with a serrated knife into ¾-in. slices. Return to the baking sheets cut side down.

**4.** Bake for 6-7 minutes on each side or until golden brown. Remove to wire racks to cool completely. Dip each cookie halfway into the melted candy coating, allowing excess to drip off. Place on waxed paper until set. Store cookies in an airtight container.

## FAST FIX Sparkling Pom-Berry Splash

A romantically red beverage is the perfect refresher on Valentine's Day. For a garnish, thread blueberries onto a drink stirrer or add a slice of lime.

**—SHIRLEY WARREN**
THIENSVILLE, WISCONSIN

**PREP/TOTAL TIME:** 5 MIN.
**MAKES:** 1 SERVING

- **2 ounces pomegranate blueberry juice, chilled**
- **1 teaspoon lime juice**
- **⅓ cup sparkling moscato wine, chilled**

Pour pomegranate blueberry juice and lime juice into a champagne flute; top with wine.

## Strawberries and Champagne Cheesecake

**PREP:** 45 MIN. **BAKE:** 55 MIN.+ CHILLING
**MAKES:** 12 SERVINGS

- **1 cup Champagne or other sparkling wine**
- **2 cups chocolate graham cracker crumbs (about 14 whole crackers)**
- **2 cups sugar, divided**
- **½ cup butter, melted**
- **1 cup sliced fresh strawberries**

- 3 packages (8 ounces each) cream cheese, softened
- ½ cup sweetened condensed milk
- 2 tablespoons cornstarch
- 2 eggs, lightly beaten
- 2 egg yolks

**TOPPING**

- 20 fresh strawberries, hulled
- ⅓ cup milk chocolate chips
- 1 teaspoon shortening, divided
- ⅓ cup white baking chips
- 1 cup heavy whipping cream
- ¼ cup confectioners' sugar

**1.** Place the Champagne in a small saucepan. Bring to a boil; cook until the liquid is reduced to about 1/4 cup, about 8 minutes. Set aside to cool.

**2.** In a small bowl, combine the cracker crumbs, 1/2 cup sugar and butter. Press onto the bottom and 1 1/2 in. up the sides of a greased 9-in. springform pan; set aside. Arrange the sliced strawberries over the bottom.

**3.** In a large bowl, beat cream cheese and remaining sugar until smooth. Beat in sweetened condensed milk, cornstarch and reduced Champagne. Add the eggs and egg yolks; beat on low speed just until combined. Pour over the strawberries. Place the pan on a baking sheet.

**4.** Bake at 325° for 55-60 minutes or until center is almost set. Cool on a wire rack for 10 minutes. Carefully run a knife around edge of pan to loosen; cool 1 hour longer. Refrigerate overnight.

**5.** Remove sides of springform pan. For the topping, wash the strawberries and gently pat with paper towels until completely dry. Slice and arrange over cheesecake. In a microwave, melt chocolate chips and 1/2 teaspoon shortening; stir until smooth. Drizzle over strawberries. Repeat melting and drizzling with white baking chips and remaining shortening.

**6.** In a small bowl, beat cream until it begins to thicken. Add confectioners' sugar; beat until soft peaks form. Serve cheesecake with whipped cream.

Strawberries and Champagne Cheesecake

I love to bake, and I believe that love—and sweetened condensed milk—are the best ingredients of all! Drizzled with chocolate, Strawberries and Champagne Cheesecake is a favorite dessert.

—**KATHRYN WORK** LOUISVILLE, KENTUCKY

## Lots of Love Cherry Pies

You'll become the Queen of Hearts when you surprise loved ones with miniature cherry pies. The Taste of Home Test Kitchen experts added a heart-shaped cutout for extra fun.

**PREP:** 30 MIN. + CHILLING
**BAKE:** 15 MIN./BATCH + COOLING
**MAKES:** 1 DOZEN

- **3¾ cups all-purpose flour**
- **¾ teaspoon salt**
- **1 cup cold butter, cubed**
- **¾ cup shortening**
- **9 to 10 tablespoons cold water**

**FILLING**

- **⅓ cup sugar**
- **¼ cup water**
- **2 tablespoons cornstarch**
- **1 tablespoon lemon juice**
- **3 cups fresh or frozen pitted dark sweet cherries, thawed, halved**
- **⅛ teaspoon almond extract**
- **1 egg, lightly beaten**
- **Coarse sugar**

**1.** In a large bowl, combine the flour and salt; cut in the butter and shortening until crumbly. Gradually add the water, tossing with a fork until the dough holds together when pressed. Divide dough in half; form each portion into a disk. Wrap separately in plastic wrap; refrigerate for 1 hour or until easy to handle.

**2.** In a large saucepan, combine the sugar, water, cornstarch and lemon juice until smooth. Add cherries. Bring to a boil; cook and stir for 1 minute or until thickened. Stir in extract. Set aside to cool.

**3.** On a lightly floured surface, roll one portion of dough to ⅛-in. thickness. Cut out 12 hearts with a floured 4-in. heart-shaped cookie cutter. Transfer half of the hearts to a parchment-lined baking sheet. Using a floured ¾-in. heart-shaped cookie cutter, cut out small hearts from the remaining large hearts. (Discard small hearts or reserve for another use.)

**4.** Spoon 2 tablespoons cherry mixture onto the center of each solid heart. Brush edges of pastry with egg. Top with cutout hearts; press the edges with a fork to seal. Brush the tops with egg; sprinkle with coarse sugar.

**5.** Bake at 400° for 15-20 minutes or until the crust is golden brown and the filling is bubbly. While pies are baking, repeat with remaining dough and filling.

**6.** Let the pies stand for 5 minutes before removing to wire racks. Serve warm.

## Key Lime Bars

I like Key lime pie, but some people are reluctant to eat a whole slice, especially after a big dinner. These scrumptious bars have all the tangy flavor of that classic dessert. They freeze well, too.

**—KRISTINE STATON**
BROOMFIELD, COLORADO

**PREP:** 25 MIN. + COOLING
**BAKE:** 35 MIN. + CHILLING
**MAKES:** 3 DOZEN

- **1¼ cups all-purpose flour**
- **30 vanilla wafers, broken into pieces**
- **½ cup confectioners' sugar**
- **½ cup chopped pecans**
- **¾ cup cold butter, cubed**

**CREAM CHEESE LAYER**

- **1 package (8 ounces) cream cheese, softened**
- **¼ cup sugar**
- **2 tablespoons 2% milk**
- **1 teaspoon vanilla extract**

**KEY LIME LAYER**

- **1½ cups sugar**
- **¼ cup all-purpose flour**
- **4 eggs**
- **½ cup Key lime juice**
- **Additional confectioners' sugar**

**1.** In a food processor, combine the flour, wafers, confectioners' sugar and pecans; cover and process until the nuts are fine. Add butter; cover and pulse until crumbly.

**2.** Press into an ungreased 13-in. x 9-in. baking dish. Bake at 350° for 15-18 minutes or until lightly browned. Cool on a wire rack.

**3.** In a bowl, beat cream cheese, sugar, milk and vanilla until blended; spread over crust to edges of pan. In another small bowl, combine sugar and flour; whisk in eggs and lime juice. Gently pour over the cream cheese layer.

**4.** Bake for 20-25 minutes or until the filling is set. Cool on a wire rack. Refrigerate for 1 hour or until chilled. Cut into bars. Just before serving, sprinkle with additional confectioners' sugar.

## Chocolate-Mint Hearts

Dip cutout cookies in minty chocolate for a special indulgence. They're so good with a cup of coffee or tea!

**—SHERI LIVERMORE**
WAUKESHA, WISCONSIN

**PREP:** 25 MIN. + CHILLING
**BAKE:** 10 MIN./BATCH + COOLING
**MAKES:** 2 DOZEN

- **1 package (10 ounces) mint chocolate chips, divided**
- **¼ cup butter, softened**
- **⅓ cup sugar**
- **1 egg**
- **½ teaspoon vanilla extract**
- **1¼ cups all-purpose flour**
- **¾ teaspoon baking powder**
- **¼ teaspoon salt**
- **¼ teaspoon baking soda**
- **¼ cup shortening**
- **Colored sprinkles, optional**

**1.** In a microwave-safe bowl, melt ½ cup chocolate chips; stir. Cool slightly. In a small bowl, cream butter and sugar. Beat in the egg, vanilla and melted chocolate. Combine the flour, baking powder, salt and baking soda; gradually add to creamed mixture.

**2.** Cover and refrigerate for 1-2 hours or until easy to handle. On a lightly floured surface, roll out the dough to ¼-in. thickness. Cut with a floured 2½-in. heart-shaped cookie cutter. Place 2 in. apart on ungreased baking sheets. Bake at 350° for 7-10 minutes or until set. Remove to wire racks to cool completely.

**3.** In a microwave, melt shortening and remaining chocolate chips; stir until smooth. Dip each cookie halfway into chocolate mixture; allow excess to drip off. Sprinkle chocolate with sprinkles if desired. Place the cookies on waxed paper; refrigerate until set.

Lots of Love Cherry Pies
Key Lime Bars
Chocolate-Mint Hearts

# FEAST FOR EASTER SUNDAY

When Peter Cottontail is hopping down that bunny trail, look here. You'll find everything you need—from the main course to delectable desserts—to serve a memorable holiday meal.

## Raspberry-Rhubarb Slab Pie

"Slab pie" is a pastry baked in a jelly roll pan and cut into slabs just like a bar cookie—or, in this case, a bar-shaped pie. My grandfather was a professional baker and sold pieces of his slab pie to customers years ago. Here is my spin, featuring the tangy combo of rhubarb and red raspberries.

**—JEANNE AMBROSE** MILWAUKEE, WISCONSIN

**PREP:** 30 MIN. + CHILLING **BAKE:** 45 MIN. + COOLING
**MAKES:** 2 DOZEN

- **3¼ cups all-purpose flour**
- **1 teaspoon salt**
- **1 cup butter**
- **¾ cup plus 1 to 2 tablespoons 2% milk**
- **1 egg yolk**
- **2 cups sugar**
- **⅓ cup cornstarch**
- **5 cups fresh or frozen unsweetened raspberries, thawed and drained**
- **3 cups sliced fresh or frozen rhubarb, thawed and drained**

Raspberry-Rhubarb Slab Pie

Polka-Dot Macaroons

**VANILLA ICING**

- **1¼ cups confectioners' sugar**
- **½ teaspoon vanilla extract**
- **5 to 6 teaspoons 2% milk**

**1.** In a large bowl, combine the flour and salt; cut in the butter until crumbly. Whisk 3/4 cup milk and the egg yolk; gradually add to flour mixture, tossing with a fork until dough forms a ball. Add additional milk, 1 tablespoon at a time, if necessary.

**2.** Divide dough in half so that one portion is slightly larger than the other; wrap each portion in plastic wrap. Refrigerate for 1 hour or until easy to handle.

**3.** Roll out larger portion of dough between two large sheets of lightly floured waxed paper into an 18-in. x 13-in. rectangle. Transfer to an ungreased 15-in. x 10-in. x 1-in. baking pan. Press onto the bottom and up the sides of pan; trim pastry to edges of pan.

**4.** In a large bowl, combine the sugar and cornstarch. Add the raspberries and rhubarb; toss to coat. Spoon into the pastry.

**5.** Roll out remaining dough; place over filling. Fold bottom pastry over edge of top pastry; seal with a fork. Prick top with a fork.

**6.** Bake at 375° for 45-55 minutes or until golden brown. Cool completely on a wire rack.

**7.** For icing, combine confectioners' sugar, vanilla and enough milk to achieve a drizzling consistency; drizzle over pie. Cut pie into squares.

**Editor's Note:** *If using frozen rhubarb, measure rhubarb while still frozen, then thaw completely. Drain in a colander, but do not press liquid out.*

## Polka-Dot Macaroons

These chewy cookies are easy to mix up in a hurry, and they go over well with everyone. For Easter or other springtime events, choose chocolate candies in pastel colors.
**—JANICE LASS** DORR, MICHIGAN

**PREP:** 15 MIN. **BAKE:** 10 MIN./BATCH
**MAKES:** ABOUT 4½ DOZEN

- **5 cups flaked coconut**
- **1 can (14 ounces) sweetened condensed milk**
- **½ cup all-purpose flour**
- **1½ cups M&M's minis**

**1.** In a large bowl, combine the coconut, milk and flour. Stir in M&M's.
**2.** Drop dough by rounded tablespoonfuls 2 in. apart onto baking sheets coated with cooking spray. Bake at 350° for 8-10 minutes or until the edges are lightly browned. Remove to wire racks.

Stuffed Pork Tenderloin with Shiitake Mushroom Sauce

## Stuffed Pork Tenderloin with Shiitake Mushroom Sauce

Pork tenderloin is a versatile cut that's ideal for busy cooks because it roasts so quickly. For a flavorful entree, the Taste of Home Test Kitchen pros filled it with a stuffing of porcini and shiitake mushrooms, sausage and fresh herbs.

**PREP:** 40 MIN. + STANDING **BAKE:** 35 MIN.
**MAKES:** 8 SERVINGS (2 CUPS SAUCE)

- **1 cup water**
- **1 ounce dried porcini mushrooms**
- **½ pound bulk pork sausage**
- **2 small onions, chopped**
- **5 cups coarsely chopped fresh shiitake mushrooms (about ¾ pound), divided**
- **1½ teaspoons minced fresh rosemary or ½ teaspoon dried rosemary, crushed**
- **1 teaspoon minced fresh sage or ¼ teaspoon rubbed sage**
- **5 cups soft bread crumbs**
- **3 tablespoons minced fresh parsley, divided**
- **2 pork tenderloins (about 1¼ pound each)**
- **1¼ teaspoons salt, divided**
- **¾ teaspoon pepper, divided**
- **2 tablespoons butter**
- **3 tablespoons all-purpose flour**
- **1½ cups chicken broth**

**1.** In a small saucepan, bring the water and porcini mushrooms to a boil. Remove from the heat; let stand 20-30 minutes or until mushrooms are softened. Using a slotted spoon, remove mushrooms; finely chop and set aside. Strain the soaking liquid through a fine mesh strainer, reserving 2/3 cup.
**2.** In a large skillet, cook the sausage and onion over medium heat until sausage is no longer pink. Remove with a slotted spoon. Remove drippings, reserving 2 tablespoons. Saute 4 cups shiitake mushrooms in reserved drippings until tender.
**3.** Add the rosemary, sage, porcini mushrooms and 1/3 cup mushroom soaking liquid; cook 2 minutes longer, stirring occasionally. Remove from the heat; stir in the bread crumbs, 2 tablespoons parsley and sausage.
**4.** Make a lengthwise slit down the center of each tenderloin to within 1/2 in. of bottom. Open so meat lies flat. Cover with plastic wrap; flatten to 1/4-in. to 1/2-in. thickness. Remove plastic wrap.
**5.** Spoon half of the stuffing down the center of each tenderloin. Close roasts; tie several times with kitchen string and secure ends with toothpicks. Sprinkle each roast with 1/2 teaspoon salt and 1/4 teaspoon pepper.
**6.** Place tenderloins on a rack in a shallow roasting pan. Bake, uncovered, at 425° for 35-45 minutes or until a thermometer inserted in pork reads 145°. Let stand for 5 minutes before slicing.
**7.** Meanwhile, in a small saucepan, saute remaining shiitake mushrooms in butter until tender. Sprinkle with the flour; stir until blended. Gradually add chicken broth and remaining 1/3 cup mushroom soaking liquid. Bring to a boil; cook and stir for 2 minutes or until thickened. Stir in the remaining parsley, salt and pepper. Serve with pork.

**Editor's Note:** *To make soft bread crumbs, tear bread into pieces and place in a food processor or blender. Cover and pulse until crumbs form. One slice of bread yields 1/2 to 3/4 cup crumbs.*

## Parmesan Potatoes Au Gratin

This recipe represents my philosophy of cooking: cook with love. Letting the au gratin rest is very important—even though it's so good, you want to jump right in! If your family likes onions, slice them thinly and add them in between the layers. Either way, you'll have a creamy, comforting side dish.

**—THERESA DANOS**
HYDE PARK, NEW YORK

**PREP:** 20 MIN.
**BAKE:** 1½ HOURS + STANDING
**MAKES:** 9 SERVINGS

- **2 cups grated Parmesan cheese**
- **1 tablespoon minced fresh thyme or 1 teaspoon dried thyme**
- **1 tablespoon grated lemon peel**
- **½ teaspoon salt**
- **½ teaspoon pepper**
- **2 pounds red potatoes, very thinly sliced**
- **2½ cups heavy whipping cream**

**1.** Combine the first five ingredients. Layer a third of the potatoes and ⅔ cup cheese mixture in a greased 8-in. square baking dish; repeat the layers. Top with the remaining potatoes; pour heavy whipping cream over the top. Sprinkle with remaining cheese mixture.

**2.** Cover and bake at 325° for 65 minutes. Increase the temperature to 375°. Uncover; bake 25-30 minutes longer or until the potatoes are tender and the top is golden brown. Let stand for 10 minutes before serving.

Parmesan Potatoes Au Gratin

## Sauteed Spring Vegetables

Sauteed Spring Vegetables

Fresh asparagus, yellow squash and red onion help usher in the tastes of springtime. To give your vegetables an Asian twist, substitute soy sauce for the balsamic vinegar (less salt will be needed because of the soy sauce). Sprinkle on extra red pepper flakes if you prefer more heat.

**—BILLY HENSLEY**
MOUNT CARMEL, TENNESSEE

**PREP:** 20 MIN. + MARINATING
**COOK:** 10 MIN. **MAKES:** 9 SERVINGS

- **2 medium yellow summer squash, sliced**
- **1 pound fresh asparagus, trimmed and cut into 1½-inch pieces**
- **1 medium zucchini, sliced**
- **1 small red onion, cut into thin wedges**
- **1 cup green pepper strips**
- **½ cup sweet red pepper strips**

**MARINADE**

- **¼ cup olive oil**
- **2 tablespoons balsamic vinegar**
- **1 tablespoon lemon juice**
- **2 garlic cloves, minced**
- **½ teaspoon salt**
- **½ teaspoon pepper**
- **⅛ to ½ teaspoon crushed red pepper flakes**

**1.** Place the vegetables in a large bowl. In a small bowl, whisk the marinade ingredients. Pour over vegetables; toss to coat. Cover and refrigerate for up to 1 hour.

**2.** In a large skillet, saute vegetable mixture in batches for 3-6 minutes or until crisp-tender.

For a festive springtime favor on your Easter dinner table, top each place setting with a small artificial bird's nest (available at most craft stores) and fill each nest with several miniature egg-shaped candies.

## Braided Onion-Potato Loaf

**PREP:** 20 MIN. + RISING **BAKE:** 25 MIN.
**MAKES:** 1 LOAF (16 SLICES)

- **1 large Yukon Gold potato, peeled and cubed**
- **1 small onion, chopped**
- **1 cup warm 2% milk (70° to 80°)**
- **1 egg**
- **2 tablespoons butter**
- **1 tablespoon honey**
- **¼ cup grated Parmesan cheese**
- **¼ cup chopped fresh parsley**
- **1½ teaspoons salt**
- **¼ teaspoon pepper**
- **4 cups bread flour**
- **1 package (¼ ounce) active dry yeast**

**TOPPING**

- **1 egg, lightly beaten**
- **Additional grated Parmesan cheese**

**1.** Place the potato and onion in a small saucepan and cover with water. Bring to a boil. Reduce heat; cover and cook for 10-15 minutes or until vegetables are tender. Mash until potato is smooth (about ¾ cup); set aside.

**2.** In bread machine pan, place the milk, mashed potato, egg, butter, honey, cheese, parsley, salt, pepper, flour and yeast in the order suggested by the manufacturer. Select the dough setting (check the dough after 5 minutes of mixing; add 1 to 2 tablespoons of water or flour if needed).

**3.** When the cycle is completed, turn dough onto a lightly floured surface. Divide into thirds. Shape each into an 18-in. rope. Place the ropes on a greased baking sheet and braid; pinch the ends to seal and tuck under.

**4.** Cover with a clean kitchen towel and let rise in a warm place until doubled, about 1 hour. Uncover; brush the top with beaten egg. Sprinkle with additional cheese. Bake at 350° for 25-35 minutes or until golden brown. Remove from pan to a wire rack.

**Braided Onion-Potato Loaf**

I use a mashed potato in my Braided Onion-Potato Loaf. With its starchy quality, the potato absorbs liquid during the kneading stage and holds onto that liquid during baking. The loaf comes out of the oven with a crisp, brown crust and flavorful, moist interior that helps the bread keep longer. It's a treat!

**—JOAN RANZINI** WAYNESBORO, VIRGINIA

# FATHER'S DAY FAVORITES

One surefire way to please Dad on his special day is with a meaty meal he can really sink his teeth into. So surprise him with a fresh-from-the-grill steak and all the fixings.

## Grilled Corn Salsa

**PREP:** 30 MIN.
**GRILL:** 30 MIN. + CHILLING
**MAKES:** 7½ CUPS

- **8 medium ears sweet corn, husks removed**
- **2 small yellow summer squash, cut into ½-inch slices**
- **1 medium sweet red pepper, cut into four wedges**
- **1 medium red onion, cut into ½-inch rings**
- **1 medium tomato, seeded and chopped**

**BASIL VINAIGRETTE**

- **½ cup olive oil**
- **⅓ cup white balsamic or cider vinegar**
- **12 fresh basil leaves, chopped**
- **1 teaspoon salt**
- **1 teaspoon garlic powder**
- **1 teaspoon dried oregano**

**1.** Fill a soup kettle two-thirds full with water; bring to a boil. Add corn. Reduce heat; cover and simmer for 5 minutes or until crisp-tender. Remove corn; cool slightly.

Grilled Corn Salsa

**2.** Moisten a paper towel with cooking oil; using long-handled tongs, lightly coat the grill rack. Grill the corn, squash, red pepper and onion, covered, over medium heat for 8-10 minutes or until lightly browned, turning occasionally.
**3.** Cut corn from cobs; cut the squash, red pepper and onion into bite-size pieces. Place the vegetables in a large bowl; add the tomato.
**4.** In a small bowl, whisk the vinaigrette ingredients. Pour over vegetables; toss to coat. Cover and refrigerate until chilled. Serve with a slotted spoon.

## FAST FIX Herbed Potato Packs

The Taste of Home Test Kitchen pros filled their packs with fingerlings—small, firm and waxy potatoes that cook faster than chunkier varieties.

**PREP/TOTAL TIME:** 25 MIN.
**MAKES:** 4 SERVINGS

- **2 pounds fingerling potatoes**
- **2 tablespoons olive oil**
- **2 garlic cloves, minced**
- **1 teaspoon salt**
- **2 teaspoons minced fresh thyme**
- **½ teaspoon coarsely ground pepper**

Herbed Potato Packs

**1.** Pierce the potatoes with a fork. Place in a large microwave-safe dish; cover and microwave for 4-7 minutes or until crisp-tender, stirring halfway. Add the remaining ingredients; toss to coat.
**2.** Place one-fourth of the potatoes on a double thickness of heavy-duty foil (about 14 in. x 12 in.). Fold foil around the potatoes and seal tightly. Repeat with the remaining potatoes.
**3.** Grill, covered, over medium-high heat for 6-9 minutes on each side or until the potatoes are tender. Open the foil carefully to allow steam to escape.

Putting the veggies on the grill gives Grilled Corn Salsa some sweetness and smoke. For even more flavor, make it the day before and refrigerate it overnight.
—**TERI KMAN** LAPORTE, COLORADO

## FAST FIX Grilled Romaine Hearts

Steak is nicely balanced by refreshing romaine. Don't leave it on the grill too long, or the leaves may scorch.

**—STUART PRITCHARD**
COMMERCE, TEXAS

**PREP/TOTAL TIME:** 10 MIN.
**MAKES:** 12 SERVINGS

- **¾ cup olive oil**
- **⅔ cup balsamic vinegar**
- **6 romaine hearts, halved lengthwise with cores intact**
- **Salt and pepper to taste**

In a small bowl, whisk the oil and vinegar. Generously brush over all surfaces of romaine. Grill romaine, uncovered, over medium-hot heat for 1-2 minutes or until slightly charred and wilted, turning once. Season with salt and pepper.

## FAST FIX Garlic-Rubbed T-Bones with Burgundy Mushrooms

**PREP/TOTAL TIME:** 25 MIN.
**MAKES:** 4 SERVINGS

- **12 garlic cloves, minced or sliced**
- **1 tablespoon olive oil**
- **1 teaspoon salt**
- **4 beef T-bone or Porterhouse steaks (¾ inch thick and 12 ounces each)**
- **½ cup butter, cubed**
- **1 pound baby portobello mushrooms, thickly sliced**
- **½ cup Burgundy wine or reduced-sodium beef broth**

**1.** In a small bowl, combine garlic, oil and salt; rub over both sides of steaks. Grill steaks, covered, over medium heat or broil 4 in. from the heat for 4-7 minutes on each side or until meat reaches desired doneness (for medium-rare, a thermometer should read 145°; medium, 160°; well-done, 170°).
**2.** Meanwhile, in a large skillet, melt butter over medium-high heat. Add the mushrooms; cook and stir for 3-5 minutes or until almost tender. Stir in the wine; bring to a boil. Cook until the liquid is reduced by half, stirring occasionally. Serve over steaks.

**Grilled Romaine Hearts**

**Grilled Corn Salsa**

**Garlic-Rubbed T-Bones with Burgundy Mushrooms**

My dad always made an amazing steak. I tweaked his recipe to add a topping and came up with Garlic-Rubbed T-Bones with Burgundy Mushrooms.
**—KEVIN BLACK** CEDAR RAPIDS, IOWA

## FAST FIX Herbed Garlic Dipping Oil

Try this as a full-flavored dipping oil with cubed bread as an appetizer. You could also spread it over halved French bread and broil until toasted...or even toss it with hot pasta.
**—DAWN EMBRY-RODRIGUEZ** FLORENCE, COLORADO

**PREP/TOTAL TIME:** 20 MIN. **MAKES:** 1 CUP PLUS 2 TABLESPOONS

- **1 cup olive oil**
- **16 to 20 fresh basil leaves**
- **¼ cup minced fresh rosemary**
- **4 teaspoons minced garlic**
- **1 teaspoon salt**
- **⅓ cup balsamic vinegar**
- **Italian bread, cubed**

Place the first five ingredients in a blender; cover and process until desired consistency. Transfer to a small bowl. Stir in vinegar. Serve with bread cubes.

## FAST FIX Peaches 'n' Cream

A great way to bond with Dad in the kitchen is to assemble a simple but luscious dessert together. My cream-topped fruit platter is light and refreshing after a big meal.
**—DORIT RITTER-HADDAD** LIVINGSTON, NEW JERSEY

**PREP/TOTAL TIME:** 15 MIN. **MAKES:** 4 SERVINGS

- **1 cup heavy whipping cream**
- **½ teaspoon vanilla extract**
- **4 medium peaches, halved and pitted**
- **1 cup sliced fresh strawberries**
- **1 large banana, peeled and sliced**
- **¼ cup packed brown sugar**

In a small bowl, beat the heavy whipping cream until it begins to thicken. Add the vanilla; beat until soft peaks form. Arrange the fruit on a platter; top with whipped cream. Sprinkle with brown sugar.

### GRILLING 101

Herbed Garlic Dipping Oil and fruit-filled Peaches 'n' Cream (recipes at left) round out the fantastic from-the-grill menu that begins on p. 194. Want to brush up on grilling before getting started? These helpful hints from the Taste of Home Test Kitchen pros will make preparing your feast a breeze on Father's Day or anytime:

- Bring foods to a cool room temperature before grilling to ensure more even cooking results. Cold foods may burn on the outside before the interior is cooked.
- Don't crowd food on the grill. Allow some space between each piece for even cooking.
- Use tongs to turn meat instead of a meat fork to avoid piercing and losing juices.
- It's best to have two pairs of long-handled tongs—one for moving the coals and one for turning food.
- Use a meat or instant-read thermometer to check the internal temperature of meat and poultry before the recommended cooking time is up.
- Always place cooked food on a clean plate—never on a plate that held uncooked food.

**Herbed Garlic Dipping Oil**

Peaches 'n' Cream

# OUTDOORS ON JULY FOURTH

Make it a grand ol' Independence Day party with this festive backyard spread. Just pop the main courses on the grill, toss together a few side dishes and whip up a cool dessert.

Creamy Red Potato Salad

## Triple Bean Bake with Bacon

Baked beans go from ordinary to extraordinary when you mix three bean varieties—kidney, butter and great northern—and add a little zing from horseradish. Delicious!

**—SHERRI MELOTIK**
OAK CREEK, WISCONSIN

**PREP:** 15 MIN. **BAKE:** 30 MIN.
**MAKES:** 8 SERVINGS

- **½ pound bacon strips, cut into ½-inch pieces**
- **⅔ cup chopped onion (about 1 medium)**
- **1 can (15½ ounces) great northern beans, undrained**
- **1 can (16 ounces) butter beans, rinsed and drained**
- **1 can (16 ounces) kidney beans, rinsed and drained**
- **¾ cup packed brown sugar**
- **1 tablespoon prepared horseradish**
- **1 tablespoon yellow mustard**

**1.** In a Dutch oven, cook bacon over medium heat until crisp. Remove to paper towels with a slotted spoon; drain, reserving 1 tablespoon drippings. Add onion to drippings; cook and stir over medium heat until tender.
**2.** Stir in the remaining ingredients; return bacon to pan. Transfer to a greased 2-qt. baking dish. Cover and bake at 325° for 30-35 minutes or until heated through. Uncover and bake until desired consistency.

Triple Bean Bake with Bacon

## Creamy Red Potato Salad

The recipe for this classic picnic side dish has been in our family for many years, and I've fixed it for countless gatherings. I love using red potatoes because of their color and shape.

**—ELIZABETH KING**
DULUTH, MINNESOTA

**PREP:** 30 MIN.
**COOK:** 20 MIN.+ CHILLING
**MAKES:** 12 SERVINGS

- **2½ pounds small red potatoes, cut into ¼-in. slices**

**VINAIGRETTE**
- **⅔ cup canola oil**
- **⅓ cup red wine vinegar**
- **2 tablespoons Dijon mustard**
- **¾ teaspoon salt**
- **½ teaspoon dill weed**
- **¼ teaspoon garlic salt**
- **¼ teaspoon pepper**

**SALAD**
- **⅔ cup mayonnaise**
- **⅔ cup sour cream**
- **2 cups sliced radishes**
- **⅔ cup thinly sliced green onions**
- **½ cup minced fresh parsley**
- **4 hard-cooked eggs, coarsely chopped**

**1.** Place the potatoes in a Dutch oven; cover with water. Bring to a boil. Reduce heat; cover and cook the potatoes for 15-18 minutes or until tender. Drain.
**2.** Transfer the potatoes to a large bowl. In a small bowl, whisk the vinaigrette ingredients. Pour over warm potatoes; gently toss to coat. Cool slightly. Cover and refrigerate until chilled.
**3.** In a small bowl, combine the mayonnaise and sour cream; stir in the radishes, onions and parsley. Add to potatoes; mix gently. Top with eggs. Chill until serving.

*MAKE AHEAD*

## Banana Split Icebox Cake

**PREP:** 30 MIN. + CHILLING
**MAKES:** 10 SERVINGS

- **1 carton (16 ounces) frozen whipped topping, thawed**
- **1 cup (8 ounces) sour cream**
- **1 package (3.4 ounces) instant vanilla pudding mix**
- **1 can (8 ounces) crushed pineapple, drained**
- **24 whole graham crackers**
- **2 medium bananas, sliced**
- **Toppings: chocolate syrup, halved fresh strawberries and additional banana slices**

**1.** In a large bowl, mix whipped topping, sour cream and vanilla pudding mix until blended; fold in pineapple. Cut a small hole in the corner of a pastry or plastic bag; fill with pudding mixture.
**2.** On a flat serving plate, arrange four whole graham crackers in a rectangle. Pipe about 1 cup vanilla pudding mixture over the graham crackers; top with about 1/4 cup banana slices. Repeat the layers five times. Cover and refrigerate overnight.
**3.** Before serving, top with the chocolate syrup, strawberries and banana slices.

Banana Split Icebox Cake transforms a favorite summertime treat into a dessert that feeds a crowd. Plus, I can finish most of the prep work the day before.
**—SHELLY FLYE** ALBION, MAINE

## Fourth of July Decorating

Want to give your outdoor Independence Day party plenty of spark? Try these simple-as-can-be ideas for patriotic decorations. Start by covering tables with red-and-white checkered tablecloths. For vases, fill Mason jars (such as the old blue ones) with water and fresh cherries for color, then add white roses, hydrangeas or daisies. Use blue or red speckled enamelware to serve food, and hang twinkle lights alongside garlands of popcorn and cherries or tiny flags.

## Juicy Watermelon Salad

**PREP:** 20 MIN. + CHILLING
**MAKES:** 10 SERVINGS

- **8 cups cubed seedless watermelon (about 1 medium)**
- **1 small red onion, cut into rings**
- **1 cup coarsely chopped macadamia nuts or slivered almonds, toasted**
- **1 cup fresh arugula or baby spinach**
- **⅓ cup balsamic vinaigrette**
- **3 tablespoons canola oil**
- **Watermelon slices, optional**
- **1 cup (4 ounces) crumbled blue cheese**

In a large bowl, combine the watermelon and red onion; cover and refrigerate until cold, about 30 minutes. Just before serving, add macadamia nuts and arugula to watermelon mixture. In a small bowl, whisk vinaigrette and oil; drizzle over salad and toss to coat. Serve over sliced watermelon, if desired. Sprinkle with cheese.

Everyone raves over the unusual mix of ingredients in Juicy Watermelon Salad. For a colorful twist, use yellow, pink and red varieties of watermelon.
—**HEIDI HAIGHT** MACOMB, MICHIGAN

**Editor's Note:** *To toast nuts, spread in a 15-in. x 10-in. x 1-in. baking pan. Bake at 350° for 5-10 minutes or until lightly browned, stirring occasionally. Or, spread in a dry nonstick skillet and heat over low heat until lightly browned, stirring occasionally.*

Juicy Watermelon Salad

## MAKE AHEAD Grilled Huli Huli Chicken

I received this flavorful chicken recipe from a friend while living in Hawaii. *Huli* means "turn" in Hawaiian.
**—SHARON BOLING** CORONADO, CALIFORNIA

**PREP:** 15 MIN. + MARINATING **GRILL:** 15 MIN.
**MAKES:** 12 SERVINGS

- **1 cup packed brown sugar**
- **¾ cup ketchup**
- **¾ cup reduced-sodium soy sauce**
- **⅓ cup sherry or chicken broth**
- **2½ teaspoons minced fresh gingerroot**
- **1½ teaspoons minced garlic**
- **24 boneless skinless chicken thighs (about 5 pounds)**

**1.** In a small bowl, mix the first six ingredients. Reserve 1⅓ cups for basting; cover and refrigerate. Divide the remaining marinade between two large resealable plastic bags. Add 12 chicken thighs to each; seal the bags and turn to coat. Refrigerate for 8 hours or overnight.
**2.** Drain and discard marinade from chicken. Moisten a paper towel with cooking oil; using long-handled tongs, lightly coat the grill rack.
**3.** Grill the chicken, covered, over medium heat for 6-8 minutes on each side or until no longer pink; baste occasionally with reserved marinade during the last 5 minutes.

Grilled Huli Huli Chicken

Saucy Grilled Pork Chops

## FAST FIX Saucy Grilled Pork Chops

My mamaw in Kentucky slathered this "dip," as she called it, on many grilled meats, including chicken and steak.
**—MISTY SCHNEIDER** BAYPORT, MINNESOTA

**PREP:** 5 MIN. **GRILL:** 10 MIN. **MAKES:** 8 SERVINGS

- **½ cup butter, cubed**
- **½ cup packed light brown sugar**
- **½ cup lemon juice**
- **8 bone-in pork loin chops (¾ inch thick)**
- **Lemon slices, optional**

**1.** In a microwave-safe dish, microwave the butter, covered, until melted; add brown sugar and lemon juice, stirring to dissolve sugar. Reserve ⅔ cup for drizzling.
**2.** Moisten a paper towel with cooking oil; using long-handled tongs, lightly coat the grill rack. Brush the pork chops with the remaining sauce. Grill, covered, over medium heat or broil 4 in. from the heat for 4-5 minutes on each side or until a thermometer reads 145°. Let stand 5 minutes before serving.
**3.** Stir the sauce to combine and gently rewarm if necessary; drizzle over the pork chops. Top with lemon slices if desired.

# HIGHLIGHTS OF HALLOWEEN

When spooky characters come around on October 31, scare up the special treats here. You'll have a frightfully fun time!

## Black & White Spider Cookies

These spiders from the Taste of Home Test Kitchen are yummy, not creepy!

**PREP:** 45 MIN.
**BAKE:** 10 MIN./BATCH + STANDING
**MAKES:** 2½ DOZEN

- **1 package (18¼ ounces) yellow cake mix**
- **2 eggs**
- **½ cup water**

**ICING**

- **⅔ cup water**
- **⅓ cup light corn syrup**
- **8 cups confectioners' sugar**
- **1½ teaspoons vanilla extract**
- **2 ounces unsweetened chocolate, chopped**
- **1 to 3 tablespoons warm water**

**1.** In a large bowl, combine the cake mix, eggs and water; beat on low speed for 30 seconds. Beat on medium for 2 minutes.

**2.** Drop by rounded tablespoonfuls 3 in. apart onto greased baking sheets. Bake at 375° for 8-10 minutes or until the edges begin to brown. Cool for 2 minutes before removing to wire racks to cool completely.

**3.** For icing, in a large heavy saucepan, combine water and corn syrup; bring just to a boil over medium heat. Remove from the heat; whisk in confectioners' sugar and vanilla until smooth.

**4.** In a small microwave-safe bowl, melt chocolate. Stir in 1 cup of icing and 1 tablespoon warm water until smooth. (Icings will thicken as they stand; stir in additional water, 1 teaspoon at a time, to thin if necessary.)

**5.** Spoon chocolate icing over half of each cookie; spread evenly. Spoon vanilla icing over the remaining half of cookies; spread evenly. Let stand until set.

**6.** Cut a small hole in the corner of a pastry or plastic bag; insert #2 round pastry tip. Fill the bag with remaining vanilla icing; pipe a spider web onto the chocolate half of each cookie.

**7.** Using another bag, pipe spiders onto cookies with remaining chocolate icing. Let stand until set. Store in an airtight container.

Bones & Blood

## Bones & Blood

"Zombies" crave these bone-shaped cookies from the Taste of Home Test Kitchen pros. Serve the chocolaty strawberry sauce for dipping.

**PREP:** 45 MIN.
**BAKE:** 25 MIN./BATCH + COOLING
**MAKES:** 40 COOKIES (2 CUPS SAUCE)

- **5 egg whites**
- **½ cup cake flour**
- **½ cup ground almonds**
- **¼ teaspoon ground cinnamon**
- **⅛ teaspoon ground cloves**
- **⅛ teaspoon ground nutmeg**
- **1 teaspoon vanilla extract**
- **¼ teaspoon cream of tartar**
- **Dash salt**
- **4 drops yellow food coloring, optional**
- **¾ cup plus 2 tablespoons sugar**

**SAUCE**

- **1¼ cups heavy whipping cream**
- **½ cup semisweet chocolate chips**
- **½ cup strawberry jelly**
- **Red food coloring, optional**

**1.** Place egg whites in a large bowl; let stand at room temperature for 30 minutes. Meanwhile, combine the flour, almonds, cinnamon, cloves and nutmeg.

**2.** Add the vanilla, cream of tartar, salt and food coloring, if desired, to egg whites. Beat on medium speed until soft peaks form. Gradually add sugar, 1 tablespoon at a time, beating on high until stiff glossy peaks form and sugar is dissolved. Fold in flour mixture.

**3.** Cut a ½-in. hole in the corner of a pastry or plastic bag. Fill bag with egg white mixture. Pipe 4-in. logs onto parchment-lined baking sheets. Pipe two ½-in. balls at both ends of each log. Bake at 300° for 25-30 minutes or until firm to the touch. Remove to wire racks. Store in an airtight container.

**4.** In a small microwave-safe bowl, combine the cream, chocolate chips and jelly. Microwave on high in 30-second intervals until melted; stir until smooth. Tint red if desired. Cool to room temperature and serve with bone cookies. Refrigerate leftover sauce.

Black & White Spider Cookies

## FAST FIX Cupcake Mummy

Alan Richardson and I featured these frightfully frosted mummy cakes in our book, *Cupcakes, Cookies, & Pie, Oh My!* You'll need just four simple ingredients to "wrap" them up. Pipe on the frosting so it resembles white bandages.
**—KAREN TACK** RIVERSIDE, CONNECTICUT

**PREP/TOTAL TIME:** 30 MIN. **MAKES:** 6 SERVINGS

- **1 can (16 ounces) vanilla frosting**
- **6 vanilla cupcakes**
- **8 to 12 large marshmallows, cut into pieces**
- **Baking cocoa and crushed chocolate wafers**

**1.** Frost the tops of the cupcakes. Arrange on a covered cake board, forming a mummy. Place the marshmallow pieces on cupcakes. Insert tip #46 into a pastry bag; fill with frosting. Pipe long bands across the mummy, creating bandages.
**2.** Dust mummy with cocoa; sprinkle the cake board with crushed wafers.

Cupcake Mummy

Body Bites

## Body Bites

Go ahead—play with your food! With Halloween fun in mind, the Taste of Home Test Kitchen experts created this jiggly, creepy-crawly treat that uses gummy body parts.

**PREP:** 20 MIN. + CHILLING **MAKES:** 2 DOZEN

- **2 envelopes unflavored gelatin**
- **1 cup cold prepared limeade**
- **2 cups boiling prepared limeade**
- **24 gummy body parts**

**1.** Sprinkle the gelatin over the cold limeade; let stand for 1 minute. Add boiling limeade; stir until gelatin is completely dissolved.
**2.** Pour into ice cube trays. Refrigerate for 30 minutes or until soft-set. Press a gummy candy into each cube; refrigerate until firm.

Halloween is my favorite part of fall, and we always find special ways to celebrate. My mom sews a homemade costume for my son each year, and I love to share fun, easy-to-make foods with friends and visitors. Our favorite "spooky" beverage is a recipe I call Poison Punch. I pour clear bubbly soda into a glass, add 1 tablespoon of orange Jell-O and stir slightly. The magic happens in front of your eyes as the carbonation and Jell-O create a little "volcano." It's a blast!
—ZIA MCNEAL MAPLE GROVE, MINNESOTA

## FAST FIX Witches' Brew

The Taste of Home Test Kitchen pros stirred up garishly green beverages that are sure to bewitch your party guests. For a nonalcoholic version, simply omit the vodka.

**PREP/TOTAL TIME:** 20 MIN.
**MAKES:** 6 SERVINGS

- **1 cup sugar**
- **1 cup water**
- **8 medium kiwifruit, peeled and quartered**
- **½ cup fresh mint leaves**
- **Green food coloring, optional**
- **1 cup vodka, optional**
- **1 liter ginger ale, chilled**
- **Ice cubes**

**1.** In a small saucepan, bring the sugar and water to a boil. Cook and stir until the sugar is dissolved; set aside to cool.
**2.** Place kiwi, mint leaves and sugar syrup in a blender; cover and process until blended. Tint green if desired. Pour into a large pitcher; stir in vodka if desired. Refrigerate until chilled.
**3.** Just before serving, stir in ginger ale. Serve over ice.

## FAST FIX Witches' Broom

Pair these edible mini brooms from the Taste of Home Test Kitchen with Witches' Brew (recipe above) for an unforgettable combo. All they require are pretzels and licorice!

**PREP/TOTAL TIME:** 30 MIN.
**MAKES:** 6 BROOMS

- **6 pieces green shoestring licorice**
- **6 pretzel rods**
- **6 pieces black licorice**

Cut one green shoestring licorice into 1-in. lengths. Arrange them around the end of one pretzel rod to form broom bristles; tightly wrap the bristles with one black shoestring licorice, tucking in the end to secure. Repeat with the remaining ingredients.

Witches' Broom
Witches' Brew

# THANKSGIVING CORNUCOPIA

On Turkey Day, dining tables overflow with an abundance of special dishes. You'll have a bountiful feast of your own to share when you turn to the unforgettable menu here.

## Cranberry Ricotta Gnocchi with Brown Butter Sauce

**PREP:** 30 MIN. + STANDING
**COOK:** 5 MIN. **MAKES:** 8 SERVINGS

- **¾ cup dried cranberries, divided**
- **2 cups ricotta cheese**
- **1 cup all-purpose flour**
- **½ cup grated Parmesan cheese**
- **1 egg, lightly beaten**
- **¾ teaspoon salt, divided**
- **4 quarts water**
- **¾ cup butter, cubed**
- **2 tablespoons minced fresh sage**
- **½ cup chopped walnuts, toasted**
- **⅛ teaspoon white pepper**

**1.** Finely chop 1/4 cup cranberries. In a large bowl, combine the ricotta cheese, flour, Parmesan cheese, egg, 1/2 teaspoon salt and chopped cranberries; mix until blended. On a lightly floured surface, knead 10-12 times, forming a soft dough. Cover and let rest for 10 minutes.

**2.** Divide the dough into four portions. On a floured surface, roll each portion into a 3/4-in.-thick rope; cut into 3/4-in. pieces. Press and roll each piece with a lightly floured fork.

**3.** In a Dutch oven, bring the water to a boil. Cook gnocchi in batches for 30-60 seconds or until they float. Remove with a slotted spoon; keep warm.

**4.** In a large heavy saucepan, cook the butter over medium heat for 5 minutes. Add the sage; cook 3-5 minutes longer or until the butter is golden brown, stirring occasionally. Stir in the walnuts, white pepper, remaining cranberries and salt. Add the gnocchi; stir gently to coat.

Cranberry Ricotta Gnocchi with Brown Butter Sauce

## FAST FIX Jalapeno Cranberry Sauce

Convenient pantry ingredients make this delightfully different, zippy sauce a favorite year-round. If you're having a cookout, slather the warm sauce on roast pork or grilled chicken.

**—ROXANNE CHAN**
ALBANY, CALIFORNIA

**PREP/TOTAL TIME:** 30 MIN.
**MAKES:** 2⅔ CUPS

- **2 cups jellied cranberry sauce**
- **½ cup cranberry juice**
- **¼ cup red wine vinegar**
- **¼ cup jalapeno pepper jelly, preferably red**
- **¼ cup dried cranberries**
- **¼ cup finely chopped red onion**
- **2 garlic cloves, minced**
- **¾ teaspoon ground allspice**

In a small saucepan, combine all ingredients. Bring to a boil over medium heat. Reduce heat; simmer, uncovered, for 10-12 minutes or until thickened, stirring occasionally.

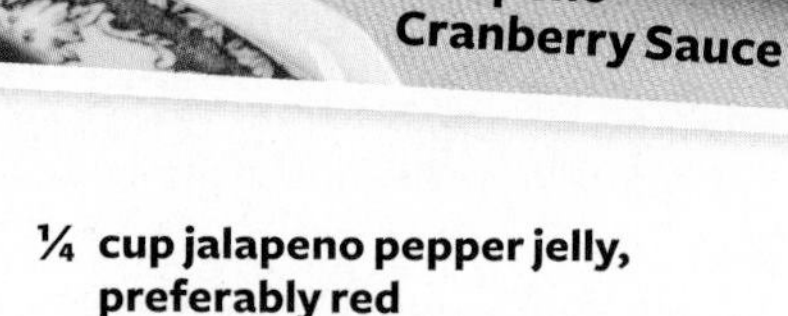

Jalapeno Cranberry Sauce

**Did you know?**

Think jalapenos are the hottest chili peppers? Not even close. Serrano, cayenne and habanero peppers all have a more "fiery" taste.

Cranberry Ricotta Gnocchi with Brown Butter Sauce is so good. Work quickly, handling the dough as little as possible, and puffy pasta pillows will result!

**—SALLY SIBTHORPE**
SHELBY TOWNSHIP, MICHIGAN

## Tangerine-Glazed Turkey

**PREP:** 30 MINUTES
**BAKE:** 3¾ HOURS + STANDING
**MAKES:** 14 SERVINGS (4 CUPS GRAVY)

- **1 turkey (14 to 16 pounds)**
- **½ cup butter, softened**
- **½ cup butter, cubed**
- **1 cup canola oil**
- **2 cups tangerine juice**

**GRAVY**

- **2 to 3 cups chicken broth**
- **5 tablespoons all-purpose flour**

**1.** Remove the giblets from the turkey; cover and refrigerate for gravy. Pat turkey dry; place breast side up on a rack in a roasting pan. Rub softened butter over turkey.
**2.** In a large saucepan, melt the cubed butter; stir in oil. Saturate a four-layered 17-in. square of cheesecloth in the butter mixture; drape over turkey.
**3.** Add the tangerine juice to the remaining butter mixture. Bake turkey, uncovered, at 325° for 3 hours; baste with tangerine juice mixture every 30 minutes, keeping cheesecloth moist at all times.
**4.** Remove and discard the cheesecloth. Bake turkey 45 minutes to 1¼ hours longer or until a meat thermometer reads 180°, basting occasionally with pan drippings. Cover loosely with foil if turkey browns too quickly.
**5.** Remove turkey to a serving platter; cover and let stand for 20 minutes before carving. Pour drippings and loosened brown bits into a measuring cup. Skim fat, reserving ⅓ cup. Add enough broth to remaining drippings to measure 4 cups.
**6.** For gravy, chop reserved giblets. In a large saucepan, saute giblets in reserved fat until browned. Stir in flour until blended; gradually stir in broth mixture. Bring to a boil; cook and stir for 2 minutes or until thickened. Serve with turkey.

**Cranberry Ricotta Gnocchi with Brown Butter Sauce**
**Jalapeno Cranberry Sauce**
**Tangerine-Glazed Turkey**

A technique passed down through the generations—drenching cheesecloth in melted butter and oil, then draping the cloth over the turkey before roasting—helps give Tangerine-Glazed Turkey beautiful golden-brown skin and juicy, moist breast meat. You'll love it!
—**JEANNE HORN** DULUTH, MICHIGAN

## Roasted Parsnip & Pear Soup

Once peeled, parsnips may turn dark when exposed to air, so be sure to roast them right after they're chopped. If you want to get a head start on the prep work, store the peeled and chopped parsnips in acidulated water (just add a bit of lemon or lime juice or vinegar to water).

—**SARA PETRIE** GRASSIE, ONTARIO

**PREP:** 1 HOUR 20 MIN. **COOK:** 45 MIN.
**MAKES:** 9 SERVINGS (2¼ QUARTS)

- **1½ pounds parsnips, peeled and coarsely chopped**
- **2 tablespoons olive oil**
- **¾ teaspoon ground nutmeg**
- **¼ teaspoon salt**
- **⅛ teaspoon pepper**
- **3 medium pears, peeled and chopped**
- **3 medium leeks (white portion only), thinly sliced**
- **2 celery ribs, chopped**
- **3 shallots, chopped**
- **¼ cup butter, cubed**
- **6 cups chicken broth**
- **¼ cup maple syrup**
- **1 bay leaf**
- **1 teaspoon minced fresh thyme**
- **½ cup heavy whipping cream**

**GARNISH**

- **2 tablespoons butter**
- **2 teaspoons brown sugar**
- **⅛ teaspoon ground cumin**
- **⅛ teaspoon ground coriander**
- **2 medium pears, thinly sliced**

Roasted Parsnip & Pear Soup

Tom Turkeys

**1.** In a large bowl, toss parsnips with oil, nutmeg, salt and pepper. Transfer to a greased 15-in. x 10-in. x 1-in. baking pan. Bake, uncovered, at 425° for 25 minutes. Stir in the pears; bake 20-25 minutes longer or until parsnips are tender, stirring occasionally.

**2.** In a large saucepan, cook leeks, celery and shallots in butter over medium heat for 4-6 minutes or until tender. Stir in the broth, maple syrup, bay leaf, thyme and parsnip mixture. Bring to a boil. Reduce the heat; simmer, uncovered for 30 minutes.

**3.** Cool slightly. Discard bay leaf. In a blender, process soup in batches until smooth. Return all to pan. Stir in cream; heat through.

**4.** For garnish, in a large skillet, heat the butter, sugar, cumin and coriander until the sugar is melted, stirring occasionally. Add pears; saute for 2-3 minutes or until crisp-tender. Arrange over servings of soup.

## Tom Turkeys

With a little help from Mom or Dad, these sweet treats from the Taste of Home Test Kitchen pros make the perfect craft project for children to enjoy on Thanksgiving. Kids will love decorating the turkeys almost as much as gobbling them up!

**PREP:** 30 MIN. **COOK:** 5 MIN. + COOLING **MAKES:** 26 TURKEYS

- **1 package (12 ounces) semisweet chocolate chips**
- **1 package (11 ounces) candy corn**
- **52 fudge-striped cookies**
- **¼ cup butter, cubed**
- **4 cups miniature marshmallows**
- **6 cups crisp rice cereal**
- **52 white confetti sprinkles**

**1.** In a microwave, melt the chocolate chips; stir until smooth. For tails, use a dab of chocolate to attach five candy corns to the chocolate side of half of the cookies in a fan shape; refrigerate until set.

**2.** In a large saucepan, melt butter. Add marshmallows; stir over low heat until melted. Stir in cereal. Cool for 10 minutes. With buttered hands, form cereal mixture into 1½-in. balls.
**3.** Remelt the chocolate if necessary. Using chocolate, attach the cereal balls to the chocolate side of the remaining cookies. Position the tails perpendicular to the base cookies; attach with chocolate. Refrigerate until set.
**4.** For feet, cut off the white tips from 52 candy corns; discard tips. Attach feet to base cookies with chocolate. Attach one candy corn to each cereal ball for heads.
**5.** With a toothpick dipped in chocolate, attach two confetti sprinkles to each head. Using chocolate, dot each sprinkle to make pupils. Let stand until set. Store in an airtight container.

Spiced Pumpkin Custard Pie

## Spiced Pumpkin Custard Pie

If it's the crust that makes you nervous about pie-making, here's the solution. The nutty, gingery crumb crust is simply patted into the pie plate. Serve each slice with a generous amount of whipped cream and a sprinkling of cinnamon.
**—CHARLENE CHAMBERS** ORMOND BEACH, FLORIDA

**PREP:** 25 MIN. **BAKE:** 40 MIN. + COOLING **MAKES:** 8 SERVINGS

- **¾ cup chopped pecans, toasted**
- **1 cup plus 2 tablespoons all-purpose flour**
- **½ teaspoon ground ginger**
- **½ teaspoon salt**
- **7 tablespoons shortening**
- **2 tablespoons plus 1 teaspoon ice water**

**FILLING**
- **2 eggs**
- **¾ cup sugar**
- **1 teaspoon ground cinnamon**
- **¾ teaspoon ground allspice**
- **½ teaspoon ground ginger**
- **½ teaspoon salt**
- **1 can (15 ounces) solid-pack pumpkin**
- **1 can (12 ounces) evaporated milk**
- **Whipped cream, optional**
- **Additional ground cinnamon, optional**

**1.** Place pecans in a food processor; cover and process until finely ground. In a large bowl, combine the pecans, flour, ginger and salt. Cut in shortening until mixture is crumbly. Gradually add water, tossing with a fork until dough forms a ball. Press dough onto the bottom and up the sides of an ungreased 9-in. pie plate.
**2.** For filling, in a large bowl, beat the eggs, sugar, spices and salt until smooth. Beat in pumpkin. Gradually beat in milk. Pour into crust.
**3.** Bake at 400° for 40-45 minutes or until a knife inserted near the center comes out clean. Cover edges with foil during the last 15 minutes to prevent overbrowning if necessary. Cool on a wire rack. Garnish with whipped cream and additional cinnamon if desired. Refrigerate leftovers.

**TIME-SAVING HOSTESS TRICKS**

*Is it your year to host a Thanksgiving dinner or other holiday meal? With a little bit of planning, you can serve up a stunning feast while avoiding unnecessary fussing and last-minute scrambling. Here are some helpful hints and tips from the experts in the Taste of Home Test Kitchen:*

- With a big crowd coming, go ahead and mix and match plates, cutlery and serving bowls. Guests will love the eclectic, cozy feel—and you won't have to buy more.
- Gather all your serving utensils the day before and place them in the mixing bowls you're using so you won't be hunting for the gravy ladle, meat fork or extra spoons at the last minute.
- As dishes rotate out of the oven, keep them toasty by covering them with dish towels. Keep the dishes in a closed cardboard box so they'll stay warm until serving.

# A MERRY CHRISTMAS DINNER

What's better on December 25 than a feast of traditional favorites? This classic menu featuring Mustard & Cranberry Glazed Ham will make your season extra bright.

## Mustard & Cranberry Glazed Ham

A delicious glaze for ham requires only four basic ingredients. It's an easy way to ensure your main course will be the star of your holiday dinner.

**—NELLA PARKER** HERSEY, MICHIGAN

**PREP:** 15 MIN.
**BAKE:** 1 HOUR 50 MIN. + STANDING
**MAKES:** 12 SERVINGS (4 CUPS SAUCE)

- **1 fully cooked bone-in ham (6 to 8 pounds)**
- **Whole cloves**
- **3 cans (14 ounces each) jellied or whole-berry cranberry sauce**
- **1½ cups packed brown sugar**
- **1½ cups dry red wine or chicken broth**
- **3 tablespoons Dijon mustard**

**1.** Place ham on a rack in a shallow roasting pan. If desired, score the surface of the ham, making diamond shapes ½ in. deep. Insert cloves into the surface. Loosely cover ham with foil; bake at 325° for 1½ hours.

**2.** In a large saucepan, combine the cranberry sauce, brown sugar and wine. Bring to a boil. Reduce heat; simmer, uncovered, for 10 minutes or until slightly thickened. Remove from the heat; whisk in mustard.

**3.** Pour 2 cups cranberry mixture over the ham. Bake 20-30 minutes longer or until a meat thermometer reads 140°. Let stand for 10 minutes before slicing. Serve with the remaining cranberry sauce.

Mustard & Cranberry Glazed Ham

Creamy Peppermint Punch

FAST FIX

## Creamy Peppermint Punch

Almost too pretty to drink, this minty pink beverage is always popular at Christmastime. Your guests can help themselves at the punch bowl, leaving you free to mingle and enjoy the party.

**—LINDA FOREMAN**
LOCUST GROVE, OKLAHOMA

**PREP/TOTAL TIME:** 10 MIN.
**MAKES:** 16 SERVINGS (¾ CUP EACH)

- **Crushed peppermint candies, optional**
- **½ gallon peppermint ice cream, softened**
- **1 bottle (1 liter) club soda, chilled**
- **4 cups eggnog**

**1.** If desired, moisten the rims of stemmed punch glasses with water. Sprinkle crushed candies on a plate; dip rims in candies. Set glasses aside.

**2.** Just before serving, combine the ice cream, soda and eggnog in a 4-qt. punch bowl. Serve in prepared glasses.

**Editor's Note:** *This recipe was tested with commercially prepared eggnog.*

## Brussels Sprouts & Cauliflower Gratin

I combined two of my favorite vegetables to come up with a creamy, family-friendly dish that takes less than 30 minutes to get in the oven. Topped with crunchy panko bread crumbs and Italian cheeses, this crowd-pleasing side is comfort food at its best and ideal for a special-occasion feast.

**—PRISCILLA GILBERT** INDIAN HARBOUR BEACH, FLORIDA

**PREP:** 25 MIN. **BAKE:** 30 MIN. **MAKES:** 8 SERVINGS

- **4 cups fresh cauliflowerets**
- **4 cups fresh Brussels sprouts, quartered**
- **4 bacon strips, chopped**
- **1 large sweet onion, chopped**
- **4 garlic cloves, minced**
- **¼ cup all-purpose flour**
- **1½ cups 2% milk**
- **⅔ cup half-and-half cream**
- **1 teaspoon salt**
- **¼ teaspoon pepper**
- **½ cup panko (Japanese) bread crumbs**
- **⅓ cup grated Parmesan and Romano cheese blend**

**1.** Place the cauliflower and Brussels sprouts in a large saucepan and cover with water. Bring to a boil. Cover and cook for 2-3 minutes or until crisp-tender; drain.

**2.** Meanwhile, in a large skillet, cook bacon over medium heat until crisp. Remove to paper towels with a slotted spoon; drain, reserving drippings. Saute onion and garlic in the drippings until tender. Stir in flour until blended; gradually add the milk, cream, salt and pepper. Bring to a boil; cook and stir for 2 minutes or until thickened.

**3.** Stir in cauliflower mixture and bacon. Transfer to a greased 2½-qt. baking dish. Cover and bake at 375° for 15 minutes.

**4.** Combine bread crumbs and cheese blend. Uncover vegetables; sprinkle with bread crumb mixture. Bake, uncovered, for 15-20 minutes or until golden brown.

Brussels Sprouts & Cauliflower Gratin

### About Sprouts

A member of the cabbage family, Brussels sprouts average 1 inch in diameter. The name originates from Brussels, Belgium, where this tiny green vegetable was first grown centuries ago.

Brussels sprouts are available from September through May; peak season is October through February. Select small, firm, tightly closed heads that have a bright green color.

Store unwashed Brussels sprouts in an open plastic bag in your refrigerator's crisper drawer for up to 3 days. To prepare Brussels sprouts, remove any loose or yellowed outer leaves, trim the stem end and rinse the sprouts.

### Cauliflower Clues

Cauliflower is enjoyed by many in both cooked dishes and veggie trays. This snowy-white vegetable has a flowerlike appearance and a mild flavor similar to cabbage.

Select firm, solid white or cream-colored heads that are heavy for their size. The florets should be clean and tightly packed, and the surrounding jacket heads should be fresh and green.

Store unwashed cauliflower in an open plastic bag in your refrigerator's crisper drawer for up to 5 days. To prepare cauliflower, trim off the leaves, then remove the base stem at an angle so the core comes out in a cone and the head remains intact. Separate it into florets if desired.

## FAST FIX Chunky Garlic Mashed Potatoes

I like to dress up my mashed potatoes with a whole bulb of roasted garlic. It may seem like overkill, but once cooked, any harshness mellows out and you're left with a sweet, delicate garlic flavor that appeals to everyone.
**—JACKIE GREGSTON** HALLSVILLE, TEXAS

**PREP/TOTAL TIME:** 30 MIN. **MAKES:** 9 SERVINGS

- **3 pounds Yukon Gold potatoes, cut into quarters**
- **1 whole garlic bulb, cloves separated and peeled**
- **½ cup butter, cubed**
- **½ cup half-and-half cream**
- **2 tablespoons prepared horseradish**
- **¾ teaspoon salt**
- **¾ teaspoon pepper**
- **Fresh thyme leaves, optional**

**1.** Place potatoes and garlic cloves in a large saucepan; cover with water. Bring to a boil. Reduce heat; cover and cook for 15-20 minutes or until potatoes are tender.
**2.** Meanwhile, in a small saucepan, heat the butter and cream; keep warm. Drain potatoes and garlic; return to pan. Add the horseradish, salt, pepper and butter mixture; mash to reach desired consistency. Garnish with thyme if desired.

Chunky Garlic Mashed Potatoes

Sweet Holiday Carrots

## FAST FIX Sweet Holiday Carrots

Here's a side dish fit for the finest Christmas table. The dried cranberries plumped in a mixture of honey and lemon juice guarantee a sweet-tart glaze for tender carrots.
**—DONNA MARIE RYAN** TOPSFIELD, MASSACHUSETTS

**PREP/TOTAL TIME:** 30 MIN. **MAKES:** 5 SERVINGS

- **8 medium carrots, sliced**
- **½ cup water**
- **1 can (8 ounces) crushed pineapple, undrained**
- **½ cup chopped peeled tart apple**
- **½ cup dried cranberries**
- **⅓ cup honey**
- **1 tablespoon lemon juice**
- **½ teaspoon salt**
- **1 tablespoon butter, melted**
- **1 tablespoon all-purpose flour**
- **½ teaspoon ground cinnamon**
- **½ cup chopped walnuts, toasted**

**1.** Place carrots and water in a large saucepan. Bring to a boil; reduce heat. Cover and simmer for 5 minutes.
**2.** Add the pineapple, apple, cranberries, honey, lemon juice and salt; cook for 3-4 minutes or until the carrots are crisp-tender, stirring occasionally.
**3.** Combine the butter, flour and cinnamon; stir into the pan. Bring to a boil; cook and stir for 2 minutes or until the sauce is thickened. Sprinkle with walnuts before serving.

To use up leftover mashed potatoes, I mix in a grated raw potato, seasonings and an egg, then shape it into patties and fry. Delicious!
**—HELEN HILLER** SHOREWOOD, WISCONSIN

Dark Chocolate Flourless Cake

## Dark Chocolate Flourless Cake

When I'm using just a few ingredients, I like to use the best ingredients—such as the good quality bittersweet chocolate I put in this rich, decadent cake. A splash of pomegranate juice gives it a subtle hint of fruitiness.
**—VIVIAN TAYLOR** MIDDLEBURG, FLORIDA

**PREP:** 40 MIN. + COOLING **BAKE:** 40 MIN. + COOLING
**MAKES:** 16 SERVINGS

- **1 cup pomegranate juice**
- **¾ cup sugar**
- **1 teaspoon vanilla extract**
- **1 pound bittersweet chocolate, chopped**
- **½ cup butter, cubed**
- **6 eggs**

**GANACHE**

- **6 ounces bittersweet chocolate, chopped**
- **¾ cup heavy whipping cream**
- **Optional garnishes: whipped cream, pomegranate seeds and confectioners' sugar**

**1.** Line the bottom of a buttered 9-in. springform pan with parchment paper; butter the paper and sides of pan. Place on a double thickness of heavy-duty foil (about 18 in. square). Securely wrap foil around pan.
**2.** In a small saucepan, bring pomegranate juice and sugar to a simmer, stirring to dissolve sugar; cook and stir 8-10 minutes or until syrupy. Remove from the heat; stir in vanilla.
**3.** In a large saucepan, melt chocolate and butter over low heat, stirring constantly. Remove from the heat; stir in pomegranate mixture. Cool to room temperature.
**4.** Whisk the eggs into chocolate mixture. Pour into prepared pan. Place in a large baking pan; add 1 in. of hot water to larger pan.
**5.** Bake at 350° for 40-50 minutes or until center is just set and top appears dull. Remove springform pan from water bath. Cool completely on a wire rack.
**6.** Carefully run a knife around the edge of the pan to loosen; remove sides of pan. Place the cake on a serving platter. For the ganache, place the chocolate in a small bowl. In a small saucepan, bring cream just to a boil. Pour over chocolate; whisk until smooth. Cool slightly, stirring occasionally.
**7.** Pour over cake, allowing ganache to drape down the sides. Let stand until set. Just before serving, garnish with whipped cream and pomegranate seeds and dust with confectioners' sugar if desired.

# HOLIDAY COOKIE EXCHANGE

Whether served on a platter or packed into gift tins, fancy cookies are a must at Christmastime. Here, you'll find six merry-as-can-be varieties your guests are sure to love.

## Thin Mint Wreaths

These popular mint-chocolate rounds will keep in a tightly sealed container in the freezer for three weeks.

**—SAMANTHA HARTZELL**
WASHINGTON, ILLINOIS

**PREP:** 35 MIN. + FREEZING
**BAKE:** 10 MIN./BATCH **MAKES:** 5 DOZEN

- **¾ cup butter, softened**
- **1 cup sugar**
- **⅓ cup 2% milk**
- **¾ teaspoon peppermint extract**
- **½ teaspoon vanilla extract**
- **2 cups all-purpose flour**
- **⅓ cup baking cocoa**
- **¼ cup cornstarch**
- **½ teaspoon salt**
- **1 pound dark chocolate or white candy coating, melted**
- **Assorted sprinkles**

**1.** In a large bowl, cream butter and sugar until light and fluffy. Beat in milk and extracts. Combine the flour, cocoa, cornstarch and salt; gradually add to the creamed mixture and mix well.

**2.** Shape into two 1½-in. diameter rolls; wrap each in plastic wrap. Freeze for 2 hours or until firm.

**3.** Unwrap and cut into ¼-in. slices. Place 1 in. apart onto parchment paper-lined baking sheets.

**4.** Bake at 375° for 10-12 minutes or until set. Remove to wire racks to cool completely.

**5.** Dip cookies in coating; allow the excess to drip off. Place on waxed paper. Decorate with sprinkles to resemble wreaths; let stand until set.

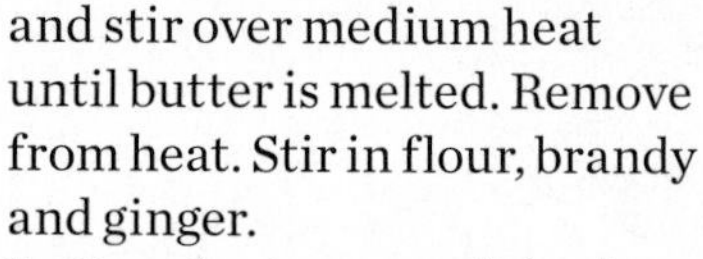

Lacy Brandy Snaps

## Lacy Brandy Snaps

Here's the perfect choice when guests crave "a little something sweet" to nibble on after a big meal.

**—NATALIE BREMSON**
PLANTATION, FLORIDA

**PREP:** 30 MIN.
**BAKE:** 10 MIN./BATCH + COOLING
**MAKES:** 4 DOZEN

- **6 tablespoons unsalted butter, cubed**
- **⅓ cup sugar**
- **3 tablespoons light corn syrup**
- **⅔ cup all-purpose flour**
- **2 teaspoons brandy**
- **1 teaspoon ground ginger**

**FILLING**

- **4 cups heavy whipping cream**
- **1¾ cups confectioners' sugar**
- **½ cup brandy**
- **Grated chocolate, optional**

**1.** In a small saucepan, combine butter, sugar and corn syrup. Cook and stir over medium heat until butter is melted. Remove from heat. Stir in flour, brandy and ginger.

**2.** Drop by teaspoonfuls, three at a time, 3 in. apart onto a parchment paper-lined baking sheet. Bake at 350° for 7-8 minutes or until golden brown.

**3.** Cool for 30-45 seconds. Working quickly, loosen each cookie and curl around a thick wooden spoon handle. (If cookies become too cool to shape, return them to the oven for 1 minute to soften.) Remove to a wire rack to cool completely.

**4.** For filling, in a large bowl, beat cream until it begins to thicken. Add the confectioners' sugar and brandy; beat until stiff peaks form. Just before serving, pipe cream mixture into cookies. Sprinkle ends with chocolate if desired.

Thin Mint Wreaths

## Flaky Creme-Filled Cookies

**PREP:** 55 MIN. + CHILLING
**BAKE:** 10 MIN./BATCH
**MAKES:** 6½ DOZEN

- **2 cups all-purpose flour**
- **¼ teaspoon salt**
- **1 cup cold butter, cubed**
- **1 package (8 ounces) cream cheese, cubed**
- **⅔ cup marshmallow creme**
- **⅔ cup butter, softened**
- **1⅓ cups confectioners' sugar**

**Optional flavoring: 2 tablespoons baking cocoa, ½ teaspoon lemon extract or ½ teaspoon peppermint extract**
**Optional filling: seedless raspberry preserves, blueberry preserves or crushed peppermint candies**
**Confectioners' sugar**

**1.** In a large bowl, combine the flour and salt. Cut in the cold butter and cream cheese until the mixture resembles coarse crumbs. Shape into a disk; wrap in plastic wrap. Refrigerate for 2 hours or until easy to handle.
**2.** On a lightly floured surface, roll the dough to ⅛-in. thickness. Cut out with a floured 1½-in. cookie cutter. Place 2 in. apart on parchment paper-lined baking sheets. Bake at 350° for 7-10 minutes or until light golden brown. Remove to wire racks to cool completely.
**3.** Meanwhile, in a large bowl, beat the marshmallow creme and softened butter until light and fluffy. Gradually beat in the confectioners' sugar.
**4. TO MAKE CHOCOLATE-RASPBERRY COOKIES:** Beat cocoa into marshmallow creme mixture. Spread on the bottoms of half of the cookies. Spread raspberry preserves on the bottoms of remaining cookies; top with matching creme-topped cookies. Sprinkle with confectioners' sugar.
**5. TO MAKE LEMON-BLUEBERRY COOKIES:** Beat lemon extract into marshmallow creme mixture. Spread on the bottoms of half of the cookies. Spread blueberry preserves on the bottoms of remaining cookies; top with matching creme-topped cookies. Sprinkle with confectioners' sugar.
**6. TO MAKE PEPPERMINT COOKIES:** Beat peppermint extract into marshmallow creme mixture. (Tint with 1 drop red food coloring if desired.) Spread on the bottoms of half of the cookies; top with remaining matching cookies. Roll sides in candies if desired. Sprinkle with confectioners' sugar.

**Flaky Creme-Filled Cookies**

The recipe for Flaky Creme-Filled Cookies gives you three different ways to make these treats. Mix and match the flavorings and fillings, and you'll have delectable goodies to suit every taste.
—**SUSAN FALK** WARREN, MICHIGAN

## Italian Rainbow Cookies

Balanced beautifully in the sweet spot between cake and cookie, these sensational slices covered with chocolate will be the centerpiece of your dessert tray.
—**SHERRY THOMPSON** SENECA, SOUTH CAROLINA

**PREP:** 45 MIN. **BAKE:** 10 MIN./BATCH + CHILLING
**MAKES:** 12 DOZEN

- **⅔ cup blanched hazelnuts or macadamia nuts**
- **⅔ cup confectioners' sugar**
- **1 egg white**
- **4 eggs**
- **1 cup sugar**
- **1 cup butter, melted and cooled**
- **1½ teaspoons rum extract**
- **1 cup all-purpose flour**
- **½ teaspoon salt**
- **6 to 8 drops red food coloring**
- **6 to 8 drops green food coloring**
- **2 tablespoons seedless strawberry jam**
- **2 tablespoons apricot preserves**
- **1 cup (6 ounces) dark chocolate chips**
- **1 teaspoon shortening**

**1.** Place the hazelnuts in a food processor; cover and process until ground. Add the confectioners' sugar and egg white; cover and process until blended.
**2.** In a large bowl, beat the eggs and sugar on high speed for 2-3 minutes or until thick and lemon-colored. Gradually beat in the hazelnut mixture, then butter. Beat in the rum extract. Combine the flour and salt; add to the egg mixture.

Italian Rainbow Cookies

Easy 3-Ingredient Shortbread Cookies

**3.** Divide the batter into thirds. Stir red food coloring into one portion of batter; stir green food coloring into another portion. Leave remaining batter plain. Spread one portion into each of three well-greased 11-in. x 7-in. baking dishes.
**4.** Bake at 375° for 10-12 minutes or until a toothpick inserted near the center comes out clean and the edges begin to brown. Cool for 10 minutes before removing from pans to wire racks to cool completely.
**5.** Place the red layer on a waxed paper-lined baking sheet; spread with strawberry jam. Top with the plain layer; spread with apricot preserves. Add the green layer; press down gently.
**6.** In a microwave, melt the dark chocolate chips and shortening; stir until smooth. Spread half over green layer. Refrigerate for 20 minutes or until set. Turn over; spread remaining chocolate over red layer. Refrigerate for 20 minutes or until set.
**7.** With a sharp knife, trim the edges of the rectangle. Cut rectangle lengthwise into fourths. Cut each portion into ¼-in. slices.

## Easy 3-Ingredient Shortbread Cookies

Buttery shortbread squares get instant holiday flair when you add delicate snowflake designs on top. To create them, see the Editor's Note at the end of the recipe.
—**PATTIE PRESCOTT** MANCHESTER, NEW HAMPSHIRE

**PREP:** 10 MIN. **BAKE:** 30 MIN. + COOLING **MAKES:** 9 COOKIES

- **1 cup unsalted butter, softened**
- **½ cup sugar**
- **2 cups all-purpose flour**
- **Confectioners' sugar**

**1.** In a large bowl, cream butter and sugar until light and fluffy. Gradually beat in flour. Press the dough into a greased 9-in. square baking pan.
**2.** Bake at 325° for 30-35 minutes or until lightly browned. Cool for 10 minutes before removing from pan to a wire rack to cool completely. Cut into nine squares; dust with confectioners' sugar.
**Editor's Note:** *We used craft store paper stencils for our snowflakes. To make the white cookie, just tap confectioners' sugar over the stencil through a fine-mesh sieve. To make blue snowflake, dip a small artist's brush in Luster Dust and paint in the stencil opening with a stippling motion.*

## Gingerbread Boy Cookies

My mom always used the same round-headed cookie cutter to shape these "boys." They came out of the oven soft and chewy, with plenty of traditional molasses-ginger flavor.
**—DONNA SASSER HINDS** MILWAUKIE, OREGON

**PREP:** 1 HOUR + CHILLING **BAKE:** 10 MIN./BATCH
**MAKES:** 3-4 DOZEN

- **½ cup butter, cubed**
- **½ cup sugar**
- **½ cup molasses**
- **2 teaspoons white vinegar**
- **1 egg, lightly beaten**
- **3 cups all-purpose flour**
- **½ teaspoon baking soda**
- **½ teaspoon ground ginger**
- **½ teaspoon ground cinnamon**
- **¼ teaspoon salt**
- **Decorating icing, nonpareils, red-hot candies or candies of your choice, optional**

**1.** In a saucepan, combine the butter, sugar, molasses and vinegar; bring to a boil, stirring constantly. Remove from the heat; cool to lukewarm. Stir in egg. Combine the flour, baking soda, ginger, cinnamon and salt; stir into molasses mixture to form a soft dough.
**2.** Divide the dough into thirds. Shape each portion into a disk; wrap in plastic wrap. Refrigerate for at least 2 hours or until easy to handle.
**3.** On a lightly floured surface, roll dough to ¼-in. thickness. Cut with a floured 3-in. gingerbread boy cookie cutter. Place on greased baking sheets. Bake at 375° for 7-9 minutes or until edges are firm. Remove to wire racks; cool completely. Decorate as desired.

**Gingerbread Boy Cookies**

# Mom's Best

When it comes to **comfort food**, no one can dish it out quite like Mom. Here, readers share the heartwarming stories behind the **treasured recipes** they still enjoy with their own families.

"Thanks to my mother's influence and encouragement, I won a recipe contest that led me to Italy. As a result, I developed this skillet dinner that's a new take on Italian Wedding Soup."

—**PATRICIA HARMON** BADEN, PENNSYLVANIA

*MOM'S BEST*

# SOUTHERN COMFORT

**Creativity in the kitchen** is passed from mother to daughter and turns a Mississippi belle into a **reality cooking show champion.**

STORY BY **WHITNEY MILLER** | RECIPES BY **MARY MILLER** POPLARVILLE, MISSISSIPPI

Creative cooking is a big bond between me and my mother. While I was growing up in Poplarville, Mississippi, she prepared mouthwatering feasts on a teacher's budget using just a few basic pantry ingredients. She also regularly did the "mystery box" challenge—putting together meals from a handful of random ingredients—long before today's competitive cooking shows made it popular to do so.

Mom always made meals a family celebration, whether they were at the dining room table, in our backyard, at the beach or in a park. Often, she'd make things extra-special with bandanna napkins or vintage tablecloths.

And holidays? Watch out! Fourth of July has always been one of our favorites. Not only is it America's birthday, it's my mom's, too, and we celebrate in style with lots of laughter, fun and, of course, great-tasting food.

I'll never forget that, after Hurricane Katrina, when we were without electricity for weeks, Mom used one of her favorite kitchen tools, a baking stone, to cook over an open fire.

She inspired me to use the baking stone to cook healthful oven-fried garden vegetables such as squash and peppers, skipping the traditional deep-fat frying.

Needless to say, she passed down the art of making sweet tea. I make a version with sugar, but I can't resist Mom's Tangerine Iced Tea because she blends it with a simple syrup. It has an unbeatable citrus twist and was always served by the gallon at my great-grandmother's house for Sunday dinner.

Another recipe that's packed with flavor is my mother's Crispy Pita BLT's. They're loaded with fresh produce and always wow guests with their just-picked taste.

I'm thankful for my mom's patience in teaching me to cook at a young age. She was one of my biggest cheerleaders while I was competing on the TV show *MasterChef.* And I'll always cherish the time we spent together devising and testing recipes for my cookbook, *Modern Hospitality.*

I am so blessed to have her helping me out now and then in the kitchen as my sous chef—and, more than that, to have her as my mom.

## Crispy Pita BLT's

**PREP:** 35 MIN. **BAKE:** 15 MIN. **MAKES:** 4 SERVINGS

- **⅓ cup mayonnaise**
- **1 garlic clove, minced**
- **¼ teaspoon grated lemon peel**
- **¼ cup all-purpose flour**
- **¾ cup fat-free milk**
- **1 cup panko (Japanese) bread crumbs**
- **2 medium yellow summer squash, cut into ¼-inch slices**
- **2 jalapeno peppers, seeds removed and cut into ¼-inch slices**
- **Cooking spray**
- **8 pita pocket halves**
- **8 romaine leaves**
- **8 slices tomato**
- **16 cooked bacon strips, halved**

**1.** In a small bowl, mix the mayonnaise, garlic and lemon peel. Cover and chill until serving.
**2.** Place flour, milk and bread crumbs in three separate shallow bowls. Coat squash and jalapeno slices with flour, then dip in milk and coat with bread crumbs. Place on baking sheets coated with cooking spray. Spritz vegetables with additional cooking spray.
**3.** Bake at 475° for 12-14 minutes or until golden brown, turning once.
**4.** Spread mayonnaise mixture inside pita halves; fill with lettuce, tomatoes, bacon and breaded vegetables. Serve immediately.

Mom's Tangerine Iced Tea

Crispy Pita BLT's

## Mom's Tangerine Iced Tea

**PREP:** 10 MIN. **COOK:** 5 MIN. + CHILLING **MAKES:** 4 SERVINGS

- **2¾ cups water, divided**
- **4 individual black tea bags**
- **⅔ cup sugar**
- **2 cups fresh tangerine juice (about 12 tangerines)**
- **Ice cubes**
- **Tangerine slices and mint sprigs, optional**

**1.** In a small saucepan, bring 2 cups water to a boil. Remove from the heat; add tea bags. Steep for 3-5 minutes. Discard tea bags; cool tea slightly.
**2.** In another saucepan, combine remaining water and sugar; bring to a boil. Cook and stir until sugar is dissolved. Remove from the heat; cool slightly.
**3.** Transfer tea and sugar syrup to a large pitcher; stir in tangerine juice. Refrigerate until chilled.
**4.** Serve over ice; add tangerine slices and mint if desired.

# *MOM'S BEST*

# SHORTCUT SECRETS

**Time-saving tricks**—and a little less butter—make it easy for this mom to maintain food traditions with a **healthier spin.**

STORY & RECIPES BY **JEAN ECOS** HARTFORD, WISCONSIN

With my family's Armenian background, I grew up around great cooks. All of our social gatherings focused on food—even church dinners were a big production. The ladies would gather weeks ahead of time to stuff grape leaves and bake cheese borag and other pastries.

It was like that—on a smaller scale—in my mom's and grandmothers' kitchens, which always smelled like lemon, mint and sauteed onions. My maternal grandmother passed away at a young age, so although Mom learned how to cook from her, she also gleaned skills from her mother-in-law and the church ladies. (Yet Mom was always partial to how *her* mom made things. It was comforting to her, I think.)

Mom entertained often. If she had friends over for dinner, the delicious homemade dishes just kept on coming. It was truly a feast!

Because Armenian cooking can be very time-consuming and labor-intensive, holidays were always very busy. Mom started cooking weeks in advance, preparing everything from scratch, including phyllo dough and even yogurt.

Mom is adept at multitasking, which she learned from her mother, who managed her kitchen with ease. Their secret? A cheat sheet!

When entertaining, they listed everything that needed to be done, including which dishes were to be used for each course. The dessert plates and coffee machine were set up in one corner; the platters for the main course waited in another. That's how I entertain now. I have a vision of how I want things done. I even know which containers will hold the leftovers.

I've revamped many of Mom's recipes to make them healthier and quicker, but I always stay true to their original flavor. Armenian Garden Salad comes together quickly, even with the homemade dressing.

When I was young, we'd spend time rolling out dough until it was paper thin. These days, I rely on time-saving flour tortillas for recipes such as Lahmajoon (Armenian Pizza).

Mom is older now but more modern than many of her friends. She sometimes comes home frustrated after cooking at church because the other cooks ignore her advice to use olive oil instead of butter. That's *my* influence on her.

## FAST FIX Armenian Garden Salad

**PREP/TOTAL TIME:** 20 MIN.
**MAKES:** 16 SERVINGS (¾ CUP EACH)

- **1 bunch romaine, torn**
- **2 medium tomatoes, chopped**
- **1 medium cucumber, seeded and chopped**
- **1 medium sweet red pepper, chopped**
- **1 small red onion, thinly sliced**
- **1 tablespoon minced fresh parsley**
- **1 teaspoon minced fresh basil**
- **1 teaspoon minced fresh mint**

**DRESSING**

- **¼ cup white wine vinegar**
- **¼ cup olive oil**
- **1 garlic clove, minced**
- **1 teaspoon lemon juice**
- **½ teaspoon dried tarragon**
- **½ teaspoon pepper**
- **¼ teaspoon salt**

In a large bowl, combine the first eight ingredients. In a small bowl, whisk the dressing ingredients. Drizzle over salad; toss to coat. Serve immediately.

Armenian Garden Salad

Lahmajoon (Armenian Pizza)

## Lahmajoon (Armenian Pizza)

**PREP:** 25 MIN. **BAKE:** 10 MIN. **MAKES:** 6 SERVINGS

- **¾ cup drained petite diced tomatoes**
- **½ cup finely chopped onion**
- **⅓ cup minced fresh parsley**
- **¼ cup finely chopped green pepper**
- **2 tablespoons tomato paste**
- **1 teaspoon dried mint**
- **1 garlic clove, minced**
- **¼ teaspoon salt**
- **¼ teaspoon paprika**
- **⅛ teaspoon cayenne pepper**
- **⅛ teaspoon pepper**
- **¾ pound extra-lean ground beef (95% lean)**
- **12 flour tortillas (8 inches)**

**1.** In a large bowl, combine the first 11 ingredients. Crumble beef over mixture and mix well.
**2.** Place tortillas on greased baking sheets. Spread 1/4 cup of meat mixture onto each tortilla to within 1/2 in. of edges (tortillas will not be completely covered). Bake at 425° for 9-12 minutes or until meat is no longer pink and edges of tortillas begin to brown.

# *MOM'S BEST*

# A TALL ORDER

**Pro basketball player Kris Humphries** has taken hits on and off the court. But his **mother's cooking** makes everything better.

STORY BY **KRIS HUMPHRIES** | RECIPES BY **DEBRA HUMPHIRES** CHANHASSEN, MINNESOTA

When I was growing up, my mom tried to get me to cook. She even signed me up for a cooking class when I was in high school. While I never did quite get the hang of it—the extent of my cooking today is limited to grilling—I did learn the importance of eating right.

Mom always encouraged my sisters and me to make healthy choices. She never kept soda in the house and always made sure there were healthy snacks on hand. Her efforts apparently worked—I'm 6 foot 9!

All kidding aside, her resolve has inspired me in a big way. Proper nutrition is one of the cornerstones of my nonprofit organization, the Kris Humphries Foundation. We are on a mission to fight childhood obesity.

At our basketball camps, for instance, we encourage participants to lead a healthy lifestyle through exercise and making good food choices. Changes don't happen overnight, but learning to eat right is a worthwhile cause that can have a positive impact on a young person for years.

As for me, I usually start off the day with a nutritious breakfast. But it's my mom's Juicy Turkey Cheeseburgers and Spiced-Up Sweet Potato Fries that always call me back home. (Being in the NBA, I don't make it home as often as I'd like.)

According to Mom, her burger recipe evolved until she found the perfect combo of ingredients and flavors. She always included chopped onion and garlic, but then she added ketchup and soy sauce to the meat for more moisture and richer flavor. They're incredible!

From the time I was a little kid, my mom has done everything she possibly could for our family. She's the one who encouraged me to go to swim practice at 6 a.m., cooked my favorite dinner after cheering me on through three basketball games in a single Saturday, and bounced back and forth from my sister's swim meet to my game in the same day. At the same time, she inspired me to be a man of character, or, as she said, "a prince among men."

To me, she's the world's best mom for putting her faith, family and beliefs first. Thanks, Mom!

## FAST FIX Juicy Turkey Cheeseburgers

**PREP/TOTAL TIME:** 30 MIN. **MAKES:** 4 SERVINGS

- **⅔ cup finely chopped onion**
- **1½ teaspoons minced garlic**
- **2 tablespoons ketchup**
- **1 tablespoon reduced-sodium soy sauce**
- **¼ teaspoon ground mustard**
- **¼ teaspoon pepper**
- **1 pound ground turkey**
- **4 slices Monterey Jack cheese**
- **4 hamburger buns, split**
- **4 turkey bacon strips, cooked**
- **4 lettuce leaves**

**1.** In a large nonstick skillet coated with cooking spray, cook and stir onion and garlic over medium heat until tender. Transfer to a large bowl; cool slightly. Mix in the ketchup, soy sauce, mustard and pepper. Crumble turkey over mixture and mix well; shape into four patties.
**2.** In the same skillet, cook burgers over medium heat for 5-7 minutes on each side or until a thermometer reads 165° and juices run clear.
**3.** Top with cheese; cover and cook 30 seconds longer or until cheese is melted. Serve on buns with bacon and lettuce.

## FAST FIX Spiced-Up Sweet Potato Fries

**PREP/TOTAL TIME:** 30 MIN. **MAKES:** 4 SERVINGS

- **3 medium sweet potatoes, peeled and cut into 1-inch wedges (about 1½ pounds)**
- **2 tablespoons olive oil**
- **1 teaspoon Cajun seasoning**
- **½ teaspoon kosher salt**
- **½ teaspoon coarsely ground pepper**

**1.** In a large bowl, combine potatoes and oil; toss to coat. Sprinkle with seasonings; toss to combine. Arrange in a single layer on a greased 15-in. x 10-in. x 1-in. baking pan.
**2.** Bake, uncovered, at 425° for 20-25 minutes or until tender and lightly browned, turning occasionally.

### Did you know?

Kosher salt is a coarse salt that's great for cooking and canning purposes. It is far coarser than table salt, which makes it desirable for seasoning foods, rubbing over meats, and using as a garnish on the rims of cocktail glasses. While the flavor of kosher salt is terrific, it is not recommended for use in baking or as a substitute for the salt you set on the table.

# *MOM'S BEST*

# FOOD FULL CIRCLE

A **hardworking mother's gift** of cooking comforting, home-style meals inspires her now-grown daughter to **do the same.**

STORY & RECIPES BY **BRYNN RADER** OLYMPIA, WASHINGTON

I am always amazed when I think back to how hard my mother worked when my younger brothers and I were growing up. She made sure we had a home-cooked family meal on the table every night.

It was easier for her when I was in elementary school and she didn't work outside the house. But then we moved to the Midwest, and she had to work full time. She'd waitress all day, then come home and be just as hospitable to us as she was to her customers. She'd insist on serving everyone else first, always waiting to serve herself last.

When I was a teenager, she started working crazy hours. She took a job as a certified nurse assistant, pulling herself out of bed at 5 a.m. so she could be home with us after school. As a kid, you don't think much about the sacrifices your parents make, but you appreciate them more as you get older. Now that I'm a stay-at-home mom with two children of my own, I truly understand how hard she worked.

Mom lives about 15 minutes away from me and my family. Even though she still works hard, we get to see her frequently. She and I share a love for *Taste of Home* magazine, and I use it to plan my family's weekly menus.

I make my mom's recipes, too. Chicken and Sweet Potato Chili reminds me of the comfort food I loved so much growing up. We like the twist of swapping in chicken for beef, and our family has always been partial to sweet potatoes.

Mom also baked batches of tender Cornmeal Dinner Rolls regularly. They're great with just about anything.

My mother definitely passed her sweet tooth on to us! She prepares a Maple Nut Twist that is so pretty and company-worthy. My brothers and I used to squabble over the center piece, which was the softest, most buttery part.

Mom has always made everyday moments special with food, and I do that now as a mother myself. It feels like a gift she's given me, and I'm happy I can pass it on to my own children.

## Cornmeal Dinner Rolls

**PREP:** 35 MIN.+ RISING
**BAKE:** 15 MIN. **MAKES:** 2½ DOZEN

- **2 cups whole milk**
- **½ cup sugar**
- **½ cup butter, cubed**
- **⅓ cup cornmeal**
- **1¼ teaspoons salt**
- **1 package (¼ ounce) active dry yeast**
- **¼ cup warm water (110° to 115°)**
- **2 eggs**
- **4¾ to 5¾ cups all-purpose flour**

**TOPPING**

- 2 tablespoons butter, melted
- 1 tablespoon cornmeal

**1.** In a large saucepan, combine the milk, sugar, butter, cornmeal and salt. Bring to a boil over medium heat, stirring constantly. Reduce heat; cook and stir 5-8 minutes or until thickened. Cool to 110°-115°.
**2.** In a small bowl, dissolve yeast in warm water. In a large bowl, combine the eggs, cornmeal mixture, yeast mixture and 2 cups flour; beat until smooth. Stir in enough remaining flour to form a soft dough (dough will be sticky).
**3.** Turn onto a floured surface; knead until smooth and elastic, about 6-8 minutes. Place in a greased bowl, turning once to grease the top. Cover with plastic wrap; let rise in a warm place until doubled, about 1 hour.
**4.** Punch dough down. Turn onto a lightly floured surface; divide into 30 balls. Place 2 in. apart on greased baking sheets. Cover with a clean kitchen towel; let rise in a warm place until doubled, about 45 minutes.
**5.** Uncover rolls; brush with melted butter and sprinkle with cornmeal. Bake at 375° for 13-17 minutes or until golden brown. Remove from pans to wire racks; serve warm.

## Chicken and Sweet Potato Chili

**PREP:** 35 MIN. **COOK:** 1½ HOURS
**MAKES:** 10 SERVINGS (3½ QUARTS)

- 1 medium onion, chopped
- 1 whole garlic bulb, cloves separated, peeled and minced
- 2 tablespoons olive oil
- 1 broiler/fryer chicken (3 to 4 pounds), cut up
- 2 cans (14½ ounces each) plus 1½ cups chicken broth, divided
- 1 tablespoon chili powder
- ¾ teaspoon salt
- ¼ teaspoon crushed red pepper flakes
- ¼ teaspoon pepper
- ½ cup quinoa, rinsed
- 3 medium sweet potatoes, peeled and cubed
- 2 cans (15 ounces each) black beans, rinsed and drained
- 2 cans (16 ounces each) kidney beans, rinsed and drained
- 1 can (14½ ounces) diced tomatoes, undrained

**1.** In a Dutch oven, saute onion and garlic in oil until tender. Add the chicken, 2 cans broth and seasonings. Bring to a boil. Reduce heat; cover and simmer for 1 hour or until chicken is tender.
**2.** Meanwhile, in a small saucepan, bring remaining broth to a boil. Add quinoa. Reduce heat; cover and simmer for 12-15 minutes or until liquid is absorbed. Remove from the heat; fluff with a fork. Set aside.
**3.** Remove chicken; cool slightly. Strain broth, reserving vegetables; skim fat from broth. Return vegetables and broth to the Dutch oven; add the sweet potatoes, beans, tomatoes and cooked quinoa. Bring to a boil. Reduce heat; simmer for 15-20 minutes or until sweet potatoes are tender.
**4.** Meanwhile, remove chicken from bones; cut into bite-size pieces. Discard bones. Stir chicken into chili; heat through.

## Maple Nut Twist

**PREP:** 55 MIN. + RISING
**BAKE:** 20 MIN. **MAKES:** 16 SERVINGS

- 1 package (16 ounces) hot roll mix
- 3 tablespoons sugar
- ¾ cup warm water (120° to 130°)
- ⅓ cup butter, melted
- 1 egg, lightly beaten
- 1 teaspoon maple flavoring

**FILLING**

- 1½ cups finely chopped walnuts
- ¾ cup packed brown sugar
- ¾ cup sugar
- 3 teaspoons ground cinnamon
- 3 teaspoons maple flavoring
- ⅓ cup butter, melted

Chicken and Sweet Potato Chili
Cornmeal Dinner Rolls

**1.** In a large bowl, combine the contents of the roll mix and yeast packets with the sugar. Stir in the water, butter, egg and maple flavoring; mix well.
**2.** Turn onto a floured surface; knead until smooth and elastic, about 5 minutes. Place in a greased bowl, turning once to grease the top. Cover with plastic wrap; let rise in a warm place until doubled, about 1 hour.
**3.** Combine the first five filling ingredients in a small bowl; set aside. Punch dough down. Turn onto a lightly floured surface; divide into thirds.
**4.** Roll one portion of dough into a 12-in. circle; transfer to a greased 12-in. pizza pan. Brush with a third of the butter; sprinkle with a third of the filling. Repeat two times with the remaining dough, butter and filling, placing each circle of dough over the previous layer. Pinch outer edges to seal.
**5.** Place a small glass at the center of the dough. With scissors, cut from the outside edge to the glass to form 16 wedges. Remove glass; twist each wedge three times. Cover with plastic wrap; let rise in a warm place until doubled, about 30 minutes.
**6.** Uncover dough. Bake at 375° for 20-25 minutes or until golden. Remove from pan to a wire rack.

# *MOM'S BEST*

# LEGACY OF A SUPER COOK

A Pennsylvania mother flaunts her **considerable culinary powers** in the kitchen—and becomes a **family hero** at dinnertime.

STORY & RECIPES BY **PATRICIA HARMON** BADEN, PENNSYLVANIA

My mother was truly a cooking superwoman. Every evening, she donned her cape and powered through the family kitchen, often cooking two dinners in one day. My father worked varying shifts, so Mom would make a meal for us kids, then cook again for him when he came home from work.

My mom learned from my grandmother, who also loved to cook, especially during the holidays. (I still use Grandma's style when preparing my Easter paska breads.) Later on, my mother honed her culinary skills by working in the kitchen of a local hospital. She was a hero of the heart as well as the stove!

She insisted on sitting down to eat as a family. Food bonds people, and we preferred to share our meals with each other rather than the TV.

When my daughter was born, I inherited the Super Cook cape. I always cooked from scratch, making many of the dishes I'd learned from my mother and also dabbling with newly discovered recipes I couldn't wait to try.

Because the creative aspect of cooking is such a joy for me, I began developing unique recipes of my own. Thanks to my mother's influence and encouragement, I started entering cooking and recipe contests. Once I even won a trip to Italy as my prize!

That country and cuisine warmed my soul, so lots of my creations are Italian. I came up with Italian Wedding Soup Supper—a skillet dinner—that's a new take on the traditional soup.

In a classic Italian Wedding Soup, the meat marries the vegetables in a savory broth. In my heartier dish, chicken goes well with the trio of onion, carrot and celery, and also complements the spinach and meatballs.

Now my children are grown, but my Super Cook duties live on. I love to do the cooking when I visit my daughter in Arizona, and I ask my nearby stepson and his family to sample many of my dinner creations.

Flexing my culinary muscles and letting loose in the kitchen remind me of my mother. I'm not making two meals, as she did, but I might as well be when I'm feeding that many people!

I've been retired for a number of years now but have yet to hang up my Super Cook cape. As I say to my husband, "We have to eat anyway!"

## Italian Wedding Soup Supper

**PREP:** 25 MIN. **COOK:** 15 MIN.
**MAKES:** 6 SERVINGS

- **2 cups small pasta shells**
- **½ pound boneless skinless chicken breasts, cut into ¾-inch cubes**
- **2 tablespoons olive oil, divided**
- **1 medium onion, chopped**
- **1 medium carrot, finely chopped**
- **1 celery rib, chopped**
- **1 package (12 ounces) frozen fully cooked Italian meatballs, thawed**
- **1 can (10¾ ounces) reduced-fat reduced-sodium condensed cream of chicken soup, undiluted**
- **1 package (10 ounces) frozen chopped spinach, thawed and squeezed dry**
- **1 cup reduced-sodium chicken broth**
- **2 teaspoons minced fresh thyme or ½ teaspoon dried thyme**
- **½ teaspoon salt**
- **⅛ teaspoon pepper**
- **¾ cup shredded Asiago cheese**

**1.** Cook pasta according to package directions. Meanwhile, in a large skillet, saute chicken in 1 tablespoon oil until no longer pink; remove and keep warm.

**2.** In the same skillet, saute the onion, carrot and celery in remaining oil until tender. Add the meatballs, soup, spinach, broth, thyme, salt, pepper and reserved chicken; cover and cook for 4-6 minutes or until heated through.

**3.** Drain pasta; stir into skillet. Sprinkle with cheese.

Frozen spinach that has been thawed typically needs to be drained and squeezed dry before it's used in a recipe. This is done to prevent the final dish from watering out. Simply set thawed spinach in a colander, and with clean hands, squeeze the water out of the spinach.

Italian Wedding Soup Supper

# Field Editor Favorites

From coast to coast, our Field Editors **love sharing** the dishes that keep their families running to the table. Here, they offer up the **tried-and-true recipes** they turn to most.

"I'm attracted to the versatility of beef Wellington, and the best part is that it's very uncomplicated to make—even though the final presentation is awesome!"

—**KERRY DINGWALL** VERDA, FLORIDA

*From the kitchen of*

# Lee Ann Miller

***Millersburg, Ohio***

Lee Ann Miller cooks for a variety of visitors at Miller Haus Bed and Breakfast in Millersburg, Ohio. "It's another way to show my guests I care," she says. "There's nothing better than watching my kitchen creations disappear."

## This Field Editor serves up **helpings of love** at her country-style bed and breakfast, located **in the heart** of Ohio's Amish country.

STORY & RECIPES BY **LEE ANN MILLER** AS TOLD TO **DEBORAH WAGMAN**

Visitors like to travel to Ohio's Amish country to experience the beauty of our landscapes and to witness our peaceful lifestyle. But most of all, they come to eat!

Holmes County, home to the world's largest Amish settlement, is known for its amazing food. Our kitchens overflow with rich and hearty fare.

My husband, Daryl, was raised by an Old Order Amish mother who divided her days between the garden and the kitchen. My Swiss-German family was always well fed by my mother, too.

Our backgrounds were perfect for the work we do. For a number of years now, Daryl and I have owned and operated Miller Haus Bed and Breakfast, a nine-room Amish-style home where we offer lodging and home-cooked meals to travelers. My husband and his uncle built the building. I furnished it with antiques and lots of country charm, and before I knew it, I was making breakfast every day for our guests.

Amish traditions—especially using wholesome, high-quality ingredients—continually influence my cooking. The idea of eating organic food is nothing new here: Amish people have lived such a lifestyle and produced their own meat, dairy, vegetables and fruits in that way for generations—long before the concepts of "organic" and "going green" even existed.

Locally produced foods are everywhere. We keep our own chickens, so the eggs we serve at our B&B couldn't be fresher. And there are Amish produce stands bursting with bountiful harvests around every corner.

One of my favorite stands is Blessings Acres, owned by two Amish widows who bottle their own honey. When I stopped there recently, the women were gone, but their wonderful honey was still there—accompanied by a pail with a sign reading, "Put money here."

I do most of the B&B cooking, but I have great helpers. My sons Ted and Joe—whose favorite dessert is Two-Chip Chocolate Chippers (recipe on page 235)—are really good in the kitchen. I don't know what I would do without them. I've always told my boys, "Don't ever let anyone tell you that real men don't cook!"

Food means many things to people, but to me, food means love. In my daily cooking, whether I'm preparing an extra-special dinner, baking a chocolate layer cake or kneading a hearty loaf of bread, I feel I'm communicating to the people at our table, "You are important to our family. You have value, and you are loved."

## Italian Sausage Quiche

This is our B&B's most popular dish. It's prepared with mild Italian sausage that's made for us by our local butcher. For the best flavor, choose sausage that is not too heavily spiced.
**—LEE ANN MILLER** MILLERSBURG, OHIO

**PREP:** 30 MIN. **BAKE:** 35 MIN. + STANDING **MAKES:** 6 SERVINGS

- **Pastry for single-crust pie (9 inches)**
- **1 pound bulk Italian sausage**
- **¼ cup chopped onion**
- **¼ cup chopped green pepper**
- **4 teaspoons chopped seeded jalapeno pepper**
- **1 cup (4 ounces) shredded sharp cheddar cheese**
- **3 eggs**
- **1 cup heavy whipping cream**
- **1 teaspoon minced fresh parsley**
- **1 teaspoon minced fresh basil**
- **¼ teaspoon pepper**
- **⅛ teaspoon salt**
- **Dash garlic powder**
- **Dash cayenne pepper**

1. Roll out pastry to fit a 9-in. pie plate. Transfer pastry to pie plate. Trim pastry to ½ in. beyond edge of plate; flute edges. Line unpricked pastry with a double thickness of heavy-duty foil. Fill with dried beans, uncooked rice or pie weights.
2. Bake at 450° for 8 minutes. Remove foil and weights; bake 5 minutes longer. Cool on a wire rack.
3. Meanwhile, in a large skillet, cook the sausage, onion, green pepper and jalapeno over medium heat until meat is no longer pink; drain. Spoon into shell and sprinkle with cheese.
4. In a large bowl, whisk the remaining ingredients; pour over cheese. Bake at 375° for 35-40 minutes or until a knife inserted near the center comes out clean. Let stand for 10 minutes before cutting.

**Editor's Note:** *Wear disposable gloves when cutting hot peppers; the oils can burn skin. Avoid touching your face.*

## Banana Pecan Loaf

We slice this bread so thick, it's almost embarrassing—but we need fat slices to deliver ample portions of the Pineapple Spread! When beating the cream cheese for the spread, beat it until it's as light and fluffy as whipped cream.
**—LEE ANN MILLER** MILLERSBURG, OHIO

**PREP:** 25 MIN. **BAKE:** 50 MIN. + COOLING
**MAKES:** 1 LOAF (16 SLICES)

- **½ cup butter, softened**
- **1 cup packed brown sugar**
- **2 eggs**
- **3 medium ripe bananas, mashed**

Italian Sausage Quiche

2 cups all-purpose flour
½ teaspoon baking powder
½ teaspoon baking soda
½ teaspoon salt
½ cup chopped pecans

**PINEAPPLE SPREAD**

1 package (8 ounces) cream cheese, softened
1 cup canned crushed pineapple, well drained

1. In a large bowl, cream butter and sugar until light and fluffy. Add eggs, one at a time, beating well after each addition. Beat in bananas. Combine the flour, baking powder, baking soda and salt; add to creamed mixture. Fold in pecans.
2. Transfer to a greased 9-in. x 5-in. loaf pan. Bake at 350° for 50-60 minutes or until a toothpick inserted near the center comes out clean. Cool for 10 minutes before removing from pan to a wire rack.
3. In a small bowl, combine cream cheese and pineapple. Serve with bread.

Banana Pecan Loaf

## Two-Chip Chocolate Chippers

When preparing this recipe, I'm a stickler for using one stick of butter and one stick of margarine. I think the combination of fats gives these treats terrific texture. And avoid using a scooper—the tool compacts the cookies too much.
**—LEE ANN MILLER** MILLERSBURG, OHIO

**PREP:** 20 MIN. **BAKE:** 10 MIN./BATCH **MAKES:** 5 DOZEN

½ cup butter, softened
½ cup stick margarine, softened
¾ cup packed brown sugar
¼ cup sugar
2 eggs
1½ teaspoons vanilla extract
2¼ cups all-purpose flour
1 package (3.4 ounces) instant vanilla pudding mix
1 teaspoon baking soda
1½ cups semisweet chocolate chips
1½ cups milk chocolate chips
1½ cups chopped pecans, optional

1. In a large bowl, cream the butter, margarine and sugars until light and fluffy. Beat in eggs and vanilla. Combine the flour, pudding mix and baking soda; gradually add to creamed mixture and mix well. Stir in chocolate chips and pecans if desired.
2. Drop by rounded tablespoonfuls 1 in. apart onto ungreased baking sheets; flatten slightly with a glass. Bake at 375° for 8-10 minutes or until lightly browned. Remove to wire racks.

Two-Chip Chocolate Chippers

*From the kitchen of*

# Debbie Johnson

***Centertown, Missouri***

Debbie Johnson happily spends much of her free time sharing her love of cooking at home, at church and all over the neighborhood.

## This Missouri mom and grandma warms hearts with **breakfast delights,** other from-scratch specialties and **sage advice** for new cooks.

STORY & RECIPES BY **DEBBIE JOHNSON**

Although I've always liked to cook, my mother truly lit a fire of inspiration in me. I'll never forget how wonderful she was at making a really grand meal out of almost nothing.

When I moved into an apartment after high school, I began cooking and experimenting in the kitchen. At first, there were a lot of phone calls to my mom for help; however, I've been cooking nonstop ever since.

I've come to realize that I'm not a fancy cook. My food tends to be more country or wholesome—family-style, you might say. I like making things from scratch. There's just something about measuring, mixing and kneading that I find very relaxing and satisfying, particularly when it comes to preparing a hearty morning meal.

I put my breakfast skills to good use at church, too. I'm part of a group of married ladies who minister to newlyweds. I teach the young brides how to fit breakfast preparation into their busy lives. My Baked French Toast with Blueberry Sauce is a favorite. (See the following pages for this recipe and a few others!)

I also started a "neighborhood plate" program. One person bakes something and delivers the plate of treats to a neighbor, who then repeats the process. Eventually, the plate makes its way back to the home of the original baker and the process starts again. We've found it to be a delightful way to share.

Needless to say, my cookbook collection has gained extra weight over the years. It's a good thing, too, because my children often call and say, "Mom, can I have that recipe for...?" I'm truly honored when they ask. Sometimes I ask them for recipes as well.

I simply adore preparing meals for them. It's just one of the ways I express my love. When my daughter, Jessica, gave birth to her son, I fixed several meals and put them in her freezer. My son-in-law joked that if he knew what it took to get so many of my home-cooked dinners, they would have had a baby sooner!

## Baked French Toast with Blueberry Sauce

French toast always seems to have a "special occasion" feel about it; however, it's one of the simplest breakfast dishes to prepare. Start your day off perfectly with this oven-baked version covered with a tangy blueberry sauce.
—**DEBBIE JOHNSON** CENTERTOWN, MISSOURI

**PREP:** 20 MIN. **BAKE:** 20 MIN. **MAKES:** 4 SERVINGS (1 CUP SAUCE)

- **¼ cup butter, melted**
- **4 eggs**
- **1 cup 2% milk**
- **1 teaspoon vanilla extract**
- **½ teaspoon ground nutmeg**
- **8 slices Texas toast**

**BLUEBERRY SAUCE**

- **¼ cup sugar**
- **1½ teaspoons cornstarch**
- **¼ teaspoon ground cinnamon**
- **⅛ teaspoon ground cloves**
- **1½ cups fresh or frozen blueberries**
- **2 tablespoons thawed orange juice concentrate**

1. Pour melted butter on a 15-in. x 10-in. x 1-in. baking pan; lift and tilt pan to coat bottom evenly. In a large shallow bowl, whisk the eggs, milk, vanilla and nutmeg. Dip both sides of Texas toast into egg mixture; place on prepared pan. Bake at 375° for 20-25 minutes or until lightly browned.

Baked French Toast with Blueberry Sauce

Easy Breakfast Strata

2. For sauce, in a large saucepan, combine the sugar, cornstarch, cinnamon and cloves. Stir in blueberries and orange juice concentrate. Bring to a boil; cook and stir for 2 minutes or until thickened. Serve with French toast.

## MAKE AHEAD Easy Breakfast Strata

Mornings are fuss-free when you can begin preparing your food the night before. Not only does a little planning help you serve something spectacular, but cleanup is a snap as well. If you like, change up my make-ahead breakfast strata by switching to brown-and-serve sausage links, diced cooked ham or diced cooked bacon. Or, try using Swiss or Monterey Jack cheese if you're not a fan of cheddar.
—**DEBBIE JOHNSON** CENTERTOWN, MISSOURI

**PREP:** 20 MIN. + CHILLING **BAKE:** 30 MIN. **MAKES:** 12 SERVINGS

- **1 pound bulk pork sausage**
- **1 large green pepper, chopped**
- **1 medium onion, chopped**
- **1 loaf (1 pound) herb or cheese bakery bread, cubed**
- **1 cup (4 ounces) shredded cheddar cheese**
- **6 eggs**
- **2 cups 2% milk**
- **1 teaspoon ground mustard**

1. In a large skillet, cook the sausage, pepper and onion over medium heat until meat is no longer pink; drain.
2. Place bread in a greased 13-in. x 9-in. baking dish. Top with sausage; sprinkle with cheese. In a large bowl, whisk the eggs, milk and mustard. Pour over the top. Cover and refrigerate overnight.

**3.** Remove from the refrigerator 30 minutes before baking. Bake, uncovered, at 350° for 30-35 minutes or until a knife inserted near the center comes out clean. Let stand 5 minutes before cutting.

## Raspberry Almond Coffee Cake

Coffee and cake are like a wink and a smile—you'll take one without the other, but given the choice, you want the pair! Raspberries and almonds lift this coffee cake to a delightfully tart and nutty place. Plus, the recipe doubles easily in a 9x13 pan to accommodate larger get-togethers.
—**DEBBIE JOHNSON** CENTERTOWN, MISSOURI

**PREP:** 20 MIN. **BAKE:** 25 MIN. + COOLING **MAKES:** 8 SERVINGS

- **1 cup fresh raspberries**
- **3 tablespoons brown sugar**
- **1 cup all-purpose flour**
- **⅓ cup sugar**
- **½ teaspoon baking powder**
- **¼ teaspoon baking soda**
- **⅛ teaspoon salt**
- **1 egg**
- **½ cup sour cream**
- **3 tablespoons butter, melted**
- **1 teaspoon vanilla extract**
- **¼ cup sliced almonds**

**ICING**

- **¼ cup confectioners' sugar**
- **1½ teaspoons 2% milk**
- **¼ teaspoon vanilla extract**

**1.** In a small bowl, combine raspberries and brown sugar; set aside.
**2.** In a large bowl, combine the flour, sugar, baking powder, baking soda and salt. In a small bowl, whisk the egg, sour cream, butter and vanilla. Stir into dry ingredients just until moistened.
**3.** Spoon half of the batter into a greased and floured 8-in. round baking pan. Top with raspberry mixture. Spoon remaining batter over raspberries; sprinkle with almonds.
**4.** Bake at 350° for 25-30 minutes or until a toothpick inserted near the center comes out clean. Cool for 10 minutes before removing from pan to a wire rack. In a small bowl, combine the icing ingredients; drizzle over coffee cake. Serve warm.

**Raspberry Almond Coffee Cake**

*From the kitchen of*

# Julie Sterchi

***Jackson, Missouri***

A big fan of grapes, Julie Sterchi successfully adds this versatile fruit to four must-try family delights and gets bunches of compliments.

## When it comes to **culinary inspiration,** this Field Editor finds it in her mom, celebrity chefs, online friends and one of her **go-to ingredients.**

STORY & RECIPES BY **JULIE STERCHI**

I have enjoyed working in the kitchen ever since I was a young girl. My mother really inspired me. She was the type of cook who didn't use a recipe; rather, she relied on a pinch of this and a handful of that to create a memorable meal.

A few months before my wedding, I began watching her more carefully. I wanted to be able to duplicate her cooking techniques and delicious dishes when I was on my own!

Today, I like to watch Ina Garten and Tyler Florence on cooking shows, but I also draw inspiration from the friends I've made on an online recipe exchange group. I've been a member of the group for a number of years now, and the sharing of recipes, tips and the details of our lives has truly been a blessing. If I need advice or an idea, someone always provides it.

I love making people feel right at home and appreciated when they come to visit me. A big part of that is feeding them, of course! When I cook for guests, I'm never afraid to experiment, especially with different seasonings, cooking methods and ingredients.

For example, I'm a big fan of grapes, so I'm happy to find new uses for them whenever I can. My inspiration for Chunky Chicken Salad with Grapes & Pecans was a delicious sandwich I tried at a tearoom. I wanted to enjoy it at home, and after a few attempts, I created this refreshing medley. (My recipes start on page 243.)

Similarly, I read about grape tartlets once, so I came up with my own take on that dessert. I also created a breakfast yogurt treat and even a grape punch for a wedding shower. Sparkling White Grape Punch gets the perfect touch of tartness from cranberry juice.

It's all about experimenting, taking advice from others and tweaking ideas to create a specialty you and your guests will enjoy time and again.

## FAST FIX Sparkling White Grape Punch

White cranberry juice adds tartness to a beverage you'll want to serve at bridal showers and teas. To give it a light blush color, use regular cranberry juice instead.
**—JULIE STERCHI** JACKSON, MISSOURI

**PREP/TOTAL TIME:** 10 MIN. **MAKES:** 24 SERVINGS (¾ CUP)

- **1 bottle (64 ounces) white grape juice, chilled**
- **1½ cups white cranberry juice, chilled**
- **2 liters lemon-lime soda, chilled**
- **Seedless red or green grapes, optional**

Just before serving, combine juices in a 5-qt. punch bowl. Stir in soda. Add grapes if desired.

## FAST FIX Grapes with Lemon-Honey Yogurt

Here's a soothing side dish that blends honey, lemon and cinnamon flavors with grapes in a light, lovely way.
**—JULIE STERCHI** JACKSON, MISSOURI

**PREP/TOTAL TIME:** 10 MIN. **MAKES:** 8 SERVINGS

- **1 cup fat-free plain Greek yogurt**
- **2 tablespoons honey**
- **1 teaspoon vanilla extract**
- **½ teaspoon grated lemon peel**
- **⅛ teaspoon ground cinnamon**
- **3 cups seedless red grapes**
- **3 cups green grapes**
- **3 tablespoons sliced almonds, toasted**

Grapes with Lemon-Honey Yogurt

In a small bowl, combine the first five ingredients. Divide grapes among eight serving bowls. Top with yogurt mixture; sprinkle with almonds.

**Editor's Note:** *To toast nuts, spread in a 15-in. x 10-in. x 1-in. baking pan. Bake at 350° for 5-10 minutes or until lightly browned, stirring occasionally. Or, spread in a dry nonstick skillet and heat over low heat until lightly browned, stirring occasionally.*

## FAST FIX Chunky Chicken Salad with Grapes & Pecans

My luncheon salad is ready in no time when you use rotisserie chicken and chopped celery from the supermarket salad bar.
**—JULIE STERCHI** JACKSON, MISSOURI

**PREP/TOTAL TIME:** 25 MIN. **MAKES:** 8 SERVINGS

- **½ cup mayonnaise**
- **2 tablespoons sour cream**
- **1 tablespoon lemon juice**
- **⅛ teaspoon salt**
- **⅛ teaspoon pepper**
- **4 cups shredded rotisserie chicken**
- **1¼ cups seedless red grapes, halved**
- **½ cup chopped pecans**
- **½ cup chopped celery**
- **¼ cup chopped sweet onion, optional**
- **Romaine leaves**

In a large bowl, combine the first five ingredients. Add the chicken, grapes, pecans, celery and, if desired, onion; mix lightly to coat. Serve on romaine.

## FAST FIX Orange-Drizzled Grape Tartlets

Refrigerated sugar cookie dough and cream cheese make it so easy to create these crunchy, tangy tartlets.
**—JULIE STERCHI** JACKSON, MISSOURI

**PREP/TOTAL TIME:** 20 MIN. **MAKES:** 1 DOZEN

- **1 tube (16½ ounces) refrigerated sugar cookie dough**
- **1 package (8 ounces) cream cheese, softened**
- **½ cup confectioners' sugar**
- **½ teaspoon vanilla extract**
- **¾ cup seedless red grapes, halved**
- **¾ cup green grapes, halved**
- **¼ cup orange marmalade**

**1.** Cut cookie dough into twelve slices, about ¾ inch thick. On ungreased baking sheets, pat each slice to form ½-in. thick circles. Bake at 350° for 10-12 minutes or until golden brown. Remove to wire racks to cool completely.

**2.** Meanwhile, in a small bowl, beat the cream cheese, confectioners' sugar and vanilla until blended. Spread over cookie crusts. Top with grapes.

**3.** In a microwave-safe dish, microwave marmalade, covered, on high for 15-20 seconds or until warmed. Drizzle over grapes.

**Chunky Chicken Salad with Grapes & Pecans**

**Orange-Drizzled Grape Tartlets**

*From the kitchen of*

# Trisha Kruise

***Eagle, Idaho***

Life is a bountiful banquet for Trisha Kruse, who uses her considerable culinary skills to tie together the tastes and traditions of Italy.

This well-rounded Field Editor keeps **fresh and flavorful** memories close while **honoring values** from her Mediterranean childhood.

STORY & RECIPES BY **TRISHA KRUSE**

If you ask me, food is like a glorious window into how other cultures and communities live. I grew up in Italy, eating *paesano* (village Italian) food. I was raised with sit-down meals for breakfast and dinner, and even lunches on the weekend.

My mother prepared everything from scratch, using ingredients from the family garden or small local markets. We wasted nothing, and food was genuinely appreciated.

I learned the basics of developing great flavors—canning, baking and preserving—and doing it on a tight budget. My mother and grandmother gathered recipes from friends and neighbors in our Genovese community. Most of these recipes were shared verbally, with no measurements or cooking times given. Some were jotted on a scrap of paper, but most were not.

To this day, many of my favorite recipes are adaptations of the specialties I learned from my mother and grandmother. The savory Italian dishes I've shared on the following pages make a wonderful special-occasion meal I often serve to dinner guests.

I usually make the potato-asparagus side dish to complement grilled chicken, pork chops or salmon. The luscious Orange Chocolate Ricotta Pie is a must-have for Easter Sunday and has become an annual tradition.

My dishes serve as reminders of my Italian childhood. At the same time, I find culinary inspiration from cookbooks and articles about foods from other cultures.

No matter what inspires you—the flavors of the Mediterranean or something else—here's a message to live by: Use your car for driving and the supper table for eating. Sit down with your family, and share time and nourishment!

FIELD EDITOR FAVORITES

## FAST FIX Sage & Prosciutto Chicken Saltimbocca

The Italian word "saltimbocca" means to "jump" into one's mouth...and this mouthwatering dish fulfills that promise with prosciutto and fresh sage leaves.
**—TRISHA KRUSE** EAGLE, IDAHO

**PREP/TOTAL TIME:** 25 MIN. **MAKES:** 4 SERVINGS

- **½ cup plus 2 teaspoons all-purpose flour, divided**
- **4 boneless skinless chicken breast halves (6 ounces each)**
- **½ teaspoon salt**
- **¼ teaspoon pepper**
- **8 fresh sage leaves**
- **8 thin slices prosciutto or deli ham**
- **2 tablespoons olive oil**
- **1 tablespoon butter**
- **½ cup chicken broth**
- **2 tablespoons lemon juice**
- **2 tablespoons white wine or additional chicken broth**
- **Lemon slices and fresh sage, optional**

1. Place 1/2 cup flour in a shallow bowl; set aside. Flatten chicken breasts to 1/4-in. thickness. Sprinkle both sides with salt and pepper; top each breast half with 2 sage leaves and 2 slices prosciutto, pressing to adhere. Dip chicken sides only in flour to coat.
2. In a large skillet, heat oil and butter over medium heat; cook chicken for 3-4 minutes on each side or until lightly browned and a thermometer reads 170°. Remove and keep warm.
3. In a small bowl, whisk the chicken broth, lemon juice, wine and remaining flour; add to the skillet, stirring to loosen browned bits from pan. Bring to a boil; cook and stir for 1 minute or until thickened. Spoon over chicken. Top chicken with lemon and sage if desired.

Sage & Prosciutto Chicken Saltimbocca

Rosemary Roasted Potatoes & Asparagus

## Rosemary Roasted Potatoes & Asparagus

Fresh rosemary and red potatoes make a wonderfully earthy counterpoint to asparagus spears in this winning recipe. Add minced garlic, and you get a gorgeous, flavorful side dish!
**—TRISHA KRUSE** EAGLE, IDAHO

**PREP:** 10 MIN. **BAKE:** 35 MIN. **MAKES:** 4 SERVINGS

- **½ pound fingerling potatoes, cut into 1-inch pieces**
- **¼ cup olive oil, divided**
- **2 tablespoons minced fresh rosemary or 2 teaspoons dried rosemary, crushed**
- **2 garlic cloves, minced**
- **1 pound fresh asparagus, trimmed**
- **¼ teaspoon salt**
- **¼ teaspoon freshly ground pepper**

1. In a small bowl, combine the potatoes, 2 tablespoons oil, rosemary and garlic; toss to coat. Transfer to a greased 15-in. x 10-in. x 1-in. baking pan. Roast at 400° for 20 minutes, stirring once.
2. Drizzle asparagus with remaining oil; add to the pan. Roast 15-20 minutes longer or until vegetables are tender, stirring occasionally. Sprinkle with salt and pepper.

## Orange Chocolate Ricotta Pie

A traditional Italian dessert served on holidays and special occasions, this pie highlights the popular combination of orange and chocolate. The filling is rich and tangy, making it the perfect finale to a Mediterranean-style dinner.
**—TRISHA KRUSE** EAGLE, IDAHO

**PREP:** 20 MIN. **BAKE:** 40 MIN. + COOLING **MAKES:** 8 SERVINGS

- **2 cartons (15 ounces each) whole milk ricotta cheese**
- **2 eggs, lightly beaten**
- **½ cup dark chocolate chips**
- **⅓ cup sugar**
- **1 tablespoon grated orange peel**
- **2 tablespoons orange liqueur, optional**
- **Pastry for double-crust pie (9 inches)**

1. In a large bowl, combine the ricotta cheese, eggs, chocolate chips, sugar, orange peel and, if desired, orange liqueur.
2. Roll out half of the pastry to fit a 9-in. pie plate; transfer pastry to pie plate. Fill with ricotta mixture.
3. Roll out remaining pastry into an 11-in. circle; cut into 1-in.-wide strips. Lay half of the strips across the pie, about 1-in. apart. Fold back every other strip halfway. Lay another strip across center of pie at a right angle. Unfold strips over center strip. Fold back the alternate strips; place a second strip across the pie. Continue to add strips until pie is covered with lattice. Trim, seal and flute edges.
4. Bake at 425° for 40-45 minutes or until crust is golden brown. Refrigerate leftovers.

Orange Chocolate Ricotta Pie

*From the kitchen of*

# Lucia Johnson

***Massena, New York***

Much to her family's delight, Lucia Johnson turned her home into a veritable test kitchen that yielded delicious, one-dish-meal results.

## More than 59 years of marriage, including one **hilarious cooking mishap**, paved the **way to perfection** for this family cook.

STORY & RECIPES BY **LUCIA JOHNSON**

I vividly remember when I first started cooking as a new bride—because one of my most important meals turned into a complete catastrophe!

In 1953, I invited my new in-laws over for a chicken dinner. I bought the chicken "fully dressed," assuming that this meant it came already stuffed, and I was thrilled that I didn't have to make the dressing myself. As we sat down to eat, I dug inside with a spoon for the promised stuffing, and instead came out with a bag full of giblets! My in-laws thought this was hysterical and had fun teasing me about it for years.

I've come a long way since that dinner disaster—with the help of my husband and three daughters. Each one of them was key in the development of my kitchen skills. They're always happy to try a new dish and give me helpful feedback.

Now, I love creating my own recipes. Part of the challenge (and joy) is trying to make each new dish turn out right. I enjoy tinkering with ingredients until I get just the flavor I want.

I also like to bake. My daughters and I are very close, and we always have a good time baking together. During the holiday season, we gather to make big batches of my mother's Italian fruitcake. Everyone's crazy about it, and I think they can taste the love of our family in every bite.

My family adores the three recipes I've shared on the next few pages. These entrees offer lots of flavor and meal-in-one convenience.

In fact, each dish makes a complete dinner when you round out the menu with a salad made from fresh tomatoes, sweet peppers and Italian seasonings. I hope your family enjoys these main courses as much as mine does.

## Crunchy Herbed Chicken Breasts

This Italian-style recipe is simply out of this world. I'm always getting requests to make it for family and friends.
**—LUCIA JOHNSON** MASSENA, NEW YORK

**PREP:** 15 MIN. **BAKE:** 25 MIN. **MAKES:** 6 SERVINGS

- **⅔ cup panko (Japanese) bread crumbs**
- **½ cup grated Parmesan cheese**
- **½ cup grated Romano cheese**
- **1 tablespoon minced fresh oregano or 1 teaspoon dried oregano**
- **1 tablespoon minced fresh basil or 1 teaspoon dried basil**
- **2 teaspoons minced fresh parsley**
- **2 garlic cloves, minced**
- **½ teaspoon salt**
- **½ teaspoon pepper**
- **½ cup all-purpose flour**
- **2 eggs, lightly beaten**
- **6 boneless skinless chicken breast halves (5 ounces each)**
- **Olive oil-flavored cooking spray**

1. In a shallow bowl, mix the first nine ingredients. Place flour and eggs in separate shallow bowls. Dip both sides of chicken in the flour, eggs, then crumb mixture, patting to help coating adhere.
2. Place on a greased baking sheet. Spritz tops with cooking spray. Bake at 375° for 25-30 minutes or until a thermometer reads 170°.

Crunchy Herbed Chicken Breasts

## FAST FIX Zucchini Onion Pie

We get a lot of zucchini when it's in season. This is a unique, delicious way to use up the bounty—and so easy.

**—LUCIA JOHNSON** MASSENA, NEW YORK

**PREP/TOTAL TIME:** 30 MIN. **MAKES:** 6 SERVINGS

- **3 eggs**
- **1 cup grated Parmesan cheese**
- **½ cup canola oil**
- **1 tablespoon minced fresh parsley**
- **1 garlic clove, minced**
- **¼ teaspoon salt**
- **⅛ teaspoon pepper**
- **3 cups sliced zucchini**
- **1 cup biscuit/baking mix**
- **1 small onion, chopped**

In a large bowl, whisk the first seven ingredients. Stir in the zucchini, baking mix and onion. Pour into a greased 9-in. deep-dish pie plate. Bake at 350° for 25-35 minutes or until lightly browned.

Zucchini Onion Pie

## FAST FIX Quick Potato Corn Chowder

Here's a satisfying first course that can also make a terrific meal all by itself. It's wonderful any time of year.

**—LUCIA JOHNSON** MASSENA, NEW YORK

**PREP/TOTAL TIME:** 30 MIN. **MAKES:** 8 SERVINGS (2 QUARTS)

- **1 medium onion, chopped**
- **1 tablespoon olive oil**
- **2 cans (14½ ounces each) chicken broth**
- **3 large Yukon Gold potatoes, peeled and cubed**
- **1 can (15¼ ounces) whole kernel corn, drained**
- **1 cup 2% milk, divided**
- **½ teaspoon salt**
- **½ teaspoon pepper**
- **⅓ cup all-purpose flour**
- **Minced fresh parsley, optional**

1. In a large saucepan, cook and stir onion in oil over medium heat until tender. Add broth and potatoes; bring to a boil. Reduce heat; cover and simmer for 10-15 minutes or until potatoes are tender.
2. Stir in the corn, ½ cup milk, salt and pepper. In a small bowl, whisk flour and remaining milk until smooth. Stir into soup; return to a boil. Cook and stir for 2-3 minutes or until thickened. Sprinkle with parsley if desired.

Quick Potato Corn Chowder

Although available in Europe and South America for centuries, Yukon Gold potatoes are now popular in North America. Yukon Golds are versatile enough for use in baked dishes as well as soups.

*From the kitchen of*

# Kerry Dingwall

***Ponte Vedra, Florida***

Kerry Dingwall may reside in Florida, but her creative experiments in the kitchen give her dinner table plenty of international appeal.

## In her all-American kitchen, this Field Editor draws **culinary inspiration** from the cuisines of **England and Australia.**

STORY & RECIPES BY **KERRY DINGWALL** AS TOLD TO **CHERYL STERNMAN RULE**

My interest in cooking dates back to when I was just 6 years old. I'd stand in my grandma's small kitchen in London, where I would watch her make fruitcakes. My favorite part was licking the bowl! My mum noticed my enthusiasm, so she'd let me help with cooking as much as possible.

I soon started making dinner for our family on Saturday nights. I remember slicing hot dogs in half, then lining them up against the side of a casserole dish and filling the center with macaroni and cheese. I topped the whole thing with fried onions and peppers, then popped it in the oven. We called it "picket fence" because the hot dogs made a fence around the macaroni! To this day, my father still asks me to make picket fence when he visits.

My father was born in Australia, so my lineage is half-Australian and half-English, and both cultures influence my cooking greatly. The Aussies are big meat eaters, so I especially love preparing beef Wellington. I'm attracted to its versatility, and the best part is that it's uncomplicated to make—even though the end result is awesome!

I make a few different versions depending on the occasion. You can use hamburger for very casual dinners or use beef tenderloin to make a holiday-worthy dish, such as my Classic Beef Wellingtons (see the recipe on page 254).

The English and Australians also tend to eat parsnips the way Americans eat carrots. That's why I developed Parsnip Potato Gratin (recipe on page 255). When you bake parsnips into a creamy gratin, the flavors blend so well.

I live near the top of Florida, just outside Jacksonville, where it can get cool in the fall. So I like to make homemade soups such as Pumpkin Bisque with Smoked Gouda (recipe on page 255) to warm up on chilly days. It fills the house with such a wonderful aroma! I also love traditional dishes such as Yorkshire puddings, toad-in-the-hole and bubble-and-squeak.

I stay busy at work during the week, but on weekends, cooking is my therapy. It's a great way to relieve stress and reconnect with my heritage.

## Classic Beef Wellingtons

Perfect for holidays, this entree is also surprisingly easy to fix. Look for ready-made puff pastry in the frozen food section.
**—KERRY DINGWALL** PONTE VEDRA, FLORIDA

**PREP:** 20 MIN. + CHILLING **BAKE:** 25 MIN. **MAKES:** 4 SERVINGS

- **4 beef tenderloin steaks (6 ounces each)**
- **¾ teaspoon salt, divided**
- **½ teaspoon pepper, divided**
- **2 tablespoons olive oil, divided**
- **1¾ cups sliced fresh mushrooms**
- **1 medium onion, chopped**
- **1 package (17.3 ounces) frozen puff pastry, thawed**
- **1 egg, lightly beaten**

1. Sprinkle steaks with ½ teaspoon salt and ¼ teaspoon pepper. In a large skillet, brown steaks in 1 tablespoon oil for 2-3 minutes on each side. Remove from skillet and refrigerate until chilled.
2. In the same skillet, saute mushrooms and onion in remaining oil until tender. Stir in remaining salt and pepper; cool to room temperature.
3. On a lightly floured surface, roll each puff pastry sheet into a 14-in. x 9½-in. rectangle. Cut into two 7-in. squares (use scraps to make decorative cutouts if desired). Place a steak in the center of each square; top with mushroom mixture. Lightly brush pastry edges with water. Bring opposite corners of pastry over steak; pinch seams to seal tightly.
4. Place on a greased 15-in. x 10-in. x 1-in. baking pan. Cut four small slits in top of pastry. Arrange cutouts over top if desired. Brush with egg.
5. Bake at 425° for 25-30 minutes or until pastry is golden brown and meat reaches desired doneness (for medium-rare, a meat thermometer should read 145°; medium, 160°; well-done, 170°).

Classic Beef Wellingtons

## Parsnip Potato Gratin

Parsnips don't get much space in the produce section. But their subtle sweetness makes them worth the hunt!
**—KERRY DINGWALL** PONTE VEDRA, FLORIDA

**PREP:** 20 MIN. **BAKE:** 50 MIN. **MAKES:** 10 SERVINGS

- **4 large potatoes, peeled and thinly sliced**
- **4 medium onions, thinly sliced**
- **3 large parsnips, peeled and thinly sliced**
- **1½ cups (6 ounces) shredded Gruyere or Swiss cheese, divided**
- **1 tablespoon all-purpose flour**
- **¾ teaspoon salt**
- **¼ teaspoon pepper**
- **2 cups heavy whipping cream**

1. Layer the potatoes, onions, parsnips and 3/4 cup cheese in a greased 13-in. x 9-in. baking dish; set aside. In a small saucepan, combine the flour, salt, pepper; gradually whisk in cream. Bring to a gentle boil, stirring occasionally. Remove from the heat; pour over vegetables. Sprinkle with remaining cheese.
2. Cover and bake at 375° for 30 minutes. Uncover; bake 20-25 minutes longer or until vegetables are tender and top is golden brown.

Parsnip Potato Gratin

## Pumpkin Bisque with Smoked Gouda

I love the aroma of this rich, cheesy soup as it bubbles on the stove. The Gouda cheese adds a delightful smokiness that, together with the pumpkin, just says autumn to me.
**—KERRY DINGWALL** PONTE VEDRA, FLORIDA

**PREP:** 20 MIN. **COOK:** 35 MIN. **MAKES:** 9 SERVINGS (2¼ QUARTS)

- **4 bacon strips, chopped**
- **1 medium onion, chopped**
- **3 garlic cloves, minced**
- **6 cups chicken broth**
- **1 can (29 ounces) solid-pack pumpkin**
- **½ teaspoon salt**
- **¼ teaspoon ground nutmeg**
- **⅛ teaspoon pepper**
- **1 cup heavy whipping cream**
- **1 cup shredded Gouda cheese**
- **2 tablespoons minced fresh parsley**
- **Additional shredded Gouda cheese, optional**

1. In a Dutch oven, cook bacon over medium heat until crisp. Remove to paper towels with a slotted spoon; drain, reserving 1 tablespoon drippings. Saute onion in drippings until tender. Add garlic; cook 1 minute longer.
2. Stir in the broth, pumpkin, salt, nutmeg and pepper. Bring to a boil. Reduce heat; simmer, uncovered, for 10 minutes. Cool slightly.
3. In a blender, process soup in batches until smooth. Return all to pan. Stir in cream; heat through. Add cheese; stir until melted. Sprinkle each serving with parsley, bacon and additional cheese if desired.

Pumpkin Bisque with Smoked Gouda

*From the kitchen of*

# Lori Stefanishion

***Drumheller, Alberta***

Someone find Lori Stefanishion a crown—she just might be the queen of appetizers (or "appys," as she likes to call them).

This Alberta Field Editor warms her house with **friends and family** every winter, making spirits bright with **bite-size favorites.**

STORY & RECIPES BY **LORI STEFANISHION**

I was raised in Red Deer, a small city in Alberta, Canada. Whenever my mother would leave my sister and me home alone, the last words out of her mouth were, "Don't touch the stove!" Of course, as soon as she was down the street, we'd run right to the stove.

While I've always liked cooking, I simply love entertaining—especially around the holidays. I throw an annual Christmas party for about 100 people. I put up five Christmas trees and do up the whole house from top to bottom.

First comes the decorating party, with the men setting up the trees and the women fluffing out the branches. The hors d'oeuvres I serve make it light and happy work. I like to put out a wide variety: There are hot dishes, cold dishes and sweet dishes—at least six of each type.

There are a few favorites people always ask for, and I'm more than happy to oblige. My Rice Paper Rolls (recipe on page 258) seem to be a crowd-pleaser, and Asian Cheese Spread (recipe on page 259) is a popular choice I can fix a few hours in advance. What a convenient time-saver, especially during the busy holiday season!

Similarly, Crispy Shrimp Cups (recipe on page 259) calls for wonton shells you can bake ahead of time and an easy-to-make filling you can spoon in at the last minute. If time allows, you could also pipe in the filling using a resealable storage bag—just snip off a corner and fill.

I also try to add a variety of new recipes to my buffet. This keeps things fun and exciting for all involved, including me! Last Christmas, for instance, I tried Smoked Trout & Hearts of Palm Bites (recipe on page 258), and it was a hit. Try it for your next get-together, and I'm sure your guests will enjoy it, too.

I love to serve "appys" when I host my monthly book club as well. We alternate houses, but the December gathering is at my home because my fellow club members kindly say that it puts them in the Christmas spirit.

As long as friends and family want to celebrate the holidays with me, I'm more than happy to set out one of my appetizer buffets for them!

## Rice Paper Rolls

I like to have a package of rice papers and noodles on hand for quick-and-easy appetizer ideas. I've used thin and thick rice noodles for these rolls with equal success.
—**LORI STEFANISHION** DRUMHELLER, ALBERTA

**PREP:** 40 MIN. **COOK:** 10 MIN. **MAKES:** 1 DOZEN

- **2 garlic cloves, minced**
- **½ teaspoon crushed red pepper flakes**
- **2 teaspoons canola oil**
- **½ cup water**
- **¼ cup creamy peanut butter**
- **¼ cup hoisin sauce**
- **2 tablespoons tomato paste**

**ROLLS**

- **4 ounces uncooked thin rice noodles**
- **2 teaspoons hoisin sauce, optional**
- **1 medium sweet red pepper, julienned**
- **1 medium cucumber, seeded and julienned**
- **1 medium carrot, julienned**
- **12 rice papers (8 inches) or spring roll wrappers**
- **½ cup dry roasted peanuts, chopped**
- **½ cup fresh cilantro leaves, optional**

1. In a small saucepan, saute the garlic and pepper flakes in oil for 1-2 minutes or until garlic is tender. Add the water, peanut butter, hoisin sauce and tomato paste; cook and stir for 2-4 minutes or until thickened. Remove from the heat; set aside.
2. For rolls, cook noodles according to package directions. Drain and rinse in cold water; drain well. Add hoisin sauce if desired; toss to coat. In a small bowl, combine the red pepper, cucumber and carrot. Set aside noodles and vegetables.
3. Fill a shallow bowl with water. Soak a rice paper in the water just until pliable, about 5-15 seconds (depending on thickness of rice papers); remove, allowing excess water to drip off.
4. Place on a flat surface. Layer vegetables and noodles down the center; top with peanuts and, if desired, cilantro. Fold both ends over filling; fold one long side over the filling, then roll up tightly. Place seam side down on a serving platter. Repeat with remaining ingredients.
5. Cover with damp paper towels until serving. Cut rolls diagonally in half; serve with peanut sauce.

Rice Paper Rolls

Smoked Trout & Hearts of Palm Bites

## FAST FIX Smoked Trout & Hearts of Palm Bites

I've had luck finding hearts of palm in the canned vegetable section at my local grocery store. In a pinch, you can use quartered artichoke hearts in place of the hearts of palm and still end up with a great-tasting dish.
—**LORI STEFANISHION** DRUMHELLER, ALBERTA

**PREP/TOTAL TIME:** 25 MIN. **MAKES:** 2 DOZEN

- **1 can (14 ounces) hearts of palm, drained**
- **4 ounces cream cheese, softened**
- **24 bagel chips**
- **6 ounces smoked trout, broken into 24 portions**
- **3 tablespoons capers, drained**

Cut hearts of palm widthwise into thin slices. Spread bagel chips with half of the cream cheese; layer with hearts of palm and trout. Garnish with remaining cream cheese and capers.

## FAST FIX Asian Cheese Spread

This recipe is pretty simple as it is, but to save even more time, leave the block of cream cheese whole and let your guests spoon up what they'd like. If you can't find crystallized ginger, simply substitute 1/4 teaspoon of ground ginger.
**—LORI STEFANISHION** DRUMHELLER, ALBERTA

**PREP/TOTAL TIME:** 15 MIN. **MAKES:** 8 SERVINGS

- **¼ cup reduced-sodium soy sauce**
- **2 tablespoons confectioners' sugar**
- **1 tablespoon finely chopped crystallized ginger**
- **1 tablespoon thinly sliced green onion**
- **½ teaspoon crushed red pepper flakes**
- **1 small garlic clove, minced**
- **1 package (8 ounces) cold cream cheese, cut into 36 cubes**
- **2 tablespoons sesame seeds**
- **Rice crackers**

In a small bowl, combine the first six ingredients. Add the cream cheese cubes; gently toss to coat. To serve, place cream cheese on crackers; sprinkle with sesame seeds.

## Crispy Shrimp Cups

The perfect party food for passing, this stuffed wonton recipe also works well with a crabmeat or mushroom filling instead of shrimp. Serve the cups hot, warm or cold.
**—LORI STEFANISHION** DRUMHELLER, ALBERTA

**PREP:** 30 MIN. **BAKE:** 15 MIN. **MAKES:** 2 DOZEN

- **24 wonton wrappers**
- **1 tablespoon butter, melted**
- **⅛ teaspoon garlic powder**
- **12 ounces cream cheese, softened**
- **4 teaspoons honey**
- **1 tablespoon minced fresh parsley**
- **2 teaspoons hot pepper sauce**
- **24 peeled and deveined cooked medium shrimp**
- **Optional garnishes: lemon slices and fresh basil leaves**

1. Press wonton wrappers into greased miniature muffin cups. Combine butter and garlic powder; brush over edges of wrappers. Bake at 350° for 8-10 minutes or until lightly browned.
2. In a small bowl, beat the cream cheese, honey, minced parsley and hot pepper sauce until blended. Spoon into cups. Bake 5-8 minutes longer or until filling is heated through. Top with shrimp. Serve warm, garnished with lemon and basil if desired.

Crispy Shrimp Cups

# Quick Fixes

Every recipe in this chapter takes just **30 minutes or less** to prepare from start to finish. But your family will never guess—they'll be too busy savoring these **fast but fantastic** dishes!

"I used to work at a restaurant that served a great variation of chicken with penne pasta. I didn't know how easy it would be to make until I gave it a shot. Now, I often get requests for this homemade version."

—**RUSTY KOLL** ELMWOOD, ILLINOIS

## Provolone-Stuffed Pork Chops with Tarragon Vinaigrette

**PREP/TOTAL TIME:** 25 MIN.
**MAKES:** 4 SERVINGS

- **½ cup olive oil**
- **¼ cup white balsamic vinegar**
- **2 tablespoons minced fresh tarragon or 2 teaspoons dried tarragon**
- **2 garlic cloves, minced**
- **¼ teaspoon salt**
- **¼ teaspoon pepper**

**PORK CHOPS**

- **4 bone-in pork loin chops (8 ounces each and ¾ inch thick)**
- **4 slices provolone cheese, cut into eighths**
- **2 tablespoons olive oil**
- **2 teaspoons minced fresh tarragon or ½ teaspoon dried tarragon**
- **¼ teaspoon salt**
- **¼ teaspoon pepper**
- **2 large tomatoes, each cut into 6 wedges**

The homemade dressing and cheese in grilled Provolone-Stuffed Pork Chops with Tarragon Vinaigrette may give you the feeling of dining in Provence.

**—BARBARA PLETZKE** HERNDON, VIRGINIA

**1.** In a small bowl, whisk the first six ingredients. Set aside 1/4 cup vinaigrette for serving.

**2.** For pork chops, cut a pocket in each chop by slicing almost to the bone; fill pockets with cheese. Combine the oil, tarragon, salt and pepper; brush onto both sides of chops.

**3.** Moisten a paper towel with cooking oil; using long-handled tongs, lightly coat the grill rack. Brush tomato wedges with some of the remaining vinaigrette. Grill, uncovered, over medium heat or broil 4 in. from the heat for 1-3 minutes on each side or until lightly browned. Set aside.

**4.** Grill chops, covered, over medium heat or broil 4 in. from the heat for 4-5 minutes on each side or until a thermometer reads 145°. Baste frequently with remaining vinaigrette during the last 3 minutes of cooking. Let stand for 5 minutes. Serve with tomatoes and reserved vinaigrette.

## Super-Quick Shrimp & Green Chili Quesadillas

If I'm really short on time, I head to the store and get prepared guacamole for my seafood quesadillas. You could also fix them with shredded rotisserie chicken in place of the shrimp.

**—ANGIE RESSA**
CHENEY, WASHINGTON

**PREP/TOTAL TIME:** 10 MIN.
**MAKES:** 4 SERVINGS (½ CUP GUACAMOLE)

- **1¾ cups shredded cheddar cheese**
- **1 cup peeled and deveined cooked small shrimp**
- **1 can (4 ounces) chopped green chilies, drained**
- **2 green onions, thinly sliced**
- **8 flour tortillas (8 inches)**
- **1 medium ripe avocado, peeled and pitted**
- **2 tablespoons salsa**
- **¼ teaspoon garlic salt**

**1.** In a bowl, combine the cheese, shrimp, green chilies and green onions. Place half of the tortillas on a greased griddle; sprinkle with cheese mixture. Top with remaining tortillas. Cook over medium heat for 1-2 minutes on each side or until golden brown and cheese is melted.

**2.** Meanwhile, in a small bowl, mash avocado with salsa and garlic salt. Serve with quesadillas.

**Super-Quick Shrimp & Green Chili Quesadillas**

## Mixed Greens with Orange Juice Vinaigrette

Like a string of pearls on a little black dress, a vinaigrette is the perfect way to dress up a bowl of ordinary salad greens. A little oil, a little vinegar, a tangy infusion of orange juice and a sprinkling of grated orange peel are just enough of an enhancement.

**—KRISTIN BATAILLE**
STAMFORD, CONNECTICUT

**PREP/TOTAL TIME:** 10 MIN.
**MAKES:** 6 SERVINGS

- **2 tablespoons olive oil**
- **2 tablespoons orange juice**
- **1 tablespoon cider vinegar**
- **1 teaspoon grated orange peel**
- **Dash salt**
- **Dash pepper**
- **1 package (5 ounces) spring mix salad greens**

In a small bowl, whisk the first six ingredients. Place salad greens in a large bowl. Drizzle with vinaigrette; toss to coat.

## Lemony Grilled Salmon Fillets with Dill Sauce

Grilled lemons add a smoky tartness to salmon fillets. A delectable butter sauce flavored with more lemon, fresh dill, chervil and a dash of cayenne pepper is the crowning touch.

**—APRIL LANE**
GREENEVILLE, TENNESSEE

**PREP/TOTAL TIME:** 30 MIN.
**MAKES:** 4 SERVINGS (¾ CUP SAUCE)

- **2 medium lemons**
- **4 salmon fillets (6 ounces each)**

**LEMON-DILL SAUCE**

- **1½ teaspoons cornstarch**
- **½ cup water**
- **⅓ cup lemon juice**
- **4 teaspoons butter**
- **3 lemon slices, quartered**
- **1 tablespoon snipped fresh dill**
- **¼ teaspoon salt**
- **⅛ teaspoon dried chervil**
- **Dash cayenne pepper**

**1.** Trim both ends from each lemon; cut lemons into thick slices. Moisten a paper towel with cooking oil; using long-handled tongs, lightly coat the grill rack. Grill salmon and lemon slices, covered, over high heat or broil 3-4 in. from the heat for 3-5 minutes on each side or until the fish flakes easily with a fork and the lemons are lightly browned.

**2.** For sauce, in a small saucepan, combine the cornstarch, water and lemon juice; add butter. Cook and stir over medium heat until thickened and bubbly. Remove from the heat; stir in quartered lemon slices and seasonings. Serve with salmon and grilled lemon slices.

## Italian Sausage & Bean Soup

With a chunky blend of sausage, beans and packaged coleslaw, this simple soup is the definition of comfort food on a cold winter's night. A steaming bowlful goes so well with a side of warm-from-the-oven bread.

**—STACEY BENNETT**
LOCUST GROVE, VIRGINIA

**PREP/TOTAL TIME:** 30 MIN.
**MAKES:** 6 SERVINGS (2 QUARTS)

- **1 pound bulk hot Italian sausage**
- **2 cans (15½ ounces each) great northern beans, rinsed and drained**
- **1 package (16 ounces) coleslaw mix**
- **1 jar (24 ounces) garlic and herb spaghetti sauce**
- **3 cups water**

In a Dutch oven, cook the sausage over medium heat until no longer pink; drain. Stir in the remaining ingredients. Bring to a boil. Reduce the heat; simmer, uncovered, for 16-20 minutes or until the flavors are blended.

## Old-Fashioned Ice Cream Sodas

I always keep the five ingredients for these classic ice cream beverages on hand so I can sip a frosty soda any time the mood strikes. The recipe is easy to double or triple for a crowd, too.

**—ANNA ERICKSON**
SILVERDALE, WASHINGTON

**Old-Fashioned Ice Cream Sodas**

**Italian Sausage & Bean Soup**

**PREP/TOTAL TIME:** 15 MIN.
**MAKES:** 4 SERVINGS

- **¾ cup chocolate syrup**
- **1 cup milk**
- **4 cups carbonated water, chilled**
- **8 scoops chocolate ice cream (about 2⅔ cups), divided**
- **Whipped cream in a can, optional**

Place 3 tablespoons syrup in each of four 16-oz. glasses. Add ¼ cup milk and 1 cup carbonated water to each; stir until foamy. Add two scoops of chocolate ice cream to each glass. Top with whipped cream if desired.

## Pizza Wraps

Savor the flavors of your favorite pie in wraps that take only a few minutes to assemble—no cooking or baking is required. They're perfect when you need a school lunch for the kids but don't have much time before the bus arrives.
**—ELIZABETH DUMONT** BOULDER, COLORADO

**PREP/TOTAL TIME:** 15 MIN. **MAKES:** 4 WRAPS

- **1 package (8 ounces) sliced pepperoni**
- **4 flour tortillas (8 inches), room temperature**
- **½ cup chopped tomatoes**
- **¼ cup each chopped sweet onion, chopped fresh mushrooms and chopped ripe olives**
- **¼ cup chopped green pepper, optional**
- **1 cup (4 ounces) shredded part-skim mozzarella cheese**

Arrange the pepperoni off center on each tortilla. Top with the remaining ingredients. Fold the sides and bottom over the filling and roll up.

Pizza Wraps

Spicy Mustard Turkey Pizza

## Spicy Mustard Turkey Pizza

Craving something different from the usual sausage and pepperoni? This pizza will become an instant hit when your family tastes the tangy sauce and crispy crust. If you're not a fan of Swiss cheese, substitute provolone or mozzarella.
**—KERI COTTON** LAKEVILLE, MINNESOTA

**PREP/TOTAL TIME:** 30 MIN. **MAKES:** 6 SLICES

- **1 prebaked 12-inch thin pizza crust**
- **3 tablespoons reduced-fat mayonnaise**
- **3 tablespoons spicy brown mustard**
- **3 tablespoons honey**
- **½ teaspoon garlic powder**
- **2 cups cubed cooked turkey**
- **1 cup chopped fresh mushrooms**
- **5 cooked bacon strips, chopped**
- **1 cup (4 ounces) shredded Swiss cheese**

**1.** Place crust on an ungreased 12-in. pizza pan. In a small bowl, combine the mayonnaise, mustard, honey and garlic powder. Add turkey; toss to coat. Spread over crust.
**2.** Top with mushrooms, bacon and cheese. Bake at 450° for 9-11 minutes or until cheese is melted.

Spicy Mustard Turkey Pizza (recipe above right) makes mouthwatering use of leftover cooked turkey from a Thanksgiving dinner or other special meal. Want more ideas for your excess turkey? Add barbecue sauce, heat it through and serve it on warmed hamburger buns for satisfying sandwiches. Or mix it with your leftover gravy and dressing, put it in a greased baking pan and bake for a family-pleasing casserole.

## Soba Noodles with Gingered-Sesame Dressing

A sweet-and-sour, gingery dressing goes hand in hand with soft soba noodles, edamame and crunchy slaw. If you like, toss in grilled shrimp or chicken for a protein-packed finish.

**—MANDY RIVERS**
LEXINGTON, SOUTH CAROLINA

**PREP/TOTAL TIME:** 30 MIN.
**MAKES:** 8 SERVINGS

- **½ cup reduced-sodium soy sauce**
- **¼ cup packed brown sugar**
- **2 tablespoons rice vinegar**
- **2 tablespoons canola oil**
- **2 tablespoons orange juice**
- **1 tablespoon minced fresh gingerroot**
- **1 teaspoon sesame oil**
- **1 garlic clove, minced**
- **1 teaspoon sriracha Asian hot chili sauce or ½ teaspoon hot pepper sauce**

**SALAD**

- **2 cups frozen shelled edamame, thawed**
- **½ pound uncooked Japanese soba noodles or whole wheat linguini**
- **1 package (14 ounces) coleslaw mix**
- **1 cup shredded carrots**
- **1 cup thinly sliced green onions**
- **3 tablespoons sesame seeds, toasted**

**1.** In a small bowl, whisk the first nine ingredients; set aside. Cook edamame and soba noodles according to package directions; drain. Rinse noodles in cold water; drain again.

**2.** Just before serving, combine the coleslaw mix, carrots, green onions, noodles and edamame in a large bowl. Add dressing; toss to coat. Garnish with sesame seeds.

Soba Noodles with Gingered-Sesame Dressing

## Stuffed Sweet Potato Casserole

Delight your holiday guests with these little individual casseroles baked right inside the sweet potato shell. Yum!

**—PAULINE DETTREY**
MONUMENT, COLORADO

**PREP/TOTAL TIME:** 30 MIN.
**MAKES:** 8 SERVINGS

- **4 large sweet potatoes**
- **½ cup hot caramel ice cream topping**
- **2 tablespoons butter**
- **1½ cups miniature marshmallows**
- **½ cup chopped pecans**

**1.** Scrub and pierce the sweet potatoes; place on a microwave-safe plate. Microwave, uncovered, on high for 15-18 minutes or until tender, turning once.

**2.** When cool enough to handle, cut each potato in half lengthwise. Scoop out the pulp, leaving thin shells. In a large bowl, mash the pulp with caramel topping and butter. Spoon into potato shells.

**3.** Place on baking sheets; sprinkle with marshmallows and pecans. Broil 3-4 in. from the heat for 2-3 minutes or until marshmallows are golden brown.

## Turkey Mushroom Sandwich Bowls

My grandmother was an incredible cook, and one of her talents was bringing new life to leftovers. I've tried to do the same by creating these creamy, turkey-packed "bowls."
**—ANGELA LEINENBACH** MECHANICSVLLE, VIRGINIA

**PREP/TOTAL TIME:** 30 MIN. **MAKES:** 4 SERVINGS

- **4 French rolls**
- **¼ cup butter, melted**
- **1½ cups sliced fresh mushrooms**
- **1 medium onion, thinly sliced**
- **2 tablespoons canola oil**
- **½ cup dry vermouth or chicken broth**
- **2 tablespoons all-purpose flour**
- **½ teaspoon salt**
- **¼ teaspoon pepper**
- **1¼ cups heavy whipping cream**
- **4 cups cubed cooked turkey**
- **Minced fresh chives**

**1.** Cut a ½-in. slice off the top of each roll; set aside tops. Hollow out the centers, leaving ¼-in. shells (discard the removed bread or save for another use). Brush the tops and inside of rolls with butter; place on a baking sheet. Bake at 325° for 10-15 minutes or until lightly browned.
**2.** Meanwhile, in a large skillet, saute mushrooms and onion in oil until tender. Add vermouth, stirring to loosen browned bits from pan. Bring to a boil; cook until liquid is almost evaporated. Combine the flour, salt, pepper and cream; stir until smooth. Stir into skillet; bring to a boil. Reduce heat; cook and stir for 1-2 minutes or until sauce is thickened. Stir in turkey; heat through. Spoon into hollowed rolls; garnish with chives. Replace tops.

Turkey Mushroom Sandwich Bowls

Mediterranean Chicken Bake

## Mediterranean Chicken Bake

What do you do when you have extra sun-dried tomatoes, feta cheese and artichoke hearts after making a Greek pasta salad? The solution is simple—bake them with chicken for a restaurant-worthy Mediterranean entree.
**—SHANNEN MAHONEY** ODESSA, MISSOURI

**PREP/TOTAL TIME:** 30 MIN. **MAKES:** 4 SERVINGS

- **4 boneless skinless chicken breast halves (5 ounces each)**
- **2 teaspoons herbes de Provence**
- **½ teaspoon salt**
- **¼ teaspoon pepper**
- **1 tablespoon olive oil**
- **1 cup marinated quartered artichoke hearts**
- **¼ cup oil-packed sun-dried tomatoes, coarsely chopped**
- **1 cup (4 ounces) crumbled feta cheese**

**1.** Flatten chicken to ½-in. thickness. Combine the herbes de Provence, salt and pepper; sprinkle over chicken. In a large skillet, brown chicken in oil on both sides.
**2.** Transfer to a greased 11-in. x 7-in. baking dish. Top with artichokes, tomatoes and cheese. Bake, uncovered, at 425° for 15-20 minutes or until a thermometer inserted in chicken reads 170°.
**Editor's Note:** *Look for herbes de Provence in the spice aisle.*

## Super Spaghetti Sauce

If you're bored with the usual store-bought spaghetti sauce but can't fit a made-from-scratch variety into your schedule, here's a happy medium that meat lovers will especially enjoy. It jazzes up a jarred version with slices of smoked kielbasa, ground beef and chunky salsa. Simply add hot pasta, side salads and fresh-baked bread for an Italian feast.
**—BELLA ANDERSON** CHESTER, SOUTH CAROLINA

**PREP/TOTAL TIME:** 30 MIN. **MAKES:** 2½ QUARTS

- **1 pound ground beef**
- **1 pound smoked kielbasa, cut into ¼-inch slices**
- **2 jars (24 ounces each) spaghetti sauce with mushrooms**
- **1 jar (16 ounces) chunky salsa**
- **Hot cooked pasta**

**1.** In a Dutch oven, cook beef over medium heat until no longer pink; drain and set aside. In the same skillet, cook sausage over medium heat for 5-6 minutes or until browned.
**2.** Stir in the spaghetti sauces, salsa and reserved beef; heat through. Serve with pasta.

## Apricot-Lemon Chicken

Chicken spiced with curry and spread with a lemony apricot sauce is elegant enough for company. I discovered this recipe in college and have been serving the delicious main dish to friends and family ever since. Because it's so easy to prepare, I can put it in my regular menu rotation, too.
**—KENDRA DOSS** KANSAS CITY, MISSOURI

**PREP/TOTAL TIME:** 30 MIN. **MAKES:** 4 SERVINGS

- **4 boneless skinless chicken breast halves (6 ounces each)**
- **1 teaspoon curry powder**
- **½ teaspoon salt**
- **¼ teaspoon coarsely ground pepper**
- **2 teaspoons canola oil**
- **⅓ cup apricot spreadable fruit**
- **2 tablespoons water**
- **2 tablespoons lemon juice**
- **2 teaspoons grated lemon peel**

**1.** Flatten chicken to ½-in. thickness. Combine the curry powder, salt and pepper; sprinkle over chicken.
**2.** In a large skillet, cook the chicken in oil over medium heat for 5-6 minutes on each side or until a thermometer reads 170°. Remove to a serving plate; keep warm.
**3.** Add the apricot spreadable fruit, water and lemon juice to the pan; cook and stir for 1-2 minutes or until syrupy. Serve the sauce over the chicken; sprinkle with lemon peel.

Roast Beef & Tomato Sandwich Pizza

## Roast Beef & Tomato Sandwich Pizza

My change-of-pace pizza has all the makings of my favorite roast beef sandwiches. If time allows, I marinate the veggies in balsamic vinaigrette just before topping the pie.
**—SETH MURDOCH** RED ROCK, TEXAS

**PREP/TOTAL TIME:** 20 MIN. **MAKES:** 6 SERVINGS

- **2 cups fresh baby spinach**
- **2 plum tomatoes, chopped**
- **½ cup thinly sliced red onion**
- **½ cup thinly sliced sweet yellow or orange pepper**
- **⅓ cup balsamic vinaigrette**
- **4 ounces reduced-fat cream cheese**
- **¼ cup mayonnaise**
- **2 tablespoons minced chives**
- **2 tablespoons horseradish sauce**
- **1 prebaked 12-inch pizza crust**
- **8 ounces sliced deli roast beef, cut into strips**
- **1 green onion, chopped**

**1.** In a small bowl, combine the spinach, tomatoes, red onion and pepper. Add the balsamic vinaigrette; toss to coat.
**2.** In a small bowl, mix the cream cheese, mayonnaise, chives and horseradish sauce until blended; spread over the pizza crust. Top with deli roast beef. Using a slotted spoon, place the spinach mixture over beef. Sprinkle with green onion.

QUICK FIXES

## Chinese Takeout-on-a-Stick

Here's a great way to enjoy Chinese "takeout" without going to a pricey restaurant. The grilled chicken and broccoli make a terrific meal with rice and a side of pineapple. Leftovers—if there are any—are ideal for a quick lunch or dinner the next day. Just toss them in a salad or wrap them in a flour tortilla with a little mayonnaise.

**—BETHANY SEELEY**
WARWICK, RHODE ISLAND

**PREP/TOTAL TIME:** 30 MIN.
**MAKES:** 4 SERVINGS

- **3 tablespoons reduced-sodium soy sauce**
- **3 tablespoons sesame oil**
- **4 teaspoons brown sugar**
- **4 teaspoons minced fresh gingerroot**
- **2 garlic cloves, minced**
- **½ teaspoon crushed red pepper flakes**
- **1 pound boneless skinless chicken breasts, cut into 1-inch cubes**
- **3 cups fresh broccoli florets**

**1.** In a large bowl, combine the first six ingredients; remove 3 tablespoons for basting. Add chicken to remaining soy sauce mixture; toss to coat. On four metal or soaked wooden skewers, alternately thread chicken and broccoli.

**2.** Moisten a paper towel with cooking oil; using long-handled tongs, lightly coat the grill rack. Grill skewers, covered, over medium heat or broil 4 in. from the heat for 10-15 minutes or until chicken is no longer pink, turning occasionally; baste with reserved soy mixture during the last 4 minutes of cooking.

Chinese Takeout-on-a-Stick

## Portobello Mushroom Pizza Cups

Serving my stuffed portobellos to guys watching hockey on TV was quite an endeavor. I fixed two dozen for six men, and as the game grew more exciting, they yelled for more! To avoid cracking the caps when removing the gills from the mushrooms, gently scrape them using a small teaspoon.

**—LORRAINE CALAND**
SHUNIAH, ONTARIO

**PREP/TOTAL TIME:** 30 MIN.
MAKES: 4 SERVINGS

- **4 large portobello mushrooms (3 inches)**
- **4 teaspoons olive oil**
- **1 cup marinara or spaghetti sauce**
- **12 slices pepperoni, finely chopped**
- **¼ cup chopped green pepper**
- **1½ teaspoons Italian seasoning, divided**
- **1 cup shredded Italian cheese blend**

**1.** Remove and discard stems and gills from the portobello mushrooms; brush the mushroom caps with oil. Place rounded sides down on an ungreased 15-in. x 10-in. x 1-in. baking pan. Bake, uncovered, at 400° for 5 minutes.

**2.** Meanwhile, in a small bowl, combine the marinara sauce, pepperoni, green pepper and 1¼ teaspoons Italian seasoning; spoon onto mushrooms. Sprinkle with cheese and remaining Italian seasoning. Bake for 8-12 minutes or until mushrooms are tender and cheese is bubbly.

Portobello Mushroom Pizza Cups

## Three-Cheese Creamed Spinach

For a crispy boost, sprinkle this with French-fried onions before baking.

**—KATHY VAZQUEZ** AMARILLO, TEXAS

**PREP/TOTAL TIME:** 20 MIN.
**MAKES:** 6 SERVINGS

- **2 packages (10 ounces each) frozen chopped spinach, thawed and squeezed dry**
- **1½ cups spreadable chive and onion cream cheese**
- **1 cup grated Parmesan cheese**
- **1 cup (4 ounces) shredded part-skim mozzarella cheese**
- **¼ cup butter, cubed**
- **¼ teaspoon pepper**

In a large saucepan, combine all ingredients. Cook and stir over medium heat for 8-10 minutes or until blended and heated through.

### Did you know?

You can soak your wooden skewers well in advance. Place them in water overnight, put them in a resealable plastic bag and freeze. When you need soaked skewers for kabobs, simply grab them from the freezer.

## Zucchini Apple Salad

You'll want to pull out your best glass bowl for this colorful, refreshing salad.
**—LOIS FRAZEE** FERNLEY, NEVADA

**PREP/TOTAL TIME:** 15 MIN.
**MAKES:** 6 SERVINGS

- **2 medium red apples, chopped**
- **2 small zucchini, chopped**
- **½ cup coarsely chopped walnuts**
- **⅔ cup Italian salad dressing**

In a large bowl, combine the apples, zucchini and walnuts. Add salad dressing; toss to coat.

## Grilled Pound Cake with Warm Amaretto Bananas

**PREP/TOTAL TIME:** 30 MIN.
**MAKES:** 4 SERVINGS

- **4 teaspoons butter, divided**
- **2 large bananas, cut into ¼-inch slices**
- **2 tablespoons brown sugar**
- **1 tablespoon Amaretto**
- **1 teaspoon lemon juice**
- **4 slices pound cake (about 1 inch thick)**
- **Sweetened whipped cream and toasted sliced almonds, optional**

**1.** Melt 2 teaspoons butter; drizzle over a double thickness of heavy-duty foil (about 10 in. square). Place bananas on foil; top with brown sugar, Amaretto and lemon juice. Dot with remaining butter. Fold foil around mixture and seal tightly.
**2.** Grill, covered, over medium heat for 8-10 minutes or until heated through. Grill cake for 1-2 minutes on each side or until lightly browned. Open foil packets carefully, allowing steam to escape. Spoon bananas over cake; top with whipped cream and almonds if desired.

**Editor's Note:** *To toast nuts, spread in a 15-in. x 10-in. x 1-in. baking pan. Bake at 350° for 5-10 minutes or until lightly browned, stirring occasionally. Or, spread in a dry nonstick skillet and heat over low heat until lightly browned, stirring occasionally.*

Grilled Pound Cake with Warm Amaretto Bananas

The flavors in Grilled Pound Cake with Warm Amaretto Bananas blend so well together. There's no better treat when a cookout calls for a fresh-air finale—just add whipped cream and almonds.
**—CAROL TRAUPMAN-CARR**
BREINIGSVILLE, PENNSYLVANIA

QUICK FIXES

# HOMEMADE PESTO, PRESTO

When fresh herbs are plentiful, put them to good use in the recipes here. Classic Pesto Sauce will give you a head start on seafood pasta, a peppery pizza and standout sandwiches.

*MAKE AHEAD*

## Classic Pesto Sauce

Store-bought pesto can't measure up to a homemade version. Use it to fix the other recipes on this page.

**—SUE JURACK** MEQUON, WISCONSIN

**PREP/TOTAL TIME:** 15 MIN.
**MAKES:** ½ CUP

- **¾ cup loosely packed basil leaves**
- **2 tablespoons pine nuts or sunflower kernels**
- **1 garlic clove, peeled**
- **½ teaspoon salt**
- **⅛ teaspoon pepper**
- **⅓ cup olive oil**
- **⅓ cup grated Parmesan cheese**

Place the first five ingredients in a small food processor; pulse until chopped. Continue processing while gradually adding the oil in a steady stream. Add the Parmesan cheese; pulse just until blended. Cover and freeze pesto for up to 3 months.

**Editor's Note:** *When freezing the pesto, leave about ¾ inch in the top of the container, then cover the top with a thin layer of olive oil so the pesto doesn't brown during freezing.*

## Pesto Vermicelli with Bay Scallops

Here's a seafood entree that tastes special but is so easy to make. With a salad, you'll have a complete dinner.

**—MARILYN LUSTGARTEN**
WENTZVILLE, MISSOURI

**PREP/TOTAL TIME:** 15 MIN.
**MAKES:** 4 SERVINGS

- **8 ounces uncooked vermicelli**
- **¼ cup butter, cubed**
- **1 teaspoon garlic powder**
- **¼ teaspoon dried oregano**
- **⅛ teaspoon pepper**
- **1 pound bay scallops**
- **¼ cup white wine or chicken broth**
- **⅓ cup prepared pesto**

**1.** Cook vermicelli according to package directions. Meanwhile, in a large skillet, heat the butter, garlic powder, oregano and pepper over medium heat. Add scallops and wine; cook and stir for 5-6 minutes or until scallops are firm and opaque.

**2.** Reduce heat to low. Stir in pesto; heat through. Drain vermicelli; add to skillet. Toss to combine.

Pesto Vermicelli with Bay Scallops

## Pesto Grilled Cheese Sandwiches

Take your usual grilled cheese to the next level with this simple recipe.

**—ARLENE REAGAN**
LIMERICK, PENNSYLVANIA

**PREP/TOTAL TIME:** 10 MIN.
**MAKES:** 4 SERVINGS

- **8 slices walnut-raisin bread**
- **3 to 4 tablespoons prepared pesto**
- **8 slices provolone and mozzarella cheese**
- **8 slices tomato**
- **¼ cup butter, softened**

**1.** Spread four slices of bread with pesto. Layer with cheese and tomato; top with remaining bread. Butter outsides of sandwiches.

**2.** In a large skillet over medium heat, toast sandwiches for 2-3 minutes on each side or until golden brown and cheese is melted.

## Pepper Lover's Pesto Pizza

My colorful appetizer pizzas are piled high with peppers, but they taste great with just about any veggies.

**—NANCY ZIMMERMAN**
CAPE MAY COURT HOUSE, NEW JERSEY

**PREP/TOTAL TIME:** 15 MIN.
**MAKES:** 4 SERVINGS

- **2 tablespoons olive oil**
- **1 each small sweet yellow, orange and red pepper, julienned**
- **1 medium onion, halved and sliced**
- **½ teaspoon Italian seasoning**
- **1 loaf (1 pound) unsliced Italian bread**
- **⅓ cup prepared pesto**
- **1 cup (4 ounces) shredded part-skim mozzarella cheese**

**1.** In a large skillet, heat oil over medium-high heat until hot. Add peppers, onion and Italian seasoning; cook and stir until vegetables are tender.

**2.** Cut bread in half lengthwise; place on a baking sheet. Spread cut sides of bread with pesto; top with pepper mixture. Top with cheese.

**3.** Broil 4-6 in. from the heat for 5-8 minutes or until cheese is melted. Cut into slices.

Pepper Lover's Pesto Pizza

## Lime Tilapia with Crisp-Tender Peppers

**PREP/TOTAL TIME:** 20 MIN.
**MAKES:** 4 SERVINGS

- **4 tilapia fillets (6 ounces each)**
- **2 teaspoons lime juice**
- **½ teaspoon grated lime peel**
- **¼ teaspoon salt**
- **¼ teaspoon pepper**
- **1 each medium sweet red, yellow and orange pepper, cut into thin strips**
- **1 tablespoon olive oil**
- **2 tablespoons minced fresh basil**

**1.** Place the tilapia fillets on a 13-in. x 9-in. baking dish. Drizzle with lime juice; sprinkle with lime peel, salt and pepper. Bake at 350° for 10-12 minutes or until fish flakes easily with a fork.
**2.** Meanwhile, in a large skillet, cook and stir peppers in oil over medium heat until crisp-tender; stir in basil. Serve with tilapia.

I love the splash of citrus in Lime Tilapia with Crisp-Tender Peppers. Replace the peppers with mushrooms, and you'll have a delightfully different entree.
**—JANEE GRAGSTON** CINCINNATI, OHIO

## Warm Goat Cheese in Marinara

Every family has a special recipe that gets pulled out time and again when the whole gang gathers together. For us, it's an appetizer of goat cheese warmed in a marinara sauce. Minced fresh basil and cracked black pepper give it the perfect finishing touch.
**—JAN VALDEZ** CHICAGO, ILLINOIS

**PREP/TOTAL TIME:** 30 MIN.
**MAKES:** 1½ CUPS

- **1 log (4 ounces) goat cheese**
- **1 cup marinara or spaghetti sauce**
- **2 tablespoons minced fresh basil**
- **¼ teaspoon cracked black pepper**
- **Toasted French bread baguette slices or assorted crackers**

**1.** Freeze cheese for 15 minutes. Unwrap and cut into ½-in. slices. In an ungreased small shallow baking dish, combine marinara sauce and basil. Top with cheese slices; sprinkle with pepper.
**2.** Bake, uncovered, at 350° for 8-10 minutes or until heated through. Serve warm with toasted baguette slices.

Lime Tilapia with Crisp-Tender Peppers

## Cheddar Bacon Chicken

It's tempting to seek out new flavors when baking chicken. But then again, with barbecue sauce, cheddar cheese and bacon so easy to grab from the fridge—and so delicious—why use anything else? Turn to this whenever you need a winning main dish.
**—BRENDA COLEMAN**
JACKSON, ALABAMA

**PREP/TOTAL TIME:** 30 MIN.
**MAKES:** 4 SERVINGS

- **4 boneless skinless chicken breast halves (5 ounces each)**
- **¼ cup reduced-sodium teriyaki sauce**
- **¼ cup barbecue sauce**
- **4 slices ready-to-serve fully cooked bacon, cut in half**
- **4 slices cheddar cheese**

**1.** Dip both sides of the chicken in teriyaki sauce; place on a greased 15-in. x 10-in. x 1-in. baking pan. Bake, uncovered, at 425° for 13-18 minutes or until a thermometer reads 170°.
**2.** Spread barbecue sauce over the chicken; top with bacon and cheese. Return to the oven and bake for 3-5 minutes or until the cheese is melted.

## B&W Vanilla Bean Puddings with Fresh Strawberries

**PREP/TOTAL TIME:** 20 MIN.
**MAKES:** 8 SERVINGS

- **4 cups cold 2% milk**
- **2 packages (3.3 ounces each) instant white chocolate pudding mix**
- **½ vanilla bean, split**
- **8 ounces semisweet chocolate**
- **1 tablespoon canola oil**
- **2 ounces white baking chocolate, chopped**
- **2 cups sliced fresh strawberries**

**1.** In a large bowl, whisk milk and pudding mixes for 2 minutes. With a sharp knife, scrape vanilla bean to remove seeds; stir seeds into pudding. Let pudding stand for 2 minutes or until soft-set. Spoon into eight 4-oz. ramekins.
**2.** In a microwave, melt semisweet chocolate with canola oil; stir until smooth. Spoon onto the puddings; refrigerate for 5-10 minutes or until chocolate is set.
**3.** In a microwave, melt the white chocolate; stir until smooth. Drizzle over tops. Serve with strawberries.

**B&W Vanilla Bean Puddings with Fresh Strawberries**

To personalize your B&W Vanilla Bean Puddings with Fresh Strawberries, add chopped candy bars to the pudding for the kids. For adults, add a tablespoon or so of your favorite liqueur.
**—KRISTY SHELLHORN** GUELPH, ONTARIO

## Ham & Zucchini Italiano

To me, dinner should be wholesome, great-tasting and simple to make. I can accomplish all three when I choose this cheesy ham-and-zucchini bake.
**—MADISON MAYBERRY** AMES, IOWA

**PREP/TOTAL TIME:** 30 MIN.
**MAKES:** 4 SERVINGS

- **3 medium zucchini, cut diagonally into ¼-inch slices**
- **1 tablespoon olive oil**
- **1 teaspoon dried basil**
- **½ teaspoon salt**
- **¼ teaspoon pepper**
- **10 slices smoked deli ham, cut into strips**
- **1 cup marinara or spaghetti sauce**
- **¾ cup shredded part-skim mozzarella cheese**

**1.** In a large skillet, saute zucchini in oil until crisp and tender. Sprinkle with basil, salt and pepper.
**2.** With a slotted spoon, transfer half of the zucchini to a greased 8-in. baking dish; spread evenly. Layer with half of the deli ham, marinara sauce and mozzarella cheese. Repeat the layers.
**3.** Bake, uncovered, at 450° for 10-12 minutes or until heated through and cheese is melted. Serve with a slotted spoon.

## Blueberry-Dijon Chicken

Blueberries and chicken may seem like a strange combination, but prepare to be pleasantly surprised!
**—SUSAN MARSHALL**
COLORADO SPRINGS, COLORADO

**PREP/TOTAL TIME:** 30 MIN.
**MAKES:** 4 SERVINGS

- **4 boneless skinless chicken breast halves (6 ounces each)**
- **¼ teaspoon salt**
- **¼ teaspoon pepper**
- **1 tablespoon butter**
- **½ cup blueberry preserves**
- **⅓ cup raspberry vinegar**
- **¼ cup fresh or frozen blueberries**
- **3 tablespoons Dijon mustard**
- **Minced fresh basil or tarragon, optional**

**1.** Sprinkle chicken with salt and pepper. In a large skillet, cook chicken in butter over medium heat for 6-8 minutes on each side or until a thermometer reads 170°. Remove and keep warm.
**2.** In the same skillet, combine the blueberry preserves, vinegar, blueberries and mustard, stirring to loosen browned bits from pan. Bring to a boil; cook and stir until thickened. Serve with chicken. Sprinkle with basil if desired.

**Blueberry-Dijon Chicken**

## Herbtastic Pork Chops

**PREP/TOTAL TIME:** 30 MIN.
**MAKES:** 4 SERVINGS

- **2/3 cup olive oil**
- **1/4 cup minced fresh sage**
- **1/4 cup minced fresh parsley**
- **8 garlic cloves, minced**
- **2 tablespoons minced fresh thyme**
- **1 tablespoon minced fresh rosemary**
- **1/4 teaspoon salt**
- **1/4 teaspoon pepper**
- **2 yellow summer squash, sliced lengthwise**
- **4 bone-in pork loin chops (3/4 inch thick)**

**1.** In a small bowl, combine the first eight ingredients; reserve 1/3 cup for serving. Rub both sides of squash and pork chops with remaining mixture.
**2.** Grill, covered, over medium heat for 4-5 minutes on each side or until a thermometer inserted in the pork reaches 145° and the squash is tender. Let pork stand 5 minutes before serving. Serve pork and squash with reserved herb mixture.

Herbtastic Pork Chops

My recipe for Herbtastic Pork Chops puts the chops on the grill and smothers them with sage, rosemary, parsley and thyme straight from the garden. Add sliced summer squash to round out a delicious, warm-weather dinner.
**—JENN TIDWELL** FAIR OAKS, CALIFORNIA

## Chicken Philly Sandwiches

A traditional Philly cheesesteak is a wonderful thing—unless you're trying to cut the fat and calories in your diet. To lighten up this classic sandwich without losing its cheesy goodness, replace the usual steak with strips of chicken. Boost nutrition with red and orange sweet peppers, too.
**—SHELLY EPLEY**
THORNTON, COLORADO

**PREP/TOTAL TIME:** 30 MIN.
**MAKES:** 4 SERVINGS

- **1/2 pound boneless skinless chicken breasts, cut into strips**
- **2 teaspoons olive oil**
- **1/2 teaspoon salt**
- **1/2 teaspoon freshly ground pepper**
- **1 large onion, halved and sliced**
- **1 medium sweet red pepper, julienned**
- **1 medium sweet orange or yellow pepper, julienned**
- **6 slices provolone cheese, cut into strips**
- **4 whole wheat hoagie buns, split and warmed**

**1.** In a large skillet, saute chicken in oil until no longer pink; sprinkle with salt and pepper. Remove and set aside. In the same skillet, saute onion and sweet peppers until crisp-tender.
**2.** Return the chicken to the pan. Reduce heat to medium. Add the provolone cheese. Cook and stir for 1-2 minutes or until cheese is melted. Serve on buns.

### Did you know?

May is National Barbecue Month and July is National Grilling Month—perfect timing for those backyard cookouts on Memorial Day and Independence Day!

Chicken Philly Sandwiches

## Italian-Style Pork Chops

An Italian-style version of pork chops was one of the first recipes I tried preparing in the early years of my marriage. Over the years, I've tossed in some vegetables and reduced the oil and fat to create a healthier main course. Serve it over rice for a complete, satisfying dinner anytime.
**—TRACI HOPPES** SPRING VALLEY, CALIFORNIA

**PREP/TOTAL TIME:** 30 MIN. **MAKES:** 4 SERVINGS

- **2 medium green peppers, cut into ¼-inch strips**
- **½ pound sliced fresh mushrooms**
- **1 tablespoon plus 1½ teaspoons olive oil, divided**
- **4 boneless pork loin chops (6 ounces each)**
- **¾ teaspoon salt, divided**
- **¾ teaspoon pepper, divided**
- **2 cups marinara or spaghetti sauce**
- **1 can (3½ ounces) sliced ripe olives, drained**

**1.** In a large skillet, saute peppers and mushrooms in 1 tablespoon oil until tender. Remove and keep warm.
**2.** Sprinkle the pork chops with 1/4 teaspoon salt and 1/4 teaspoon pepper. In the same skillet, brown pork chops in remaining oil. Add the marinara sauce, ripe olives, remaining salt and pepper and reserved pepper mixture. Bring to a boil. Reduce heat; cover and simmer for 10-15 minutes or until a thermometer reads 145°. Let stand for 5 minutes before serving.

Italian-Style Pork Chops

Mediterranean Turkey Panini

## Mediterranean Turkey Panini

I love fixing these turkey paninis for my fellow teachers and friends. Need something for a party or potluck? Cook several of these sandwiches and cut them into fourths. The smaller pieces work wonderfully as an appetizer.
**—MARTHA MUELLENBERG** VERMILLION, SOUTH DAKOTA

**PREP/TOTAL TIME:** 25 MIN. **MAKES:** 4 SERVINGS

- **4 ciabatta rolls, split**
- **1 jar (24 ounces) marinara or spaghetti sauce, divided**
- **1 container (4 ounces) crumbled feta cheese**
- **1 jar (7½ ounces) marinated quartered artichoke hearts, drained and chopped**
- **2 plum tomatoes, sliced**
- **1 pound sliced deli turkey**

**1.** Spread each ciabatta bottom with 2 tablespoons marinara sauce. Top with cheese, artichokes, tomatoes and turkey. Spread each ciabatta top with 2 tablespoons marinara sauce; place over turkey.
**2.** Cook on a panini maker or indoor grill for 4-5 minutes or until the cheese is melted. Place remaining marinara sauce in a small microwave-safe bowl; cover and microwave on high until heated through. Serve with sandwiches.

### Fuss-Free Shopping

I save time—and my sanity—at the grocery store by writing my list on a junk-mail envelope and putting the coupons I'll need in the envelope. That way, I don't have to fumble with my coupons and list in the store.
**—JILL BEDNAREK** MADISON HEIGHTS, MICHIGAN

## Pesto Chicken & Asparagus

With just five simple ingredients, I can put a beautiful entree on the table for my family or guests in very little time. This one-skillet dish is also the only way I can get my 3-year-old son to eat asparagus! Use store-bought pesto or your own made-from-scratch favorite.

**—BROOKE ICENHOUR**
EASLEY, SOUTH CAROLINA

**PREP/TOTAL TIME:** 30 MIN.
**MAKES:** 4 SERVINGS

- **1 pound boneless skinless chicken breasts, cut into 1-inch cubes**
- **1 tablespoon olive oil**
- **1 pound fresh asparagus, trimmed and cut into 1-inch pieces**
- **1 cup heavy whipping cream**
- **½ cup prepared pesto**
- **⅛ teaspoon pepper**
- **Hot cooked couscous**

In a large skillet, saute chicken in oil until no longer pink. Remove and set aside. In same skillet, saute asparagus until crisp-tender. Stir in cream, pesto and pepper until blended. Return chicken to pan; heat through. Serve with couscous.

## Pineapple-Mango Chicken

Combining pineapple, spices and mango creates a delicious sauce for grilled chicken. We like to round out the meal with veggie kabobs.

**—KIM WAITES**
RUTHERFORDTON, NORTH CAROLINA

**PREP/TOTAL TIME:** 30 MIN.
**MAKES:** 4 SERVINGS

- **1½ cups undrained crushed pineapple**
- **½ cup golden raisins**
- **¼ teaspoon ground cinnamon**
- **¼ teaspoon ground cloves**
- **⅛ teaspoon ground nutmeg**
- **2 medium mangoes, peeled and chopped**
- **4 boneless skinless chicken breast halves (5 ounces each)**
- **½ teaspoon salt**
- **⅛ teaspoon pepper**
- **Hot cooked rice**

**1.** In a small saucepan, combine the first five ingredients; bring to a boil over medium heat. Reduce heat; simmer, uncovered, for 4-6 minutes or until sauce is thickened and raisins are plumped, stirring occasionally. Stir in mangoes; heat through. Set aside.

**2.** Moisten a paper towel with cooking oil; using long-handled tongs, lightly coat the grill rack. Sprinkle chicken with salt and pepper. Grill chicken, covered, over medium heat or broil 4 in. from the heat for 5-8 minutes on each side or until a thermometer reads 170°. Serve with sauce and rice.

Quick Cajun Chicken Penne

## Quick Cajun Chicken Penne

I used to work at a restaurant that served a great variation of chicken with penne pasta. I didn't know how easy it would be to make until I gave it a shot. Now, I often get requests for this homemade version.

**—RUSTY KOLL** ELMWOOD, ILLINOIS

**PREP/TOTAL TIME:** 30 MIN.
**MAKES:** 6 SERVINGS

- **1 package (16 ounces) penne pasta**
- **4 boneless skinless chicken breast halves (5 ounces each)**
- **2 teaspoons blackened seasoning**
- **2 containers (10 ounces each) refrigerated Alfredo sauce**
- **2 plum tomatoes, chopped**
- **3 green onions, thinly sliced**

**1.** Cook the pasta according to the package directions; drain.

**2.** Moisten a paper towel with cooking oil; using long-handled tongs, lightly coat the grill rack. Sprinkle chicken with blackened seasoning. Grill chicken, covered, over medium heat or broil 4 in. from the heat for 5-8 minutes on each side or until a thermometer reads 170°. Cut into bite-size pieces.

**3.** In a large skillet, heat sauce over medium heat until warm, stirring frequently. Add tomatoes, onions, pasta and chicken; toss to coat and heat through.

# Cooking Lighter

It's easy to **trim the fat** with this hearty collection of mealtime standbys. Whether you're trying to cut back on calories or simply want to eat healthier, give these **family favorites** a try!

"Here's a cozy meal in one that's sure to warm your family on the coldest winter night. Ground beef, a host of vegetables and savory herbs make it a winner with everyone at the table."

—**JOSEPHINE PIRO** EASTON, PENNSYLVANIA

## Pecan Bread Pudding with Rum Custard Sauce

Fat-free ingredients, though not suitable for all baking recipes, work like a charm in my homey dessert.

**—VIRGINIA ANTHONY**
JACKSONVILLE, FLORIDA

**PREP:** 25 MIN. + STANDING
**BAKE:** 30 MIN.
**MAKES:** 6 SERVINGS (1½ CUPS SAUCE)

- **¾ cup fat-free milk**
- **¾ cup fat-free evaporated milk**
- **½ cup egg substitute**
- **⅓ cup sugar**
- **½ teaspoon vanilla extract**
- **¼ teaspoon salt**
- **¼ teaspoon ground cinnamon**
- **¼ teaspoon ground nutmeg**
- **4 cups cubed day-old French bread**
- **⅓ cup chopped pecans, toasted**

**RUM CUSTARD SAUCE**

- **¼ cup sugar**
- **4 teaspoons cornstarch**
- **⅛ teaspoon salt**
- **½ cup fat-free milk**
- **½ cup fat-free evaporated milk**
- **2 tablespoons egg substitute**
- **1 tablespoon butter**
- **1 tablespoon rum or ½ teaspoon rum extract**
- **¼ teaspoon vanilla extract**
- **⅛ teaspoon butter flavoring**

**1.** In a large bowl, whisk the first eight ingredients. Gently stir in bread and pecans; let stand for 10 minutes or until bread is softened.

Pecan Bread Pudding with Rum Custard Sauce

**2.** Transfer to an 8-in. square baking dish coated with cooking spray. Bake, uncovered, at 350° for 30-35 minutes or until a knife inserted near the center comes out clean.
**3.** For sauce, combine the sugar, cornstarch and salt in a small heavy saucepan. Stir in milk and evaporated milk until smooth. Cook and stir over medium-high heat until thickened and bubbly. Reduce heat; cook and stir 2 minutes longer.
**4.** Remove from the heat. Whisk a small amount of the hot mixture into the egg substitute; return all to the pan, whisking constantly. Bring to a gentle boil; cook and stir 2 minutes longer. Remove from the heat. Stir in the remaining ingredients. Serve warm with bread pudding. Refrigerate leftovers.

**Nutritional Facts:** ¾ cup pudding with ¼ cup sauce equals 286 calories, 8 g fat (2 g saturated fat), 8 mg cholesterol, 455 mg sodium, 43 g carbohydrate, 1 g fiber, 11 g protein.

## FAST FIX Spinach Penne Salad

This bridal shower beauty will shine as is, or you can double the vinaigrette and use half to marinate and grill chicken breasts to add to the salad.
**—BENICE SILVER** CARMEL, INDIANA

**PREP/TOTAL TIME:** 30 MIN.
**MAKES:** 10 SERVINGS

- **1 package (16 ounces) uncooked whole wheat penne pasta**

**VINAIGRETTE**

- **½ cup olive oil**
- **½ cup white wine vinegar**
- **⅓ cup grated Parmesan cheese**
- **1 tablespoon Dijon mustard**
- **2 garlic cloves, minced**
- **1 teaspoon dried oregano**
- **¼ teaspoon salt**
- **¼ teaspoon pepper**

**SALAD**

- **1 package (6 ounces) fresh baby spinach**
- **3 medium tomatoes, seeded and chopped**
- **¾ cup (6 ounces) crumbled feta cheese**
- **4 green onions, thinly sliced**
- **½ cup sliced ripe or Greek olives**

Lentil-Tomato Soup

**1.** In a Dutch oven, cook pasta according to package directions. Drain and rinse in cold water; drain a second time.
**2.** Meanwhile, in a small bowl, whisk the vinaigrette ingredients. In a large bowl, combine the pasta, spinach, tomatoes, feta cheese, onions and olives. Add vinaigrette; toss to coat. Serve immediately.

**Nutritional Facts:** 1½ cups equals 327 calories, 15 g fat (3 g saturated fat), 7 mg cholesterol, 233 mg sodium, 38 g carbohydrate, 7 g fiber, 11 g protein.

## Lentil-Tomato Soup

Double the recipe and share this hearty soup with neighbors and loved ones on cold winter nights. I like to serve it with corn bread for dunking.

**—MICHELLE CURTIS**
BAKER CITY, OREGON

**PREP:** 15 MIN. **COOK:** 30 MIN.
**MAKES:** 6 SERVINGS

- **4½ cups water**
- **4 medium carrots, sliced**
- **1 medium onion, chopped**
- **⅔ cup dried lentils, rinsed**
- **1 can (6 ounces) tomato paste**
- **2 tablespoons minced fresh parsley**
- **1 tablespoon brown sugar**
- **1 tablespoon white vinegar**
- **1 teaspoon garlic salt**
- **½ teaspoon dried thyme**
- **¼ teaspoon dill weed**
- **¼ teaspoon dried tarragon**
- **¼ teaspoon pepper**

In a large saucepan, combine the water, carrots, onion and lentils; bring to a boil. Reduce heat; cover and simmer for 20-25 minutes or until vegetables and lentils are tender. Stir in the remaining ingredients; return to a boil. Reduce heat; simmer, uncovered, for 5 minutes to allow flavors to blend.

**FOR SAUSAGE VARIATION:** *Stir in 1/2 pound chopped fully cooked turkey sausage; heat through.*

**FOR KALE VARIATION:** *Stir in 3 cups chopped fresh kale; cook, uncovered, until kale is tender.*

**FOR SPICED VARIATION:** *Add 3/4 teaspoon garam masala when adding other seasonings.*

**Nutritional Facts:** 3/4 cup equals 138 calories, trace fat (trace saturated fat), 0 cholesterol, 351 mg sodium, 27 g carbohydrate, 9 g fiber, 8 g protein. **Diabetic Exchanges:** 1 starch, 1 lean meat, 1 vegetable.

## Chocolate-Pumpkin Cheesecake Bars

**PREP:** 30 MIN. **BAKE:** 20 MIN.
**MAKES:** 2 DOZEN

- **1/3 cup butter, cubed**
- **1 1/2 ounces unsweetened chocolate, coarsely chopped**
- **1 tablespoon instant coffee granules**
- **1/2 cup boiling water**
- **1 cup canned pumpkin**
- **2 eggs, lightly beaten**
- **2 cups all-purpose flour**
- **1 1/2 cups sugar**
- **3/4 teaspoon baking soda**
- **1/2 teaspoon salt**

**CHEESECAKE BATTER**

- **1 package (8 ounces) reduced-fat cream cheese**
- **1/2 cup canned pumpkin**
- **1/4 cup sugar**
- **1 teaspoon vanilla extract**
- **3/4 teaspoon ground cinnamon**
- **3/4 teaspoon ground ginger**
- **1/8 teaspoon ground cloves**
- **1 egg**
- **1 cup (6 ounces) semisweet chocolate chips**

**1.** In a microwave, melt butter and chocolate; stir until smooth. Cool slightly.

**2.** In a large bowl, dissolve coffee in water. Stir in the pumpkin, eggs and chocolate mixture. Combine the flour, sugar, baking soda and salt; gradually add to chocolate mixture. Transfer to a 15-in. x 10-in. x 1-in. baking pan coated with cooking spray.

Chocolate-Pumpkin Cheesecake Bars

I created this by taking my favorite cheesecake brownie recipe, which is about 40 years old, and kicking it up a bit with pumpkin and spices. These bars disappear fast, so consider doubling the recipe.

**—JUDY CASTRANOVA**
NEW BERN, NORTH CAROLINA

**3.** For cheesecake batter, in a small bowl, beat cream cheese and pumpkin until smooth. Beat in the sugar, vanilla and spices. Add egg; beat on low speed just until combined. Spoon over chocolate batter. Cut through the batter with a knife to swirl cheesecake portion. Sprinkle with chocolate chips.

**4.** Bake at 350° for 20-25 minutes or until a toothpick inserted near the center comes out with moist crumbs (do not overbake). Cool on a wire rack. Cut into bars. Refrigerate the leftovers.

**Nutritional Facts:** 1 bar equals 197 calories, 8 g fat (5 g saturated fat), 40 mg cholesterol, 157 mg sodium, 29 g carbohydrate, 2 g fiber, 4 g protein. **Diabetic Exchanges:** 2 starch, 1 fat.

Try "pie pumpkins" in your baked goods. Wash, peel and remove seeds. Cut pumpkin into chunks and steam until soft. Puree and pack into freezer bags or containers in 1 cup servings. Use cup-for-cup in place of canned pumpkin.

## MAKE AHEAD Almond Torte

Reduced-fat sour cream, egg whites and applesauce lighten up this gorgeous torte. A creamy custard filling lends richness.
—**KATHY OLSEN** MARLBOROUGH, NEW HAMPSHIRE

**PREP:** 45 MIN. + CHILLING **BAKE:** 25 MIN. + COOLING
**MAKES:** 16 SERVINGS

- **⅓ cup sugar**
- **1 tablespoon cornstarch**
- **½ cup reduced-fat sour cream**
- **3 egg yolks**
- **1 tablespoon butter**
- **1 teaspoon vanilla extract**
- **½ teaspoon almond extract**

**CAKE**

- **4 egg whites**
- **⅓ cup butter, softened**
- **1½ cups sugar, divided**
- **2 egg yolks**
- **⅓ cup fat-free milk**
- **¼ cup unsweetened applesauce**
- **1 teaspoon vanilla extract**
- **1 cup cake flour**
- **1 teaspoon baking powder**
- **⅛ teaspoon salt**
- **½ cup sliced almonds**
- **½ teaspoon ground cinnamon**

**1.** In a double boiler or metal bowl over simmering water, constantly whisk the sugar, cornstarch, sour cream and egg yolks until mixture reaches 160° or is thick enough to coat the back of a spoon.

**Almond Torte**

**2.** Remove from the heat; stir in butter and extracts until blended. Press waxed paper onto surface of custard. Refrigerate for several hours or overnight.
**3.** Place egg whites in a large bowl; let stand at room temperature for 30 minutes. Line two 8-in. round baking pans with waxed paper. Coat sides and paper with cooking spray; sprinkle with flour and set aside.
**4.** In a large bowl, beat butter and ½ cup sugar until blended, about 2 minutes. Add egg yolks; mix well. Beat in the milk, applesauce and vanilla (mixture may appear curdled). Combine the flour, baking powder and salt; add to butter mixture. Transfer to prepared pans; set aside.
**5.** Using clean beaters, beat egg whites on medium speed until soft peaks form. Gradually beat in remaining sugar, 2 tablespoons at a time, on high until stiff glossy peaks form and sugar is dissolved. Spread evenly over batter; sprinkle with almonds and cinnamon.
**6.** Bake at 350° for 25-30 minutes or until meringue is lightly browned. Cool in pans on wire racks for 10 minutes (meringue will crack). Loosen edges of cakes from pans with a knife. Using two large spatulas, carefully remove one cake to a serving plate, meringue side up; remove remaining cake to a wire rack, meringue side up. Cool cakes completely.
**7.** Carefully spread custard over cake on serving plate; top with remaining cake. Store in the refrigerator.

**Nutritional Facts:** 1 slice equals 215 calories, 8 g fat (4 g saturated fat), 79 mg cholesterol, 99 mg sodium, 32 g carbohydrate, 1 g fiber, 4 g protein. **Diabetic Exchanges:** 2 starch, 1 fat.

## MAKE AHEAD Strawberry Spinach Salad with Poppy Seed Dressing

Spinach salad looks best dressed with luscious red strawberries and accents of toasted pecans. Finish it up with a sweet poppy seed dressing.
—**ERIN LOUGHMILLER** RIDGECREST, CALIFORNIA

**PREP:** 25 MIN. + CHILLING **MAKES:** 10 SERVINGS

- **⅓ cup olive oil**
- **¼ cup sugar**
- **3 tablespoons white or balsamic vinegar**
- **2 tablespoons sesame seeds**
- **1 tablespoon poppy seeds**
- **1 tablespoon chopped onion**
- **¼ teaspoon paprika**
- **¼ teaspoon Worcestershire sauce**
- **1 package (9 ounces) fresh spinach, trimmed**
- **4 cups fresh strawberries, sliced**
- **¼ cup chopped pecans, toasted**

**1.** Place the first eight ingredients in a jar with a tight-fitting lid; shake well. Refrigerate for 1 hour.
**2.** Just before serving, combine the remaining ingredients in a large bowl. Shake dressing and drizzle over salad; toss to coat.

**Nutritional Facts:** 1 cup equals 141 calories, 11 g fat (1 g saturated fat), 0 cholesterol, 23 mg sodium, 11 g carbohydrate, 2 g fiber, 2 g protein. **Diabetic Exchanges:** 1½ fat, ½ starch.

## Biscuit-Topped Shepherd's Pies

Here's a cozy meal in one that's sure to warm your family on the coldest winter night. Ground beef, veggies and savory herbs make it a winner with everyone at the table.
**—JOSEPHINE PIRO** EASTON, PENNSYLVANIA

**PREP:** 30 MIN. **BAKE:** 10 MIN. **MAKES:** 6 SERVINGS

- **1 pound lean ground beef (90% lean)**
- **1 medium onion, chopped**
- **1 celery rib, finely chopped**
- **1 package (16 ounces) frozen peas and carrots, thawed and drained**
- **1 can (15 ounces) Italian tomato sauce**
- **¼ teaspoon pepper**
- **1 cup reduced-fat biscuit/baking mix**
- **2 tablespoons grated Parmesan cheese**
- **¼ teaspoon dried rosemary, crushed**
- **½ cup fat-free milk**
- **2 tablespoons butter, melted**

**1.** In a large nonstick skillet, cook the beef, onion and celery over medium heat until meat is no longer pink; drain. Add the vegetables, tomato sauce and pepper; cook and stir for 5-6 minutes or until heated through. Spoon into six 8-oz. ramekins coated with cooking spray; set aside.
**2.** In a small bowl, combine the biscuit mix, cheese and rosemary. Stir in milk and butter just until moistened. Spoon dough over meat mixture; place ramekins on a baking sheet.
**3.** Bake at 425° for 10-12 minutes or until golden brown.

**Nutritional Facts:** 1 serving equals 311 calories, 12 g fat (5 g saturated fat), 59 mg cholesterol, 771 mg sodium, 31 g carbohydrate, 5 g fiber, 22 g protein. **Diabetic Exchanges:** 2 lean meat, 1½ starch, 1 vegetable, 1 fat.

## Peanut Butter Snack Bars

These deliciously portable bars combine protein and whole grains to fuel workouts or to simply get you through the day whenever hunger hits.
**—NETTIE HOGAN** WADSWORTH, OHIO

**PREP:** 25 MIN. + COOLING **MAKES:** 3 DOZEN

- **3¼ cups Kashi Heart to Heart honey toasted oat cereal**
- **2¾ cups old-fashioned oats**
- **1 cup unblanched almonds**
- **½ cup sunflower kernels**
- **¼ cup ground flaxseed**
- **¼ cup uncooked oat bran cereal**
- **¼ cup wheat bran**
- **¼ cup flaxseed**
- **3 tablespoons sesame seeds**
- **2 cups creamy peanut butter**
- **1½ cups honey**
- **1 teaspoon vanilla extract**

**1.** In a large bowl, combine the first nine ingredients. In a small saucepan, combine peanut butter and honey. Cook over medium heat until peanut butter is melted, stirring occasionally. Remove from the heat. Stir in vanilla. Pour over cereal mixture; mix well.
**2.** Transfer to a greased 15-in. x 10-in. x 1-in. baking pan; gently press into pan. Cool completely. Cut into bars. Store in an airtight container.

**Nutritional Facts:** 1 bar equals 215 calories, 12 g fat (2 g saturated fat), 0 cholesterol, 87 mg sodium, 24 g carbohydrate, 3 g fiber, 7 g protein. **Diabetic Exchanges:** 1½ starch, 1 high-fat meat.

**Editor's Note:** *Look for oat bran cereal near the hot cereals or in the natural foods section.*

Biscuit-Topped Shepherd's Pies

## FAST FIX Arugula Salad with Shaved Parmesan

A mother deserves a beautiful salad that combines her favorite flavors, like peppery arugula, golden raisins, crunchy almonds and shredded Parmesan. I put this simple salad together for my mom, and the whole family ended up loving it!
**—NICOLE RASH** BOISE, IDAHO

**PREP/TOTAL TIME:** 15 MIN. **MAKES:** 4 SERVINGS

- **6 cups fresh arugula**
- **¼ cup golden raisins**
- **¼ cup sliced almonds, toasted**
- **3 tablespoons olive oil**
- **1 tablespoon lemon juice**
- **¼ teaspoon salt**
- **¼ teaspoon freshly ground pepper**
- **⅓ cup shaved Parmesan cheese**

In a large bowl, combine the arugula, raisins and almonds. Drizzle with oil and lemon juice. Sprinkle with salt and pepper; toss to coat. Divide among four plates; top with cheese.

**Nutritional Facts:** 1 cup equals 181 calories, 15 g fat (3 g saturated fat), 4 mg cholesterol, 242 mg sodium, 10 g carbohydrate, 2 g fiber, 4 g protein. **Diabetic Exchanges:** 3 fat, ½ starch.

**Editor's Note:** *To toast nuts, spread in a 15-in. x 10-in. x 1-in. baking pan. Bake at 350° for 5-10 minutes or until lightly browned, stirring occasionally. Or, spread in a dry nonstick skillet and heat over low heat until lightly browned, stirring occasionally.*

## FAST FIX Lemon-Lime Salmon with Veggie Saute

A fresh squeeze of lemon juice brightens so many items! Add a little lime juice, too, and you're really in for a sensational meal. Here, I add citrus to salmon fillets, and I saute a supporting cast of vegetables separately until they're crisp-tender. What a tasty dinner!

**—BRIAN HILL** WEST HOLLYWOOD, CALIFORNIA

**PREP/TOTAL TIME:** 30 MIN. **MAKES:** 6 SERVINGS

- **6 salmon fillets (4 ounces each)**
- **½ cup lemon juice**
- **½ cup lime juice**
- **1 teaspoon seafood seasoning**
- **¼ teaspoon salt**
- **2 medium sweet red peppers, sliced**
- **2 medium sweet yellow peppers, sliced**
- **1 large red onion, halved and sliced**
- **2 teaspoons olive oil**
- **1 package (10 ounces) frozen corn, thawed**
- **2 cups baby portobello mushrooms, halved**
- **2 cups cut fresh asparagus (1-inch pieces)**
- **2 tablespoons minced fresh tarragon or 2 teaspoons dried tarragon**

**1.** Place salmon in a 13-in. x 9-in. baking dish; add lemon and lime juices. Sprinkle with seafood seasoning and salt. Bake, uncovered, at 425° for 10-15 minutes or until fish flakes easily with a fork.

**2.** Meanwhile, in a large nonstick skillet coated with cooking spray, saute peppers and onion in oil for 3 minutes. Add the corn, mushrooms and asparagus; cook and stir 3-4 minutes longer or just until vegetables reach desired doneness. Stir in tarragon. Serve with salmon.

**Nutritional Facts:** 1 fillet with 1¼ cups vegetables equals 329 calories, 15 g fat (3 g saturated fat), 67 mg cholesterol, 283 mg sodium, 25 g carbohydrate, 4 g fiber, 27 g protein. **Diabetic Exchanges:** 3 lean meat, 1½ starch, 1½ fat.

Citrus Vinaigrette

## FAST FIX Brown Sugar & Banana Oatmeal

Oatmeal is a favorite breakfast food, quick, easy and filling. I came up with this version by using some of the same ingredients from my favorite breakfast smoothie. Add bran cereal for a heartier taste and more fiber. A brown sugar substitute and soy milk also blend in well.

**—JESSI RIZZI** ODENTON, MARYLAND

**PREP/TOTAL TIME:** 15 MIN. **MAKES:** 3 SERVINGS

- **2 cups fat-free milk**
- **1 cup quick-cooking oats**
- **1 large ripe banana, sliced**
- **2 teaspoons brown sugar**
- **1 teaspoon honey**
- **½ teaspoon ground cinnamon**
- **Additional fat-free milk or ground cinnamon, optional**

**1.** In a small saucepan, bring milk to a boil; stir in oats. Cook over medium heat for 1-2 minutes or until thickened, stirring occasionally.

**2.** Stir in the banana, brown sugar, honey and cinnamon. Divide among three serving bowls. Serve with additional milk and cinnamon if desired.

**Nutritional Facts:** 1 cup (calculated without additional milk) equals 215 calories, 2 g fat (trace saturated fat), 3 mg cholesterol, 71 mg sodium, 42 g carbohydrate, 4 g fiber, 10 g protein.

## FAST FIX Citrus Vinaigrette

Tart, tangy and citrusy flavors abound in this quick vinaigrette you can whisk together any night of the week you have the greens to go with it. Our Test Kitchen staff members couldn't wait to share the recipe!

**PREP/TOTAL TIME:** 5 MIN. **MAKES:** ½ CUP

- **¼ cup orange juice**
- **3 tablespoons red wine vinegar**
- **2 teaspoons honey**
- **1½ teaspoons Dijon mustard**
- **1 tablespoon olive oil**

Place all ingredients in a jar with a tight-fitting lid; shake well. Chill until serving. Just before serving, shake dressing and drizzle over salad.

**Nutritional Facts:** 2 tablespoon equals 53 calories, 4 g fat (trace saturated fat), 0 cholesterol, 47 mg sodium, 5 g carbohydrate, trace fiber, trace protein.

## FAST FIX Cranberry-Grape Spritzer

The bold colors of cranberries and grapes make them standouts in the juice aisle, but in this recipe, club soda lends a sparkle that delivers true refreshment. Add ice cubes and a slice of lemon for the full effect.

**—KAREN SCHWABENLENDER**
WAXHAW, NORTH

**PREP/TOTAL TIME:** 5 MIN.
**MAKES:** 1 SERVING

- **½ cup cranberry-apple juice**
- **½ cup grape juice**
- **¼ cup club soda**
- **Lemon slice**

Combine juices and club soda in a tall glass; add ice. Garnish with lemon.

**Nutritional Facts:** 1¼ cups (calculated without lemon slice) equals 134 calories, trace fat (trace saturated fat), 0 cholesterol, 37 mg sodium, 33 g carbohydrate, trace fiber, 1 g protein.

## FAST FIX Rosemary Walnuts

My aunt Mary started making this recipe years ago, and each time we visited her she would have a batch ready for us. The use of cayenne adds an unexpected zing to the savory combo of rosemary and walnuts. When you need a good housewarming or hostess gift, double the batch and save one for yourself!

**—RENEE CIANCIO**
NEW BERN, NORTH CAROLINA

**PREP/TOTAL TIME:** 20 MIN
**MAKES:** 2 CUPS

- **2 cups walnut halves**
- **Cooking spray**
- **2 teaspoons dried rosemary, crushed**
- **½ teaspoon kosher salt**
- **¼ to ½ teaspoon cayenne pepper**

**1.** Place walnuts in a small bowl. Spritz with cooking spray. Add the seasonings; toss to coat. Place in a single layer on a baking sheet.
**2.** Bake at 350° for 10 minutes. Serve warm.

**Nutritional Facts:** ¼ cup equals 166 calories, 17 g fat (2 g saturated fat), 0 cholesterol, 118 mg sodium, 4 g carbohydrate, 2 g fiber, 4 g protein. **Diabetic Exchange:** 3 fat.

## FAST FIX Easy Southwestern Veggie Wraps

I developed this recipe when corn was at the farmers market and big red juicy tomatoes were in my garden. To make this wrap light and healthy, I use fat-free sour cream, whole grain tortillas and brown rice. Although it's meatless by nature, you can change it up with a large chicken breast cut into small strips or cubes.

**—CINDY BEBERMAN**
ORLAND PARK, ILLINOIS

**PREP/TOTAL TIME:** 30 MIN.
**MAKES:** 6 SERVINGS

- **2 large tomatoes, seeded and diced**
- **1 can (15 ounces) black beans, rinsed and drained**
- **1 cup frozen corn, thawed**
- **1 cup cooked brown rice, cooled**
- **2 shallots, chopped**
- **1 jalapeno pepper, seeded and chopped**
- **⅓ cup fat-free sour cream**
- **¼ cup minced fresh cilantro**
- **2 tablespoons lime juice**
- **½ teaspoon ground cumin**
- **½ teaspoon chili powder**
- **½ teaspoon salt**
- **6 romaine leaves**
- **6 whole wheat tortillas (8 inches), at room temperature**

**1.** In a large bowl, combine the first six ingredients. In a small bowl, combine the sour cream, cilantro, lime juice and seasonings. Gently stir into tomato mixture.
**2.** Place romaine on tortillas; top with filling. Roll up and secure with toothpicks. Cut each in half.

**Nutritional Facts:** 2 halves equals 295 calories, 4 g fat (trace saturated fat), 2 mg cholesterol, 525 mg sodium, 53 g carbohydrate, 7 g fiber, 11 g protein.

**Editor's Note:** *Wear disposable gloves when cutting hot peppers; the oils can burn skin. Avoid touching your face.*

## Veggie Nicoise Salad

**PREP:** 40 MIN. **COOK:** 25 MIN.
**MAKES:** 6 SERVINGS

- **⅓ cup olive oil**
- **¼ cup lemon juice**
- **2 teaspoons minced fresh oregano**
- **2 teaspoons minced fresh thyme**
- **1 teaspoon Dijon mustard**
- **1 garlic clove, minced**
- **¼ teaspoon coarsely ground pepper**
- **⅛ teaspoon salt**
- **1 pound small red potatoes, halved**
- **1 pound fresh asparagus, trimmed**
- **½ pound fresh green beans, trimmed**
- **1 can (16 ounces) kidney beans, rinsed and drained**
- **1 small red onion, halved and thinly sliced**
- **2 bunches romaine, torn**
- **6 hard-cooked eggs, quartered**
- **1 jar (6½ ounces) marinated quartered artichoke hearts, drained**
- **½ cup Nicoise or Kalamata olives**

**1.** In a small bowl, whisk the first eight ingredients; set aside.
**2.** Place potatoes in a small saucepan and cover with water. Bring to a boil. Reduce heat; cover and simmer for 10-15 minutes or until tender. Drain. Drizzle warm potatoes with 1 tablespoon vinaigrette; toss to coat and set aside.
**3.** In a large saucepan, bring 4 cups water to a boil. Add asparagus; cook for 2-4 minutes or until crisp-tender. With tongs, remove asparagus and immediately place in ice water. Drain and pat dry.
**4.** Return water to a boil. Add green beans; cook for 3-4 minutes or until crisp-tender. Remove beans and place in ice water. Drain and pat dry.
**5.** In a small bowl, combine the kidney beans, onion and 1 tablespoon vinaigrette; toss to coat. Set aside.
**6.** Just before serving, toss asparagus with 1 tablespoon vinaigrette; toss green beans with 2 teaspoons vinaigrette. Place romaine in a large bowl; drizzle with remaining vinaigrette and toss to coat. Transfer to a serving platter; arrange vegetables, kidney bean mixture, eggs, artichoke hearts and olives over lettuce.

More people in my workplace are becoming vegetarians. When we are together, the focus is on fresh produce. This salad combines our favorite ingredients in one dish... and the hard-boiled eggs and kidney beans deliver enough protein to satisfy those who are vegetarian skeptics.
**—ELIZABETH KELLEY** CHICAGO, ILLINOIS

**Nutritional Facts:** 1 serving equals 431 calories, 26 g fat (5 g saturated fat), 212 mg cholesterol, 565 mg sodium, 37 g carbohydrate, 9 g fiber, 17 g protein. **Diabetic Exchanges:** 3 fat, 2 medium-fat meat, 2 vegetable, 1½ starch.

## Curried Cashews

Spiced cashews contrast with sweet dried cranberries in this quick combo made on the stovetop. Feel free to swap walnuts, almonds and/or pecans for the cashews.
**—LOUISE GILBERT**
QUESNEL, BRITISH COLUMBIA

**PREP:** 20 MIN. + COOLING
**MAKES:** 2½ CUPS

- **2 cups salted cashews**
- **1 tablespoon olive oil**
- **2 teaspoons curry powder**
- **1 garlic clove, minced**
- **1 teaspoon Worcestershire sauce**
- **¾ teaspoon ground cumin**
- **¼ teaspoon cayenne pepper**
- **½ cup dried cranberries**

In a large nonstick skillet, cook cashews over medium heat until toasted, about 4 minutes. Add the oil, curry powder, garlic, Worcestershire sauce, cumin and cayenne. Cook and stir for 2-4 minutes or until cashews are well coated. Spread on foil to cool completely. Stir in cranberries; store in an airtight container.

**Nutritional Facts:** ⅓ cup equals 322 calories, 25 g fat (5 g saturated fat), 0 cholesterol, 298 mg sodium, 19 g carbohydrate, 2 g fiber, 8 g protein.

## FAST FIX Leah's Party Popcorn

Popcorn gets a special treatment when tossed with sesame breadsticks, mixed nuts, sunflower kernels and potato sticks. Pile it in bowls for parties or spoon individual portions into sealed bags or containers for anytime snacks.
**—LEAH STEENBERG**
CIRCLE PINES, MINNESOTA

**PREP/TOTAL TIME:** 30 MIN.
**MAKES:** 4 QUARTS

- **4 quarts popped popcorn**
- **2 cups miniature sesame breadsticks or sesame sticks**
- **2 cups mixed nuts**
- **1 cup sunflower kernels**
- **1 cup salted pumpkin seeds or pepitas**
- **1 cup potato sticks, optional**
- **¼ cup olive oil**
- **2 tablespoons lemon juice**
- **1 tablespoon Worcestershire sauce**
- **1 teaspoon salt**
- **1 teaspoon dill weed**
- **1 teaspoon coarsely ground pepper**
- **½ teaspoon onion powder**
- **½ teaspoon garlic powder**
- **½ teaspoon hot pepper sauce**

**1.** In a large bowl, combine the first five ingredients. Stir in the potato sticks if desired. In a small bowl, combine the remaining ingredients. Drizzle over popcorn mixture and toss to coat.
**2.** Spread into two greased 15-in. x 10-in. x 1-in. baking pans. Bake at 325° for 15 minutes, stirring every 5 minutes. Cool completely on a wire rack. Store in an airtight container.

**Nutritional Facts:** ½ cup (calculated without potato sticks) equals 184 calories, 14 g fat (2 g saturated fat), 0 cholesterol, 299 mg sodium, 11 g carbohydrate, 2 g fiber, 6 g protein.

Veggie Nicoise Salad

## MAKE AHEAD Heavenly Chocolate Pie

I lightened this up with fat-free, sugar-free and reduced-fat products. What a lovely way to satisfy chocolate cravings!

—**DONNA ROBERTS**
MANHATTAN, KANSAS

**PREP:** 15 MIN. + CHILLING
**MAKES:** 8 SERVINGS

- **1 cup fat-free vanilla frozen yogurt, softened**
- **2 cups fat-free milk**
- **1 package (1.4 ounces) sugar-free instant chocolate pudding mix**
- **1 package (1 ounce) sugar-free instant vanilla pudding mix**
- **1 carton (8 ounces) frozen reduced-fat whipped topping, thawed, divided**
- **Chocolate curls, optional**
- **1 reduced-fat graham cracker crust (8 inches)**

**1.** In a large bowl, whisk yogurt until soft and smooth. Gradually whisk in milk until blended. Add pudding mixes; whisk 2 minutes longer. Let stand for 2 minutes or until soft-set.

**2.** Fold in 1 cup whipped topping. Transfer to crust. Top with remaining whipped topping and chocolate curls if desired. Refrigerate for at least 4 hours.

**Nutritional Facts:** 1 piece equals 235 calories, 6 g fat (4 g saturated fat), 2 mg cholesterol, 433 mg sodium, 40 g carbohydrate, trace fiber, 5 g protein.

Heavenly Chocolate Pie

## FAST FIX Crisp and Nutty Mix

Whether you're running on the track or running to class, this mixture of dried fruit, cereal, nuts and more is the ultimate combination for munching. It's perfect for busy days!

—**MIKE TCHOU** PEPPER PIKE, OHIO

**PREP/TOTAL TIME:** 20 MIN.
**MAKES:** 2 QUARTS

- **1 cup Wheat Chex**
- **1 cup Multi Grain Cheerios**
- **1 cup reduced-fat Triscuits, broken**
- **1 cup yogurt-covered pretzels**
- **½ cup blanched almonds**
- **½ cup dried apples, chopped**
- **½ cup dried banana chips**
- **½ cup dried blueberries**
- **½ cup salted cashews**
- **½ cup dark chocolate M&M's**
- **⅓ cup finely shredded unsweetened coconut**
- **⅓ cup sunflower kernels**
- **⅓ cup salted pumpkin seeds or pepitas**

In a large bowl, combine all ingredients. Store in an airtight container.

**Nutritional Facts:** ½ cup equals 250 calories, 14 g fat (6 g saturated fat), 1 mg cholesterol, 157 mg sodium, 28 g carbohydrate, 3 g fiber, 6 g protein.

**Editor's Note:** *Look for unsweetened coconut in the baking or health food section.*

## FAST FIX Nuts and Seeds Trail Mix

The amount of protein and fiber in a handful of this yummy combo helps offset the fact that it's a bit high in fat and calories. Simply take care to eat healthy portions throughout the day to control your calorie intake.

—**KRISTIN RIMKUS**
SNOHOMISH, WASHINGTON

**PREP/TOTAL TIME:** 15 MIN.
**MAKES:** 5 CUPS

- **1 cup salted pumpkin seeds or pepitas**
- **1 cup unblanched almonds**
- **1 cup unsalted sunflower kernels**
- **1 cup shelled walnuts**
- **1 cup chopped dried apricots**
- **1 cup dark chocolate chips**

Gluten-Free Apple Cider Doughnuts

In a large bowl, combine all ingredients. Store in an airtight container.

**Nutritional Facts:** ⅓ cup equals 336 calories, 25 g fat (6 g saturated fat), 0 cholesterol, 96 mg sodium, 22 g carbohydrate, 4 g fiber, 11 g protein.

## MAKE AHEAD Gluten-Free Apple Cider Doughnuts

I wanted to create a gluten-free doughnut that tasted so good, the fact that it's gluten-free was beside the point!

—**KATHRYN CONRAD** MILWAUKEE

**PREP:** 20 MIN. + STANDING
**BAKE:** 15 MIN. + COOLING
**MAKES:** 10 DOUGHNUTS

- **2 cups gluten-free biscuit/baking mix**
- **¾ cup sugar**
- **1 package (¼ ounce) quick-rise yeast**
- **1½ teaspoons baking powder**
- **½ teaspoon salt**
- **½ teaspoon apple pie spice**
- **¼ teaspoon ground cinnamon**
- **⅛ teaspoon baking soda**
- **½ cup warm water (110° to 115°)**
- **6 tablespoons butter, melted**
- **¼ cup unsweetened applesauce, room temperature**
- **1 tablespoon vanilla extract**

**GLAZE**

- **1 cup apple cider or juice**
- **1 tablespoon butter, softened**
- **⅔ to ¾ cup confectioners' sugar**

**1.** In a large bowl, mix the first eight ingredients. In another bowl, whisk the water, butter, applesauce and vanilla until blended. Add to the dry ingredients; stir until blended. Cover and let rest for 10 minutes.
**2.** Cut a small hole in the corner of a food-safe plastic bag; fill with batter. Pipe into a 6-cavity doughnut pan coated with cooking spray, filling cavities three-fourths full.
**3.** Bake at 325° for 11-14 minutes or until golden brown. Cool for 5 minutes before removing from pan to a wire rack. Repeat with remaining batter.
**4.** For glaze, in a small saucepan, bring apple cider to a boil; cook until liquid is reduced to 3 tablespoons. Transfer to a small bowl; stir in butter until melted. Stir in enough confectioners' sugar to reach glaze consistency. Dip each doughnut halfway, allowing excess to drip off. Place on wire rack; let stand until set.

## Thin-Crust Gluten-Free Pepperoni Pizza

**PREP:** 20 MIN. **BAKE:** 20 MIN.
**MAKES:** 8 SERVINGS

- **1½ cups almond flour**
- **¼ teaspoon salt**
- **¼ teaspoon baking soda**
- **1 egg**
- **1 tablespoon grapeseed or olive oil**
- **¼ pound Italian turkey sausage links, casings removed**
- **1 medium onion, chopped**
- **½ cup pizza sauce**
- **1 garlic clove, minced**
- **½ cup julienned roasted sweet red peppers**
- **¼ cup sliced ripe olives**
- **1 cup (4 ounces) shredded part-skim mozzarella cheese**
- **17 slices turkey pepperoni**

**1.** In a small bowl, mix the almond flour, salt and baking soda. In another bowl, whisk egg and oil; stir into dry ingredients. Press onto a 12-in. pizza pan coated with cooking spray; build up edges slightly. Bake crust at 350° for 8-10 minutes or until the edges are lightly browned.
**2.** Meanwhile, in a large skillet, cook and stir sausage and onion over medium heat for 4-6 minutes or until sausage is no longer pink. Spread pizza sauce over crust; sprinkle with garlic. Top with the sausage mixture, red peppers, olives, cheese and pepperoni. Bake 18-20 minutes longer or until cheese is melted.

Thin-Crust Gluten-Free Pepperoni Pizza

My husband can't eat pizza with gluten or sugar in the crust. Because that leaves out boxed mixes and frozen pizzas, I decided to simply make my own.

—**ANGELA SAGE** WAXHAW, NORTH CAROLINA

top tip

The key to a perfect pizza crust is a hot oven. Always preheat your oven to the appropriate temperature (per the recipe directions) before baking the crust.

# Tasteful Get-Togethers

Gather with **friends and family** for a festive, unforgettable event. Thanks to the themed party menus and special treats featured in this chapter, you'll be having a **great time** in no time!

"A delightful dessert for a summer birthday party or patriotic holiday, this poke cake is a fun one to make with the kids. If you have a little extra time, add the eye-catching stars that stand on top."

—**JEANNE AMBROSE** MILWAUKEE, WISCONSIN

# FOR THE BIG GAME

When that can't-miss sporting event is on TV, invite the whole gang over for a fan-friendly bonanza. Your star players? Special snacks and munchies that are sure to win over the crowd.

## March Madness Miniature Peppers

I changed up my mother's recipe for stuffed peppers to make it a little bit healthier, using brown rice and ground turkey. I think the lighter version is just as good as similar recipes made with white rice, pork and beans.

**—ROSE MUCCIO**
LOWELL, MASSACHUSETTS

**PREP:** 55 MIN. **BAKE:** 20 MIN.
**MAKES:** 2 DOZEN

- **24 miniature sweet red peppers**
- **4 ounces ground turkey**
- **½ cup finely chopped fresh mushrooms**
- **¼ cup chopped sweet onion**
- **1 garlic clove, minced**
- **1 can (15 ounces) tomato sauce, divided**
- **¼ cup cooked brown rice**
- **1 tablespoon grated Parmesan cheese**
- **1 tablespoon shredded part-skim mozzarella cheese**
- **½ teaspoon dried basil**
- **¼ teaspoon salt**
- **¼ teaspoon cayenne pepper**
- **¼ teaspoon pepper**

**1.** Cut and reserve the tops off the peppers; remove the seeds. If necessary, cut thin slices from the pepper bottoms to level; set aside the peppers.

**2.** In a large skillet, cook the ground turkey, mushrooms, sweet onion and garlic over medium heat until the meat is no longer pink. Remove from the heat; let stand for 5 minutes.

**3.** Stir in 1/4 cup tomato sauce, rice, cheeses and seasonings; spoon into peppers. Place upright in a greased 11-in. x 7-in. baking dish. Spoon remaining tomato sauce over peppers; replace pepper tops. Cover and bake at 400° for 18-22 minutes or until heated through and peppers are crisp-tender.

March Madness Miniature Peppers

Jalapeno Ranch Dip

FAST FIX

## Jalapeno Ranch Dip

Ranch dressing got its start on a real dude ranch in California. I give that West-Coast classic a boost with salsa, green chilies, jalapenos and cilantro. They add color, spice and volume to feed a hungry party crowd.

**—LINDSAY DUKE** GOODRICH, TEXAS

**PREP/TOTAL TIME:** 10 MIN.
**MAKES:** 2¼ CUPS

- **1⅓ cups mayonnaise**
- **⅓ cup buttermilk**
- **⅓ cup salsa verde**
- **3 tablespoons canned chopped green chilies**
- **¾ cup fresh cilantro leaves**
- **2 jalapeno peppers, halved and seeded**
- **1 envelope ranch salad dressing mix**
- **Hot cooked buffalo-style chicken wings**
- **Celery sticks, optional**

Place the first seven ingredients in a blender; cover and process until smooth. Chill until serving. Serve with chicken wings and, if desired, celery sticks.

**Editor's Note:** *Wear disposable gloves when cutting hot peppers; the oils can burn skin. Avoid touching your face.*

## FAST FIX Cheese & Pepperoni Pizza Dip

You know those times when you want to use up a few extra ingredients in the refrigerator, but nothing comes to mind? When you have spaghetti sauce, a prebaked pizza crust, assorted cheeses and pepperoni, look here. In less than 30 minutes, you can turn the crust into strips for dipping and use the remaining items to mix up a fast, warm dip.

**—JULIE PUDERBAUGH** BERWICK, PENNSYLVANIA

**PREP/TOTAL TIME:** 25 MIN. **MAKES:** ABOUT 2 CUPS

- **Prebaked 12-inch pizza crust**
- **1 cup roasted garlic and Parmesan spaghetti sauce**
- **1½ cups shredded part-skim mozzarella cheese**
- **4 slices Muenster cheese, cut into thin strips**
- **20 slices pepperoni, chopped**
- **Dried oregano, optional**

**1.** Place the prebaked pizza crust on an ungreased baking sheet; bake at 350° for 9-12 minutes or until heated through.
**2.** Meanwhile, in a small saucepan, heat the spaghetti sauce over medium-low heat. Add the cheeses and pepperoni. Cook and stir until the cheeses are melted and the sauce is heated through; sprinkle with oregano, if desired.
**3.** Cut the pizza crust into 1½-in. strips; serve warm with sauce.

## Chipotle Focaccia with Garlic-Onion Topping

Chipotle peppers leave some people scrambling for a cold beverage; others can't get enough of the smoky heat. I'm a fan and came up with this peppery homemade focaccia topped with chipotle, roasted garlic and caramelized onion. Some guests who sampled it wanted it spicier—chipotle is only a medium-heat pepper—and some liked it just the way it is. Feel free to add more if you crave more "fire."

**—FRANCES "KAY" BOUMA** TRAIL, BRITISH COLUMBIA

**PREP:** 1¼ HOURS + RISING **BAKE:** 20 MIN. **MAKES:** 16 SERVINGS

- **1 cup water (70° to 80°)**
- **2 tablespoons olive oil**
- **2½ cups all-purpose flour**
- **1 teaspoon salt**
- **1 tablespoon chopped chipotle pepper in adobo sauce**
- **1½ teaspoons active dry yeast**

**TOPPING**

- **6 garlic cloves, peeled**
- **¼ teaspoon plus 7 tablespoons olive oil, divided**
- **4 large onions, cut into ¼-inch slices**
- **2 tablespoons chopped chipotle peppers in adobo sauce**
- **¼ teaspoon salt**

**1.** In bread machine pan, place the first six ingredients in the order suggested by the manufacturer. Select the dough setting (check dough after 5 minutes of mixing; add 1 to 2 tablespoons of water or flour if needed).

Chipotle Focaccia with Garlic-Onion Topping

**2.** When cycle is completed, turn dough onto a lightly floured surface. Punch down dough; cover and let rest for 15 minutes.
**3.** Meanwhile, place garlic in a small microwave-safe bowl. Drizzle with ¼ teaspoon oil. Microwave on high for 20-60 seconds or until softened. Mash the garlic.
**4.** Roll dough into a 12-in. x 10-in. rectangle. Transfer to a well-greased baking sheet. Cover and let rise in a warm place until slightly risen, about 20 minutes.
**5.** With your fingertips, make several dimples over top of dough. Brush dough with 1 tablespoon oil. Bake at 400° for 10 minutes or until lightly browned.
**6.** Meanwhile, in a large skillet, saute the onions in the remaining oil until tender. Add the chipotle peppers, salt and mashed garlic; saute 2-3 minutes longer. Sprinkle over the dough.
**7.** Bake 10-15 minutes longer or until golden brown. Cut into squares; serve warm.

## Chive Mascarpone Dip with Herbed Pita Chips

**PREP:** 25 MIN. **BAKE:** 10 MIN.
**MAKES:** 2 CUPS (48 CHIPS)

- **1 carton (8 ounces) mascarpone cheese**
- **¾ cup minced fresh chives**
- **¾ cup sour cream**
- **4 bacon strips, cooked and crumbled**
- **¼ teaspoon salt**
- **¼ teaspoon pepper**

**PITA CHIPS**

- **8 whole wheat pita breads (6 inches)**
- **¼ cup minced fresh oregano**
- **¼ cup olive oil**
- **½ teaspoon salt**
- **½ teaspoon pepper**
- **Assorted fresh vegetables**

**1.** In a small bowl, combine the first six ingredients. Chill until serving.

Chive Mascarpone Dip with Herbed Pita Chips

I have a massive herb garden in the summer. Chive Mascarpone Dip with Herbed Pita Chips is a scrumptious way to use up some of my seasonal harvest. I prepare this yummy appetizer 2-3 days in advance for the best flavor.
—**SARAH VASQUES** MILFORD, NEW HAMPSHIRE

**2.** Cut each pita bread into six wedges; arrange in a single layer on ungreased baking sheets. In a small bowl, combine the oregano, oil, salt and pepper; brush on the pita wedges. Bake pita wedges at 400° for 8-10 minutes or until crisp, turning once. Serve pita chips and vegetables with dip.

## *MAKE AHEAD* Buffalo-Style Chicken Chili Dip

**PREP:** 30 MIN. **COOK:** 30 MIN.
**MAKES:** 11 CUPS

- **3 celery ribs, finely chopped**
- **1 large onion, chopped**
- **1 large carrot, finely chopped**
- **5 garlic cloves, minced**
- **2 tablespoons butter**
- **2 pounds ground chicken**
- **1 tablespoon olive oil**
- **2 cups chicken broth**
- **1 can (16 ounces) kidney beans, rinsed and drained**
- **1 can (15 ounces) white kidney or cannellini beans, rinsed and drained**
- **1 can (15 ounces) crushed tomatoes**
- **1 can (15 ounces) tomato sauce**
- **1 can (6 ounces) tomato paste**
- **¼ cup Louisiana-style hot sauce**
- **3 teaspoons smoked paprika**
- **1 bay leaf**
- **¾ teaspoon salt**
- **¼ teaspoon pepper**
- **Crumbled blue cheese and tortilla chips**

**1.** In a Dutch oven, saute the celery, onion, carrot and garlic in butter until tender. Remove and set aside. In the same pan, cook the chicken in oil until no longer pink; drain.

**2.** Stir in chicken broth, beans, tomatoes, tomato sauce, tomato paste, hot sauce, paprika, bay leaf, salt, pepper and vegetable mixture. Bring to a boil; reduce heat. Simmer, uncovered, for 12-15 minutes or until slightly thickened. Discard bay leaf.

**3.** Serve the desired amount of dip; sprinkle with blue cheese and serve with tortilla chips. Cool remaining dip; transfer to freezer containers. Cover and freeze for up to 3 months.

**4. TO USE FROZEN DIP:** Thaw the dip in the refrigerator. Place in a saucepan; heat through. Sprinkle with cheese and serve with chips.

Craving that buffalo wing goodness without the bones? My Buffalo-Style Chicken Chili Dip freezes nicely in individual containers. Just pull it out at party time and let the fun begin!
—**BRENDA CALANDRILLO** MAHWAH, NEW JERSEY

## Football Fest Empanadas

**PREP:** 30 MIN. **BAKE:** 10 MIN./BATCH
**MAKES:** 2 DOZEN

- **1 jar (16 ounces) black bean and corn salsa**
- **½ cup frozen corn, thawed**
- **2 jalapeno peppers, seeded and minced**
- **3 tablespoons minced fresh cilantro, divided**
- **2 teaspoons lime juice**
- **1 package (9 ounces) ready-to-use Southwestern chicken strips, chopped**
- **2 packages (14.1 ounces each) refrigerated pie pastry**
- **4 ounces quesadilla cheese, shredded**
- **1 egg, lightly beaten**

**1.** In a large bowl, combine the salsa, corn, jalapeno peppers, 2 tablespoons cilantro and lime juice. In another bowl, combine the chicken, remaining cilantro and 1/2 cup salsa mixture; set aside. Reserve the remaining salsa for serving.

**2.** Unroll a pastry sheet onto a lightly floured surface. Using a floured 4-in. round cookie cutter placed halfway on the edge of the pastry, cut 4-in. x 3-in. football shapes. Repeat with the remaining dough, chilling and rerolling the scraps as needed.

**3.** Transfer half of the cutouts to greased baking sheets. Place 1 tablespoon chicken mixture in the center of each; top each with 1 1/2 teaspoons cheese. Brush the edges of the pastry with egg. Top with the remaining cutouts; press edges with a fork to seal. Cut slits in the tops to resemble football laces. Brush the tops with egg.

**4.** Bake at 450° for 8-12 minutes or until golden brown. Serve warm with reserved salsa mixture. Refrigerate leftovers.

**Editor's Note:** *Wear disposable gloves when cutting hot peppers; the oils can burn skin. Avoid touching your face.*

Classic empanadas from South America are stuffed pastries of beef or chicken and are usually fried. Football Fest Empanadas are baked instead and have a Southwestern spin. Serve them with the extra salsa mixture on the side.

**—JANE MCMILLAN** DANIA BEACH, FLORIDA

# A BOUNTIFUL BAKE SALE

Planning to sell baked treats for a charity, school or church? Take your sale from standard to super with the yummy favorites found here. Browsing buyers won't be able to resist!

Chocolate-Dipped Pretzel Rods

## Frosted Red Velvet Cookies

During college, my student job was in the bakery. Red velvet cookies always take me back to that place and time.
**—CHRISTINA PETRI** ALEXANDRIA, MINNESOTA

**PREP:** 20 MIN. **BAKE:** 10 MIN./BATCH
**MAKES:** 5 DOZEN

- **2 ounces unsweetened chocolate, chopped**
- **½ cup butter, softened**
- **⅔ cup packed brown sugar**
- **⅓ cup sugar**
- **1 egg**
- **1 tablespoon red food coloring**
- **1 teaspoon vanilla extract**
- **2 cups all-purpose flour**
- **½ teaspoon baking soda**
- **½ teaspoon salt**
- **1 cup sour cream**
- **1 cup (6 ounces) semisweet chocolate chips**
- **1 can (16 ounces) cream cheese frosting**

**1.** In a microwave, melt the unsweetened chocolate; stir until smooth. Cool.
**2.** In a large bowl, cream butter and sugars until light and fluffy. Beat in the egg, red food coloring and vanilla. Add the cooled unsweetened chocolate; beat until blended. In another bowl, mix the flour, baking soda and salt; add to the creamed mixture alternately with the sour cream, beating well after each addition. Stir in the chocolate chips.
**3.** Drop by tablespoonfuls 2 in. apart onto parchment paper-lined baking sheets. Bake at 375° for 6-9 minutes or until set. Remove to wire racks to cool completely. Spread with frosting.

Frosted Red Velvet Cookies

## Chocolate-Dipped Pretzel Rods

Kids of all ages will go crazy for these fun-to-eat, sweet-and-salty sticks. For a bake sale, tie the decorated rods into bundles and slip them into cellophane gift bags. Or stand the pretzels in a big glass jar if you're selling singles.
**—KAY WATERS** BENLD, ILLINOIS

**PREP:** 25 MIN. + STANDING
**COOK:** 10 MIN.
**MAKES:** ABOUT 4½ DOZEN

- **3 cups chopped toasted almonds**
- **2 packages (14 ounces each) caramels, unwrapped**
- **2 tablespoons water**
- **2 packages (10 ounces each) pretzel rods**
- **2 packages (10 to 12 ounces each) white baking chips**
- **2 packages (10 to 12 ounces each) dark chocolate chips**
- **Assorted sprinkles, optional**

**1.** Place almonds in a shallow dish. In a large glass measuring cup, microwave caramels and water on high until the caramels are melted, stirring every minute.
**2.** Dip three-fourths of each pretzel rod into caramel, allowing the excess to drip off. (Reheat the caramel in microwave if mixture becomes too thick for dipping.) Roll in almonds. Place on waxed paper until set.
**3.** In a microwave, melt white baking chips; stir until smooth.

Dip half of the caramel-coated pretzels in white baking chips, allowing the excess to drip off. Add sprinkles if desired; return to waxed paper to set. Repeat with chocolate chips and remaining pretzels.
**4.** Store in airtight containers or wrap in cellophane gift bags and tie with ribbon.

## Chocolate Caramel Cracker Bars

Here's a real disappearing act! Made on Saturday and gone by Sunday, the chocolaty caramel bars are truly that good. No one can believe that the recipe requires just crackers and five other ingredients that are kitchen staples.
**—ALLYSA BILLHORN** WILTON, IOWA

**PREP:** 15 MIN. **COOK:** 10 MIN. + CHILLING **MAKES:** 27 BARS

- **1 teaspoon plus ¾ cup butter, cubed**
- **45 Club crackers (2½-inches x 1-inch)**
- **1 can (14 ounces) sweetened condensed milk**
- **½ cup packed brown sugar**
- **3 tablespoons light corn syrup**
- **1 cup (6 ounces) semisweet chocolate chips**

**1.** Line a 9-in. square baking pan with foil and grease the foil with 1 teaspoon butter. Arrange a single layer of crackers in the pan.
**2.** In a large saucepan, combine sweetened condensed milk, brown sugar, corn syrup and remaining butter. Bring to a boil over medium heat, stirring occasionally. Reduce the heat to maintain a low boil; cook and stir for 7 minutes. Remove from the heat. Evenly spread a third of the mixture over the crackers. Repeat cracker and caramel layers twice.
**3.** Immediately sprinkle the chocolate chips over the caramel; let stand 3-5 minutes or until glossy. Spread over the top. Cover and refrigerate for 2 hours or until the chocolate is set. Using the foil, lift the layers out of the pan; cut into 3-in. x 1-in. bars.

**Chocolate Caramel Cracker Bars**

**Sweet & Salty Marshmallow Popcorn Treats**

## Sweet & Salty Marshmallow Popcorn Treats

Popcorn balls get even yummier when you add colorful milk chocolate candies and peanuts. The crisp goodies are great for children's parties and school events, too.
**—NINA VILHAUER** MINA, SOUTH DAKOTA

**PREP:** 20 MIN. + COOLING **MAKES:** ABOUT 5 DOZEN

- **4 quarts popped popcorn**
- **3 cups salted peanuts**
- **1 package (12.6 ounces) milk chocolate M&M's**
- **1 package (16 ounces) large marshmallows**
- **1 cup butter, cubed**

**1.** In a large bowl, combine the popcorn, peanuts and M&M's. In a large saucepan, combine marshmallows and butter. Cook and stir over medium-low heat until melted. Add to popcorn mixture; mix well.
**2.** When cool enough to handle, shape the popcorn mixture into 2-in. popcorn balls. Let stand until firm before wrapping in plastic.

Wondering what to charge for the goodies at your bake sale? Stick with simple prices in increments of 25 cents, so making change for customers goes quickly. For example, you could price large cookies and bars at $1 to $2, cupcakes and muffins at $2 to $3, small loaf breads at $5 and pies and small cakes at $10. Or, try this—let customers name their price. Buyers may pay more than what you'd charge because they'd consider it a donation.

## Lemon-on-Lemon Iced Cookies

I collect recipes from all over the world. When I find a great one—like this—it goes in a binder to use again and again!

**—SHARON DELANEY-CHRONIS**
SOUTH MILWAUKEE, WISCONSIN

**PREP:** 20 MIN.
**BAKE:** 15 MIN./BATCH + COOLING
**MAKES:** 4 DOZEN

- **2½ cups all-purpose flour**
- **⅓ cup sugar**
- **1 tablespoon grated lemon peel**
- **1 cup cold butter, cubed**

**ICING**

- **1 cup confectioners' sugar**
- **½ teaspoon grated lemon peel**
- **4 to 6 teaspoons lemon juice**

**1.** In a large bowl, combine the flour, sugar and lemon peel; cut in butter until crumbly. Transfer to a clean work surface; knead gently until the mixture forms a smooth dough, about 2 minutes. Divide in half.
**2.** On a lightly floured surface, roll or pat each portion into an 8-in. x 6-in. rectangle. Cut each into twelve 2-in. squares; cut squares diagonally in half to form twenty-four triangles. Place 1-in. apart on ungreased baking sheets.
**3.** Bake at 325° for 15-18 minutes or until lightly browned. Remove to wire racks to cool completely.
**4.** In a small bowl, mix the confectioners' sugar, lemon peel and enough lemon juice to achieve desired consistency. Drizzle over cookies; let stand until set.

Lemon-on-Lemon Iced Cookies

Nana's Rocky Road Fudge

## Nana's Rocky Road Fudge

It's a tradition for us to make a batch of rocky road-style fudge every year at Christmastime. But why wait until the holidays for a treat this yummy?

**—ASHLEY BERRY**
MONTGOMERY VILLAGE, MARYLAND

**PREP:** 15 MIN. **COOK:** 5 MIN. + CHILLING
**MAKES:** ABOUT 2½ POUNDS

- **1½ teaspoons plus 1 tablespoon butter, divided**
- **2 cups (12 ounces) semisweet chocolate chips**
- **1 can (14 ounces) sweetened condensed milk**
- **2 cups salted peanuts**
- **1 package (10½ ounces) miniature marshmallows**

**1.** Line a 13-in. x 9-in. baking pan with foil and grease the foil with 1½ teaspoons butter; set aside.
**2.** In a large saucepan, combine the chocolate chips, milk and remaining butter. Cook and stir over medium heat until mixture is smooth. Remove from the heat; stir in peanuts. Place marshmallows in a large bowl; add chocolate mixture and stir well. Spread into prepared pan. Refrigerate until firm.
**3.** Using foil, lift fudge out of pan. Cut into 1½-in. squares.

## Angela's XOXO Shortbread Brownies

Everyone loves a brownie. This one has a buttery crust and a fun finish, thanks to the colorful candy on top.

**—ANGELA KAMAKANA BAPTISTA**
HILO, HAWAII

**PREP:** 20 MIN. + COOLING
**BAKE:** 25 MIN. **MAKES:** 16 SERVINGS

- **2 cups all-purpose flour**
- **½ cup sugar**
- **1 cup cold butter, cubed**
- **1 package fudge brownie mix (13-inch x 9-inch pan size)**
- **8 striped chocolate kisses, unwrapped**
- **8 milk chocolate kisses, unwrapped**
- **½ cup M&M's minis**

**1.** In a large bowl, mix flour and sugar; cut in butter until crumbly. Press onto the bottom of a greased 13-in. x 9-in. baking pan. Bake at 350° for 17-20 minutes or until lightly browned. Cool on a wire rack.
**2.** Prepare brownie mix batter according to package directions; spread over the crust. Bake 23-28 minutes longer or until a toothpick inserted in center comes out clean (do not overbake). Immediately top with kisses and M&M's, spacing evenly and pressing down lightly to adhere. Cool in pan on a wire rack.

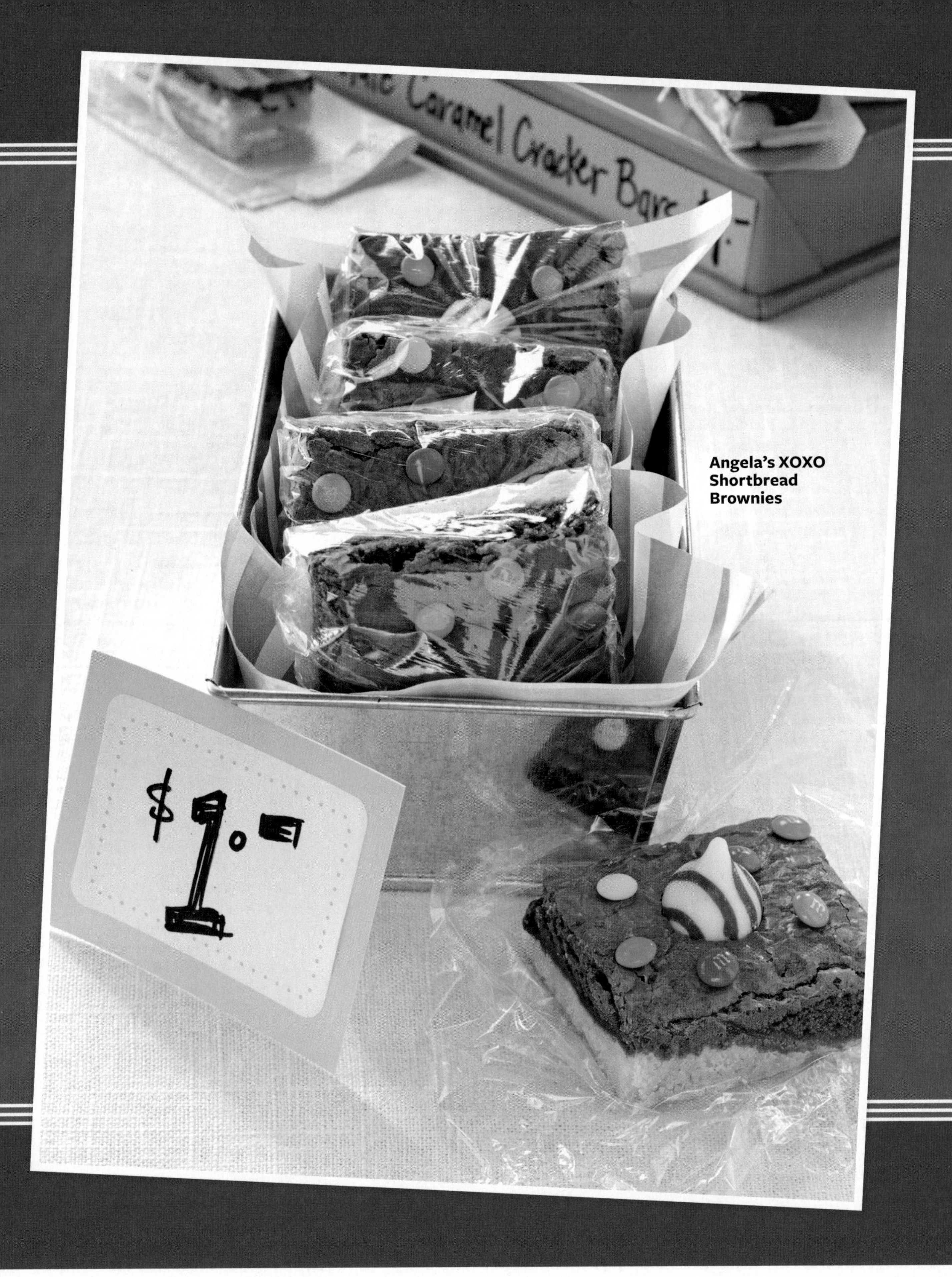


**Angela's XOXO Shortbread Brownies**

# HAPPY BIRTHDAY TO YOU

A cake with candles—that's all it takes to transform an ordinary event into a festive birthday party. Start the singing!

## Lemony Daffodil Cake

My grandma made this dessert. The marshmallow flowers are extra fun.
**—LORI KAMPSTRA**
FRANKLIN, WISCONSIN

**PREP:** 45 MIN. + COOLING
**BAKE:** 45 MIN. + COOLING
**MAKES:** 12 SERVINGS

- **1¼ cups egg whites (about 9)**
- **1 package (2.9 ounces) cook-and-serve lemon pudding mix**
- **1 teaspoon cream of tartar**
- **½ teaspoon salt**
- **1⅓ cups sugar**
- **1 cup all-purpose flour**
- **½ teaspoon vanilla extract**
- **4 egg yolks**
- **¼ teaspoon almond extract**
- **1 cup heavy whipping cream**
- **¼ cup confectioners' sugar**

**DAFFODILS**

- **21 Kraft StackerMallows**
- **2 tablespoons light corn syrup, warmed**
- **2 tablespoons yellow colored sugar**

**1.** Place egg whites in a large bowl; let stand at room temperature for 30 minutes. Meanwhile, prepare pudding according to package directions, reducing water to 2 cups. Transfer to a large bowl; cover and cool to room temperature.

**2.** Add cream of tartar and salt to egg whites; beat on medium speed until soft peaks form. Gradually add sugar, 2 tablespoons at a time, beating on high until stiff glossy peaks form. Gradually fold in flour, 1/4 cup at a time.

**3.** Divide mixture in half. Fold vanilla into one portion; set aside. In another bowl, beat yolks on high speed until thick and lemon-colored. Stir in almond extract. Fold in unflavored egg white batter.

**4.** Alternately spoon white and yellow batters into an ungreased 10-in. tube pan. Gently cut through batter with a knife to swirl. Bake on the lowest rack at 325° for 45-55 minutes or until top springs back when lightly touched. Immediately invert the pan; cool completely, about 1 hour.

**5.** In a small bowl, beat cream until it begins to thicken. Add confectioners' sugar; beat until stiff peaks form. Using a whisk, fold into cooled pudding. Cover and refrigerate until chilled.

**6.** Cut six marshmallows with a 1 1/4-in. scalloped round cookie cutter; cut holes in centers with an apple corer or 3/4-in. round cutter. Brush tops with warm corn syrup; dip tops and sides in sugar. Cut 15 marshmallows with 2-in. teardrop-shaped cookie cutter; brush with corn syrup and coat with sugar.

**7.** Run a knife around sides and center tube of pan. Remove cake to a serving plate; split into two horizontal layers. Spread pudding mixture between layers and over top and sides of cake. Just before serving, decorate with cutouts to make daffodils.

Lemony Daffodil Cake

Banana Cake with Chocolate Frosting

## Banana Cake with Chocolate Frosting

Banana and chocolate—what a winning combination! Everyone loves it.
**—JEANNE AMBROSE**
MILWAUKEE, WISCONSIN

**PREP:** 45 MIN. **BAKE:** 45 MIN. + COOLING
**MAKES:** 16 SERVINGS

- **¾ cup unsalted butter, softened**
- **2 cups sugar**
- **3 eggs**
- **1½ cups mashed ripe bananas (2 to 3 large)**
- **1½ teaspoons vanilla extract**
- **3 cups all-purpose flour**
- **1½ teaspoons baking powder**
- **1½ teaspoons baking soda**
- **1 teaspoon salt**
- **¾ cup buttermilk**
- **¾ cup chopped unsalted pistachios, toasted**

**CREAM CHEESE FROSTING**

- **2 containers (8 ounces each) whipped cream cheese, room temperature**
- **½ cup butter, softened**
- **½ cup baking cocoa**
- **4½ cups confectioners' sugar**
- **2 teaspoons vanilla extract**
- **Additional chopped unsalted pistachios, toasted, optional**

**1.** In a large bowl, cream butter and sugar until light and fluffy. Add eggs, one at a time, beating well after each addition. Beat in bananas and vanilla. Combine the flour, baking powder, baking soda and salt; add to the creamed mixture alternately with buttermilk, beating well after each addition. Fold in 3/4 cup pistachios.

**2.** Transfer to two greased and floured 8-in. round baking pans. Bake at 350° for 45-55 minutes or until a toothpick inserted near the center comes out clean. Cool for 10 minutes before removing from pans to wire racks to cool completely.

**3.** For frosting, in a large bowl, beat cream cheese and butter until smooth. Add cocoa; mix until blended. Add confectioners' sugar and vanilla; beat until creamy.

**4.** Place one cake layer on a serving plate; spread top with 1 cup frosting. Top with remaining cake. Spread top and sides with 2 cups frosting. Press pistachios into sides of cake if desired.

**5.** Cut a small hole in the corner of a large pastry or plastic bag; insert #127 petal pastry tip. Fill the bag with remaining frosting. Pipe concentric circles of frosting over top of cake. Refrigerate for at least 1 hour or until frosting is set.

Red, White & Blueberry Poke Cake

## Red, White & Blueberry Poke Cake

To add the fun candy stars on top, see the tip box below right. Just let the stars on the skewers cool completely, then slide straws over the skewers and stand them in the cake.
**—ELISABETH SCHULZ** BLOSSVALE, NEW YORK

**PREP:** 40 MIN. + COOLING **BAKE:** 30 MIN. + CHILLING
**MAKES:** 12 SERVINGS

- **1 package (18¼ ounces) white cake mix**
- **1¼ cups water**
- **2 eggs**
- **¼ cup canola oil**

**STRAWBERRY GELATIN**

- **1½ cups fresh strawberries**
- **½ cup water**
- **1 cup plus 2 tablespoons sugar**
- **1 tablespoon strawberry gelatin**

**BLUEBERRY GELATIN**

- **1 cup fresh blueberries**
- **¾ cup water**
- **2 tablespoons sugar**
- **2 tablespoons berry blue gelatin**

**FROSTING AND FILLING**

- **2½ cups heavy whipping cream**
- **⅓ cup confectioners' sugar**

**1.** Line bottoms of two greased 8-in. round baking pans with parchment or waxed paper. In a large bowl, beat the cake mix, water, eggs and oil; beat on low speed for 30 seconds. Beat on medium for 2 minutes.

**2.** Pour into prepared pans. Bake at 350° for 30-35 minutes or until a toothpick inserted near the center comes out clean. Cool completely in pans on wire racks.

**3.** For strawberry gelatin, in a small saucepan, combine the strawberries, water and sugar; bring to a boil. Reduce heat; simmer, uncovered, for 2-3 minutes or until berries are soft. Strain into a small bowl; discard pulp. Add gelatin to syrup; stirring to dissolve. Cool completely. Repeat steps to make blueberry gelatin.

**4.** Pierce top of cakes with a wooden skewer 1/2-in. deep at 1/2-in. intervals. Pour cooled strawberry mixture over one cake. Pour cooled blueberry mixture over remaining cake. Cover cakes with plastic wrap; refrigerate until gelatin is set, about 2 hours.

**5.** In a large bowl, beat cream until it begins to thicken. Add confectioners' sugar; beat until soft peaks form.

**6.** Run a knife around edge of pans to loosen. Invert strawberry cake onto a serving plate; remove paper. Spread with 1 cup whipped cream. Remove blueberry cake; remove paper. Place cake over whipped cream layer. Frost top and sides with remaining cream. Chill for at least 1 hour before serving.

To make a candy star, lightly coat a microwave-safe bowl and the inside of a 2-inch metal star cookie cutter with cooking spray. Put the cutter on a foil-lined baking sheet coated with spray. Place 2 hard candies in the bowl; microwave for 10 seconds at a time until just melted; pour into the cutter. When the candy is slightly set, lift the cutter, pushing the edges with the flat end of a wooden skewer. Insert the skewer's pointed end into the star and cool.

# CAN'T MISS THE COOKOUT!

That sizzling main course hot off the grill...those summer-perfect salads...alfresco fare just can't be beat. For your next backyard gathering, fire up with the outdoorsy recipes here.

## Cookout Potato Salad

I replace some of the mayonnaise in the dressing of my potato salad with plain yogurt. It's a lighter addition and has a pleasing tang, too.

—ANN GROVE
GREENWOOD, MISSISSIPPI

**PREP:** 10 MIN.
**COOK:** 20 MIN. + CHILLING
**MAKES:** 6 SERVINGS

- **2 pounds medium Yukon Gold potatoes, cut into ½-inch cubes**
- **1 garlic clove, chopped**
- **½ cup plain yogurt**
- **3 tablespoons mayonnaise**
- **1 tablespoon olive oil**
- **2 teaspoons white wine vinegar**
- **¾ teaspoon salt**
- **¼ teaspoon pepper**
- **1 tablespoon minced fresh parsley**
- **Optional toppings: chopped hard-cooked eggs, blanched green beans and salad croutons**

**1.** Place potatoes and garlic in a large saucepan and cover with water. Bring to a boil. Reduce heat; cover and simmer for 13-18 minutes or until tender. Drain potatoes; cool completely.

**2.** Place potatoes in a large bowl. In a small bowl, whisk the yogurt, mayonnaise, oil, vinegar, salt and pepper; pour over potatoes and toss to coat. Refrigerate, covered, until chilled. Sprinkle with parsley; serve with toppings if desired.

## Honey Chipotle Ribs

**PREP:** 5 MIN. **COOK:** 1½ HOURS
**MAKES:** 12 SERVINGS

- **6 pounds pork baby back ribs**

**BARBECUE SAUCE**

- **3 cups ketchup**
- **2 bottles (11.2 ounces each) Guinness beer**
- **2 cups barbecue sauce**
- **⅔ cup honey**
- **1 small onion, chopped**
- **¼ cup Worcestershire sauce**
- **2 tablespoons Dijon mustard**
- **2 tablespoons chopped chipotle peppers in adobo sauce**
- **4 teaspoons ground chipotle pepper**
- **1 teaspoon salt**
- **1 teaspoon garlic powder**
- **½ teaspoon pepper**

**1.** Wrap the ribs in large pieces of heavy-duty foil; seal edges of foil. Grill, covered, over indirect medium heat for 1 to 1½ hours or until tender.

**2.** In a large saucepan, combine sauce ingredients; bring to a boil. Reduce heat; simmer, uncovered, for about 45 minutes or until thickened, stirring occasionally.

**3.** Carefully remove ribs from foil. Place over direct heat; baste with some of the sauce. Grill, covered, over medium heat for about 30 minutes or until browned, turning once and basting occasionally with additional sauce. Serve with remaining sauce.

Nothing's better than a lip-smacking barbecue sauce with the perfect slather consistency. That's just what you get with Honey Chipotle Ribs. Feel free to make the sauce up to a week ahead of time.
—CAITLIN HAWES WESTWOOD, MASSACHUSETTS

## Almond & Apple Wild Rice Salad

Here's a wholesome, delicious side dish. Use a mixture of red and green apples to give it a pop of color.

—DAN WELLBERG
ELK RIVER, MINNESOTA

**PREP:** 5 MIN. **COOK:** 1 HOUR + CHILLING
**MAKES:** 10 SERVINGS

Almond & Apple Wild Rice Salad

- **1½ cups uncooked wild rice**
- **2 medium apples, chopped**
- **2 tablespoons plus ½ cup orange juice**
- **4 teaspoons olive oil**
- **4 teaspoons red wine vinegar**
- **1 tablespoon honey**
- **¾ teaspoon salt**
- **¼ teaspoon white pepper**
- **2 celery ribs, chopped**
- **½ cup unblanched almonds, coarsely chopped**
- **Optional toppings: halved green grapes, cubed cheddar cheese and chopped red onion**

**1.** Cook wild rice according to package directions. Transfer to a large bowl; cool completely.

**2.** Meanwhile, in a small bowl, toss apples with 2 tablespoons orange juice. In another bowl, whisk the remaining orange juice, oil, vinegar, honey, salt and pepper.

**3.** Add the apples and celery to rice. Drizzle with the dressing; toss to combine. Refrigerate, covered, until chilled. Sprinkle with almonds; serve with toppings if desired.

Cookout Potato Salad
Honey Chipotle Ribs

# Substitutions & Equivalents

## EQUIVALENT MEASURES

| | | | | | |
|---|---|---|---|---|---|
| **3 teaspoons** | = 1 tablespoon | | **16 tablespoons** | = 1 cup | |
| **4 tablespoons** | = 1/4 cup | | **2 cups** | = 1 pint | |
| **5-1/3 tablespoons** | = 1/3 cup | | **4 cups** | = 1 quart | |
| **8 tablespoons** | = 1/2 cup | | **4 quarts** | = 1 gallon | |

## FOOD EQUIVALENTS

| | | | |
|---|---|---|---|
| GRAINS | **Macaroni** | 1 cup (3-1/2 ounces) uncooked | = 2-1/2 cups cooked |
| | **Noodles, Medium** | 3 cups (4 ounces) uncooked | = 4 cups cooked |
| | **Popcorn** | 1/3 to 1/2 cup unpopped | = 8 cups popped |
| | **Rice, Long Grain** | 1 cup uncooked | = 3 cups cooked |
| | **Rice, Quick-Cooking** | 1 cup uncooked | = 2 cups cooked |
| | **Spaghetti** | 8 ounces uncooked | = 4 cups cooked |
| CRUMBS | **Bread** | 1 slice | = 3/4 cup soft crumbs, 1/4 cup fine dry crumbs |
| | **Graham Crackers** | 7 squares | = 1/2 cup finely crushed |
| | **Buttery Round Crackers** | 12 crackers | = 1/2 cup finely crushed |
| | **Saltine Crackers** | 14 crackers | = 1/2 cup finely crushed |
| FRUITS | **Bananas** | 1 medium | = 1/3 cup mashed |
| | **Lemons** | 1 medium | = 3 tablespoons juice, 2 teaspoons grated peel |
| | **Limes** | 1 medium | = 2 tablespoons juice, 1-1/2 teaspoons grated peel |
| | **Oranges** | 1 medium | = 1/4 to 1/3 cup juice, 4 teaspoons grated peel |

| | | | | | | |
|---|---|---|---|---|---|---|
| VEGETABLES | **Cabbage** | 1 head | = 5 cups shredded | **Green Pepper** | 1 large | = 1 cup chopped |
| | **Carrots** | 1 pound | = 3 cups shredded | **Mushrooms** | 1/2 pound | = 3 cups sliced |
| | **Celery** | 1 rib | = 1/2 cup chopped | **Onions** | 1 medium | = 1/2 cup chopped |
| | **Corn** | 1 ear fresh | = 2/3 cup kernels | **Potatoes** | 3 medium | = 2 cups cubed |
| NUTS | **Almonds** | 1 pound | = 3 cups chopped | **Pecan Halves** | 1 pound | = 4-1/2 cups chopped |
| | **Ground Nuts** | 3-3/4 ounces | = 1 cup | **Walnuts** | 1 pound | = 3-3/4 cups chopped |

## EASY SUBSTITUTIONS

| When you need... | | Use... |
|---|---|---|
| **Baking Powder** | 1 teaspoon | 1/2 teaspoon cream of tartar + 1/4 teaspoon baking soda |
| **Buttermilk** | 1 cup | 1 tablespoon lemon juice or vinegar + enough milk to measure 1 cup (let stand 5 minutes before using) |
| **Cornstarch** | 1 tablespoon | 2 tablespoons all-purpose flour |
| **Honey** | 1 cup | 1-1/4 cups sugar + 1/4 cup water |
| **Half-and-Half Cream** | 1 cup | 1 tablespoon melted butter + enough whole milk to measure 1 cup |
| **Onion** | 1 small, chopped (1/3 cup) | 1 teaspoon onion powder or 1 tablespoon dried minced onion |
| **Tomato Juice** | 1 cup | 1/2 cup tomato sauce + 1/2 cup water |
| **Tomato Sauce** | 2 cups | 3/4 cup tomato paste + 1 cup water |
| **Unsweetened Chocolate** | 1 square (1 ounce) | 3 tablespoons baking cocoa + 1 tablespoon shortening or oil |
| **Whole Milk** | 1 cup | 1/2 cup evaporated milk + 1/2 cup water |

# Cooking Terms

Here's a quick reference for some of the cooking terms used in Taste of Home recipes:

**BASTE** To moisten food with melted butter, pan drippings, marinades or other liquid to add more flavor and juiciness.

**BEAT** To combine ingredients with a rapid movement using a fork, spoon, wire whisk or electric mixer.

**BLEND** To combine ingredients until *just* mixed.

**BOIL** To heat liquids until bubbles form that cannot be "stirred down." In the case of water, the temperature will reach 212°.

**BONE** To remove all meat from the bone before cooking.

**CREAM** To beat ingredients together to a smooth consistency, usually in the case of butter and sugar for baking.

**DASH** A small amount of seasoning, less than 1/8 teaspoon. If using a shaker, a dash would comprise a quick flip of the container.

**DREDGE** To coat foods with flour or other dry ingredients. Most often done with pot roasts and stew meat before browning.

**FOLD** To incorporate several ingredients by careful and gentle turning with a spatula. Used generally with beaten egg whites or whipped cream when mixing into the rest of the ingredients to keep the batter light.

**JULIENNE** To cut foods into long thin strips much like matchsticks. Used most often for salads and stir-fry dishes.

**MARINATE** To tenderize and/or flavor foods, usually meat or raw vegetables, by placing in a liquid mixture of oil, vinegar, wine, lime or lemon juice, herbs and spices.

**MINCE** To cut into very fine pieces. Used often for garlic or fresh herbs.

**PARBOIL** To cook partially, usually used in the case of chicken, sausages and vegetables.

**PARTIALLY SET** Describes the consistency of gelatin after it has been chilled for a short amount of time. Mixture should resemble the consistency of egg whites.

**PUREE** To process foods to a smooth mixture. Can be prepared in an electric blender, food processor, food mill or sieve.

**SAUTE** To fry quickly in a small amount of fat, stirring almost constantly. Most often done with onions, mushrooms and other chopped vegetables.

**SCORE** To cut slits partway through the outer surface of foods. Often used with ham or flank steak.

**STIR-FRY** To cook meats and/or vegetables with a constant stirring motion in a small amount of oil in a wok or skillet over high heat.

# General Recipe Index

This handy index lists every recipe by food category, major ingredient and/or cooking method, so you can easily locate recipes to suit your needs.

✓*Recipe includes Nutrition Facts and Diabetic Exchanges*

## SLOW COOKER RECIPES



## SOUPS, CHILI & STEWS



## SPINACH



## SQUASH (also see Zucchini)



## STRAWBERRIES



## SWEET POTATOES



## TOMATOES



## TURKEY & TURKEY SAUSAGE



## VEGETABLES (also see specific kinds)



## YEAST BREADS



## ZUCCHINI

# Alphabetical Recipe Index

This handy index lists every recipe in alphabetical order so you can easily find your favorites.

✓*Recipe includes Nutrition Facts and Diabetic Exchanges*

## A



## B



## C

## D



## E



## F



## G

## T



## U



## V



## W



## Z